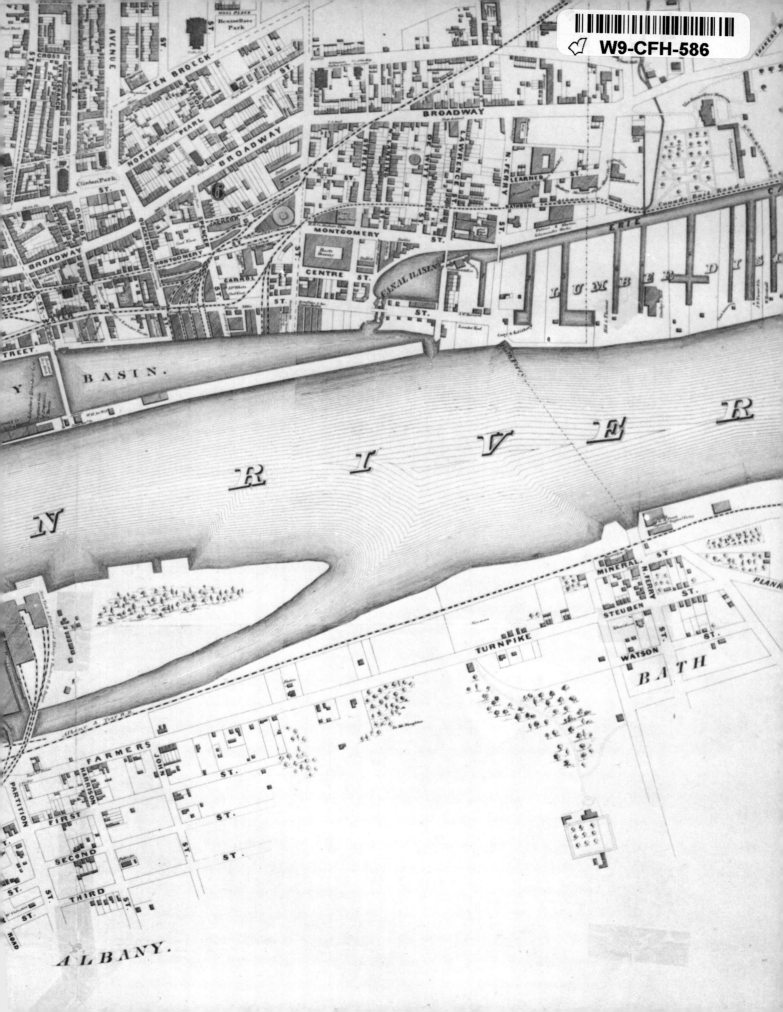

ALBANY

CAPITAL CITY ON THE HUDSON

An Illustrated History by John J. McEneny

Picture research by Dennis Holzman
Chronology by Robert W. Arnold III
Editorial coordination by Margaret Tropp

American Historical Press
Sun Valley, California

DEDICATED TO
MY BROTHER -IN-LAW
PATRICK JOSEPH LEONARD
1941 - 1980
A LOVER OF
LOYAL FRIENDSHIPS,
GOOD BOOKS, AND
HISTORY, IN ALL ITS EXPRESSIONS

Endpapers: Depicted is a Map of the City of Albany, with Villages of Greenbush, East Albany & Bath, N.Y. Surveyed and drawn by E. Jacob, 1857. Courtesy, McKinney Library, Albany Institute of History & Art.

PHOTOGRAPHS CREDIT CORRECTIONS:
All photos credited to: Erastus Corning 2nd, Dennis Holzman, the Knox Family, Morris Gerber and Albany County Historical are Courtesy of the Collection of the Albany Institute of History and Art.

FROM:	TO:
Albany League of Arts	Albany/Schenectady League of Arts
Albany Medical	Archives of Albany Medical Center
Capital Newspapers	*Times Union*, Albany, N.Y.
Greater Albany Jewish Federation	Jewish Federation of Northeast N.Y.
Rutgers University	James Voorhees Zimmerelli Art Mus., Rutgers
St. Sophia	St. Sophia Greek Greek Orthodox Church
	Libr. & Archives

Library of Congress Catalogue Card Number: 98-74147

ISBN: 0-9654754-9-2

Includes Index

TABLE OF CONTENTS

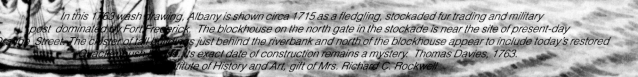

In this 1763 wash drawing, Albany is shown circa 1715 as a fledgling, stockaded fur trading and military post dominated by Fort Frederick. The blockhouse on the north gate in the stockade is near the site of present-day Orange Street. The cluster of tall buildings just behind the riverbank and north of the blockhouse appear to include today's restored Quackenbush House, its exact date of construction remains a mystery. Thomas Davies, 1763. Institute of History and Art, gift of Mrs. Richard C. Rockwell.

FOREWORD

Albany, as it extends westward from the great river where it was first established as a Dutch fur-trading post, to the dunes and pitch pine of the sand plains on the city's outskirts, is a celebration of contrasts. In many ways Albany is a 19th-century city, yet it is now crowned by Nelson Rockefeller's architectural vision of the 21st century.

Like other settlements that cover America, Albany can be regarded as a patchwork quilt. The varied colors of Albany's distinctive neighborhoods, the diverse cultural textures, and the many shapes of its topography make it wonderfully unique. The myriad fabrics that have been pieced and sewn together through time have mostly proven strong and durable. Some wear and tear, however, have resulted from the city's occupying an important place in the course of history, so that portions have been replaced or restored. Beneath the design is an interlining composed of the lives and dreams of immigrants drawn from many lands, whose labors have firmly stitched in the swatches representing the city's basic industries. Some design elements look arbitrary or haphazard, as in a crazy-quilt. In other places they seem consciously shaped and deliberately placed.

Each passing glance at Albany invites another look, for there are many features which should draw the intrigued attention of both lovers and critics of the city. Here is a special hue, a curious texture, a new addition, or an unnoticed embellishment; perhaps something comes sharply and suddenly into focus, to be scrutinized in a new way by an informed eye that now can translate what once seemed dull, ugly, or commonplace.

Like some treasured, oft-mended patchwork quilt passed on from family forebears, today's Albany transmits a special warmth and value to those who seek to understand its design and handiwork.

Since I approach Albany history in an eclectic way, I have informally and discursively recounted the city's past. After presenting Albany's foundations in the colonial and early federal periods, I gathered together aspects of the city's development and character into units which do not strictly adhere to a chronological format. Therefore, Robert W. Arnold III has created, specially for this book, an initial chapter that serves as a timeline for the rest of the tale of Albany.

John J. McEneny
Albany, New York

INTRODUCTION

Although there have been many excellent works published in the last few years on particular facets of Albany's past and present, Albanians for more than a generation have lacked an updated, comprehensive, and readable presentation of their city's history. Through sponsoring this book, the Albany Institute of History and Art has taken the initiative to fill an important need in our community.

When I first heard of the plans for this project, I could think of no one better suited than John McEneny to tell the story of Albany in an absorbing way that would also make it relevant to today's generations. Commissioner McEneny has long been renowned among us for his enthusiastic and thorough knowledge of Albany's past, especially in its connections with the present city and its citizens.

Jack shows both originality and insight in portraying and explaining the unique, diverse, and enduring qualities in his native city. His personal style of narration, coupled with the wide variety of illustrations painstakingly gathered by Dennis Holzman, has guaranteed this book's role for years to come as a valuable and attractive illumination of Albany's evolution and character. Its chronology will help to make it a standard reference work.

I congratulate the author and his writing assistants, the picture researcher, the sponsor, and all others who have worked so long and well on this fine book that is sure to increase our appreciation of Albany.

—Erastus Corning 2nd Mayor of Albany
August 1981

Jack McEneny is not unusual in the sense that he is a politician who loves his native city. Albany cannot count the politicians who fall into this category, just as it cannot really encompass in the mind its own spectacular history—as long before the revolution as since.

But Jack is a rare bird in that he has chosen not only to revel in this history but to try to cope with it by writing about it. This book joins the company of Joel Munsell's *Annals of Albany* and Cuyler Reynold's *Albany Chronicles,* as an indispensable book on any proper Albany bookshelf. Munsell took us back to our earliest history by reprinting primary and secondary documents of this city, and also gave a cue to Reynolds in his Notes from the Newspapers—a daily chronology in the *Annals* from selected early papers. Reynolds used the city's numerous newspapers as the source of his own valuable chronological history up through 1906.

Jack's book is also chronological but different in that he gives us a series of essays about the city in manageable time blocs—as a colony, a river port, a political capital, and much more. It is a most readable, accessible rendering of time, made visible by a splendid and abundant chronology of images—dioramas, sketches, posters, paintings, photos —from a corn harvest by native Americans in the 17th century to Albany's unique skyline on the eve of the 21st century.

This is a panorama of where we came from, how we were an what we look like now, and we who live here know that we've always inhabited a devilishly handsome town, architecturally wondrous, politically important, raffishly busy and vital.

But don't take my word for it. Read Jack's book.

—William Kennedy
August, 1998

CHAPTER 1

ALBANY THROUGH TIME:
A CHRONOLOGICAL NARRATIVE

by Robert W. Arnold III

Wilderness and Tribes: Before the 17th Century

In the Northeastern section of North America, the dominant element was the forest: trees in their millions stretching in almost unbroken ranks from the Atlantic Ocean to the Mississippi River in the interior. These woodlands, and the waterways within them, would shape the cultures of their earliest human inhabitants and affect the lives and livelihoods of the first white settlers from Europe.

ca. A.D. 1000 – A.D. 1300: The place that would become Albany was in the heart of the Eastern Woodlands, nearly at the confluence of this region's two principal navigable rivers, later called the Hudson and the Mohawk. The last great immigration of Algonkian-speaking people had rolled into the area of what is now New York State shortly before 1000 A.D., and for more than three centuries would dominate the region.

Of the widely dispersed Algonkian

nations the most dominant in the Albany vicinity was the Mahikan, whose people called the land *Mahikanaki*. Their principal town was at Schodack, and a satellite community occupied the site of Albany, a place they called *Pempotowwuthut–Muhhcanneuw,* meaning "the fireplace of the Mahikan nation." From Schodack, their sachem (chief) ruled a

---

Corn harvest at Mount Morris (a diorama)

dominion reaching from Lake Champlain to the Catskill Creek. On the east bank of the Hudson River Mahikan power extended south to present-day Poughkeepsie. To Schodack and the primordial site of Albany came the Indian traders, diplomats, and chieftains of the surrounding nations. From the first Albany was an intersection of commercial and political traffic.

ca. A.D. 1300 – A.D. 1600:

Threatening the Mahikan-aki were Iroquoian-speaking people who around A.D. 1300 began filtering into the area that became New York. Iroquoian nations included the Senecas, their offshoot Cayuagas, the Onondagas, the Mohawks and their cadet branch Oneidas, the Eries, the Hurons, the Susquehannocks, and many others. Wherever they came, the Algonkians were pushed out, killed, or assimilated.

Sometime between 1450 and 1570 the Huron chief Deganawidah came to the Iroquois people of the New York State area to settle the differences among them. He brought a plan for peace based on harmony, law, and justice. Iroquois legend tells that Deganawidah converted Hiawatha (a Mohawk or an Onondaga), who agreed to spread the message among the tribes, resulting finally in formation of the League of the Five Nations.

By 1600 the Five Nations occupied most of central New York west of the Genesee River to Lake Champlain, with the Mohawks and the Oneidas nearest Albany. During the coming European colonization, the Iroquois would assume a position of major influence; they would be the anvil on which the French and the English in North America tried one another for a century. The Iroquois shared a common fate with their ancient Algonkian enemies: both faced a sociological and demographic catastrophe brought on by white colonization.

Exposure to European civilization created a social revolution among the American Indians; the encounter involved two cultures with mutually unintelligible world views. The Indian and the white man had different concepts of property ownership; Indian life was largely communal; European, individualistic and competitive. The whites possessed a written language,

New York State Archives

Seneca hunter's lodge (a diorama)

were advanced in the organization of business, possessed sophisticated weapons and machinery, and were urban-inclined. Indian time sense was cyclical; European, linear.

The Voyagers: 1524-1624

1524: White men first saw the Hudson River, that vast drain of the virgin woodlands' interior, when Giovanni de Verrazano, sailing for Francois de Valois, King of France, steered into New York Bay. His ship's small boat was rowed into the upper bay, which Verrazano described as a beautiful lake formed by a larger river. The land was named by Francis I as *La Nouvelle France,* the Hudson *La Grande Rivière.*

1540: Albany tradition maintains that in this year French fur traders in barques sailed upriver as far as Cohoes, to erect a fortified post on an island on the west side of the Hudson just south of the present city of Albany. But before their fort was completed, a freshet carried away its walls and the project was abandoned. (Its outline, however, was visible to Jasper Danckaerts nearly 150 years later.)

Then Deganawidah and Hiawatha together created the laws of the Great Peace, and for each part of the law, they talked the words into wampum so that they could better remember it.

When they had created the Great Law, Deganawidah and Hiawatha, together with chiefs of the Mohawk Nation, brought the Good Message to the Mohawks' less powerful neighbors, the Oneidas, who lived to the west. Gladly did the Oneidas accept the New Mind.

Next Deganawidah and Hiawatha approached the Cayugas, a small nation living between the Onondagas and the Senecas. They were glad of the protection of the Great Peace and quickly took hold of it. Then Deganawidah and Hiawatha persuaded all the Onondaga chiefs except Atotarho to grasp the Good Message. The two leaders together with the chiefs of the four nations, were now able to persuade the warlike Seneca, the nation farthest to the west, to take hold of the Great Peace.

Paul A.W. Wallace. *The White Roots of Peace.* Philadelphia: University of Pennsylvania Press, 1946.

1609: As Holland's long war for independence from Spain slowed to a truce, the Dutch entered their golden age of economic prosperity, religious toleration, and artistic florescence. An English mariner, Henry Hudson, was engaged by the Dutch East India Company to seek La Grande Rivière and press along its channel to India, land of exotic spices and beautiful textiles. The company "shall in the first place equip a small vessel or yacht of about 30 lasts [60 tons] burden with which, well provided with men, provisions, and other necessaries, . . . Hudson shall . . . sail in order to search for a passage by the North. . . ."

Henry Hudson's ship Half Moon

Hudson's *Half Moon* sailed up the great river as far as the Albany area, which was visited in September. Around Albany, where the contact with Indians was friendly, the Dutch would later establish fairly amicable relations with the Indians; but downstream, where the crew's treatment of the natives had been less gentle, the Indians would remember, so that the Dutch relationship with those tribes remained uneasy. A Dutch historian afterwards reporting on Hudson's voyage commented that: "They found this a good place for cod-fishing, as also for traffic in good skins and furs, which were to be got there at a very low price." Clearly, though, Hudson's River did not provide the sought-for Northwest Passage to the Orient.

Only weeks after Hudson's departure, French explorer Samuel de Champlain, moving down from Canada with two Frenchmen and 60 Hurons, had a significant encounter with a band of 200 Iroquois near Ticonderoga. Champlain's treatment of the Iroquois earned the French their enmity, although French priests, traders, and envoys would at times wield considerable influence among the Five Nations.

Trade alone attracted the Dutch to Hudson's River, not the promise of colonizing some Zion in the wilderness. While God, gold, and glory motivated the Spaniards, gold alone did nicely for the Dutch. Veterans of Hudson's voyage soon persuaded Amsterdam merchants to send a vessel to trade for furs with the natives. By 1614 a Dutch map showed "Fort Nassoureen," built by Hendrick Christiaensen on the site of the French post on Castle Island, inside a stockade 50 feet square. In 1618 it too would be wrecked by a freshet, and the transient population of fur traders abandoned it for a new location at the mouth of the Normanskill.

1621: The Lord States-General of the Netherlands (Holland) chartered the Dutch West India Company, granting exclusive 24-year trading privileges on the West African coast and in the West Indies and America, as well as the right to make contacts and alliances with the nations of those places. The Company soon afterwards founded New Netherland in North America; it would jealously guard its territories and cultivate good relations with the fur-selling Indians of the regions it claimed along the Hudson, Connecticut, and Delaware rivers. Since their colony was mainly maritime, its principal settlements would be built on waterways navigable by ship. It established a main office later at New Amsterdam (now New York City).

The Dutch: 1624–1664

1624: Thirty families of French-speaking Walloons, Protestant refugees from the Spanish, sailed from Amsterdam in the *Nieu Nederlandt*. A dozen families were landed to counter a threatened French settlement at Manhattan; instead, they located New Amsterdam at first on Governors Island. The remainder continued upriver to land at the site of Albany and there constructed Fort Orange, named in honor of Maurice, Prince of Orange.

1626: Pieter Minuit, a shrewd and determined man whose coarseness at times offended those he governed, became director of New Netherland for the Dutch West India Company. Minuit purchased Manhattan Island from the Indians. The total European population of the New Netherland colony was about 200 persons.

A crude little settlement grew up around the small fort at Fort Orange. It was recommended that families arrive in New Netherland in spring, so that in their first year they could clear land, build shelters, and grow subsistence crops. In the winter the settler would be able to fell timber, and the next summer acquire livestock and erect houses, barns, and outbuildings.

In the ongoing friction between Algonkian and Iroquois, the war between the local Mahikans and Mohawks led the Mahikans to seek Dutch support. The commander of Fort Orange, Daniel Van Krieckebeck, and six soldiers advanced west against the Mohawks; they fell into an ambush somewhere in the vicinity of what is now Lincoln Park.

1629: The directors of the Dutch West India Company decided that its expense in sending ships and troops

"I, ——-, promise and swear that I shall be true and faithful to the noble Patroon and Co-directors, or those who represent them here, and to the Hon'ble Director, Commissioners and Council, subjecting myself to the Court of the Colonie; and I promise to demean myself as a good and faithful inhabitant or Burgher, without exciting any opposition, tumult or noise; but on the contrary, as a loyal inhabitant, to maintain and support offensively and defensively, against every one, the Right and Jurisdiction of the Colonie. And with reverence and fear of the Lord, and uplifting of both the first fingers of the right hand, I say—SO TRULY HELP ME GOD ALMIGHTY."—Oath taken by the Colonists of Rensselaerswyck to the Patroon.

Fort Orange Club

and building fortifications was cutting too deeply into their profit margin and stopped sending settlers. They adopted a new concept of colonization, the *patroon* system, in which members of the Dutch West India Company who established a settlement of 50 adult tenants in New Netherland could obtain tracts of land 16 miles along one shore of a navigable waterway, or 8 miles on each bank. The patroon was lord of his domain; as in Europe, tenants were not to hunt, fish, trade, or mill lumber or grain without his consent.

The first patroon was an Amsterdam pearl and diamond merchant, Kiliaen Van Rensselaer; he selected land on the west bank of the Hudson River and bought title to it from the Indians. A patroon had to lay out large sums of money in sending out cattle, horses, brewing vats, tools, and millstones and in recruiting artisans and indenturing others. Of the five patroonships granted, only Van Rensselaer's would endure; his property included present-day Albany, Rensselaer, and Columbia counties, all or in part—700,000 acres, altogether.

1640: Failing to populate New Netherland rapidly, the Dutch West India Company modified its criteria for colonization.

New Netherland offered a lucrative fur trade and religious toleration rare in the Counter-Reformation era. Its rich and fertile land was much touted by recruitment literature distributed by the Dutch West India Company and the patroons. Settlers came from throughout Europe under Dutch sponsorship. Although the patroon system is better known, most settlers were independent proprietors who owned their own land. By the time the colony was seized by England in 1664, it was populated by 8,000 Europeans. At this time New Netherland claimed parts of present-day New York, New Jersey, Connecticut, Delaware, and Pennsylvania—claims disputed by England, France, and Spain.

The quick and considerable money to be made in the fur trade steadily diverted the energies of those artisans and farmers who were induced to settle. The effects of European contact were also beginning to be felt by the Indians: the brass kettle replaced traditional ceramic vessels, and

Dutch soldier, 1630

firearms, the bow; steel tools superseded worked flint, bone, or antler. Already the hunting grounds of the Five Nations were drained of beaver (in 1633 alone 30,000 pelts were shipped out), and the Iroquois pressured the Hurons for control of the Great Lakes fur trade.

1642: A French Jesuit missionary, Father Jogues, was taken captive by the Mohawks and tortured. Escaping, he took refuge in Albany. Based on his stay there, Jogues provided an early description of Albany: "There are two things in this settlement . . . first, a miserable little fort called Fort Orange, built of logs, with four or five pieces of Breteuil cannon and as many swivels. . . . Second, a colony sent here by this Rensselaer, who is the Patroon.

This colony is composed of about a hundred persons, who reside in some twenty-five or thirty houses . . . solely of boards and thatched, with no mason-work except the chimneys."

1647: Pieter Stuyvesant arrived at New Amsterdam to serve as Governor of New Netherland. Resolute, quick-witted, hot-tempered, and vitriolic, he had an autocratic philosophy of government already becoming obsolete in the more fluid American environment. More successful in external affairs than with New Netherland, Stuyvesant would resist Spanish and English ambitions, capture New Sweden on the Delaware for the Dutch, and establish peace with the Indians, with whom relations had been ghastly under his predecessor, Willem Kieft.

1648: Conflict between Stuyvesant and the director of the Van Rensselaer patroonship, Brant Van Slichtenhorst, developed when Stuyvesant ordered the demolition of all buildings within cannon shot of Fort Orange. After Van Slichtenhorst refused to execute the command, troops were sent to arrest him. The colonists quickly took sides.

1652: As the tension in the upper Hudson Valley area became explosive, Stuyvesant ordered posts erected 600 paces on all sides of Fort Orange. On April 1, 1652, he proclaimed the village of Beverwyck and disassociated it from the patroonship colony of tenant farmers clustered around what became known as Rensselaerswyck.

1657: Beverwyck residents who enrolled for the *Burghers Recht* paid 50 guilders for the right to hold office, which exempted them from the confiscation of property and attainder when convicted of a capital offense. Small burghers, buying the right to engage in trade and join guilds, paid 20 guilders; they had to be native-born or wed to the native-born daughter of a burgher, and keep fire and light in the community for a year and six weeks. The future Albany now growing north of Fort Orange began to take shape and substance.

1663: A smallpox epidemic at Fort Orange and Beverwyck killed about one settler each day; in the Hudson River Valley about 1,000 Indians died, joining hundreds of Iroquois killed by a plague the year before.

The English: 1664–1776

1664: Charles II, King of England, began to assert English claims to New Netherland that were based on the Cabot voyages in the late 15th century. His Majesty granted the territories of New Netherland, Long Island, New England, and land stretching to Delaware Bay to his royal brother James, Duke of York and Albany. Four warships and 450 troops were dispatched to New Netherland to settle the issue. With Stuyvesant's garrison outnumbered 6 to 1, New Amsterdam surrendered to the English without fighting. Shortly thereafter Fort Orange and Beverwyck as well were promptly renamed Albany.

1673: In the course of a third Anglo-Dutch commercial war, the Dutch retook New Netherland. Under brief Dutch rule, Albany became Willemstadt and local government was again in a state of flux. The 1674 Treaty of Westminster restored to England all "lands, islands, cities, havens, castles, and fortresses" taken by the Dutch. The English did little to disturb the bureaucratic status quo in Albany upon their return.

1675–1676: King Philip's War erupted in New England, where Indians burned a number of settlements and killed hundreds of colonists. With the Hudson frozen and 1,000 hostile Indians reported 40 miles east of Albany, the village's garrison was strengthened and the Mohawk allies sent to harry King Philip's warriors. A new fort was built overlooking Albany, with four bastions mounting 6 guns each. This installation, called Fort Frederick, stood on State Street near Lodge.

1677: In their effort to control the fur trade, the Five Nations raided the Chesapeake Bay region. New York attempted to halt these raids and held a major meeting in Albany between the Five Nations and delegates from Virginia and Maryland. A compact resulted which halted these Iroquois forays.

1678: Governor Edmund Andros issued a patent to the Van Rensselaers, confirming their possession of Rensselaerswyck but *not* of Albany, making the separation complete.

1683: Colonel Thomas Dongan, who had become Governor of New York in 1682, ordered Albany and Rensselaerswyck to send two delegates (out of a total of 18) to attend the first meeting of the General Assembly in New York. A "Charter of Libertys and Privileges" was passed, and 12 counties were established in the colony, among them Albany County, much larger than it is today.

1686: Governor Dongan, visiting Albany, was petitioned by local leaders to enlarge the town's boundaries and to give sounder guarantee to land titles. To define Albany better, he "got the Ranslaers to release their pretence to the Town and sixteen miles into the Country for Commons for the King. . . . After I had obtained this release of the Ranslaers I passed the Patent for Albany." Dongan signed the Charter on July 22, 1686, making Albany a city for the first time.

The city was given a full set of officials and divided into three wards. Pieter Schuyler was appointed mayor, "Clerk

Pieter Schuyler, the first mayor of Albany

The Empire State

of ye market and Coroner of ye citty of Albany. . . ." Among the new government's first ordinances were prohibitions against watering horses from buckets hanging at the city wells and carrying sand from near the old burying-ground (so much had been taken that the coffins were exposed to view). And tavern-keepers were ordered to provide the constable with the name and business of any guest staying two days.

1689: News was received of the "Glorious Revolution" in England, which tumbled James II from the throne and replaced him with his Protestant son-in-law, William of Orange. Uprisings throughout the Dominion of New England—then including New York—ensued, and Governor Edmund Andros was arrested. During this period of wide popular unrest and dissatisfaction over the policies of James II, Jacob Leisler seized control of New York in the name of William and Mary and formed a Committee of Safety there under his leadership as self-proclaimed lieutenant governor. Leisler had arrived from Germany in 1660 in *The Golden Otter,* too poor to pay for his musket, bed, and chest. By 1689 he had become a prosperous New York City merchant who was seen as a firebrand by the conservative establishment but as a champion of Protestantism and the lower classes by others.

In Albany, William and Mary's ascent to England's throne was greeted with jubilation. At Fort Frederick "there Majts were proclaimed in solemn manner in English and Dutch, ye gunns fyreing from ye fort & volley of small arms, ye People with Loude acclamations crying God Save King Wm. & Queen Mary. . . ."

Leisler's authority over Albany, however, was rejected, demonstrating the city's growing particularism. Leisler demanded surrender of Albany's fort and garrison for resisting him. A force of Leisler's men came to Albany in three sloops, but was turned back, first by Pieter Schuyler and then by a band of Mohawks encamped on the site of Academy Park. Connecticut militia came to reinforce Schuyler against both Leisler and threatened French attack. With a Leisler plan to invade Canada and amid rumours of the Comte de Frontenac's projected invasion from Montreal, Albany finally accepted Leisler's governorship, although local government remained unchanged.

1690: After Leisler's invasion attempt petered out, the French and their Indians, 200 men in all, swept down to attack Schenectady, 20 miles northwest of Albany. "The whole village was instantly in a blaze," Mayor Schuyler wrote. "Women with child [were] riped open, and their Infants cast into the Flames, or dashed against Posts of Doors. Sixty persons perished in the Massacre, and twenty-seven were carried into Captivity. The rest fled naked towards Albany thro' a deep

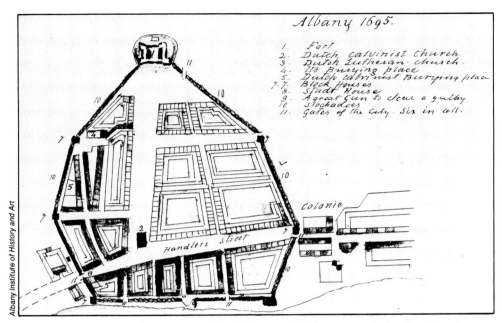

Albany in 1695

Snow which fell that very Night in a Terrible Storm; and twenty-five of these fugitives lost their Limbs in flight, thro' the Severity of the Frost." Symen Schermerhorn had ridden wounded through the night to warn Albany, which rallied for the expected French attack. The French made for Montreal, itself an epic trek, in which they ate most of the horses taken at Schenectady. The Albany militia buried Schenectady's dead and gave fruitless chase to the French.

1691: Colonel Henry Sloughter ended Leisler's Rebellion. Leisler was arrested in New York and eventually was hanged. New York concerned itself now with the war with the French, King William's War. About Albany Sloughter wrote to neighboring governors: "I need not relate unto you of how great import the preservacon of this place is, being the only bulkwork and safeguard of all Their Majesty's plantacons on the main (coast) of America. . . ."

A preventive (and vengeful) attack on French Canada was launched by Pieter Schuyler, who with Albany militia and allied Mohawks attacked and burned La Prairie de la Madeleine, killing 200. As Albany itself was increasingly fortified, thousands of pine trees were consumed.

1697: The population count of Albany County was 379 men, 270 women, and 803 children, mostly in the city of Albany. (The population of the province of New York was 18,067.) During the 1689–1697 war with the French, King William's War, 419 people had fled Albany, 84 were killed, 38 died, and 16 were taken as prisoners of war.

1700: To counter French influence with the Iroquois, the English paid court to the Five Nations, soliciting their help against Montreal. But the garrison at Albany was not turned out in a way that would impress the tribes. By the next year, however, Pieter Schuyler had succeeded in winning over the Iroquois, even though Albany's fort remained "in a miserable condition." The outbreak of Queen Anne's War in 1702 revealed that Schuyler had also made Albany's militia the only adequate unit in New York.

1708: Over four decades after the English came to power, Albany gradually began to conform to the society which controlled it. Intermarriage between the English soldiers of the garrison and the Dutch women of Albany increased and English slowly became the language of commerce and government. In 1708 the Reverend Thomas Barclay inaugurated services of the Church of England in Albany.

1710: Pieter Schuyler, after leading an abortive expedition against Canada, sailed for England, bringing four Mohawk sachems with him so they might be suitably impressed by English strength. The Indians created an immensely popular sensation, were accorded many attentions, and even received an audience with Queen Anne.

1714: The Peace of Utrecht had ended Queen Anne's War in 1713. A year later the population of Albany was 1,136, including 495 white males, 47 black males, and 528 white and 66 black women; the population of Albany County totaled 3,029, including 458 slaves.

1723: Governor Burnet reported to the Lords of Trade that he had induced Indians to bring their furs to Albany, some from "above a thousand miles to Albany from Mislimakenak which lyes between Lac Superieur and Lac Huron." Upon his recommendation, Albany built some small houses outside the stockade to shelter Indians who came to trade. Fur traders, mainly of Dutch ancestry, who had dominated both civil and economic life in Albany since the Dongan Charter, were now rivaled by an emergent class of successful general merchants who supplied the needs of the people of the upper Hudson River Valley.

1744: Once again, there was war with France. The Iroquois, Six Nations since the Tuscarora had joined their League, were at the apex of their power, their role pivotal in the perpetual Anglo-French competition for an American empire. Governor George Clinton

The Reverend Thomas Barclay

cautioned them against the French, and a French attack was greatly feared by Albanians, especially after the burning of Schuylerville in 1745. A terrorized Albany filled with refugees, and the three market houses became barracks. Although Governor Clinton had ordered the Iroquois out against the French, their chiefs remained reluctant until Indian Agent William Johnson brought the Mohawks to Albany and lavishly entertained them.

Again, war drained population away from an Albany too close to the enemy, and a postwar census in 1749 counted 9,154 whites in the county, down from 1737's 10,681. Albany would remain uneasily aware of its frontier exposure until the French were at last smashed in North America.

1754: The famed Albany Plan of Union came about partly from Albany's significance in Colonial-Indian relations. In 1753 the Lords of Trade requested Governors of Massachusetts, New Hampshire, New Jersey, Pennsylvania, Maryland, and Virginia to send delegates to Albany for discussion of possible confederation for mutual defense against the French. In June of 1754, 24 delegates from seven colonies, including William Johnson and James Delancey of New York and Benjamin Franklin of Pennsylvania, met at Albany's *Stadt Huys,* the City Hall that stood where Hudson Avenue now meets Broadway. The Plan of Union that evolved, although never ratified by Parliament, was the first wide acknowledgment of common colonial interests and the need for concerted action to realize them.

1757: The Seven Years War, a world war known in America as the French and Indian War, had begun. The French massacre of the English garrison at Fort William Henry on Lake George again packed Albany with refugees and arriving British and colonial troops.

1758: At age 34, Lord Howe, commanding the 56th regiment, was killed in a skirmish during the advance on French positions at Ticonderoga. Howe's body was brought back to Albany, to be interred in St. Peter's Church—the only British Lord buried in North America. When another unit of Abercrombie's army, the Black Watch, was horribly mauled by the French, the army fell back on Albany.

Benjamin Franklin at the Stadt Huys, 1754

1759: General Jeffrey Amherst camped at Albany and moved his troops north to take Ticonderoga and Crown Point, abandoned by the French. Elsewhere, after the British captured Montreal and Quebec, the French were finished as a colonial power in North America. The Iroquois from this point onward were diminished in their strategic importance. Victory brought the high point of British power, a time of elation shared with colonists who still saw themselves as English. In Albany, King George II's birthday was celebrated with a bonfire to which the municipal government provided wood.

1761: Schuyler Mansion, an Albany landmark henceforward, was constructed by British troops directed by Philip Schuyler's friend Colonel John Bradstreet. (Schuyler himself was in England at the time.) The city's leading citizen, Schuyler now led the way for integration of the Dutch into mainstream Anglo-American society. Yet in various ways Dutch folkways and vernacular would persist until today.

1765: Sir William Johnson observed that the Stamp Act—passed that year to raise Crown revenues by requiring the affixing of stamps to all commercial and legal documents—had revitalized a strong desire in the colonies for a representative form of government, such as that proposed by the Albany Congress of 1754. Unless checked, this spirit would soon be out of control. In 1766 Albany merchants, who had applied for the right to distribute these stamps, were forced to renounce their intentions by a group of young men

from the Dutch merchant families then dominating city politics.

1766: Albany's Common Council voted to construct three stone docks on the Hudson River, tangibly acknowledging the benefit of the waterway to the community.

1770–1772: Albany was undergoing a transformation which shaped its future, becoming a purveyor of goods and a center for services. By 1771 the county would have a population of 42,706 persons, 3,877 of them black. In 1772, Tryon and Charlotte counties were formed from Albany County. The city's first newspaper, the *Albany Gazette,* was published, and printers James and Alexander Robertson later apologized for the irregularity of its appearance. Paper delivery came by stage coach from New York, and a heavy snowfall had frozen their paper into a large mass.

1774: Mother Ann Lee, regarded by her followers as a manifestation of God, arrived from Manchester, England, and settled four miles west of Albany. The Shaker community she founded at Watervliet would last until the 1930s. The Shakers were celibate but their sect grew through conversion and by absorbing orphans from the Watervliet area.

The old order was passing, symbolized by the deaths of Sir William Johnson and General John Bradstreet. Albany's freeholders assembled in support of the

First Continental Congress, then meeting in Philadelphia.

Revolutionary Albany: 1775–1783

1775: The news of the Battle of Lexington brought matters to a head in Albany. A meeting was held at the city's market house, "that sense of the citizens should be taken on the line of conduct they propose to hold in this Critical Juncture. . . ." The people proved enthusiastic in the cause and formed a Committee of Safety, Protection, and Correspondence. The Provincial Congress unanimously recommended Philip Schuyler as "the most proper person" in New York to be appointed a Major General. Schuyler was given command of the Army of the Northern Department and entered negotiations with sachems of the Six Nations as men straggled into Albany to join his forces. Albany was again crowded with strangers, and for the first time the Dutch Reformed Church held services in English.

1776: Popular sentiment became increasingly violent. As Mayor Abraham Cuyler and others celebrated King George III's birthday at Richard Cartwright's Tavern, another party with more radical sentiments set upon them. The swinging sign outside the King's Arms Tavern, at the corner of Green and Beaver streets, was ripped from its hinges and burned on State Street by a mob.

Albany-born Philip Livingston signed the Declaration of Independence. The Albany Committee of Correspondence

Peter Gansevoort

Munson/Williams, Proctor Institute

"Resolved that the Declaration of Independence be published and declared in this City . . . and that Colonel Van Schaick be requested to review the Continental troops in this City to appear under arms. . . ."

1777: General Burgoyne landed in Quebec with 8,000 British and German mercenary troops. Four hundred Indians joined Burgoyne, and Tory leader John Johnson was ready to advance into the Mohawk Valley. Philip Schuyler's few troops in a blocking position north of Albany desperately needed supplies of all sorts. Schuyler ordered his troops to fell trees across roads and navigable waterways on Burgoyne's line of march, cutting British speed to a mile per day. The murder of Jane McCrea by Burgoyne's Indians provided an incident with great propaganda value to the patriots. Whether McCrea's murder was cause or not, New England troops began to arrive, reinforcing Schuyler. Nonetheless, as Lord Howe (brother and successor to the title of the Lord Howe killed at Ticonderoga nine years earlier) sent his troops up the Hudson River toward Albany, Schuyler had only 2,000 troops. Soon after, General Horatio Gates replaced Schuyler in command.

At Fort Stanwix, near present-day Rome, New York Colonel Peter Gansevoort of Albany was besieged by British forces under Barry St. Leger. Nicholas Herkimer and his Tryon County Militia, hurrying to reinforce Gansevoort, collided with Indians and Tories at Oriskany in the bloodiest afternoon of fighting of the Revolution. Benedict Arnold finally came to the relief of Fort Stanwix.

In Burgoyne's path was Philip Schuyler's wife, Catherine, at the Schuylers' Stillwater Farm. Instructed by her husband to burn their wheatfields, she did so, and sent off their horses to deny them to the British.

The clash between Burgoyne's main force and the Americans came at Freeman's farm on September 19, 1777, an intense day with high casualties for the units engaged. On October 7 the Battle of Saratoga was decided at Bemis Heights, in part due to Albany's General Abraham Ten Broeck, who appeared at a critical moment with 3,000 fresh troops. Having lost his

artillery, Burgoyne retreated, on his way churlishly burning Schuyler's house and outbuildings at Stillwater. On October 17 Burgoyne surrendered, escorted into captivity by Col. Henry Quackenbush and his 5th Regiment of Albany County militia. Refreshed briefly at the Quackenbush House on Broadway, Burgoyne for a time enjoyed a genteel captivity at the Schuyler Mansion.

1778: The New York State Legislature passed an act restoring Albany's municipal government, its continuity broken by the institution of the Committee of Safety, Protection, and Correspondence and by expulsion of Mayor Abraham Cuyler, last mayor by royal commission. Abraham Ten Broeck became mayor in 1779 and Philip Schuyler went to the Continental Congress.

Albany County Historical Association

General Abraham Ten Broeck

1780: Alexander Hamilton and Elizabeth, daughter of Philip Schuyler, were married at the Schuyler Mansion. The bride's father would be among Hamilton's staunchest allies in New York Federalist politics. A year later a party of Tories raided the mansion in a vain attempt to kill or capture Philip Schuyler. Another facet in Hamilton's life in Albany came in 1782, when Aaron Burr opened his law office on Norton Street two doors east of South Pearl. Hamilton would be Burr's *bête noir;* Burr, Hamilton's killer.

1783: George Washington, visiting Albany, was presented with a gold box containing the "Freedom of the City." About a month after Washington's visit, the Peace of Paris was signed, ending the American Revolution.

The New Day: 1784–1807

After the end of the American Revolution, Albany found itself an old city in a new nation. Despite gradual assimilation into the Anglo mainstream of American life, Dutch folkways—custom, language, and architecture—were still prominent. The end of French, Indian, and, for the moment, British military threats, also meant the end of Albany as a frontier community. Consequently, the city now began to outgrow the limits imposed on it, literally and figuratively, by stockades and topography. While the Hudson River remained critically important, new developments in transportation and a rapid growth in population would ultimately shift the city's axis from its traditional North and South to East and West. As the fur trade diminished in its economic importance to Albany, receding to far north and far west, Albany industrialized. New technologies and new societal stresses would transform the old city.

1784: Albany established its first post office on Broadway, north of Maiden Lane. The community was returning to normal after the war. Hard money remained scarce: at least one Albany mercantile firm, Henry, McClallen & Henry, advertised that it would take payment in wheat, corn, pease, flax, seeds, boards, planks, or peltries. Albany's Common Council proposed the demolition of Fort Frederick, its stones to be used for public improvements and in building various churches.

1786: Albany celebrated its centennial with a procession of municipal officers; 13 toasts were offered at the crest of State Street hill, and "the countenances of the inhabitants bespoke great satisfaction on the occasion." With its 550 houses, Albany was the new nation's sixth largest city.

1787: "Cherry Hill" was built by Philip Van Rensselaer on the south side of the city—today the museum of the Van Rensselaer-Rankin families.

1788: Albany's growing importance was reflected in the founding of three newspapers, and throughout the ensuing century papers would commence, merge, or vanish with feverish frequency. The political climate of the city was often volatile.

When New York State ratified the Constitution, a procession celebrating the occasion was set upon by Anti-Federalists who threw stones torn from a nearby house; the city's Light-Horse troop dispersed the mob.

1790: Stage lines connected Albany with Springfield and Lansingburgh; within the next two decades Albany was the locus of most of New York State's major turnpikes. The federal census of 1790 counted 3,500 Albanians at a time when changing street names were expressing nationalist spirit. Streets named for the British heroes of the past were renamed for animals, birds, or the heroes of the American present. Some streets were paved and a new public market was erected on Broadway. Albanians formed the Albany Library.

The opening of South Ferry Street in the late 1780s was shortly thereafter followed by the laying out of a geometric grid of streets along its axis—very different from the narrow streets of the old part of Albany. Low-lying and often swampy ground, this area was formerly pasture land belonging to the Dutch Reformed Church, subsequently auctioned as building lots. The new streets were initially named for church ministers or local fish or trees. Later, as Yankee elements grew dominant in local affairs, many of the names would change to reflect more American associations, as when Frelinghuysen became Franklin Street in 1828. This Pastures area became a densely built-up neighborhood containing commercial, industrial, and residential properties, and included stores, schools, synagogues, and churches.

1793: Slaves were suspected of starting a fire in a stable which consumed most of a block bounded by Maiden Lane, State Street, Broadway, and James Street. Four slaves—a man and three women—were convicted and executed for arson, and the Common Council set a 9 o'clock curfew for Albany's slaves. Later law established a citizen night watch drawn from all males over 16. By 1799 the combined cost of this night watch, whale oil for Albany's street lamps, maintenance of the poor, and of public schools, would exceed $4,100.

1795: Because of its fortunate geographic position, Albany was, and

would long remain, a conduit to the west. Stage fare for the two-day trip to New York City was $7.25, but much traffic was westward, into New York State's interior and to the "Old West." In three days, 1,200 sleighs passed through Albany loaded with families and their goods leaving stony New England for the promise of the fertile west.

1797: Albany became New York State's capital and assumed a political significance matched by its economic one. Governors and state officials gathering in the city transformed a rather staid social life and, by maintaining homes in Albany, lent the city a new sense of importance and responsibility. Growing to a work force of many thousands, the state's payroll would one day become pivotal to Albany's economic welfare. Architect Philip Hooker designed a lasting Albany landmark: the Dutch Reformed Church on North Pearl Street. Its twin spires that puncture the skyline are featured in almost all artists' views of the riverfront. The Ten Broeck Mansion was also erected in this period.

1799: Although a post road's mean and rutted track had long connected Albany with New York City, it was the turnpikes which would intimately link Albany to the west and make the city a significant emporium in westward expansion. Albany's roads soon reached north, west, and southwest; a road down the Hudson's west bank touched Catskill; by ferry across the river, the traveler could reach a road south to New York City.

The business of feeding, lodging, and supplying westward-bound emigrants coming through Albany by turnpike was lucrative; of more lasting importance, Albany's manufacturers could receive raw materials and ship products by road. River and roads gave Albany's industry a marked advantage. By 1800 Albany's population was over 50 percent larger than a decade earlier. Architect William Sander designed the State Hall, which housed New York's government in 1799.

1803: A customs house was established, indicative of Albany's commercial significance. New concentrations of population required new social services of many types. The Albany Waterworks Company

A LAW,

To regulate the Use, and restrain the Waste, of the Water of the Albany Water-Works. *Passed 21st October,* 1803.

BE it Ordained by the Truſtees of the Albany Water-Works, That no Perſon entitled to the Uſe of the ſaid Water, ſhall ſupply or furniſh any other Perſon, not ſo entitled to be ſupplied, with Water from any Penſtock in his or her Houſe or other Building or Lot; and that for every Neglect or Refuſal to conform to this Proviſion, the Perſon ſo neglecting or refuſing, ſhall forfeit the Sum of One Dollar.

And be it further Ordained, That every Perſon uſing the ſaid Water ſhall, at all Times during the Day Time, permit the Superintendent of the ſaid Water-Works, to enter into the Houſe, Building or Lot, in or on which any ſuch Penſtock or Aperture ſhall be erected or made, and to examine his or her lateral Pipes, Penſtock or other Devices connected with the ſaid Water-Works, without Hindrance or Moleſtation: And if it ſhall appear to ſuch Superintendent that any Part of ſuch lateral Pipes, Penſtocks or other Devices, are not well and ſufficiently ſecured to prevent the Waſte of Water, and ſuch Superintendent ſhall require the ſame to be repaired, that then and in every ſuch Caſe the Perſon entitled to the uſe of ſuch Penſtock or Aperture ſhall within ſuch reaſonable Time thereafter, as the Superintendent in his Diſcretion ſhall appoint, cauſe the ſame to be well and effectually repaired under the Direction of ſuch Superintendent; and if ſuch Repairs ſhall not have been made within the Time preſcribed for that Purpoſe, the Superintendent ſhall further require ſuch Perſon ſo neglecting or refuſing to repair, to appear before the Preſident of the ſaid Truſtees, and ſhall forthwith make Report thereof to him, and the Preſident ſhall in a ſummary Manner, enquire whether ſuch Repairs were neceſſary, and whether ſuch Notice to repair ſhall have been given and was not complied with, and in his Diſcretion, either allow a further Time to make ſuch Reparation, or cauſe ſuch lateral Pipe to be cut off.

And be it further Ordained, That no Perſon, other than the Preſident, one of the ſaid Truſtees, or the Superintendent, ſhall be permitted to open any of the Fire-Stops connected with the ſaid Water-Works, unleſs in Caſe of Fire; and that if any Perſon ſhall open any Fire-Stop, the Superintendent ſhall forthwith make report thereof to the Clerk; to the End, that the Perſons opening the ſame may be proſecuted for the ſame, which it ſhall be the Duty of the Clerk to do, as ſoon as poſſible after receiving ſuch Report.

And be it further Ordained, That if after the paſſing of this Law, any Perſon, other than the Superintendent, ſhall perforate any of the Conduits belonging to the ſaid Water-Works, or the lateral Pipes connected therewith, with intent to uſe or enable any other Perſon to uſe the Water conducted through the ſame, without the Conſent of the ſaid Truſtees firſt had and obtained, every ſuch Perſon ſhall forfeit for every ſuch Perforation the Sum of Five Dollars; and that the Superintendent ſhall not connect any lateral Pipe with the Conduits aforeſaid, unleſs he ſhall have carefully inſpected the Logs, the iron Hoops and connecting Pipes compoſing the ſame, ſo as to be ſatisfied that the ſame are found, well jointed, ſtrong and well calculated to prevent a Waſte of Water.

A true Copy,

PETER EDM. ELMENDORF, *Clerk.*

An Albany Waterworks Company broadside of 1803

employed large tree trunks, bored out and joined by iron collars, to bring water to the community. In 1803 the Albany Medical Society offered free "kine-pox" vaccination to the city's poor, and a County Medical Society was founded three years later.

1804: Changes were coming to Albany. Transplanted Yankee Elkanah Watson, a force for modernization not always appreciated by Albany's Dutch traditionalists, revived Philip Schuyler's concept of the Erie Canal. Watson was also prime mover in organizing the State Bank of Albany, Albany's oldest surviving bank.

The New Industrial Age: 1807–1860

1807: Significant to both Albany and to the world at large, the *Clermont* tied up at a wharf at the foot of Madison Avenue at 11:27 on the morning of September 5, 1807. Robert Fulton's sidewheeler steamboat had made the 150 miles from New York City in under 29 hours and, by harnessing steampower to transportation, ushered

in the age of steam. Passage on the maiden trip: $7. A number of steamboats soon traveled the Hudson and the resultant competition over the years would cause the price of a trip to New York to fluctuate between $10 and 6¾ ¢. These boats, requiring tons of cordwood, denuded the Hudson River Valley of thousands of trees.

President Jefferson's Embargo of 1807 proved injurious to merchants, manufacturers, and workers, and its lifting two years later sparked day-long ringing of the city's bells, impromptu parades, and speechifying.

1812: Once again the nation was at war with Great Britain, and once again Albany was target of a British offensive, blunted at Plattsburg. At Queenstown Heights, Albany's Colonel Solomon Van Rensselaer was wounded four times when leading American troops against British positions, only to be forced back when New York State militia refused to cross the Canadian border to reinforce him. The war would have a dramatic aftermath for Albany.

1813: A Lancastrian School—an English system in which student proctors aided a single teacher in teaching many pupils—had also been established; by 1816, 400 students were being taught there at an average annual cost of $2.50 each. To boost local industry, the Common Council pledged $1,000 to anyone who discovered a seam of coal four feet thick within five miles of the navigable Hudson. As the forests receded, coal became a vital fuel source. In 1813, Joseph Fry issued the first city directory, a 60-page listing of 1,638 names—not quite 15 percent of Albany's population.

1815: British merchants, after the War of 1812, dumped quantities of cheap goods on the American market in an attempt to regain their dominant trading position. Many local manufacturers were ruined. Albany's newspapers—then including the city's first daily, the Albany *Daily Advertiser*—recorded financial disasters. The Common Council moved to set aside 50 acres of land on the south side of Albany for an almshouse. Debtors in the city jail petitioned the city's well-to-do "for such broken meats and vegetables as the opulent have in their power to spare." In the meantime, Albany Academy laid the

cornerstone of its Philip Hooker building, still in Academy Park.

1817: Of enormous import to Albany was the bill passed by the New York State Legislature for construction of the Erie Canal, which would make Albany the terminus for the produce of the West and products of the East by connecting the Hudson River to the Great Lakes. Laborers were recruited in Ireland to build the Erie Canal, and Albany thereby gained a substantial Irish population.

At a time when there were nearly 10,000 slaves in New York State, the legislature also passed a law abolishing slavery after July 4, 1827.

1820: The Albany Savings Bank was founded, with silversmith Joseph Rice making the first deposit. Stagecoaches carried the mail to New York City; one broke through the ice and sank while crossing the frozen Hudson. Albany had five newspapers; its Apprentices' Library, founded to aid young mechanics, by 1822 had 1,585 volumes and 350 readers. Isaiah Townsend was president of Albany's first Chamber of Commerce.

1825: *The Seneca Chief* was the first boat to negotiate the full length of the Erie Canal, reaching Albany from Buffalo. Cannon were placed at intervals from Albany to New York and fired in notice of the *Seneca Chief's* arrival; it took less than an hour for this signal to reach New York and then be returned to Albany. Albany celebrated with parades, special church

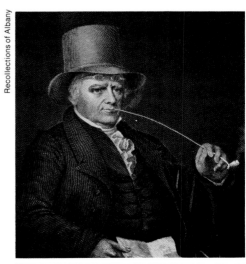

Elkanah Watson, who revived the idea of building the Erie Canal

The De Witt Clinton, *first steam passenger train in America*

services, a huge collation, and a grand ball. Seven thousand boats used the Erie Canal in its first year, almost 13,000 its second. Albany's population in 1825, nearly 16,000, would now grow dramatically, thanks to the Erie Canal. Eleven steamboats were regularly running to New York City.

1827: This year marked the emancipation of all slaves in the State of New York. . .Jesse Strang, murderer of John Whipple, was the last person publicly executed in Albany. The occasion drew an immense crowd, with 1,100 vehicles coming into Albany from the North alone. Ballads were hawked in the crowd and a largely festive atmosphere prevailed.

1828: The city was building. The Common Council received bids for leveling Robinson's Hill (Eagle Street between Hudson and Madison avenues), the soil to be used as fill in low-lying land below South Ferry Street. The contractor awarded the job was paid with three-quarters of the building lots thus created. Petitioners also requested the Common Council to improve the area of North Pearl Street between Orange and Patroon streets, where stood a row of "miserable hovels." This redevelopment, a sort of primordial urban renewal, resulted in the creation of Clinton Square, shortly afterwards the residence of young Herman Melville and his family.

1829: Both the Albany Orphan Asylum and St. Vincent's Female Orphan Society were organized. A temperance society was founded; in 1830 temperance people estimated that Albany's 415 taverns and groceries sold 200,000 gallons of alcohol annually. The city, they said, had 500 habitual drunkards, 4,000 "tipplers," and 200 deaths yearly from "intemperance." In 1829 Albanians drank 12,000 of the

42,000 barrels of beer brewed in the city, exporting the rest.

1830: The ills of urbanization were beginning to affect Albany. To maintain public services for a population of 24,238 persons, city expenditures of more than $174,000 exceeded revenues by over $18,000. Albany, author Nathaniel P. Willis quipped, looked "so well in the distance, that you half forgive it for its hogs, offals, broken pavements, and the score of other nuisances more Dutch than decent."

Most important for Albany, Stephen Van Rensselaer broke ground for the construction of the nation's first steam-powered railroad, the Mohawk & Hudson, that connected Albany to Schenectady, the first link in an eventual nationwide web of tracks.

1831: When the first train passed over the completed tracks, the people of Albany flocked to see this technological marvel, a wonder of the age. By 1833 the trains would run from the head of State Street, the cars drawn by horses to the junction of Madison and Western Avenue, where the engines were fueled. It cost $42,600 per mile to build the Mohawk & Hudson Railroad, and subscription books were immediately opened to finance a rail connection to New York City.

1832: Cholera appeared in Albany, brought in by French-Canadian

The Eagle Tavern, located on Court Street

emigrants. The first victim died in early July. Fearing the night air, the Common Council met by day and churches canceled evening services. Travelers avoided Albany, and boats and stages arrived half empty. Since farmers stopped bringing produce in to market, foodstocks were alarmingly low, and the bushel price of potatoes rose 300 percent. Most stores were closed; the mayor proclaimed a time of mourning. As citizens burned tar "to abate the plague," a gloomy pall of oily smoke hung over Albany. By the time the epidemic ended in mid-September, 1,147 cases of cholera had been diagnosed, more than a third of them fatal.

1833: With the idea of erecting a statue of George Washington there, the triangle of land at the junction of Washington and Central avenues was fenced in and named Washington Park. Its name was later changed to Townsend Park in commemoration of Mayor John Townsend.

1837: The onset of a national financial panic saw Albany's banks cease payments in specie, an action taken by New York City's banks a day earlier. Albany businessmen petitioned the Common Council to issue bills in denominations less than one dollar so that change could be made. Although State Bank of Albany was first to resume specie payment in 1838, unemployment was rife, 639 people in the city's almshouse. In three months one soup kitchen fed 1,530 persons at a cost of one third of a cent each.

1839: There was other unrest. Farmers defied the county sheriff when he attempted to collect rents due the patroonship. Turned back by several hundred assembled antirenters, the sheriff obtained the aid of Albany's militia and, after a long series of civil disturbances, was able to enforce the law. The antirenters, however, had sounded the patroonship's death-knell;

several years later a state constitutional convention abolished feudal tenure.

1840: Albany's population was 33,627 (with less than 3 percent black) and would increase by nearly 24 percent in the next five years. One May day's traffic count on a Broadway corner listed 9,762 pedestrians, 407 wagons, 146 stages, and 234 other vehicles. When the first locomotive arrived in Greenbush on the new track from Boston the next year, an all-weather route to the east was at last opened. Its Albany-bound passengers transferred from train to ferry at Greenbush.

1843–47: The Perry Stove Works opened. The stove industry became huge in 19th century Albany. City institutions were developing. Albany Hospital incorporated in 1843, five years after the medical college. The New York State Normal School, ancestor of the State University, was established in 1844. Albany Rural Cemetery supplanted several burial grounds within the city limits in 1845. In 1847 the Rev. John McCloskey became Albany's first Roman Catholic Bishop.

Albany's Irish, German, and Jewish populations were on the verge of dramatic growth. Acknowledging urban needs, in 1846 the Common Council began to search for an adequate water supply for Albany. In the same year a telegraphic link with New York City was made. Technology was beginning to shrink distance, and this communication invention owed much to Albany resident Joseph Henry's pioneering work in electromagnetic induction. In 1845 Henry was invited to become the first Secretary of the Smithsonian Institution in Washington, D.C.

1848: Albany's firemen, who were volunteers, had organized in 11 engine, two hook-and-ladder, and separate axe and hose companies. Since their rivalries were often explosive, brawls between companies, as buildings blazed, were commonplace. In 1848 large fires, including one that consumed 600 buildings on 37 acres near the river, led to a Common Council ban on construction of wooden buildings in the congested areas east of Lark Street. Another ordinance, much resented by firemen, put Albany's fire companies under command of a full-time chief, who was paid an annual $700 salary.

The Albany Republican Artillery was

An incident of anti-rentism, 1838

away in the Mexican War, in action at Chapultepec. Of the unit's 70 privates, more than one-third died. When the survivors returned to Albany, they found Albanians radically altering the topography of their city as it spread along the river and west toward the Pine Bush. Congregation Beth Jacob had built a synagogue at Madison Avenue and Fulton Street, and Joel Munsell had begun publication of his *Annals of Albany.*

1849: Zachary Taylor made a presidential visit to an Albany whose population would soon exceed 50,000— not counting those citizens who left for the goldfields of California. Albany's real estate was valued at more than $8.2 million.

1850s: The City Water Commission in 1850 purchased land and water leases for Patroon's Creek, damming it a year later to form 40-acre reservoir Rensselaer Lake (Six Mile Waterworks).

In 1851 the first train to travel the full length of the Hudson River Railroad made the journey, New York City to Albany, in less than three and a half hours. The Albany to Susquehanna Railroad was also incorporated in that year, and by 1855 the last building east of Montgomery Street made way for a dense matrix of railroad tracks. By 1854 there was heavy rail traffic, with 2,000 immigrants passing west one day, 1,380 cattle leaving Albany another. Albany's lumber district loaded 44 cargo vessels in a day.

As a state capital at the intersection of several major transportation systems, Albany was a frequent site for conventions as well as a target of orators and entertainers. Ralph Waldo Emerson addressed the Young Men's Association in 1850; Jenny Lind first triumphantly sang in Albany in 1851; and Lajos Kossuth raised $2,000 for the Magyar cause in 1852. Black Albanians met in City Hall to discuss the Fugitive Slave Law in 1850; seven years later Albany hosted an abolitionists' convention addressed "with great earnestness" by Susan B. Anthony.

Archbishop Hughes dedicated the Cathedral of the Immaculate Conception in 1852. The widow of late Mayor Charles E. Dudley gave $63,000 toward the Dudley Observatory, built in 1856 on a northern Albany hilltop

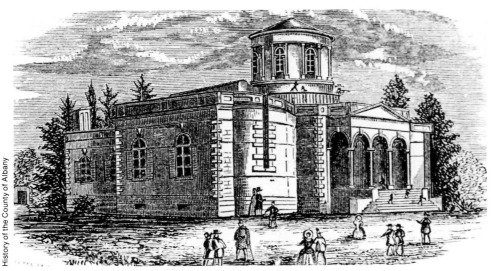

The Dudley Observatory, located on the highest point in Albany

donated by Stephen Van Rensselaer. In 1852 Albany created a regular police corps with four precincts, succeeding the old constabulary system.

1860: Kerosene was first marketed in Albany as a lighting fuel. The visiting Prince of Wales, later King Edward VII, was lionized by Albanians. St. Joseph's Roman Catholic Church, an example of 13th-century Benedictine architecture, was dedicated—a gem in the setting of prosperous Ten Broeck Square. Also in 1860, St. Peter's present building was under construction on State Street.

Late antebellum Albany sat atop the nation's sociological iceberg; its citizens would soon participate in a four-year fratricidal war fought on safely distant battlefields.

Albany's Civil War: 1861–1865

Abolitionists had been active in Albany in an effort to arouse public opinion against the institution of slavery abiding in the South. Commerce with the South was more incidental. The possibility of Union troops' actually fighting Southern Americans was approached with much soul-searching. Thurlow Weed—publisher of the Albany *Evening Journal*, confidant of William A. Seward, advisor to Abraham Lincoln, and a nationally heard voice in Republican politics—in editorials written during the pre- and post-election months shifted his tone along with events. "No Compromise— No Back Down," he said. "It is a new

and novel position, for we have been all our life showing up the dark side of the Slavery Picture. But in view of a fearful calamity, there is no want of consistency, or of fidelity, in going to the verge of conciliation with the hope of averting it." In Albany's Tweddle Hall, a mass meeting took place to promote "conciliation, concession, and compromise" on the slavery issue about to tear the states asunder.

1861: The year opened with the state's antislavery convention. Frederick Douglass, Gerrit Smith, and Lucretia Mott were among those to appear. Other cities had denied the abolitionists their rights to peaceful assembly and free speech, especially in the tense post-election period. Some Albany elements approached Mayor George H. Thacher to decline hospitality, but Thacher replied with an emphatic negative: "Let at least the

Capital of the Empire State be kept free from the disgraceful proceedings which, in other localities, have brought dishonor upon our institutions. At all events, come what may, mob law shall never prevail in our good city with my consent and connivance. . . ." Local hoodlums created a riot when the convention began in the hall of the Young Men's Association, but were soon subdued by police.

A few days later Abraham Lincoln visited the city. Albany's Burgesses' Corps would act as military escort at the inauguration. When Fort Sumter fell to the Confederacy, the 25th Regiment entrained for Washington almost immediately, and the Burgesses' Corps answered Lincoln's first call for volunteers. Other Albany regiments would follow: 3rd, 10th, 43rd, and 91st, as well as the Albany Zouaves.

Mechanicsville's 24-year-old Ephraim Elmer Ellsworth, who had organized a Zouave unit of firemen, was shot pulling down a Confederate flag at an Alexandria, Virginia, hotel. Three days later a procession of 2,000 troops escorted his body to the Capitol, where it rested in state. The martyred Ellsworth's bloody uniform became a military relic. Other Albany casualties would follow, but fresh troops of eager volunteers succeeded them. When the 10th Regiment departed for the war in 1862, fervid crowds swarmed the streets, crowding windows and rooftops to watch; in this soldiers' *bon voyage*, martial music blared and women wept.

In April 1861 the first guns were fired from the batteries of treason upon Fort Sumter. The sound of those guns startled the nation, and revealed the existence of a deep, widespread and malignant rebellion. After a long period of peace, unity, and uninterrupted prosperity—during which the arts had been advanced, the resources of the country developed, manufactures and commerce increased, and the national domain extended, with a rapidity almost unparalleled in history—there burst upon us the storm of war . . .

Rufus W. Clark. *The Heroes of Albany: A Memorial of the Patriot-Martyrs Who Sacrificed Their Lives During the Late War in Defense of the Union, 1861–1863*. Albany, 1867.

Albany Institute of History and Art

Ominously, by late summer Albany's recruiting offices were open on Sundays in an attempt to maintain a steady flow of replacements to add to the bloodshed in the South. To finance the war, an Internal Revenue office appeared in Albany. Meanwhile, unstable fiscal conditions caused the sudden and startling failure of four city banks.

1863: Recruiting tents were set up on State Street, and the National Commercial Bank (now Key Bank) guaranteed $3.5 million in enlistment bonuses. The 25th Regiment, returned from Washington, was called out to quash 1,000 striking dockers and railroad workers. The presence of troops quelled the disturbance. "This, we hope," wrote the Albany *Argus,* "has ended the strike—the most formidable one in our city."

1864: Between the end of 1863 and mid-July of 1864, Albany County paid well over a million dollars in enlistment bonuses as the Civil War dragged on and Union casualties mounted. An Army Relief Bazaar in Academy Park sent nearly $82,000 to the U. S. Sanitary Commission. The Common Council authorized Albany's first steam-operated fire engine. In 1864 the city had a baseball team, the Nationals, and also heard a performance of "Lucrezia Borgia," its first grand opera.

1865: At the war's end, Albany's population of 62,613 barely exceeded its total of five years earlier. On its winding way back to Illinois, Abraham Lincoln's body briefly rested in state in the Capitol. Blacks were now admitted to the Young Men's Association. Albany's regiments filtered back from a conflict which had cost their county nearly $4.5 million.

The Army Relief Bazaar, held from February 22 to March 10, 1864

The end of the Civil War shifted civil priorities. The state legislature authorized construction of a new Capitol. The Great Western Turnpike became Western Avenue, perhaps a change in nuance as well as in name.

Albany Enters the Gilded Age: 1866–1875

As it was for the United States generally, the aftermath of the American Civil War was a time of considerable change for Albany. The city once again experienced substantial, accelerated growth in population and commerce, which strained existing urban systems and necessitated enlarged or wholly new municipal services. Industry, too, changed, and this period saw the Erie Canal dwindling in its economic significance. Albany became more specialized in many ways, more emphatically capital city and financial center, more identifiable with the Albany of the late 20th century.

1866: For decades hundreds of dockers and teamsters had worked to unload freight trains on the shores of the Hudson River, ferry the goods across the water, and warehouse or reload them on trains on the opposite bank. A $1.1 million railroad bridge was completed, although it had been strongly opposed by those whose interests it threatened. The Hudson was no longer Albany's commercial barrier to the East; freight could now ship on through trains.

Albany's horse-drawn streetcars began operating. This railway became vital to

the growth of neighborhoods farther from the city's ancient core. Eventually residential areas would become differentiated from commercial or industrial ones.

Albany's Board of Public Instruction came into being in 1866. Responding to the need for a standardized education for Albany's children, new public schools were built with marked regularity around the city.

1867–69: A paid Fire Department was on the job by 1867, the Common Council also voting $15,000 to install fire alarms at strategic points in the city—75 were in place by the next year. In 1868 the center market on South Pearl Street was demolished for the erection of a new City Building to house expanded municipal services. Broadway was being paved with blocks of Canada pine, soon superseded by granite pavement. A Parks Commission was appointed in 1869, when the property tax rate was $3.54 per $100 of assessed value, with mandate to acquire the Washington Parade Ground and an adjacent cemetery, genesis of Washington Park. Like the municipal government which had outgrown its existing City Hall, New York State required a new Capitol, and its foundation commenced in 1869.

St. Agnes' Cemetery was established in 1867, the year St. Patrick's Roman Catholic Church was constructed; St. Ann's followed in 1868. Albany's Episcopal Diocese, its first Bishop 36-year-old William Croswell Doane, was set off from the New York Diocese in 1868. A $130,000 Congregational Church was dedicated in 1869, the same year that Christian Brothers

Daughters of Charity Archives

Kitchen of St. Vincent's Asylum for Girls

Academy was chartered. St. Vincent's Asylum for Girls opened on Elm Street.

1870–1875: The 1870 federal census counted 69,442 Albanians; 4.38 million people in New York State. Five years later another 17,000 persons had settled in the city and more than 16 percent of its total population was Irish-born. City government was undergoing modifications as the Dongan Charter was amended: the western boundary was fixed 4.25 miles from the Hudson River, instead of Governor Dongan's 16 mile corridor into the Pine Bush; the mayor received the power of the veto, polling places were designated, and election inspectors appointed.

Construction began on Washington Park, with bodies exhumed from the old burial ground interred in Albany Rural Cemetery—the final count was 40,000, according to one source. The Park opened in 1872; its lake was excavated in 1873, and bridged, and the original Lake House was built two years after that. In Albany's South End, School 15 opened, modeled on Boston's Shurtliff Grammar School by Albany architects Ogden and Wright. The building, dedicated in 1871 after a year under construction, was the city's first modern, scientifically planned school building, a landmark development in local public education.

The city's first high school, at Eagle, Columbia, and Steuben streets, was in operation in 1876.

Railroads were becoming increasingly important to Albany's economy. The first train crossed the Maiden Lane railroad bridge in 1871; another railroad bridge, with a 400-ton drawbridge, opened a year later. By 1875 the West Albany stockyards shipped a daily average of 103 carloads of livestock, nearly 38,000 that year, almost 25,000 of cattle, 8,500 of hogs. Rail transport was so rapid that New York City newspapers were in Albany by 8 a.m.

As the railroads waxed, the canals waned; in 1873 the Albany Dock Association adjourned indefinitely. Business along the pier and along Quay Street was at a virtual standstill, buildings there renting for half their former price, if rented at all. Through-rail transport had halted much of the warehouse business and many merchants moved to Broadway. National financial panic in 1873 hardly benefited the deteriorating basin area.

The cornerstone of the new State Capitol was laid in 1871, and in 1872 Congress authorized construction of

Three Albany boys enjoying their "bicycles"

Architect H.H. Richardson, designer of 1883 Albany City Hall

Albany's Federal building on Broadway. Just north of the city, the Albany Gaslight Company, capitalized at a million dollars, constructed its plant.

Albany's German community celebrated Prussia's victory over France in 1871 with a *Friedens Fest,* the 10th and 25th Regiments parading for the occasion. Albany's Martin Opera House opened in 1870, and the Albany Musical Association was organized; late 19th century Albany abounded in singers and musicians.

Nation's Centennial to City's Bicentennial: 1876–1886

1876: America's centennial year was celebrated by Albanians with a midnight parade on January 1. Albany's women later sent a "magnificent state banner" to the Philadelphia Centennial Exposition. Governor Samuel Tilden hosted the first reception held at the Eagle Street Governor's Mansion. Albany's Mayor Judson, however, appealed for donations for Albany's poor— unemployed since the financial reverses of the Panic of 1873.

1877–1885: In 1880 there were nearly 91,000 Albanians, 12,575 of them Irish-born. There were 3,325 farms in Albany County and almost 9,500 horses. Dramatic population growth was reflected in the westward extension of the street railway, up Madison Avenue to Quail Street in 1877, and along Lark Street in 1885. In

the course of repaving, workmen cut down the huge elm so long a landmark at the corner of North Pearl and State streets—a tree, as Albany folklore had it, planted in 1735 by Philip Livingston. There were 54 miles of paved streets in the city of 1885, 44 of those miles cobbled. That year, too, Albany contained 6,833 brick and 6,581 wooden structures and 111 "manufactures."

The old City Hall (on the Eagle Street site of the present one) burned in 1880, but by 1881 Masons ceremoniously laid the cornerstone of a new one designed by nationally prominent architect Henry Hobson Richardson. By 1883 the building was complete, to serve as the center of city government for the century to follow. The seven million gallon Prospect Hill reservoir was completed in 1878; a public bath opened at the foot of Columbia Street in 1882. Albany's Police Department had its telephones in operation in 1877, and the next year the city had the nation's third working telephone exchange, with 100 subscribers (the first seven had been physicians). By 1879 the Commercial Telephone Company was in business; Hudson River Telephone Company in 1883. Also in that year Albany's Board of Health was endorsing municipal sewage and garbage disposal systems, visiting nurses, and vaccination of school children.

Albany Medical College obtained the Lancastrian School building in 1877,

---

Tombstone of President Chester A. Arthur

Lou Carol Lecce

four years later granting laboratory and classroom space to Albany College of Pharmacy, the 15th college of pharmacy in the United States, second in New York; it had 21 students.

The new Capitol building was officially declared such in 1878, and opened, in part, the following year. In 1879 the cornerstone of the Federal Building was laid.

Grover Cleveland, then governor, was serenaded by the 10th Regiment's Band the night he was nominated for President in 1884, while his opponent, James G. Blaine, subsequently spoke to 7,000 Albanians during a 20 minute whistle-stop. The city was spreading west; of 20 new churches built between 1872 and 1890, the majority were located in western portions of Albany. By 1885 there were more than 87,500 Albanians. "West" was west of Washington Park, and much of Madison, Western, and Central avenues was built up during this general period.

As early as 1881 the Albany Electric Illuminating Company had contracted to light city streets, generating its electricity at a Trinity Place powerhouse. The advent of electrical power launched vertical architecture in Albany; electric motors would power the elevators that made tall buildings feasible—for the first time interrupting Albany's skyline with something besides hills, steeples, and domes.

The New York Central's Broadway crossing at Colonie Street, long a danger to the frequent north-bound funeral processions, gave way to a viaduct in 1882 and a passenger bridge was opened across the Hudson. Tolls: pedestrian, 2 cents; single team, 10 cents; double team, 15 cents. By 1883 the West Shore Railroad also linked Albany to New York City, then to Syracuse and Buffalo.

1886: By now Albany had endured two centuries as a city. It celebrated its bicentennial with the innocent fervor of parades, canoe races, regattas, and a thousand school children singing a specially composed song. Books were printed and medallions struck. Albany's blacks planted a commemorative elm in Washington Park; the Germans, of course, an oak. Significantly, one day of the week-long celebration eulogized Albany's trades

and manufactures.

In that bicentennial year Albany produced a panoply of Victorian consumer and industrial goods, from saddlery to dredges, drain tiles, tinwares, emery wheels, whale and elephant oils, ice boxes, monumental stonework, and sawsets.

Albany's middle class had many diversions. Rollerskating enjoyed a first popularity, as did bicycles. Albany's Wheelmen, part of a national fad, had productive goals—lobbying for better roads. There were clubs for chess, tennis, curling, canoeing, boating; baby shows and dog shows; orchestras and, inevitably, singing societies. Germans formed a Young Men's Democratic Club. Cricket was a popular game. The Holland Society, the Albany Press Club, and the Ridgefield Athletic Club were all founded in 1885. In 1886 a new YMCA was under construction on North Pearl Street; that year an Elks Club formed, as well as the Episcopal Women's Diocesan League and the Albany Historical and Art Society, the latter given impetus by the city's bicentennial celebration. The bicentennial year witnessed the funeral of ex-President Chester A. Arthur, who was buried at Albany Rural Cemetery.

Two Wars and a New Century: 1887–1916

1887–1890: The Albany Railway reduced its Pearl Street fare to a nickel in 1887; citizens were now long accustomed to the horsecars. A few years earlier, Richmond, Virginia, had experimented with electric trolleys; now electric streetcars were tried in Albany's neighboring communities. Well over four million fares in 1889 justified conversion to electricity and in 1890 the street railway sold 200 of its horses. New York's railroad workers were organizing and West Albany railroaders rioted in 1877; some Albany workers organized in the Ancient Order of United Workmen in 1878. Perhaps following the example of Jersey City and New York City railroad Knights of Labor, the New York Central's brakemen struck in 1882 as did Albany and Troy stovemolders in 1884–1885.

By 1890 the U.S. Census would count nearly 95,000 Albanians; almost 2,200 more would be added in the next two years. A north-south artery was needed further west to carry increasing traffic,

Erastus Corning 2nd

A portion of the silver presented to the U.S.S. Albany

and the Hilton Bridge Construction Company bridged the Sheridan Hollow with the Hawk Street Viaduct in 1890. Asphalt pavement was first used on Albany's streets that year, on Madison Avenue. The Albany Police Department was placed under a new Department of Public Safety. The sewer project sought by the Board of Health—Patroon's Creek—had been completed by contractors two years earlier.

The stonework began on the Washington Avenue Armory in 1889, the year William J. Milne became first president of Albany Normal School; in 1890 the Normal School was chartered as a college.

1891–1894: Mayor James H. Manning welcomed President Benjamin Harrison to Albany in 1891. In 1892 architect Marcus T. Reynolds supervised the careful dismantling, numbering, shipping, and rebuilding of the Van Rensselaer Manor House. Its site was cleared for railroad tracks and business use while the structure itself was assembled as a Williams College fraternity house. Golf was introduced in Albany in 1894 and a year later the Albany Country Club bought a Western Avenue property.

1895–1897: At this time Albany's women seemed increasingly involved in social issues. The Albany branch of the Indian Association voted to fund the education of Sophie High Dog at the Rosebud Sioux Agency. The Mohawk Chapter of the Daughters of the American Revolution organized. Other women got the loan of the Albany *Argus* for a day, proceeds of that day's edition to benefit Child's Hospital. Suffragettes Elizabeth Cady Stanton and Susan B. Anthony, frequent lobbyists in Albany, were opposed by a group of Albany women, led by Mrs. John V. L. Pruyn, and by Bishop Doane, who were against "woman suffragist agitators."

In 1896 another north-south viaduct was built, crossing the Sheridan Avenue ravine at Northern Boulevard. The police installed their signal-box system that year and the Fire Department acquired three chemical fire engines in 1897.

1898–1899: The effects of America's brief and venal little war with Spain were minimal in Albany. Albany Academy graduate Charles Dwight Sigsbee was in command of the U.S.S. *Maine* when it exploded in Havana harbor. Albanians responded with jingoistic enthusiasm to the prospect of war with Spain, feeling President McKinley held back for lack of adequate munitions. Albany Chemical Company speedily doubled its capacity, round-the-clock shifts producing a substance used in gunpowder. A year later the $25 million

General Chemical Company formed, consolidating the productions of a dozen smaller Albany County firms. A Brazilian Navy cruiser under construction at a British shipyard was purchased by the U.S. and named the U.S.S. *Albany* at the petition of Albany's citizens. The *Albany*, first U.S. Navy vessel launched abroad, was finished too late for combat but remained an object of pride to Albanians, who in 1903 collected $10,000 for an elaborate silver service for the *Albany*.

The Washington Avenue Armory was crowded with volunteers taking physicals. They were to form the First Provisional Regiment and leave for Long Island, then San Francisco and Honolulu, but never see battle. The few Albany men who died in the war were in Regular Army units that fought sporadic engagements. Domestic patriotic fervor remained at high pitch. Albanians collected money and sent delicacies to its troops, presented commemorative swords, celebrated the first shots fired, the victory at Manila Bay, and the surrender of Santiago.

The State Capitol was at last finished, at a cost much greater than estimated decades earlier. The stonecutters' sheds, 20 years *in situ,* were removed and Capitol Park improved.

In 1896 Albany's street railway carried more than 9.5 million fares—on one Decoration Day a decade later, 175,000 fares totaling nearly $8,000. Albany Railway and Troy Street Railway (combined as United Traction Company in 1899), sold its franchise and assets worth $7.5 million to the Delaware and Hudson Railroad in 1905. Construction started in 1898 on the beaux arts Union Station on Broadway, which opened in 1900.

1900–1905: The new century was greeted with St. Peter's chimes ringing, cannon firing, special church services. Bishop Burke celebrated mass in a greatly crowded Cathedral of the Immaculate Conception.

Municipal Albany undertook progressive public improvements to serve its still-growing population, more than 94,000 in 1900; 4,200 more in 1905. City real property had a total assessed value of nearly $60 million. Albany Trust Company organized in

1900, as did the Chamber of Commerce and the County Bar Association.

William F. Barnes, Jr., grandson of Thurlow Weed, at age 25 became the "Boy Leader" of Albany's Republicans. By controlling the *Albany Evening Journal*, subduing intraparty factionalism, and taking advantage of Democratic schisms, Barnes rapidly gained ascendancy in Albany politics with the 1900 election of James H. Blessing as mayor.

Construction of Beaver Park was underway—later to be Lincoln Park. Dana Park was dedicated by Mayor Blessing on Arbor Day, 1901, before the Dana Natural History Society. Riverside Park, from Broadway to the Hudson River, was sodded and planted with trees two years later. Also near the river, the North Albany Filtration Plant went into operation, and in 1905 work began on a new river intake for the city water supply.

The Superintendent of Schools recommended a second high school be created in the western part of the city. The Eagle Street High School had a

City Hall decorated for the 1909 Hudson-Fulton celebration

capacity of 719 pupils, a daily attendance of 883, and an enrollment of 981.

Albany bicycle mechanic Christian Weeber, who in 1898 became an automotive pioneer by building a car that could carry a half-ton and in which he eventually logged 50,000 miles, established a first in 1904—a motorized honeymoon.

By 1900 motormen and conductors of United Traction Company were on strike, as were the men of the Painters and Decorators Union and the carpenters and plumbers. In 1901 United Traction Company employees struck again, the 10th Batallion patrolling U.T.C. routes and the city under martial law. Another unit, the 23rd Regiment from Brooklyn, reinforced the 10th, firing on a rock-throwing Broadway crowd, killing two men. The "White Rats" strike—Vaudeville's union—spread from New York to Albany and theaters were stilled. Stovemounters walked out of Rathbone, Sard in 1905, printers left the city's publishers, and the compositors at the *Argus* struck in sympathy. U.T.C. employees were on strike again in 1905. Master plumbers walked out in 1906.

While Governor Charles Evans Hughes actively campaigned to better the lot of workers, Albany's 157 police were coping with the gritty side of industri-alized society. The freshet of 1900, 20 feet above normal, was the worst in 43 years, causing great suffering in the densely settled South End. The John

G. Myers Company store on North Pearl Street collapsed, entombing 80, killing 13—all victims of negligent contractors. An army of railroad men dug in the wreckage, directed by Mayor Gaus.

Germans, who organized a Liederkranz Singing Society in 1897, figured prominently in the elaborate welcome given the Kaiser's brother, Prince Heinrich von Hohenzollern, in 1902; 1904 saw the city's first German Day with Mayor Gaus its chairman. In 1905 Albany's Italian societies paraded on Columbus Day.

In 1901 Albany mourned the deaths of Queen Victoria and President McKinley with elaborate shows of crepe; McKinley was an Albany Law School graduate. Organization of the University Club and the appearances of both Mark Twain and Irish agitator Maude Gonne also took place in 1901.

1906: The Albany Institute and the Albany Historical and Art Society merged in 1900 and in 1906 accepted the plans of architects Fuller and Pitcher for a building to be constructed on Washington Avenue near Dove Street.

Dr. Mary Walker, in her usual male attire, spoke out against capital punishment in a legislative hearing. Sarah Bernhardt appeared in two plays at Harmanus Bleecker Hall. Albany's baseball team began its season in To-ronto; five years earlier it had won the State League pennant. Some young baseball players were arrested at the behest of a few Albany clergymen for playing ball in Beaver Park on Sunday. Judges dismissed the case and Sunday baseball resumed without hindrance.

Dr. Mary Walker, opponent of capital punishment

1909: Albany commemorated two epic voyages: one taken at the dusk of the age of reconnaissance, the other in the dawn of the age of steam. The Hudson-Fulton celebration caught the imaginations of communities the length of the Hudson River; it was coordinated by a governor-appointed panel of persons with impeccable Hudson Valley social credentials.

Albany's Mayor Henry F. Snyder claimed he had devoted fully half his time to readying the patriotic, week-long festival. Preparations included creation of a massive, if transitory, "Court of Honor" on Broadway.

For the event, the people of the Netherlands had constructed a fine reproduction of the *Half Moon* from the plans of a contemporary sister ship and presented it to New York State. A reproduction of Fulton's *Clermont* accompanied "Hudson's" ship up the river. After the celebration, both vessels were moored near Kingston. Diminished in their mass appeal, the *Clermont* rotted; the *Half Moon* was eventually towed to Cohoes, where it too rotted and finally burned.

1910: In 1910 (and again in 1916) Albany annexed large portions of the Pine Bush area from the town of Guilderland. The population of Albany in 1910 was more than 100,000 persons, at a time when the state's residents as a whole were about 26 percent foreign born and 33 percent of foreign-born parentage. The Hudson-Fulton celebration partly expressed a long-term civic concern in Albany: the

Americanization of a heterogeneous population, increasingly of Eastern or Southern European origins. (Trinity Institute, Albany's oldest settlement house, would be founded in 1912 with the goal of improving neighborhood living conditions and acculturating its clients. In planning a community center at School 14 in 1915, folk dancing and Americanization were parts of the programs; by 1920 the Board of Education annually budgeted $4,000 for Americanization classes.)

Seeking a $10,000 prize offered by the *New York World* for a flight between Albany and New York City in less than 24 hours, pioneer aviator Glenn Curtiss took off from a field on the present site of the Port of Albany. He made two refueling stops in this first long-distance flight by man in a heavier-than-air machine; the speed averaged about 53 miles per hour. Three years later, the nation's first municipal airfield was created in Albany, at his takeoff place.

Automotive technology made dramatic gains between 1900 and 1920. In 1910 there were six automobile dealers in Albany, soon to be followed by others. The increasing use of automobiles necessitated better roads, at the same time outmoding electric street cars. Albany's first concrete pavement was laid. The Suburban Transportation Bus Co. was operating in 1912, and in 1913 the Albany and Guilderland

Crowd on Hudson Avenue listening to a World Series broadcast over PA system

Center Bus Line charged a nickel fare. The fire horses were disappearing, and some city departments considered motorizing.

Glenn Curtiss, early aviator

Until about 1900, most heavy freight had been waterborne, although by then the Erie Canal no longer held prime economic importance for Albany. The Lumber District, once a major exporter of timber, had also declined, becoming moribund as the logging-off of the Adirondacks shifted the lumber industry west to the Great Lakes area. By 1910 Albany's waterfront area consisted of ramshackle, partially abandoned commercial buildings—a crumbling vestige of its active past, a tenderloin district in which nighttime travel could be hazardous. This unsightly waterfront, in view of the State Capitol, bloomed at the foot of State Street, to be traversed by virtually every arriving steamboat or railroad passenger coming to Albany. The City of Albany, the Chamber of Commerce, and the D & H Railroad, among others, coalesced in the Albany Beautiful Movement, to plan beautification of the waterfront. Under the aesthetic guidance of architect Marcus T. Reynolds, a screen of new buildings would replace the existing structures by 1916. The D & H Plaza was cleared to enable construction of the superb D & H and Albany Evening Journal buildings, both in a monumental Flemish High Gothic Style.

Capital Newspapers

Albany Public Library

A contemporary Chamber of Commerce yearbook endorsed this Albany Beautiful Movement and the establishment of an Albany Barge Canal terminal. It also approved construction of low-cost housing.

1911: The Woodlawn Avenue Improvement Association petitioned the United Traction Company for trolley lines. The Albany Orphan Asylum—now the campus of Junior College of Albany—had been built in 1907, and a year later the Chamber of Commerce promoted the extension of trolley lines into the Woodlawn Avenue district, to encourage development there. But the tracks were never laid. Eventually the Association formed its own transportation corporation, a bus line.

In an epic 1911 fire, part of the New York State Capitol's premises, including the State Library, burned. The entire city fire department fought the blaze, which smoldered for a week afterward. Losses were computed in the millions of dollars, but the value of historical materials destroyed could not be calculated. Ironically, the new State Education Building, to house the State Library and Museum, was already under construction. Its plans had been selected by Governor Charles Evans Hughes after an architectural competition. In 1911 the State also acquired the Schuyler Mansion as an historic site.

In 1911 William F. Barnes became State Republican Chairman after Republican boss Thomas C. Platt waned in power. From 1912 to 1916, as National Chairman of the party, Barnes was at the apex of his political power.

1912: The mercurial William Sulzer, a Tammany Democrat, became governor of New York, but quarrels with Tammany boss Charles E. Murphy resulted in Sulzer's impeachment and conviction in 1913. Sulzer was succeeded by Albany newspaper publisher Martin H. Glynn, then lieutenant governor.

Admission to the Empire Burlesque Review cost a dime in 1912; the theater even had a ladies' matinee. Albanians, enthusiastic about baseball, had a number of teams. A large crowd of Albanians listened to the 1912 World Series between the Boston Red Sox

Flood of 1913

and the New York Giants over a primitive public address system.

1913: Ice jams south of Albany caused periodic downtown flooding, and waiters at Keeler's Broadway "Hotel for Men Only" actually rowed a boat into the hotel's street-level dining room. This year's flood inundated the municipal water-filtration system, to pollute the water supply and cause a typhoid epidemic. By 1915 the cause of such flooding (near Coeymans) was removed and the Hudson's channel there was deepened.

Suffragettes were increasingly aggressive and successful; in 1913 and 1915 the state legislature passed a women's suffrage bill, to be rejected later in popular referenda. Voters finally approved it in 1917, and two years later New York State ratified the

WWI Albany medical unit ready to depart for National Guard camp

19th Amendment to the United States Constitution.

New York State also worked to improve labor conditions, while Albany's fractious United Traction Company men struck three times between 1910 and 1916. In 1914 Albany's public schools had an enrollment well over 12,000; 97 percent attendance was the norm.

1914–1916: Charles Ogden designed the massive grey stone Academy of Holy Names on Madison Avenue in 1914. Albany's business community prospered in a time of economic growth. The Municipal Gas Company built its State Street building to Marcus T. Reynolds' design in 1915—a building now housing Niagara Mohawk. The deBeer Baseball Factory relocated from Johnstown in 1916. And in a dress rehearsal of horrors soon to come for American soldiers in the other hemisphere, Albany National Guardsmen chased Pancho Villa along the Mexican border.

The interior of City Hall was renovated by architects Gander, Gander and Gander in 1916, the year Albany annexed portions of Bethlehem and Colonie.

World War I and Its Aftermath: 1917–1920

1917–1918: Albany had a large, long-established, and prosperous German-American community. By 1913 at least two German-language newspapers were printed in the city, including the *Albany Sonntags Journal.* The widespread hysterical and vitriolic anti-German sentiment manifested in many American communities during the European conflict was tempered in Albany. When the United States itself entered the First World War, 10,000 Albany men registered for the draft; under the provisions of the Stivers Act, Albany's National Guard units were called up in July 1917.

World War I accelerated the development of some business and civic procedures. Small firms grew large and new industries evolved. "Four-minute men" made their speeches, one Liberty Loan Drive followed another, and there were plans to conserve food; "Tag Days" raised money for Armenian relief, for the Salvation Army, and for the Red Cross. Albany Hospital launched a medical unit, Base Hospital 33, which served with distinction in England. Mayor Watt appointed a War Advisory Commission. A "Melting Pot Day" was organized to collect tinfoil and scrap metal. Before the Armistice, 300 Albany men died. Henry Johnson of Albany won the French Croix de Guerre while serving with the 15th New York (Colored) Infantry Regiment. Late in 1918 and into 1919, the nationwide epidemic of "Spanish influenza" struck Albany just as the veterans of the war were filtering home.

1918–1919: The election of Alfred E. Smith as governor bolstered the spirits of New York State Democrats, who in Albany made a strong, determined effort in the 1919 municipal elections, using the issues of the high costs of Republican administration, alleged vote frauds, and the lack of basic city services such as garbage and ash collection. The new South End political team of the O'Connell brothers organized a solid reform campaign, but the Democrats narrowly lost the mayoral election, 23,553 to 22,145. Daniel P. O'Connell, however, was elected to the Board of Assessors, one of the few Democratic victors; it was the only elected office he would hold in an extraordinary political career spanning nearly six decades.

The Roaring '20s: 1920–1929

1920: Albany was at the threshold of a new era. The federal census counted 113,344 Albanians in 1920. The city budget was $3.1 million, of that more than $2.8 million to be raised through taxes. The mayor's salary was $4,000

per annum; the Board of Education's teachers, *in toto,* received more than $620,000; $2,500 was expended on truants, $70,000 for the school system's fuel. Temporary relief for Albany's indigent poor was budgeted at $15,000 in 1920, and various related activities— free dispensary, infant home, etc.— received another $4,700.

Among the things returning servicemen encountered was the prospect, at least in theory, of an Albany without alcohol. By 1914 a quarter of the states had gone "dry," and during World War I, the argument that sober servicemen and factory workers promoted victory, and that many brewers were of German ancestry, did much to advance the cause of Prohibition. In 1919 the 18th Amendment to the Constitution was ratified, in a great surge of Progressivism. The Volstead Act of 1920, providing Federal enforcement of the Amendment, went into effect on the same day as Prohibition. Overnight, some 200,000 "private" clubs opened, selling illicit liquor nationwide. In Albany saloons or "speakeasies" ranged from the desperately sordid to the elegant and were soon an open secret. Bootleggers maintained a steady supply of liquor smuggled in from Canada. Many Albany drugstores clandestinely sold liquor; Albanians made home brew or "bathtub gin."

The law-breaking climate of the times, with attendant high risks and big profits, encouraged gangsterism. The best-known incident during Albany's Prohibition era was the murder of bootlegger Legs Diamond.

Bootlegger Jack "Legs" Diamond (right), wife, and Daniel Prior

Capital Newspapers

Boss Barnes reputedly was among those Republican stalwarts in the "smoke-filled room" who, in 1920, made the cynical trade-offs that brought Warren G. Harding to the Presidency. But by this time William Barnes was slipping in his control of the Albany Republican organization because of his reactionary attitudes. Meanwhile, in the Democratic primary election of 1920, the O'Connell brothers' faction defeated that of Patrick McCabe, the oldtime Democratic boss who had worked out accommodations with Barnes. The O'Connells, now controlling the Democratic organization, prepared to challenge Barnes and the Republicans, who enjoyed a three to one advantage in voter strength.

1921: There were 98 strikes nationwide; for the men of United Traction Company, 1921 brought their fifth walkout since 1900. With the trolleys not running and 1,200 to 1,400 men striking, Albany businessmen were bound to lose money. The State Public Service Commission ordered resumption of trolley service. The company brought in strikebreakers; William Barnes supported United Traction's position. Battles broke out along the trolley lines, in the West End, along North Pearl Street and Central Avenue, and at the Quail Street trolley barns. Violence was crushed by state troopers. Public sympathy went generally with the strikers; ridership on the trolleys fell off sharply. The slack in public transportation was taken up by jitneys and autos of all sorts pressed into service as *ad hoc* cabs, and 130 taxi licenses were issued during the first 90 days of the strike. As sentiment grew for the strikers, a rift between Barnes and Republican Mayor Watt developed. By the time the strike ended months later, Barnes was an unpopular figure; his mayoral choice, William Van Rensselaer Erving, barely eked out a Republican primary victory. In its dramatic acknowledgment of the rights of labor, the Trolley Strike of 1921 was Albany's largest, and last, manifestation of Progressivism.

In the mayoral election of 1921, the Democrats nominated William S. Hackett, a lawyer and banker whose New York Mortgage and Home Building Company had aided low- and medium-income people in building affordable homes. During the campaign scandals involving fraudulent billings for coal not delivered to the city, unsafe construction of School 14, shoddy paving and sewer construction jobs became issues. When Hackett beat Erving by 7,200 votes, the Democrats returned to City Hall after an absence of more than 20 years.

1922–1924: Hackett's administration was conducted in a businesslike, cash-on-delivery manner. Consultants revamped the city's property assessment system; public schools were renovated and four new ones constructed. Ash and garbage collection was instituted and steps were taken to revamp the municipal water supply. The 1922 budget topped $3.45 million, of which more than $3 million would be raised through taxes. City revenues were close to $5 million, costs of government $5.62 million.

Albany's 1920s witnessed a continuing pattern of busline franchises encouraged by outlying neighborhoods and furthering population dispersement. The Trolley Strike had engendered a marked increase in both business and pleasure use of automobiles; gas prices rose to 35 cents a gallon. Mayor Hackett appointed a City Planning Commission to study the extension of city streets, purchase new land for boulevards, and resolve traffic problems. Traffic lights were installed in 1927. A Zoning Commission was created in 1922.

The Harmanus Bleecker Library was built in 1923 at Washington Avenue on Dove Street; in 1924 the Municipal Building was put up on Eagle Street. The College of St. Rose erected a four-story brick building in 1924; four years earlier it had begun a degree program. On New Scotland Avenue, Bishop Gibbons had chosen a 56-acre site for St. Peter's Hospital, which was joined later by Mercy College, Mercy High School, Immaculate Conception Seminary, the Motherhouse of the Sisters of Mercy, and the Villa. Governor Alfred E. Smith's statewide public works program was realized locally by construction of the State Health Laboratories on New Scotland Avenue and expansion of the State Teachers College.

1925: Governor Smith created the Albany Port District in 1925, and Congress voted more than $11 million to dredge a 27-foot-deep, 30-mile-long channel up the Hudson River capable of floating 85 percent of the world's oceangoing ships. In 1926, before the port was officially opened, it had receipts totaling about $63,000. The cities of Albany and Rensselaer expended $10 million in constructing wharves, sheds, and the world's largest single-unit grain elevator. Albany annexed Westerlo Island in the port. Both D & H and New York Central Railroads cooperated in development of the port, laying a 25-mile web of tracks; a third of the American population could be reached within a 250-mile radius of the Port of Albany.

During the 1920s Albany's last horsecar disappeared. The demise of the trolley was also approaching as buses began to replace the trolleys in the nationwide trend toward motorized transportation. Between buses and automobiles, commuting became a truly viable possibility resulting in a more convenient suburban life. In the future this trend would have immense impact on life in Albany; coupled with better roads and a national prosperity locally shared, it would be cause for a dramatic demographic change.

1926–1929: By the late 1920s Albany's Democrats had achieved a two-to-one dominance over the city's Republicans in voter registration, a reversal of the situation in 1921. Aviator Charles Lindbergh was cheered by thousands of Albanians in 1927 when he made an appearance in Lincoln Park. A year later, when Albany created the first city-owned airport in the nation, it was named "Lindbergh Field," then "Quentin Roosevelt Field."—located at the site of the present Albany County Airport.

The Albany College of Pharmacy moved into its building near Albany Hospital in 1927. The city built the John A. Howe Library in 1928; in 1929 it closed the Almshouse, transferring many of its residents to the newly opened Ann Lee Home. Albany Law School was built in 1929.

Empty Pockets: 1929–1940

1929–1934: The Stock Market Crash in late 1929 commenced the epic decline of an American economy already precarious on a foundation of overextended credit, endemic speculation, and a consumer buying power too weak to support high production and high employment. By the end of 1929, Albany had spent more than $35,000 on relief for the unemployed, an amount that would mushroom in the difficult times to follow.

In 1930, entering the Depression, Albany's population was over 127,000—98 percent white, 85.5 percent native-born.

The Depression struck with an appalling rapidity. By April 1930 an estimated 2,000 to 4,000 Albanians were out of work, up from a past average of 800 to 1,000. By November, West Albany alone had 2,000 unemployed, and 25 percent of the city's total work force was looking for work, compared to 20 percent statewide. A year after the Crash, 538 families sought aid at City Hall, where meal tickets were issued, each good for two daily meals per person. In a month, 500 men lined up for meal tickets, and the city was aiding 2,200 families. The Salvation Army set up a "Municipal Barracks" in a former Bleecker Street nightclub and served 500 meals daily.

Total wages paid Albany's work force in 1930 fell more than 27 percent; total value of goods manufactured by nearly 33 percent. By 1931 aid requests for fuel, food, and rent were up almost 38 percent at City Hall; 35 to 45 new families sought help each day. Mayor John Boyd Thacher II stretched the municipal-relief dollar as far as possible, then made funds available for labor-intensive public works projects. By 1932 the "Arbor Hill School"—Philip Livingston—was built. The Hannacroix and Basic Creeks were dammed to increase Albany's water supply, creating Alcove and Basic Reservoirs; 12.8 billion gallons were piped through a 20-mile gravity feed at a cost of $11 million. Albany built 144 miles of paved streets in 1934—28 in concrete, 40 in dressed granite, and 4 in cobbles.

Albany's Academy opened its new building on Academy Road in 1930; designed by Marcus T. Reynolds, part of its interior arrangement and woodwork duplicated the original Philip Hooker structure. (Hooker's Academy building, near City Hall, was restored five years later with the help of Reynolds and the WPA.)

The Depression at least was a golden

age for the movies. Theater attendance was high as people sought escape from a sober reality. In fact, movies were used by Albany's mayor as relief fund-raisers. In 1931 Albany's Palace Theater opened—probably the last opulent-style movie theater constructed in the city. Radio was at its zenith. WOKO, a CBS station, went on the air from the Ten Eyck Hotel in 1931, and WABY moved to Albany shortly thereafter, affiliating with the National Broadcasting System's Blue Network. (Both stations eventually relocated in "Radio Center," an Elk Street townhouse revamped in Art Moderne style in 1939.)

In 1932 the first cars poured across the Dunn Memorial Bridge, named for Rensselaer's World War I Medal of Honor winner, Sergeant Parker F. Dunn. The Dunn Memorial replaced the old Greenbush Bridge over the Hudson River at a cost of more than $2.5 million. Actively boosted by the Albany Chamber of Commerce, it could handle a daily traffic flow of 30,000 vehicles. Indicative too of the new supremacy of motorized transportation was the opening of a Greyhound terminal on Broadway in 1932; 46 buses left Albany daily, bound mainly west or south.

The Port of Albany officially opened in 1932. At the intersection of six major railroads, with miles of track of its own, the port had a capacity of 20,000 freight cars in its yards, an annual pass-through total of a million. Rail travel was ever more rapid; the Twentieth Century Limited made its record 2-hour and 35-minute New York City-Albany run in 1935. The port was also fed by the revamped New York State Barge Canal System, which in 1931 had carried 3.7 million tons of freight, an increase of 220 percent over 1918.

1935: President Franklin D. Roosevelt created the Works Progress Administration, which eventually employed eight million Americans. That year in Albany, 1,881 men and 183 women were employed by the WPA.

1936–1939: Albany's Department of Public Safety in 1936 consisted of six police precincts and a Fire Department of 200 men and 16 fire trucks. The City operated 25 public parks, a municipal golf course, skating rinks, Bleecker Stadium (converted from a former reservoir by WPA workers), the Lincoln Park Pool, and several public baths. The Public Library had 130,000 books in circulation. Albany had 20 theaters, one of them—the Palace—seating 2,800 people. There were 99 churches, 10 hotels, and 5 hospitals.

1937 aerial view of Albany

The Depression ground on. In 1937 the Albany Council of Social Agencies provided Christmas dinners for 5,525 families, toys for 368. In 1939, Trinity Institute served 52,324 clients. The Depression's effects were mirrored in the statistics of the Port of Albany. Despite the decline in the number of ships, the port remained a steady source of employment in Albany throughout the Depression.

1940–1941: In the 1940 federal census, Albany's population was 130,577 persons; the city's rate of growth of 2.5 percent since the previous decade had been slowed by the Depression. Nearly 20 percent of Albany's employed men worked in transportation and communications; 16 percent were in manufacturing. Interestingly, 17.8 percent of Albany's women workers were classed as "professional," and only 6 percent of the men. New York State employed significant numbers of Albanians.

Albany had remained a large producer of iron and steel; in 1941 it had the largest machine tool repair facility in the U.S. The city with its diverse industries produced paper goods, chemicals, brushes, toys and games, caps and gowns, baseballs, pianos, billiard balls, lye, textiles, blankets, papermakers' felts, and automobile heating equipment. The total assessed value of Albany's real property was $242,525,079. John Boyd Thacher II resigned as mayor in 1941, after 14 years—then Albany's longest mayoral tenure since colonial times.

World War II: 1941–1945

1941: December 7, 1941, began as a conventional day. Jimmy Dorsey's band was headlined on the Palace Theater's marquee; and at the Leland, Charlie Chaplin's film *The Great Dictator* was playing. The Christmas tree in Capitol Park was to be lit on December 8. The New York Central Railroad advertised excursions to New York City for two dollars. Steak was 25 cents per pound, butter 35 cents, eggs 32 cents per dozen.

Many Albanians, living in peace and returning prosperity, were shocked at the news of the Japanese raid on Pearl Harbor, although many Albany men had already been conscripted and the National Guard called up. Soon blackouts and air-raid drills were

New York State Archives

Harmanus Bleecker Hall, one of Albany's 20 movie theaters in the 1930s

supervised by Civil Defense wardens in brassards and "pancake" helmets; theater screens were filled with Pathé newsreels of the war and war movies. Flags bearing small blue (and later gold) stars sometimes hung in the windows of Albany's houses where men had left for the war. Shortages developed—of canvas, straight pins, cardboard, buttons, molding sand, paper, brushes, and mattresses. Only Albany's production of baseballs seemed unaffected as the war effort snapped up building materials and defense plants added 30 percent to the drain on Albany utilities. City government created a bombproof shelter in the basement of the police headquarters, and 500 volunteers prepared to staff it.

1941-1944: An "Avenge Pearl Harbor Day" celebrated on the Capitol steps resulted in 118 recruits being sworn into the Marine Corps and Navy. An "I Am An American Day" was held later. Stationed at Steamboat Square, a military police battalion benefitted Albany businesses by purchasing coal and groceries and paying for utilities.

Erastus Corning 2nd was elected mayor of Albany in 1941, winning by a margin of nearly five to one. Corning would eventually have one of the longest mayoral tenures in American history. In 1944 Mayor Corning entered the Army as an infantry private; under the La Guardia Act he was able to appoint an acting mayor in his absence.

Eighteen Albany-area banks participated in 1942's two-month experimental trial of ration banking; based on its outcome, ration banking went nationwide in the beginning of 1943, to prevent the counterfeiting and misuse of ration stamps. National Commercial Bank entered War Bond subscriptions of more than $238.4 million during the war; these were instrumental in financing the U.S.S. *Albany,* the last ship to bear that name (and decommissioned in 1980). Sailings from the Port of Albany diminished during the war, but revenues increased as wartime ships grew larger. By 1945 larger ships mandated further deepening of the Hudson River's channel.

Postwar Era: 1945–1959

1945–1950: By the war's end 556 Albanians had died in the service. One Albany bank alone had an investment list 94 percent committed to government bonds. The city was so geared to the war effort that disengagement would be difficult. "People expect wishfully that reconversion could be completed in less than six months after the terrific struggle which ended in August," one banker remarked. The City of Albany now found it possible, at last, to purchase much-needed equipment to replace items worn out and unavailable during the war years.

The phenomenal postwar baby boom began, the birth of a generation which by its sheer numbers would strain every institution it would encounter. Returning GIs built homes, and property owners were at last able to obtain materials for alterations and repairs. The extreme postwar housing shortage presented problems nationwide; a federal housing act in 1949 led to the creation of the Albany Housing Authority. In the early 1950s the Housing Authority began to build a succession of housing developments,

Nurses teaching infant care classes at Albany Medical Center in the 1940s

especially in the older, congested parts of Albany.

The last trolleys ran the West Albany, Belt, Pine Hills, Delaware Avenue, and Second Avenue routes in 1946; the United Traction Company's 38 remaining trolleys and five remaining service cars were sold to a Broadway scrap dealer. Many Albany businessmen, feeling the commercial pull to go westward in the city, eventually acted on that impulse, although immediate postwar development took place along Pearl Street and other traditional commercial arteries. Albany Airport's runways were lengthened to handle larger aircraft and additions were planned for or in progress on the public schools in 1949.

1950–1954: By 1950 the population of Albany was almost 135,000. In that year 357 single-family houses were built in the city. A $100,000 supermarket and a $250,000 cafeteria were erected on Central Avenue; W.T. Grant's opened on North Pearl Street, with a "handsome television set" as door prize. The gross city debt was at its lowest since 1929 and prosperity was at hand, even though the New York Central Railroad began moving part of its West Albany shops away from the city. The opening of the New York State Thruway and other improved highways gave automotive traffic competitive advantage over railroads. In 1954 the West Albany shops closed down completely and the railroads seemed doomed.

1956–1959: Albany was changing; the character of its downtown in flux. While the Center Square Association, oldest of Albany's present neighborhood associations, was

founded in 1956, many Albanians were moving to outlying residential portions of the city—notably Altamont, Voorheesville, Bethlehem, Colonie, and Guilderland. Schools followed suit. In 1958 the Albany area's first shopping centers were operating: Stuyvesant Plaza in Westmere, and Westgate on Central Avenue, "a suburban center within an urban area, bringing the advantage of a suburban center's spacious parking to city residents." Movie theaters in downtown Albany were closing. By 1958 only 168 factories were operating in the city, with some 4,900 workers.

Albany's first official urban renewal project was in northern Albany in the 1950s, the first such project to be completed in the state. School 13 and "slums" were razed on the site. Further to the north, the St. Lawrence Seaway opened in 1959, posing heavy competition for the Port of Albany, which in that year handled 867,151 tons of cargo, including huge quantities of grain and molasses, from 177 oceangoing ships, 282 barges, and 21,739 railroad cars.

Decline and Revival: 1960–1980

1960: Downtown Albany's familiar, major commercial arteries were hardening, the flow of vital economic activity beginning to slow, and Pearl Street falling slowly more silent. More stores emptied as the exodus to the suburbs and the shopping malls accelerated, as businesses decades old closed their doors or relocated. The demographic shift to the suburb was evident in the new federal census, which counted 129,726 people in Albany, down 5,200 persons since 1950.

The resuscitation of decaying downtown Albany was clearly essential. Albany now created its Urban Renewal Agency, a local outgrowth of President Kennedy's newly formed Department of Housing and Urban Development.

1962: The State of New York made public its plan to acquire a large tract of land in the center of Albany for the South Mall Project. The Project was viewed with alarm and skepticism locally. Wrote Mayor Corning: "The state is planning to carve out from the heart of the city a large sterile area for a monumental group of buildings which will look spectacular on postcards all over the world, but will, in fact, hurt the people of Albany." Seven thousand people—more than 3,100 families—would be displaced by the Mall, 1,500 buildings demolished, 3.1 million cubic yards of earth excavated.

A densely settled portion of Albany now vanished as if it had never existed. In "Rockefeller's Quarry" thousands of laborers poured the 900,000 cubic yards of concrete, erected the 232,000 tons of steel and a half-million cubic feet of marble, with miles of wiring. Only in the late 1970s did this massive island of white marble begin to assume a human dimension. If the Mall's cost can ever be accurately assessed, the figures will exceed $2 billion.

Construction of the Mall reflected Albany's increasing stature as administrative nexus of an expanding State government. State jobs were an ever more important source of employment in the local economy; by

The abandoned West Albany shops, 1956

Arthur J. O'keefe

1963 only 24 percent of Albany's work force was involved in manufacturing, well below the national average.

1967: Work began on the Northside, Riverside, and Crosstown Arterial highways—frank acknowledgments of Albany's importance as workplace to thousands of commuters. With the new Northway, they would make possible a much wider dispersion of area population away from the capital city. Within Albany, the Urban Renewal Agency had received federal approval for rehabilitation of houses on Livingston Avenue and the demolition of others for a renewal site. In 1967 Albany annexed the Karlsfeld section at the city outskirts, bringing the city line to its natural border along the Normanskill Creek.

Demonstrations for civil rights and against the Viet Nam War marked the late 1960s in Albany, making national political issues more intimate and crucial to local citizens. Despite some incidents of racial violence, the city was not badly riven as others were.

The youth culture also erupted, becoming highly visible (the first "head shop" opened in 1966). It enjoyed a short-lived flowering that faded with the less prosperous economy of the decade to follow.

1970–1980: The 1970s were marked by falling enrollments in public and parochial schools; a number of city elementary and high schools closed, casualties of a declining birth rate.

Albany High moved to its ultra-modern Washington Avenue campus; when Philip Schuyler High School closed down, its student population joined Albany High. Milne and St. Joseph's Academy closed; other parochial schools were combined.

As school enrollments sagged, jobs declined. The city's new Department of Human Resources was created to administer the federally-subsidized public employment programs that appeared again in Albany. Under one grant or another, more than 17,000 persons worked in public employment programs in the decade after 1971.

The Urban Renewal Agency developed the Pastures Preservation District, a rejuvenation of one of Albany's earliest postcolonial neighborhoods still largely

architecturally intact. The State University of New York acquired the D & H, Albany Journal, and Old Federal buildings to use as its central administrative headquarters, the best form of historic preservation. Other recent and revived efforts included the colonial Quackenbush house, the Steuben Place and Ten Eyck projects, and the Water Department complex.

In 1975 the federally funded Community Development Program included the rehabilitation of housing,

A "Free the Panthers" demonstration on the steps of the State Capitol

downtown improvements, and "economic development." Coupled with tax incentives passed by Congress in 1976, rehabilitation of Albany's older structures became feasible, attractive, and, finally, trendy; by 1981, nearly $20.5 million in Community Development money had been granted Albany. Individual houses, then city blocks, and finally whole neighborhoods began to revitalize. The post-World War II babies had grown up to penetrate the housing market; they found the ambience and convenience of the old central city attractive, especially as high fuel costs began to make suburban living, and commuting, less so. Neighborhood associations, numbering more than 20 by 1981, represented almost every geographic area; growing larger and more vocal, they are demanding, and receiving, more complex and professional services from the City of Albany.

In 1973 the new, controversial Mall had been dedicated as the "Empire State Plaza" by Governor Rockefeller. In 1976, in a flurry of local and state

national bicentennial activities, the Empire State Plaza's Cultural Resources Center—housing State Archives, Library, and Museum—was opened. (In 1978, a rededication named the Mall the Governor Nelson A. Rockefeller Empire State Plaza.) As one side effect, the completion of the Mall Project meant the loss of jobs among many locals in the city's building trades, who for a decade had been busily employed.

Development of the ANSWERS Project—Albany, New York, Solid Waste Energy Recovery System—pointed one direction for Albany's future. As an old city in a climate not noted for mild winters, this unique regional facility was designed to process 750 tons of municipal solid waste daily, at once producing fuel for steam generation and recovering all recyclable materials. ANSWERS, its concepts sound, both fiscally and morally, was essentially complete by 1980.

The 1980s began with a favorable prognosis for Albany's future. New life was beginning to breathe along Pearl Street, the new State offices disgorged crowds of workers into the central city, old banks and new lined State Street. As Albany moved toward its tricentennial as a city in 1986, it showed ample signs of renewed health and vigor while yielding none of its distinctive and ancient character.

1980-1983: The final years of the Corning administration were marked by a rebirth of the city's downtown. Corning himself was re-elected without effort in 1981 but his health had begun to fail. In June 1992 he entered Albany Medical Center.

The 1980 holiday season saw the first "Melodies of Christmas" concert held at the Palace Theater. The annual event created by James Delmonico of WRGB featured the Empire State Youth Orchestra and Youth Chorale and would become a tradition, benefiting the Child Cancer Program at Albany Med.

The results of the 1980 U.S.Census were released in 1981-2. For the first time, citizens were asked to list ancestry. The count showed 101,727 souls, reflecting over three centuries of American immigration and settlement. Albany County reported 285,909 residents.

In 1982, Queen Beatrix of the Netherlands was hosted by Governor Carey with a dinner in the Governor's Mansion. The old YMCA became the Steuben Athletic Club.

In 1983, Mario Cuomo succeeded retiring Governor Hugh Carey.

On June 28, 1983, Mayor Erastus Corning 2nd died in the Boston hospital where he had been treated since October. Common Council President, Thomas M. Whalen, III succeeded as Mayor, and J. Leo O'Brien, Mayor of Watervliet, succeeded as Democratic County Chairman.

1984-85: Crossgates Mall constructed. Union Station was saved by Norstar (now Fleet) Bank, for its new headquarters.

1986: Events were dominated by the year-long Tricentennial Celebration of the Dongan Charter.

An ancient Dutch burial ground was discovered during construction of a parking garage on lower Hudson Avenue. Vestiges of a seventeenth century chapel and wampum factory were also found.

1987: The film, "Ironweed," based on William Kennedy's novel about the homeless in depression-era Albany premiered at the Palace. It was filmed on location, to the delight of residents.

1988: Michael McNulty replaced retiring long-time Congressman Samuel Stratton. Ronald Canestrari, Mayor of Cohoes, succeeded McNulty in the Assembly.

1990: The 1990 Census counted 100,082 citizens; Albany County tallied 292,594. City residents included Irish, 32%; Italians 23%, Germans, 22%; and African Americans 21%; English, 10%; Polish 9%; French, 8%; Russians, 5%; Dutch, 4%; "Non-Hispanic West Indians," Puerto Ricans, Scots and Scotch-Irish, 2% each; Austrians, Chinese, Greeks, Hungarians, Lithuanians, Slovaks, Sub-continent Indians, Swedes, Ukrainians and Welsh, about 1% each. Collectively Hispanic ancestry was 3%, and Asian ancestry was claimed by 2%. The longer any group was settled in America, the more likely its members were to claim multiple ancestry.

Enthusiastic residents flocked to downtown to attend the long awaited January 31st opening of the 18,000 seat Knickerbocker Arena.

1991: Republican Michael J. Hoblock wrested the County Executive's seat from Democratic control. Democratic Chairman Harold Joyce undertook major reforms in 1992 as directed by the (Michael) Hickey Commission. John J. McEneny replaced retiring veteran Assemblyman Richard Conners, following a four-way primary.

1993: Alderman Gerald Jennings was elected Mayor, following a close primary victory over Harold Joyce. The State bought the ANSWERS recycling/energy facility in Sheridan Hollow. Once heralded as a model environmental facility, the facility was closed because of pollution and health risks to neighbors.

1994-1995: Republican State Senator George Pataki defeated Governor Cuomo, ending 20 years of Democratic control of the Governorship.

The first two years of the Pataki administration brought much tension to area residents because of cutbacks to the state workforce and threatened relocation of state offices and reductions in services. The second two years, bolstered by a boom on Wall Street, witnessed a better relationship between the State and the Capital District including several major state construction initiatives in downtown and at the University campus.

In 1994 Michael Hoblock was elected State Senator, replacing retiring 20-year incumbent Howard Nolan. Michael Breslin was appointed County Executive by the County Legislature in 1995 to fill out the last year of Hoblock's term. His brother Neil Breslin, defeated Hoblock to return the Senate seat to the Democrats. With Thomas Breslin, a third brother a County Court Judge, the Breslin family has created a family record not seen since the O'Connell brothers and Corning brothers founded the present Democratic regime nearly eighty years before.

1996: Construction of the new Empire State Development Corporation building on Broadway revealed the remains of seventeenth century Albany within the boundries of the colonial stockade. Archaeology took several months. The New York Giants establish the University at Albany as their summer training camp.

1997-1998: The "Slater" a World War II Destroyer Escort made its permanent home on the Albany riverfront. The CESTM high-tech building opens at the University. The City celebrated its 200th anniversary as the permanent State Capital.

In 1997, Mayor Jennings was easily re-elected following a primary victory over Assemblyman McEneny. In 1998, McEneny won a primary race defeating a Jennings backed opponent.

Above
"Fort Orange, 1635" by Leonard Tantillo draws heavily on the ongoing research of the New Netherlands Project, headed by Dr. Charles Gehring in the New York State Library. The historically accurate painting depicts the military and administrative head-quarters of the Dutch West India Company, a private corporation licensed by the Dutch government. In the foreground is The Eendracht, a merchant ship flying the flag of the company. To the right, on shore, the ship Omwall, awaits completion by master carpenter and shipwright, Tymen Jansen. Fort Orange was the headquarters of Albany's defense from 1624 until it was re-placed by the British with the construction of Fort Frederick at the top of State Street hill in June 1676. The original painting is owned by Michael Picotte, an Albany business-man.

Right
Pemberton Corner was constructed in 1710 in traditional Dutch style on the corner of North Pearl and Columbia streets. At the end of the 19th century it was replaced with the Brewster Building (old Albany Business College). Painting by James Eights.

Above
This James Eights watercolor painted circa 1875 depicts the east side of Market Street (Broadway) as it appeared in 1805. Note the Public Market in the middle of the street.
Left
Dr. John Stevenson's house, built in 1780 in the Georgian style, provides a great contrast to the 1716 home built in the traditional urban Dutch fashion by Harman Wendell. The gabled end of the older house faced the street. Both houses stood on the south side of State Street just above Pearl. They were demolished in 1841. Painting by James Eights.

Clockwise from top left
The city of "Albony" was carved into this colonial powder horn, probably by provincial soldiers during the great summer campaigns of the French and Indian war.

Whitehall, shown here in an 1872 painting on brick by Ten Eyck, was destroyed by fire 11 years later. Major General John Bradstreet and the British Army used the mansion, which was seized as Tory property and became the home of the celebrated Gansevoort-Ten Eyck families.

Old Centre Market was located on South Pearl Street between Howard and Beaver streets.

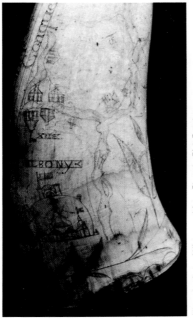

Above
Thomas Cole painted this view of the Van Rensselaer Manor House in 1841. Constructed in 1767, the great mansion in North Albany was the location from which the Van Rensselaer family ruled one of the greatest estates in the colonies. It included most of Albany and Rensselaer counties. In 1893 the building was moved to the Williams College for use by a fraternity.
Right
A Staffordshire plate is decorated with a view of Albany from Van Rensselaers (Westerlo) Island. The design was copied from a painting by William Guy Wall, circa 1830.

Left
Victorian iron work decorates the roof of this Woodlawn Avenue structure.
Below
Broadway, across from University Plaza, was once a hub of Hudson River commerce.
Bottom
Albany as a city on a hill is boldly depicted in this 19th-century oil painting made after an engraving by William Bartlett.

Albany D.H.R.   Photo by Lindsey Watson

Albany D.H.R.   Photo by Lindsey Watson

McLean Gallery, Inc.

Above
James Eights painted this view of State Street as it looked from the front of St. Peter's Church, opposite Chapel Street. Its Dutch Reformed equivalent, visible at the foot of the hill, also stood in the middle of State Street.

Right
This bas relief by Charles Calverly appears on the base of the Robert Burns statue in Washington Park.

"TAM O' SHANTER"

Albany Institute of History and Art.   Photo by Rich Frutchey

Albany Institute of History and Art.   Photo by Rich Frutchey

Albany D.H.R.   Photo by Lindsey Watson

Albany D.H.R.   Photo by Lindsey Watson

Clockwise from top
Albany's first capitol, designed by Philip Hooker, towers over the city in this 1846 painting by William Hart.

This Staffordshire bowl depicting the entrance of the Erie Canal at Albany is one of a series produced after the opening of the canal in 1825 honoring cities along that waterway. This view was taken from a watercolor by James Eights.

J. Massey Rhind's bronze statue of Moses is surrounded by smaller sculptures of several of his followers, one of which is pictured here. The statue, which stands in Washington Park, was given to the city in 1893.

The pineapple was a popular Georgian architectural detail symbolizing hospitality. This fence on South Pearl Street below 2nd Avenue incorporates the exotic fruit in its design.

Right
The Jewish Cemetery on Fuller Road memorializes an active Jewish community that has flourished in Albany from the early 19th century.

Far right, top
Pictured here is one of the carved wooden angels that looks down on the congregation of St. Joseph's Church from 80 feet above. The angels were said to remind Irish immigrants of the prows of the ships on which they came. The church, on Arbor Hill, was constructed from 1856-1860.

Far right, bottom
The third St. Peter's Church, constructed in 1856 on State Street, boasts distinctive Gothic architecture, including bronze doors, gargoyles on its bell tower, beautiful stained glass windows, painted ceiling beams, and delicate mosaic aisles, a detail of which is shown here.

Below
This depiction of State Street below North Pearl was painted by Dr. James Eights. The State Bank of Albany, whose 1806 building was designed by Philip Hooker, stands on this site today, incorporating the original facade shown in the center of the picture just above James Street. When the office building was constructed, the facade was moved up the hill to serve as the center entrance for the building.

Photo by Rich Frutchey

Albany D.H.R.   Photo by Lindsey Watson

Albany D.H.R.   Photo by Lindsey Watson

Albany Institute of History and Art

CHAPTER 2
COLONIZATION AND CONFLICT

Fifteen years after Henry Hudson sailed up the great estuary that would later bear his name, the city of Albany was founded—not by a self-governing religious fellowship, as Plymouth was, nor by the Dutch government, but by a private company. The Dutch West India Company, chartered in Amsterdam in 1621, had been granted a trading monopoly that extended all the way across the Atlantic, from the west coast of Africa to the east coast of America, including the Caribbean and, of course, Hudson's River; the company was empowered to build forts, maintain a private army, encourage settlement, and establish colonial governments.

A fort had been maintained by Dutch traders at Albany since 1614, but the first real settlers arrived in 1624, under the auspices of the new company. Consisting primarily of French-speaking Walloons from the southern provinces of Hainaut, Namur, Luxembourg, and Liege, this first group of pioneer families set to work clearing a tiny corner of the seemingly endless North American wilderness, planting crops of corn and wheat on land assigned to them by the company, building their first crude shelters, and helping to fortify a new garrison for their common defense to be known as Fort Orange. Their transportation to America had been without cost but not without obligations—among them, to obey the officers of the company, to profess the approved Reformed Calvinist faith, to live only where the company permitted, and to do nothing that might jeopardize friendly (and profitable) relations with the natives. All trade for export, as well as all mining and mineral rights, remained in the hands of the company.

Scarcely three years had passed after the first settlers arrived at Fort Orange when it became readily apparent that something was wrong. The small group of Walloon families were becoming rapidly disenchanted with their new adventure in the North American wilderness. Several, in fact, had already retreated downriver to New Amsterdam, while others were casting a lingering eye homeward to the Europe they had left behind. Meanwhile, within the corporate structure of the Dutch West India

Facing page
Fort Frederick, which was built in 1676 by the Crown to replace the badly deteriorated Fort Orange at the river's edge, stood just below the crest of State Street Hill for over a century. It was demolished after the Revolution and its stones were used in the construction of various churches and other buildings.
Above
In 1609 English navigator Henry Hudson, sailing for the Dutch East India Company in his 90-ton yacht Half Moon, traveled 160 miles up the river that now bears his name.
Right
Hudson's attempt to find the Northwest Passage to the Orient brought him to the site of Albany in 1609.

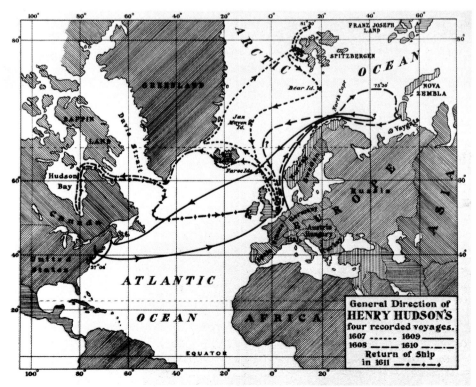

Company, opinion was by no means universal that the proper role of the company was to continue to supply, at considerable cost, a few isolated settlers in the interior of the colony of New Netherland. Was it not enough expense, many directors wondered, to provide for the garrison at Fort Orange—necessary to protect the fur trade—without taking on the additional burden of sending food, tools, and livestock to sustain a colony of would-be farmers?

Fortunately for the future of Albany, there was another opinion within the corporate mind of the Dutch West India Company—that there was a larger purpose, a more permanent mission, in the establishment of New Netherland. This opinion was shared by Kiliaen Van Rensselaer, a Dutch director of the company who had made a fortune partly by trading in gemstones. Van Rensselaer and other directors realized that there was no incentive for the average Dutch settler to go to the New World and stay for any length of time. Some organized plan had to be established that would attract colonists in greater numbers—colonists who would identify with the land and with settlement, rather than with the fur trade.

Patroonship

The plan that was developed was unique in the history of the American colonies. In 1629 the company approved a Charter of Exemptions and Privileges permitting any directors who so desired to invest their own capital in a plan of permanent settlement that would establish them as hereditary overlords of their own private fiefdoms. This was a purely voluntary plan that would not be an expense to the company; directors who did not wish to invest in colonization were free to participate in the company as before, reaping profits from the fur trade.

The Netherlands had long been dominated by foreign rulers, principally those of Spain, the dukes of Burgundy, and the Hapsburg monarchy. The great fortunes made in the lucrative trade with the East Indies and by profiteering were the fortunes of merchants and not of noblemen, based upon mercantile interests and not upon hereditary landed estates. The new plan offered these wealthy but landless men of Amsterdam an unprecedented opportunity to acquire the traditional trappings of aristocracy—a hereditary, semifeudal estate in the intriguing land of America.

Each grant had to be located along a river or other navigable body of water, extending up to 16 miles along one shore or eight miles on each side of the waterway; the depth of the estate extending back from the river or stream was open to negotiation with the Indians. The principal condition was that the investor sponsor the settlement of 50 people over the age of 15 years, to be transported to the New World within four years.

The patroon, or patron, was granted broad powers over his vassals. All mineral rights, for example, were reserved to the patroon—as they had been until recently in Holland to the Spanish king. The patroon controlled all fishing and hunting rights and could grant or deny licenses as he pleased. He conducted his own courts, serving as his own chief justice. Theoretically any case involving more than 50 guilders could be appealed to the directors of the company, but settlers were made to agree in advance of coming to the New World that they would not appeal the decisions of the patroon. Settlers coming to the patroon's estate were promised 10 years free of taxes, but, like the serfs of old, they were denied the right to move from one estate to another or to quit the land by moving into a town.

Trade on the estate was controlled in every detail. Industry of any kind, including grain and lumber milling, was strictly the prerogative of the patroon. Even handicrafts, such as blankets or clothing woven by the wife of a settler, had to be offered first to the patroon's agent before they could be sold to a next-door neighbor. The discouragement of industry in favor of agriculture in its purest form, in addition to enhancing the power of the patroon, was designed to protect Holland's home industry, in which the directors of the Dutch West India Company also had personal interests.

The patroon for his part invested heavily in establishing the settlers upon his land, providing labor to help clear the forest, as well as livestock, tools, and initial supplies of food. African slaves were to be provided for all who wanted them—supplied, of course, by the Dutch West India Company, from ships that they had captured. In order to assure the safety of the settlers and to keep peace in the patroonship, the company required that Indian claims be satisfied through purchase before title to the land would actually be granted. The company further required that the religious needs of settlers be met by a "comforter of the sick," to be followed as soon as possible by a minister of the Dutch Reformed Church.

Once the plan had been approved by the States-General of the Netherlands, Kiliaen Van Rensselaer wasted no time. He instructed Sebastian Jansen Krol (Crol), comforter of the sick and head of the garrison at Fort Orange, to purchase the land that would later be known as Rensselaerswyck. The Van Rensselaer grant—which was to prove the only successful patroonship in the Hudson Valley—extended from the Cohoes Falls southward along the Hudson River to Beeren Island in the vicinity of present-day Coeymans, ultimately extending back 24 miles on each side of the Hudson River, encompassing most of today's Albany County and southern Rensselaer County. The holdings were expanded by subsequent generations of Van Rensselaers through additional purchases, particularly in present-day Columbia County, until they totaled more than a million acres. Van Rensselaer knew what he was doing when he chose this particular location for his estate. It was situated at the head of the tidewater of the Hudson River, and it had the military protection of Fort Orange.

As soon as title to some land was obtained, an elaborate advertising campaign was launched in Holland and other parts of northern Europe. Rensselaerswyck was described in glamorous broadsides as a "Heaven in the Wilderness"; maps were drawn to show settlements presumably already in existence. The first party of Van Rensselaer settlers arrived in March 1630.

In 1640 Van Rensselaer and his partners reevaluated their plan of settlement and made major reforms, granting a new charter to their tenants. Under the extreme paternalism of the old system, particularly the restraint in trade, recruitment in Holland had been successful only among the impoverished, failing to attract prosperous, established farmers. The revised charter for the first time allowed the resale of Dutch goods, the trade of homecrafts between the settlers without the aid of a Van Rensselaer agent, and the exploitation by settlers of fisheries and salt deposits. Some degree of self-government, carefully supervised, was also introduced. And for the first time tenants, as well as other independent traders, were permitted to engage in the fur trade.

Van Rensselaer would have preferred that the majority of his tenants settle on the east bank of the Hudson, where present-day Rensselaer is

Albany's first settlers, 18 families of Walloons, arrived aboard the ship New Netherland *in 1624. Commanded by Captain Adriaen Joris, the ship carried 260 tons.*

Lossing, *The Empire State*

located and where the original Fort Crailo was built. Settlement there, it was hoped, would divert some of the fur trade from Montreal by establishing relations with the Mahican Indians—deadly enemies of the Mohawks, who brought their furs from the west. Nonetheless, most of the settlers wanted to be on the west bank, if only for the protection of Fort Orange.

In 1646 Kiliaen Van Rensselaer died, without ever having visited his American holdings. He had not only assured the continuation of the colony, but he had established a unique American dynasty that would endure well into the 19th century. Even today in the deeds of properties in Albany and Rensselaer counties, it is not uncommon to find a requirement that the owner provide annually to the successors of the Van Rensselaers 34 bushels of wheat, two fat fowl, and the use of a wagon and team one day per year as tribute to the patroon.

Fort and Manor
In 1648, shortly after assuming the governorship of New Netherland, a crusty, peg-legged Pieter Stuyvesant visited his northernmost outpost at Fort Orange. The affairs of the surrounding patroonship of Rensselaerswyck were then in the hands of Brant Aertse Van Slichtenhorst, who had been appointed director of the domain in 1646. As stubborn in defense of the prerogatives of the patroon as Stuyvesant was in the assertion of those of the Dutch West India Company, Van Slichtenhorst was to prove a formidable adversary in the forthcoming conflict between the company and the patroonship.

The principal focus of the conflict was the question of jurisdiction over the small settlement, then known as the Fuyck, that had sprung up in the immediate vicinity of Fort Orange—and indeed over the site of the fort itself. Settlers under the jurisdiction of the patroon sought to build their houses as close as possible to the fort—not only for the meager protection it offered, but also in the hope of cashing in on the fur trade. Stuyvesant insisted that no further building should take place within range of a cannon shot from the fort (approximately 1,000 yards)—ostensibly in the name of military security, but also presumably in an effort to defend the company's profits. As a matter of fact, soldiers and settlers alike, equally disloyal to their respective overlords, participated in the smuggling of furs to Connecticut, where the rival English held sway.

The conflict dragged on year after year, with Stuyvesant's agents posting notices and Van Slichtenhorst tearing them down, new buildings being

John J. McEneny

Above
Fort Crailo, on the east bank of the Hudson, was erected in 1680 by Hendrich Van Rensselaer. During the French and Indian Wars Albany residents inhabited the stockaded grounds for protection. This view of the building, which appeared on an 1848 sheet music cover, was made when it was used as a private academy for boys.
Right
Pieter Stuyvesant, known as "Old Wooden Leg," served as Dutch governor of New Netherland from 1648 to 1664. He upheld the rights of the Dutch West India Company against the equally obstinate patroon's agent, Brant Van Slichtenhorst, by establishing, in 1652, Beverwyck as an independent municipality with a "city line" one cannon shot's distance from Fort Orange.

Albany Institute of History and Art

started and Stuyvesant threatening to dismantle them. The patroon's agent claimed that Rensselaerswyck included every inch of territory outside the walls of the fort, the governor that company jurisdiction extended to a perimeter sufficient to defend the fort and to supply it with food—"the ancient and uninterrupted use of the gardens and fields near the fort." Once again the bottom line was profit: Whoever controlled the area surrounding the fort would largely control the fur trade.

Finally, in March 1652, Stuyvesant stormed up the river and proclaimed the town of Beverwyck, including the Fuyck and the fort, as an independent entity, totally outside the jurisdiction of the patroon. A month later he issued a proclamation establishing a court of justice for the town, separate from and independent of the patroon's court. Though Van Slichtenhorst protested vehemently, the establishment of this tribunal in fact marked the birth of the political entity that was to become Albany.

More than 30 years would pass, however—and the fort change hands three times—before the matter was ultimately resolved. In September 1664 a British force under Colonel George Cartwright seized Fort Orange, and fort and settlement alike were renamed Albany; eight years later the Dutch reclaimed their former colony, and the name Albany was changed to Willemstadt. Finally, under the Treaty of Westminster, February 19, 1674, all of New Netherland was ceded to the British, and Albany became Albany for good.

Meanwhile the Van Rensselaers were still seeking to clarify and confirm their rights to Rensselaerswyck—including, if possible, the area immediately surrounding the fort. During the brief interlude of Dutch rule, in 1673, the patroon's agents obtained a ruling from the directors of the Dutch West India Company that Pieter Stuyvesant had acted illegally and Beverwyck/Willemstadt was in fact part of the patroon's domain. On this basis they petitioned the Duke of York in July of 1674 to confirm their proprietary rights to "the said Colony [Rensselaerswyck] with the neighborhood called ye Fuijck which according to ye ancient priviledges and prerogatives hath been comprehended within ye said jurisdiction & limits of ye said Colony." Governor Andros, newly arrived in New York, issued a proclamation generally confirming preexisting property rights, but refused to issue any specific new patent to the Van Rensselaers.

On April 27, 1678, another lengthy and detailed petition, signed by Jan Baptist Van Rensselaer, was presented to the Duke of York. In June Governor Andros received orders to issue a patent, but he continued to stall—as did his successor, Colonel Thomas Dongan. Dongan confidently justified disobeying orders from London "which I thought not convenient to execute, judging it not for his Majesty's interest that the second town of the government and which brings his Majesty so great a revenue should be in the hands of any particular men."

At last, on November 4, 1685, Governor Dongan issued a patent formally establishing the manor of Rensselaerswyck under the suzerainty of the British Crown. The estate granted by the Dongan patent comprised an area on both sides of the Hudson River totaling upwards of one million acres—but specifically excluding not only the town of Albany, but an additional strip of land extending northwest 16 miles from the fort. In the city charter which Dongan granted to the inhabitants of Albany the following year, the direction and dimensions of this 16-mile corridor to Schenectady were further specified, and a full structure of municipal government was established at Albany.

Pieter Schuyler

He was known to the Indians as "Quidor"; to the Dutch burghers as one of their own touched with destiny; to the French garrison at Montreal as a courageous enemy; to the court of Queen Anne as a charming, sophisticated advocate of the colonists' cause.

Colonel Pieter Schuyler assumed many roles as he responded to the events shaping his native valley. Schuyler was at once a merchant, a judge, a politician extraordinaire, a cavalry officer, a wilderness fighter. He was a rare leader, a Renaissance man who was as much at ease in a crude bark canoe as in the perfumed salons of European diplomacy.

He was, above all, a patrician of the people who, as Albany's first mayor, so strongly molded the office that an unmistakable aura of prestige and power has surrounded the position for nearly 300 years. In Albany's modern-day city hall, Schuyler's portrait hangs over the fireplace opposite the mayor's desk, a near lifelike reminder of the powerful threads of history tying the present to the past and a symbol of the office's influence throughout the region.

Schuyler was only 29 and already a judge when the city charter granted by the British governor, Thomas Dongan, in 1686 formally ended Albany's existence as a Dutch village. Sensitive to the power of Albany's ruling class, Dongan appointed Schuyler, a Dutchman, as the city's first mayor.

As mayor, his meticulous attention to the people's smallest needs earned him their lasting support. Among his first acts as mayor were replacement of the rotting spouts in the city's crude water system, provision of grazing land for the burghers' cattle, and promulgation of regulations for tavern keepers. He also presided over Albany's first murder trial.

At the same time, he was curiously attuned to the needs of the area's Indians. When Schuyler became mayor, there were more Indians than Europeans in Albany County. This population was swelled by the unceasing traffic of the Iroquois and their allies who were drawn to Erie's marketplaces. In a sense, Schuyler was a prototype Sir William Johnson, who later came to prominence in the Mohawk Valley and fell heir to Schuyler's trusted epithet of "Quidor."

Schuyler spoke the Indians' language with skill and respect and understood the mysteries of their culture. He fought next to them in battle, he saw that they bartered with honest merchants, and he sheltered them in the mammoth barn of his country home on the Watervliet Flatts. Most important, Schuyler commanded the Iroquois's loyalty, thus guaranteeing their loyalty to the British Crown and ensuring the security of Albany from the French threat.

The threat was constant throughout Schuyler's years. In 1687 one of every 10 men had to be conscripted into the ranks of the local militia. In 1689, after James Stuart was driven from the British throne, Louis XIV ordered an expedition of French Canadians and Indians to descend upon Albany. In response to the emergency, Schuyler ordered that no person capable of bearing arms be allowed to leave Albany without permission from a justice of the peace.

In February 1690 the worst fears were realized when Simon Schermerhorn, bloodied and clad only in a nightshirt, rode exhausted into the stockade at Albany with word of the butcherous attack on settlers at Schenectady, 16 miles to the west.

Throughout the next months the need to counter the French menace preoccupied Albany's mayor. For the duration of his term, he would never be able to separate his military duties from his civil role. In the summer of 1690 he led a force north toward Lake Champlain to launch a campaign against the French at Montreal; the mission was aborted. A year later Schuyler successfully invaded Canada, attacking a settlement outside Montreal. The French lost 200; Schuyler lost only 21 militiamen and 20 Mohawks.

This oil painting of Pieter Schuyler hangs in the mayor's office.

Albany Public Library

Schuyler was replaced as mayor in 1694, but he remained active and influential throughout the province. Though out of office, his skills as a diplomat were still needed. In late 1709 he sailed for England, accompanied by four Mohawk sachems, to personally plead the New Yorkers' need for greater military assistance from England. Schuyler's powers of persuasion were critical in the Crown's decision to bolster the colony's defenses. The sachems, in the meantime, became the vogue of the court's artists, and their portraits were displayed throughout a curious Europe.

Pieter Schuyler's force of character and personality helped define the nature of Albany's mayoralty for all time. His influence extended far beyond the city itself and long after his own death, which came in 1724 at the age of 67.

The St. Francis de Sales Orphan Asylum once occupied the Schuyler Mansion. In the drawing room, shown here circa 1895, Alexander Hamilton married Elizabeth Schuyler.

Daughters of Charity Archives

The Dongan Charter

The significance of the city charter granted by Governor Thomas Dongan to the people of Albany on July 22, 1686, cannot be overstated. The document, conferred in the name of his "Most Sacred Majesty," James II, confirmed the importance of Albany as the second largest city in the province of New York and ended the claims of the Van Rensselaer family to ownership of the land and authority over the people resident within the city boundaries.

Stating that Albany was "an ancient town" even then, the charter reaffirmed old rights and privileges that had been granted to the burghers of Beverwyck, Fort Orange, and Willemstadt by a series of civic and military officials representing Dutch and British governments over several decades of development. It confirmed public ownership of property and land used by the people in common, including the Stadt Huys (statehouse), the burial grounds, the adjacent palisades, the watch house, and the pastures south of the old fort, and bestowed on the city control over the ferry rights to Greenbush. The economic security of Albanians was guaranteed by the granting of all fishing, hunting, and mining rights to the city government (with the specific exemption of any gold or silver mines, which were presumably reserved to the Crown). Permission also was granted to purchase from the Indians meadowland at "Schaittecoque" and "Tionondorogue," which could later be sold to farmers as a means of raising revenue.

Left
The first seal of the city of Albany was affixed to the 1686 Dongan Charter. The crown, symbolizing British royalty, surmounts the lettering ALB. Seals that were adopted in 1752 and 1797 incorporated the beaver to symbolize the city's early history as a fur trading center.
Facing page
The Staats House was originally constructed in 1667 as a double house on the corner of State and South Pearl streets. It was a typical Dutch urban town house and was the traditional birthplace of General Philip Schuyler. Half demolished for the widening of South Pearl Street, the building was finally removed for the construction of a bank building in 1881.

Albany Institute of History and Art

The municipal offices established by Thomas Dongan were those of mayor, recorder, chamberlain, six aldermen, six assistant aldermen, town clerk, sheriff, coroner, clerk of the market, high constable, three subconstables, and a sergeant-at-mace. Albany's city government traces its roots to this ancient document, thus making Albany the oldest city in the original 13 colonies still operating on its original charter.

There have been changes, of course, over the last 300 years. The size of the Common Council has been increased on several occasions, while the office of assistant alderman has been dispensed with. The mayor is no longer nominated "upon the feast day of St. Michael the Archangel," and the recorder and clerk no longer require the appointment of the lieutenant governor of New York before taking office. The chamberlain (treasurer) is now chosen by the people at the polls rather than by the mayor, and the sheriff's office maintains a separate existence within the county's bureaucracy. The duties of the clerk of the market each Wednesday and Saturday have also been removed from the responsibilities of the mayor— a change that no doubt brings much relief to the modern incumbent of that ancient office.

Most radically changed is the administration of justice—once dispensed by several city officials acting together on cases ranging from the short-weighting of groceries to capital offenses—now carried out by individual, elected judges serving on a variety of specialized courts. City Court, Police

Howell and Tenney

Court, Traffic Court, County Court, Family Court, the State Supreme Court, and the Court of Appeals are all part of a complex, multilevel system of justice undreamed of in 1686.

In 1688 Governor Dongan—Gaelic-speaking younger son of an Irish Catholic baronet, and later to become the Earl of Limerick—was succeeded by Sir Edmund Andros, appointed governor of New York for the second time. Shortly thereafter James II's Catholic regime collapsed, throwing New York's leaderless provincial government into chaos with the accession of the Protestant regime of William and Mary.

Dongan's Jesuit assistants and Stuart counselors were "hunted like a fox" by the anti-Papist followers of Jacob Leisler, the German deacon of a New York City Reform church who sought to fill the sudden void in provincial leadership with his own zealous drive to preserve the Protestant faith and control the colonial militia. Major Jervis Baster, the Catholic commander of Albany, fled the fort in the face of the Protestant purge, ending any hope of fulfilling two of Governor Dongan's old aspirations—sending English-speaking Jesuit missionaries to the Iroquois and persuading the Crown to sponsor, with the proferred aid of Dongan's nephew, a wave of Irish immigration.

In the course of the next century, Albany would be buffeted by four major colonial conflicts with the French, followed by the colonists' own War of Independence. Throughout this long period of trial, the Dongan Charter would stand as a bulwark of stability, a strong if subtle factor in the city's ability to survive.

A Century of Warfare
While there were advantages to joining the British Empire, there were disadvantages as well. England's archenemy was France, which happened to be the colony's neighbor to the north.

Alliances with the Indians, recognized from earliest Dutch times as essential to the success of the settlement at Albany, now became even more important. The British took care to maintain the treaties of mutual defense known as the "Chain of Friendship" and to keep alive the long-standing hostility of the Iroquois toward the French and Canadians. In 1675, Mohawk sachems were contracted by the British government to fight against New England tribes under a chief known as King Philip. The Mohawks carried out these obligations with such relish that a year later the New England Indian commissioners came to Albany to dissuade them from continuing their raiding expeditions long after they were needed.

Governor Andros visited Albany in 1676, at the time when most of the local Indians were off fighting in New England. He found the fort to be in a very poor state of defense, its structure literally crumbling in a state of hopeless disrepair. He ordered that Fort Orange, which had served the settlement for half a century, be abandoned and that a new fort, larger and more formidable, be constructed toward the top of what is now State Street hill (but still below the peak—a decision criticized by some). Named Fort Frederick, it was originally constructed of logs but was rebuilt of stone in the first third of the 18th century.

Fort Orange was allowed to deteriorate into a shapeless ruin and today exists only in memory. After an archaeological dig in the early 1970s, all that remains of the fort is buried under sand, partially obscured by an arterial highway access ramp. A bronze plaque on the cement retaining

Facing page
Top left
The Iroquois Indians considered most of New York State and part of Pennsylvania as their hunting grounds. They were divided into six tribes: the Mohawks, Oneidas, Onondagas, Cayugas, Senecas, and Tuscaroras.
Top right
Governor of New York Edmund Andros traveled to Albany in 1676. He organized the first Board of Commissioners for Indian Affairs and appointed Albany town clerk Robert Livingston as its secretary.
Bottom
This Dutch cannon was used at Fort Frederick, built after Governor Edmund Andros ordered the settlers to abandon Fort Orange.

Lossing, *The Empire State*

Dictionary of American Portraits

New York State Museum

wall of the highway opposite the present Inn Town Motor Hotel is all that marks its location.

By the winter of 1687–88, the volume of trade in beaver pelts, normally upwards of 40,000 pelts in a single season, had been reduced to less than one fourth that number. The members of the colony were expending their energies and treasure on militia activities and on the fortification of their inadequate stockades.

In 1690, guarded only by a few soldiers sent over from Connecticut and by snowmen constructed by the children of the settlement, the small stockaded village of Schenectady was raided at night by a party of Canadian Indians under French command. The residents, more than 400 of them, were killed, captured, or scattered within a matter of hours, and 80 houses were burned. One of the legendary heroes of Albany history, Symen Schermerhorn, rode for hours that night in a driving snowstorm, wounded and bleeding, to warn the citizens of Albany that they might be next—though, fortunately, the anticipated attack on Albany never came. Most Albanians today are familiar with the burning of Schenectady from a drawing—a silhouette of the burning village and the small snowmen— that was shown every night for years on local television.

Facing page
David Lithgow's mural depicts Albany as a trading post around 1695. Outside of the stockade Indians traded furs for silver ornaments, trinkets, and cloth.

Right
After a night raid on Schenectady by Canadian Indians under the French in 1690, a wounded Symen Schermerhorn rode through the snow to warn Albany residents of a probable attack. Fortunately it did not materialize. This modern-day mural is by Owen Rhodes.

Albany City Hall

The wars of Europe were bewildering to the settlers of North America, as they were to many throughout the far-flung empires of France and England. The War of the League of Augsburg, the War of the Spanish Succession, and the War of the Austrian Succession to the Americans were known simply as King William's War, Queen Anne's War, and King George's War, after the reigning monarch of the day. And what European history knows as the Seven Years War, Americans referred to as the French and Indian War, after those who presented an immediate threat to the colonies.

The long series of wars had the effect of bankrupting the mother country, and too often military and financial aid required by the colonies failed to materialize. According to Governor Bellomont, who visited Albany several times toward the end of the 17th century,

" The soldiers in the garrison of Albany are in such a shameful condition for the want of clothes that the women when passing them are obliged to cover their eyes. The Indians ask with significance, "Do you think us such fools as to believe that the king who cannot clothe his soldiers can protect us from the French with their 1400 men all in good condition?"

The seeds of disaffection between colony and mother country were being sown. From a European perspective, the defense of the struggling colony seemed a great burden and expense, of lesser importance than matters closer to home; to the colonists, the paltry amount of aid that finally made its way up the Hudson Valley seemed woefully inadequate, reflecting a distant monarch's unconcern with the reality of North American survival.

The population of Albany and its environs fluctuated wildly during the colonial wars of the 17th and 18th centuries. During King William's War alone, the population shrank by 25 percent, leaving many areas populated largely by male settlers and slaves. Women and children were routinely sent down to New York City for safety, while slaves harnessed to the task of clearing the wilderness lacked the mobility to leave the dangerous frontier territory even if they wanted to.

King William's War (1688–1697) was soon followed by Queen Anne's War (1701–1714). The next quarter-century of relative peace was marked by the ongoing competition between French and English for the fur trade and, even more important, for the loyalty of the Indians that each side hoped to use as its pawns in the next round of battle that was sure to come. During this period the French succeeded in making considerable inroads with the Indians, gaining the firm allegiance of the Senecas, the westernmost tribe of the Iroquois Confederacy, and some support from other tribes.

War broke out again in 1739, this time under King George II. The European issues were of little interest to the citizens of Albany, the majority of whom wished only for peace. In 1745, however, the reality of the situation was brought home with a shock. In the month of November, at a time folklore refers to as "Indian summer," French, Canadians, and Indians fell upon old Saratoga (now Schuylerville) and obliterated the settlement there, killing or capturing more than 100 people.

Still the Indian commissioners at Albany were reluctant to take definite action. The assembly voted more money to strengthen defenses on the frontier, but no action took place. By 1746 the lack of credibility with the Indians on the part of the British government had become a major problem.

What finally tilted the tables was the coming to power in the Mohawk Valley of William Johnson. Born in Ireland, Johnson had come over as a young man to protect and administer the large landed estate of his uncle, Admiral Sir Peter Warren. Acquiring land in his own name, he imported Scottish and Irish settlers from whom he won great loyalty and admiration. At the same time, he gained a remarkable rapport with the Six Nations of the Iroquois, in some ways becoming almost one of them. By 1746 he controlled the whole western frontier, and Johnson and his Indian followers assembled at Albany for a great march up to Canada that summer.

Once again, as in the two previous wars, the great hope of conquering Canada was dashed upon the rocks of international politics. The European war was not going well for the British, and the luxury of sending a fleet up the St. Lawrence—ships that could be better used in Europe—was an expense the admiralty was not about to bear. The fleet was canceled, and to the great mortification of Governor Clinton and Colonel Johnson, the news had to be spread to the Indians that King George had once again failed to send the promised help and all soldiers and warriors were to disband.

Knox Family

From his baronial seat at Johnson Hall in the Mohawk Valley, west of Albany, Sir William Johnson maintained the balance of power between the British and French empires by earning the loyalty of the Iroquois Confederacy. His mansion, shown in this E.L. Henry painting, was the site of frequent gatherings of Indians from the time of its construction in 1763.

The Treaty of Aix-la-Chapelle which ended the war in 1748 did not impart much feeling of confidence or security to the settlers of the Hudson Valley. Most people knew that it would be only a matter of time before France and Britain would be at war again.

The British government did little to ease the colonists' fear of renewed attack, as the French established garrisons at Crown Point on Lake Champlain and at Niagara, regularly penetrating the British sphere of influence in the West and wooing the Indians with French trade and religion. It seemed to the colonists that the British Crown was more interested in the future of Gibraltar, Madras, and the Caribbean than in the wilderness defense of a less glamorous North America. Ineffectual and disunited, the colonists could do nothing alone, while their appeals to London seemed to fall on deaf ears.

By 1753 a few colonial leaders, recognizing that Great Britain could no longer be relied upon for their defense, were arguing for greater military and political organization and mutual support among the American colonies. A plan for common defense, one that would be initiated and controlled by the colonists themselves, became more and more the subject of discussion in the coffeehouses and meetinghouses of America. This movement, spearheaded by Benjamin Franklin, found its first public forum at the Albany Congress of 1754, called to negotiate a new general treaty with the Iroquois Confederacy. The result was the highly prophetic Albany Plan of Union.

The French and Indian War

Even as the delegates discussed the need for a strong common defense against the French and their Indian allies, far to the west of them, after a 10-hour siege in the forests of the Pennsylvania wilderness, a force of 150 young Virginia militiamen commanded by a 22-year-old lieutenant colonel named George Washington, were forced to abandon the hastily erected Fort Necessity and return home in defeat. The date of Washington's defeat was a prophetic one—July 4, 1754.

The final chapter in the epic battle between Bourbon France and the British Empire of the German-speaking Hanoverian kings had begun. At its end, in the Treaty of Paris of 1783, the French threat that had so long shadowed Albany's history and retarded its growth was removed for all time.

British military strategy during these years depended on Albany as the headquarters and quartermaster of the northern department. The city designated as the assembly point for armies marching on to Canada also served as a supply depot, winter quarters for regular troops, and a behind-the-lines hospital for the inevitable wounded and dying of armies all too vulnerable to epidemics of typhoid, typhus, smallpox, and dysentery.

In 1755, as soon as the spring planting season was over and young farmers could be spared from the land, an army composed of militiamen from New York, New Jersey, and New England was formed at Albany to march against the French Fort St. Frederic (Crown Point), a small castlelike structure whose ruins have lately been excavated on the banks of Lake Champlain. The expedition, augmented by a small contingent of British regulars as well as the usual warriors from the Iroquois Confederacy, was placed under the command of William Johnson.

The army met the enemy at Lake George in a bloody confrontation that saw the death of the aged chief, King Hendrick, one of the Mohawk sachems who had traveled to England with Pieter Schuyler nearly half a century before, as well as the enemy commander, Baron Ludwig August Dieskau, a German mercenary in command of French and Indian troops.

Dictionary of American Portraits

In a year filled with British defeats, the victory at Lake George was welcome news, and Johnson was made a "Baronet of the British Empire in New York"—a title still held by his descendants in Canada today. Following his victory, Johnson built Fort William Henry, named diplomatically after two dukes of the royal family; for the next two years the log fortress would stand as Albany's northernmost bulwark against the inevitable onslaught of New France. The French, for their part, further narrowed the no-man's-land to the length of Lake George by building the log citadel of Fort Carillon at Ticonderoga. Albany's role in supplying Fort William Henry as well as a fort at Oswego overshadowed all other considerations in the northern colonies.

From their great country mansion at Whitehall, whose foundation now supports an apartment house on Whitehall Road in Albany, the British commanders planned and launched several attacks against the French. War was conducted almost exclusively during the summer months, when the primitive military roads were not muddy, washed out and, most important, when the boys and young men could be spared from the farms. War or no war, the worst enemy was crop failure, which in those days meant famine.

Albany Institute of History and Art

Facing page

Top
Indian commissioner William Johnson was extremely well liked by the Iroquois. In 1755 he led an expedition of British soldiers and Iroquois warriors to victory over the French at Lake George and earned the title of Baronet of the British Empire in New York.

Bottom
Decorated with handcarved drawings of various Northeast forts, this soldier's pewter-top powder horn dates from the French and Indian Wars.

Right
Chief Hendrick was one of the four Mohawk sachems brought to London to the court of Queen Anne in 1710 with Colonel Pieter Schuyler to plead for more military aid to the colonies. This mezzotint, one of several made after the celebrated visit, was widely circulated among Europeans, who were fascinated by the Indians of North America. Years later, in 1755, Hendrick would serve as a portly and aging senior officer to William Johnson at the Battle of Lake George. There he would meet death by a French bullet while still wearing a medal given him by the Queen.

The Albany Plan of Union

In 1754, startled into action by reports of the imminence of what was to be the French and Indian War, the Lords of Trade in London called for a convention of colonial leaders in Albany to negotiate a new general treaty with the Iroquois. Known today as the Albany Congress of 1754, this conference was by far the most significant gathering in Albany in colonial times.

A total of 24 delegates, including military leaders, public officials, lawyers, and clergymen, represented seven colonies—New York, Massachusetts Bay, Pennsylvania, Rhode Island, Connecticut, New Hampshire, and Maryland; the southern colonies of Virginia and North Carolina, unable to send delegations over such a long distance, also asked to be considered as participants. The conference met from June 9 to July 25 in Albany's Stadt Huys on the northeast corner of Hudson and Court streets (today's University Plaza).

The Iroquois, by now clearly skeptical of the colonies' ability to fend for themselves, were slow in arriving. Their leader, the aged Mohawk chieftain known as King Hendrick, delivered an eloquent oration in which he spoke as much to the British monarchy as he did to the colonial leaders:

" 'Tis your own fault, brethren," the chief declared, "that we are not strengthened by conquest, for we would have gone and taken Crown Point, but you hindered us. You have no fortifications about you, no, not even to this city. 'Tis but one step from Canada thither, and the French may easily come and turn you out of doors.

"Look at the French, they are men, they are fortifying everywhere—but, we are ashamed to say it, you are all like women."

Despite this harsh rebuke, King Hendrick entered into the new treaty, and the delegates, stung by his words, turned their attention to the need for a common colonial defense.

The debate, which went on for days,

JOIN, or DIE.

soon moved beyond creating a union of colonial defense to creating a colonial union. Benjamin Franklin, then a 48-year-old Pennsylvania provincial assemblyman, had brought with him to Albany a plan of unity appropriately reminiscent of Hiawatha's Confederacy. At a time when separation from Britain was undreamed of, Franklin was about to plant the seeds of a national government for America.

Franklin's plan called for a general government of 11 colonies, with a Grand Council of 48 members presided over by a President-General—the first hint of an American Presidency. The colonies would jointly maintain an army and levy taxes to pay for a united colonial defense.

On July 9 the delegates agreed "that there be a union of His Majesty's several governments on this continent, to act against their common enemy." The following day Franklin's "Plan of a Proposed Union of the Several Colonies" was approved and forwarded to the colonial assemblies—all of which ultimately refused ratification.

The idea of a united America was born out of the colonists' recognition that they could survive against the common enemy, France, only by standing together. Twenty-two years later, Benjamin Franklin, still devoted to the concept of unity presented at Albany, would sign another declaration in Philadelphia—only this time the common enemy would be not France, but England.

Franklin's divided snake illustrated the importance of the Albany Plan of Union.

During the French and Indian War, General James Abercrombie led his British troops to horrible defeat against the French garrison at Ticonderoga.

The disruption of the city by the quartering of troops in the homes of its burghers, the arrogance and revelries of unruly soldiers far from home, and the congestion of its narrow streets with a seemingly endless procession of cannon, military stores, and barrels of food and provisions were reluctantly tolerated, as Albanians contemplated the possible alternative. Too well they remembered the massacres of Schenectady, Deerfield, and old Saratoga. The war had grown particularly brutal since both sides had offered a bounty for the scalps of their respective enemies—a practice engaged in by whites and Indians alike.

In August 1757 a new wave of horror swept through the city. Not only had the famed Fort William Henry fallen, but—in a catastrophe related in James Fenimore Cooper's *Last of the Mohicans*—almost its entire garrison, along with several hundred unarmed men, women, and children, had been massacred by scalp-hungry Indians, completely out of control, who comprised the greater part of the army of the outraged but helpless Marquis de Montcalm. As the shattered survivors of the massacre trickled into Albany from their original haven at Fort Edward, the citizenry was in a state of near panic.

But the disaster was not without its benefit to the British cause. From within the British Parliament, a strong leader arose in the person of William Pitt, a magnificent orator and devoted friend of the American cause. Pitt's commitment to defend the colonies, coupled with the righteous longing of the colonists to revenge the bloody massacre at Lake George, led the following year to the formation in Albany of the largest army yet assembled on North American soil. In the early summer of 1758, some 15,000 troops, plus a motley assortment of camp followers, gathered under the command of General James Abercrombie, filling the fields near Whitehall and above Fort Frederic, as well as much of Greenbush on the east bank of the Hudson, with an accumulation of humanity that exceeded by five times the resident population of the city.

Abercrombie's mission was to advance northward along the traditional "Warpath of Nations," first defeating the French garrison at Ticonderoga, then effecting a similar victory at Crown Point, and finally moving on north to take Montreal and, if possible, Quebec. The mission failed. Wave after wave of the massive force, marching to the wail of Scottish Black Watch bagpipes, were horribly cut up by the grapeshot and musket fire of the much smaller but well-entrenched Ticonderoga garrison, by now protected by massive stone walls.

But the days of the French in North America were numbered. The vast empire of New France was held together by an extensive chain of forts strategically placed along the waterways that encircled the British colonies from Quebec to New Orleans. This thin line of French civilization was protected by alliances with most of the surrounding Indian tribes, reinforced by the zealous efforts of missionaries and trappers. Farmers and settlers, however, were rare indeed outside the narrow trading/ military corridor. The French, unlike the English, had never created a large reservoir of dissidents, such as the suppressed Scots and Irish, anxious to emigrate to America; because of their long-standing commitment to the spread of Roman Catholicism throughout the New World, in fact, they had driven one potential immigrant group, the Huguenots, into the camp of the enemy. As a result, French settlers in North America were outnumbered by their British counterparts 10 to one, and there was simply no appreciable native militia to mobilize in defense of French territory.

In the next expedition based in Albany, in 1759, some 9,000 troops under the command of Lord Jeffrey Amherst produced a series of victories that placed both Ticonderoga and Crown Point under the Union Jack. The fall of Montreal and Quebec the following year ended a long and painful chapter in Albany's history.

The victories of 1759 were overshadowed by the loss of a great friend of Albany and the American colonies, Viscount George Augustus Howe, who had been killed in 1758 at Ticonderoga. Howe had a genuine sympathy with the colonists's feelings of estrangement from the mother country. Displaying none of the arrogance shown by so many other commanders, he got to know the provincial leaders and local militiamen with whom he fought the common enemy. He appreciated the ways of the forest by which the Americans lived and fought, realizing that the close-order lines and formal discipline of European soldiery had little place in America. He encouraged his men to simplify their elaborate uniforms, to cover their gaudy colors with mud, and to hide behind the trees and rocks of the Adirondacks. Had he survived, the course of American history might well have been different. As it was, however, his remains, brought back to Albany by Philip Schuyler, were laid to rest beneath St. Peter's Anglican Church, and the question of future Anglo-American relations would be left to lesser men of little vision.

Albany in the Revolution

Following the signing of the Treaty of Paris of 1763, the people of Albany experienced a peace they had not known for generations. The new sense of security from external attack, however, made them less tolerant than ever of British officials, military or civil, at the same time that Britain was determined to begin recouping some of the huge expenses of defending and maintaining her American colonies.

The Navigation Acts, on the books for decades but enforced with new vigor after 1763, infuriated Albanians, to whom smuggling was a time-honored tradition. The Stamp Act, passed by the British Parliament in 1765, intruded even more directly into the lives of the people, and opposition throughout the colonies was virtually unanimous. In Albany a group of young men, many of them members of the city's most prominent families, began calling themselves the Sons of Liberty. Protected by older relatives on the Common Council, they regularly harassed would-be tax collectors, effectively blocking implementation of the act. Over the next few years, Committees of Correspondence disseminated to the most remote settlements news of the mounting confrontations between the American colonists and British officialdom.

The reality of armed revolt was brought home to Albany on May 1, 1775, when the news of Lexington and Concord reached the city. That afternoon members of the local Committee of Correspondence addressed a large crowd at the old marketplace, located in the middle of today's Broadway in front of the present post office. A new Committee of Safety, Protection, and Correspondence was formed, with full powers to act in support of the patriot cause. Chaired by Abraham Yates, this extralegal committee almost immediately began filling the void left by a vacillating and generally pro-British Common Council under Mayor Abraham Cuyler. Meeting daily in the old Stadt Huys, the committee regulated everything from fire watches and the raising of militia to price gouging and the suppression of conspiracies.

Albany's role in the War of Independence was essentially the same as it

Facing page

Top

In 1759, as commander-in-chief of the British forces in America, Jeffrey Amherst and his troops drove the French from Lake Champlain. He completed the conquest of Canada the following year when he captured Montreal. Painting by Joseph Blackburn.

Middle

Major General Philip Schuyler, who served as quartermaster general of the Northern Department of the Continental Army, was the father-in-law of Alexander Hamilton. This portrait of Schuyler was painted by John Trumbull in 1792.

Bottom

Lord George Augustus Howe, who accompanied James Abercrombie on his expedition against Ticonderoga, was killed in battle at the age of 34. He was buried beneath St. Peter's Church.

Above

In 1775 Richard Montgomery became a brigadier general in the Continental Army. When Albany's Philip Schuyler became ill during the siege of St. Johns, he turned over command of the Montreal expedition to Montgomery. After capturing the city, he joined forces with Benedict Arnold. On December 31, 1775, Montgomery was killed during the attack on Quebec.

had been in the earlier wars against the French. Its geographic position remained pivotal, and once again the city served as a vital center of military supply, intelligence gathering, and Indian diplomacy.

In June of 1775, the great stone fortress at Ticonderoga was taken by Ethan Allen and the Green Mountain Boys of Vermont. In the same month, the Continental Congress commissioned Albany's Philip Schuyler a major general and, in a replay of previous wars, directed him to attack Canada before the British could move south and capture the Hudson Valley, thus splitting the colonies in two.

The generations-old trading connections of Albany merchants engaged in the illegal smuggling trade with Canada would prove invaluable to the invasion force. Even so, the going was slow. The American troops, despite the blandishments of the increasingly unpopular General Schuyler, were poorly trained and undisciplined. The problems of supplying an army extended so far into the wilderness were staggering. Dysentery, smallpox, and other diseases were rampant. In the siege of St. Johns, which lasted into November, Schuyler became so ill that he turned over his command to General Richard Montgomery, the Irish-born son-in-law of Robert Livingston, who 16 years previously, as a British adjutant under General Amherst, had traveled the same path northward against the French army of Montcalm.

While Schuyler saw to the badly disrupted supply lines from his base at Ticonderoga, Montgomery pushed on to capture Montreal in mid-November. At Quebec he joined forces with General Benedict Arnold, whose weary troops had defied all odds by penetrating the still uncharted wilderness of northern Maine. With barely 800 men left, they advanced against Quebec in a desperate New Year's Eve attack. The gamble failed, Montgomery was fatally wounded, and the army retreated back down its invasion route to the Champlain Valley. Nearly 5,000 American soldiers had lost their lives in the ill-fated expedition, the overwhelming majority having perished from disease or exposure.

The one bright spot in the winter of 1776 was the successful movement of 59 pieces of ordnance from Ticonderoga over an arduous route down Lake George and the old military road to Albany, across the frozen Hudson, and through the Berkshires to Cambridge, where they played a key role in the siege of Boston. A bronze plaque in Albany's Loudon Shopping Center is one of several that mark that tortuous journey, made with the help of ox-drawn sleds, which gave new hope to the patriot cause and led to the British evacuation of Boston that March.

Meanwhile the loyalist mayor and Common Council remained in office, seemingly oblivious to the daily recruitment of troops and frantic garnering of supplies to support the Continental Army to the north. Albany County, like most of the country, was at least one-third loyalist, with perhaps as many again uncertain which side to support. Many families were disunited; Mayor Cuyler, in fact, was a first cousin of General Schuyler. Sheriff Henry Ten Eyck refused use of the jail for loyalist prisoners being questioned by the Committee of Safety, which used two rooms of the deteriorating Fort Frederick instead.

This strange dual administration lasted until June 5, 1776, when the mayor and several of his followers, ignoring all patriotic sensibilities, publicly celebrated the king's birthday at Cartwright's Tavern, at the corner of today's Green and Beaver streets. The offending loyalists were arrested the following day. Abraham Cuyler and his brother Henry were sent into exile in Hartford, Connecticut; the others were released at intervals ranging from a few days to three months. Albany's city government had ceased to exist and would remain in legal limbo for nearly two years.

On July 19, 1776, John Barclay, then chairman of the Committee of Safety, stood on the steps of the old Stadt Huys and, amid the firing of muskets and the tolling of church bells, read the Declaration of Independence. Among its signers was Albany-born Philip Livingston.

Early in the summer of 1777, Albanians learned the terrifying news that General John Burgoyne, with a force of 8,000 British and German regular troops, 150 Canadian militiamen, and about 400 Indians, was advancing down Lake Champlain to capture Albany. From the west, Colonel Barry St. Leger was approaching with a smaller but highly motivated force made up largely of Mohawk Valley loyalists who had fled to Canada and were now making one last desperate effort to regain their homes and farms. This contingent was met at Fort Stanwix by Albany's Colonel Peter Gansevoort, who managed to hold his ground with a garrison only one-third the size of the attacking force. Three days later, American reinforcements under General Nicholas Herkimer engaged the enemy at Oriskany. This bitter fight, which pitted neighbor against neighbor, was among the bloodiest of the Revolution. Herkimer, after whom Herkimer Street in the Pastures is named, showed indomitable bravery as he lay mortally wounded, propped up against a beech tree, calmly smoking his pipe and directing his troops to the end.

> *We have neither tents, houses, barns, boards, or any shelter except a little brush. Every rain that falls, and we have it in great abundance almost every day, wets the men to the skin. We are besides in great want of every kind of necessities, provisions excepted. Camp kettles we have so few, that we cannot afford one to 20 men.*
>
> —Letter to General Washington from General Philip Schuyler.

By mid-August 1,200 relief troops under Benedict Arnold had reached the hostilities, throwing St. Leger into retreat and freeing both Arnold's men and the Mohawk Valley militiamen for service against Burgoyne.

From a historical perspective, General Philip Schuyler's approach to the advance of his seasoned British opponent was nothing short of brilliant. The forts at Crown Point and Ticonderoga had originally been built by the French to repel an assault from the south; the British were coming from the north by a waterway which they had controlled since Arnold's defeat the year before. Schuyler abandoned Crown Point without a shot, and when British cannon were hauled to the top of Mount Defiance overlooking Ticonderoga, he again withdrew.

Now the invaders would have to meet Schuyler on his own terms, in a forested no-man's-land known to the frontier trappers and traders of Albany since the earliest days of Fort Orange. The American commander had his men fell great trees across the narrow portage trail that linked the Hudson and Mohawk valleys. Encumbered by bulky supply wagons, too

Dictionary of American Portraits

Dictionary of American Portraits

Dictionary of American Portraits

Dictionary of American Portraits

Facing page

Top

Major General Horatio Gates, who replaced General Philip Schuyler as commander of the Northern Department of the Continental Army, led his troops to victory at Saratoga in 1777.

Middle

Born in Albany in 1716, Philip Livingston was among those who signed the Declaration of Independence. A successful merchant, Livingston protested against British trade restrictions.

Bottom

While leading reinforcements for the Americans at Fort Stanwix, General Nicholas Herkimer was mortally wounded by Loyalists and Indians in an ambush at Oriskany Creek. Herkimer Street in the Pastures neighborhood is named for him.

Above

British General John Burgoyne was forced to surrender at Saratoga after Barry St. Leger failed to reach Albany with his troops, leaving Burgoyne to face 17,000 Americans with fewer than 5,000 able-bodied men.

wide for the portage route even in the best of circumstances, and by hundreds of civilian camp followers, the would-be conquering army slowed almost to a halt. It took Burgoyne three weeks to move 20 miles to Fort Edward. When his army finally emerged from the wilderness, it was greeted not by the anticipated cheers of loyal subjects, but by the scorched fields and deserted homesteads of refugees now on their way to Albany or to join the Continental Army.

Meanwhile the Continental Congress, stung by the loss of the legendary Ticonderoga, had relieved the veteran Dutch general of his command, replacing him with Horatio Gates, a popular leader who had succeeded the slain Montgomery as Schuyler's second in command. History would ultimately vindicate Schuyler's decision to withdraw in the face of the advancing army, thereby shortening his supply lines while lengthening those of the enemy; but in the time purchased by Schuyler, Gates, who succeeded him in early August, was able to bolster recruitments in a way that the less popular Schuyler could never have done. As Burgoyne's weary troops made their way down the once-fertile riverbank of old Saratoga, the British commander now found himself facing an army swelled to more than 17,000 while fewer than 5,000 of his own men were fit for combat.

The battles at Bemis Heights and Freeman's Farm stopped the British advance on the city. Finally, on October 17, 1777, hopelessly outnumbered and with no possibility of withdrawal, Burgoyne surrendered at Saratoga. With Burgoyne's entire army taken prisoner, a British force advancing northward up the Hudson turned back, returning to New York City, which remained in British hands for the duration of the war.

More than 5,800 military prisoners were taken at Saratoga, and most of them were marched through Albany on their way to New England. Tradition has it that Burgoyne stopped at the home of Colonel Henry Quackenbush, which still stands on Broadway, before entering the city gate only a few yards away. In Albany, he and the other staff officers, with sidearms intact, were housed in the Schuyler Mansion. Over a gracious dinner provided by their Dutch hosts, Burgoyne personally apologized for the burning of the general's home at Schuylerville, which had been located in the path of the fighting. Catherine Van Rensselaer Schuyler, wife of the general, had supervised the evacuation and had herself set fire to the fields, lest their rich harvest give sustenance to the enemy she now entertained in her Albany mansion. Even as they spoke, however, American soldiers were sawing timbers to construct a new building before the army withdrew from Schuylerville. Such were the genteel ups and downs of 18th-century warfare.

The remainder of the war saw little to rival the threat that Burgoyne had posed. The city government was restored on February 19, 1778, led by Mayor John Barclay, who was appointed by Governor George Clinton. A new body, the Committee for Detecting and Defeating Conspiracies, was appointed in April of that year. Rumors of loyalist plots were constant, and trials, pardons, imprisonment, and hangings were all part of the tense atmosphere of the remaining war years.

Albany, exhausted by its active part in the first three years of the war, remained in a state of siege for seven years in all, with both ends of the Hudson-Champlain waterway held by enemy forces. The news of the signing of the Treaty of Paris in 1783 was greeted with relief, and Albanians looked forward to playing a key role in the rise of the new Empire State.

CHAPTER 3
PATTERNS OF SETTLEMENT

The street patterns of downtown Albany still retain much of the 17th-century character created by their Dutch builders. The lower blocks of Hudson Avenue and little Beaver Street still curve to parallel a log stockade that has long since faded into history.

To the native as well as the visitor, the great breadth of State Street seems an anachronism. Most people are unaware that, in the middle of the street, the foundation ruins of the city's first Reformed and Anglican churches sleep undisturbed beneath the macadam world of modern Albany.

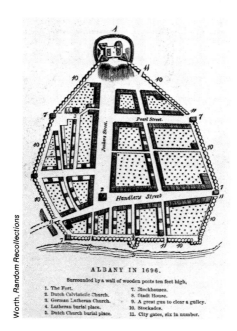

Worth, *Random Recollections*

ALBANY IN 1696.

Surrounded by a wall of wooden posts ten feet high.

1. The Fort.
2. Dutch Calvinistic Church.
3. German Lutheran Church.
4. Lutheran burial place.
5. Dutch Church burial place.
7. Blockhouses.
8. Stadt House.
9. A great gun to clear a gulley.
10. Stockades.
11. City gates, six in number.

Facing page
This 1848 watercolor by John Wilson depicts State Street as seen from Broadway (then called Market Street). The spire of St. Peter's Church and the State Capitol, both designed by architect Philip Hooker, can be seen in the distance.
Above
In 1696 Albany was surrounded by a 10-foot-high wall of wooden posts. This plat of the town shows the fort, Dutch Calvinist Church, German Lutheran Church and cemetery, Dutch Church cemetery, and blockhouses.
Right
State Street storekeepers in the late 1800s apparently had no compunction about using their own stoops and city sidewalks to display their wares. Joel Munsell Books and Printing, V.P. Douw's Albany Seed Store, T.J. Wendover, Photographer, and Stratton Auctioneers and Real Estate occupied 80 and 82 State Street, circa 1870.

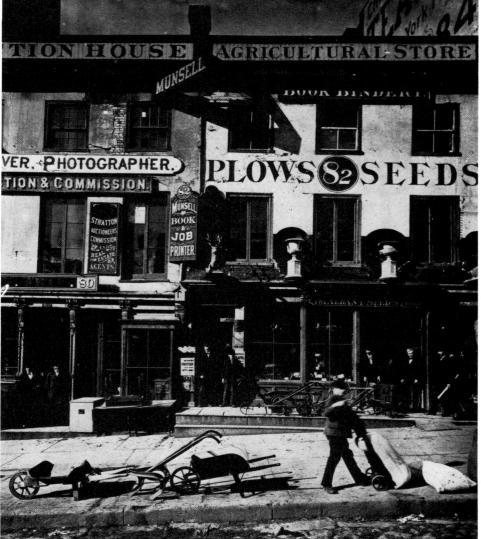

Albany Institute of History and Art

North Broadway, from State Street to Union Station, also retains a width uncommon to the age of its origin—a legacy of its function as the "Market Street" where colonial and early 19th-century Albanians bought and sold produce, poultry, and small livestock from an open-air market in the middle of the street. North Pearl Street is also comparatively wide, in this case belying its traditional role as a prime residential, professional, and commercial street that with State Street formed the principal crossroads of downtown Albany and the capital district.

Excluding these three major streets, the urban map contains exceptionally narrow streets with a design more comfortable in the 17th century than our own. The narrowness of Maiden Lane and James, Norton, Beaver, Steuben, and Division streets remains as a visible legacy of a people who kept their homes, shops, and gardens huddled together within a small area for mutual protection from the wilderness. Progress and commerce have not always been compatible to this weblike pattern. In recent years several of the streets have been closed off to traffic or obliterated entirely to accommodate large building projects such as the new Ten Eyck Project on State Street. Other streets, such as South Pearl Street—the original "Cow Lane," the path to the common pastureland in the city's South End—retained a narrowness so extreme for modern traffic that they could only be widened by demolishing the buildings along one side of the street.

Howell and Tenney

One frequently heard lament is that nothing remains of the riverfront streets that must surely have existed between University Plaza and the waters of the Hudson. The fact is that for all of its history Broadway has been the city's "River Road." The blocks to the east of it, the great rows of warehouses and wide piers, the quays, docks, railroad tracks, and modern arterial highways are virtually all built on land created by filling in the Hudson River in an attempt to service the city's ever-expanding business and commercial needs. No ancient cobblestoned streets or crumbling foundations lie beneath Interstate 787—only the same river bottom and mud flats that have always existed in the natural environment.

Colonial Times

One of the earliest descriptions of Albany comes from Jasper Danckaerts, a Dutch missionary who visited the area in 1680—after the British had assumed control of the colony but before Albany received its charter from Governor Dongan. Danckaerts' journal entry for April 30, 1680, includes the following observations:

Before we quit Albany, we must say a word about the place. It was formerly named the Fuyck by the Hollanders, who first settled there, on account of two rows of houses standing there, opposite to each other, which being wide enough apart in the beginning, finally ran quite together like a "fuyck" [a funnel-shaped fishing net], and, therefore, they gave it this name, especially the Dutch and Indians living there. It is nearly square, and lies against the hill, with several good streets, on which there may be about eighty or ninety houses. Fort Orange, constructed by the Dutch, lies below on the bank of the river, and is set off with palisades, filled in with earth on the inside. It is now abandoned by the English, who have built a similar one behind the town, high up on the declivity of the hill, from whence it can command the place. From the other side of this fort the inhabitants have brought a spring or fountain of water, under the fort, and under ground into the town, where they now have in several places always fountains of clear, fresh, cool water. The town is surrounded by palisades, and has several gates corresponding with the streets. It has a Dutch Reformed and a Lutheran church. The Lutheran minister lives up here in the winter, and down in New York in the summer. There is no English church or place of meeting, to my knowledge. As this is the principal trading-post with the Indians . . .there are houses or lodges erected on both sides of the town, where the Indians, who come from the far interior to trade, live during the time they are there.

Albany's Old English Church was located east of Fort Frederick.

Perhaps the best-known description of the city in colonial times is that of Peter Kalm , the Swedish naturalist, who visited Albany in June of 1749. After 85 years of British rule, Dutch influence was still clearly apparent.

The town extends along the river, which flows here from N.N.E. to S.S.W. The high mountains in the west, above the town, bound the view on that side. There are two churches in Albany, one English and the other Dutch. The Dutch church stands a short distance from the river on the east side of the market. It is built of stone and in the middle it has a small steeple with a bell. It has but one minister who preaches twice every Sunday. The English church is situated on the hill at the west end of the market, directly under the fort. It is likewise built of stone but has no steeple. There is no service at the church at this time because they have no minister, but all the people understand Dutch, the garrison excepted. . . .The town hall lies to the south of the Dutch church, close by the riverside. It is a fine building of stone, three stories high it has a small tower or steeple, with a bell, and a gilt ball and vane at the top of it.

The houses in this town are very neat, and partly built of stones covered with shingles of white pine. Some are slated with tile from Holland, because the clay of this neighborhood is not considered fit for tiles. Most of the houses are built in the old Frankish way, with the gable-end towards the street, except for a few, which were recently built in the modern style. . . .The eaves on the roofs reach almost to the middle of the street. This preserves the walls from being damaged by the rain, but it is extremely disagreeable in rainy weather for the people in the streets, there being hardly any means of avoiding the water from the eaves. The front doors are generally in the middle of the houses, and on both sides are porches with seats, on which during fair weather the people spend almost the whole day, especially on those porches which are in the shade. . . .The streets are broad, and some of them paved. In some parts they are lined with trees. The long streets are almost parallel to the river, and the others intersect them at right angles. The street which goes between the two churches is five times broader than the others and serves as a marketplace. The streets upon the whole are very dirty because the people leave their cattle in them during the summer nights. There are two marketplaces in town, to which the country people come twice a week. There are no city gates here but for the most part just open holes through which people pass in and out of the town.

Twenty years later, in 1769, Richard Smith of New Jersey, a native-born American and later a member of the Continental Congress, recorded his impressions of pre-Revolutionary Albany.

At Half after 10 oCloc we arrived at Albany estimated to be 164 Miles by Water from N.York and by Land 157. In the afternoon we viewed the Town which contains according to several Gentlemen residing there, about 500 Dwelling Houses besides Stores and Out Houses. The Streets are irregular and badly laid out, some paved others not, Two or Three are broad and the rest narrow and not straight. Most of the Buildings are pyramidically shaped like the old Dutch Houses of N.York....

We did not note any extraordinary Edifices in the Town....The Fort is in ruinous neglected Condition and nothing now to be seen of Fort Orange built by the Dutch but part of the Fosse or Ditch which surrounded it. The Barracks are built of Wood and of ordinary Workmanship; the same may be said of the King's Store Houses. The Court House is large and the Jail under it....There are 4 Houses of Worship for different denominations and a Public Library which we did not visit. Most of the Houses are built of Brick or faced with Brick. The Inhabitants generally speak both Dutch and English and some do not understand the latter. The Shore and Wharves 3 in Number abounded in Lumber.

Imposing Order

After the American Revolution, Albany was the sixth largest city in the United States and growing rapidly. The extension of the ancient, haphazard street pattern of Beverwyck was a practical impossibility.

In an attempt to impose some sort of order on the development of the city, the Common Council adopted the comprehensive grid pattern of straight streets and rectangular blocks upon which subsequent generations of Albanians have placed their homes, businesses, and institutions. This division of the vast uptown plains of the city into a simple grid provided clear reference points from which the farms and forests to the west might be developed and absorbed into the settled community. In recent years, this post-Revolutionary street plan has become familiar to area residents in the form of a 1794 map of the city by Simeon De Witt, which was used as a paper placemat at Farnham's restaurant downtown.

Starting from the site of the city's west gate in the now-demolished palisade, the grid pattern divided the entire city—more than a mile wide and 16 miles long—into spacious city blocks and larger "great lots," to be developed at a later date. Roads leading away from the old city were named after animals; only one of these, Elk Street, remains today. Crossing these streets were the "bird streets"—Eagle, Hawk, Swan, Dove, Lark, Snipe (now Lexington), Quail, and Partridge.

The grid system, however, made no provision for the natural terrain of rolling hills that lay to the west of the original settlement. Great ravines and wide bogs formed by the numerous streams that meandered through what is now Pine Hills and midtown Albany were all crisscrossed by "paper streets." Such undesirable land was inevitably developed last or not at all, leaving great gaps in the development of neighborhoods. Interruptions in the grid pattern, many of them now occupied by highways, parks, and campuses, have long caused confusion to postmen, cab drivers, and visitors. Albany is no doubt unique in having, for example, three Spring Streets, four Providence Streets, and five Hudson Avenues—each of which is actually a single street with vast gaps in house numbers.

The original city lines, as described in the Dongan Charter of 1686, coincided with Clinton Avenue and its imaginary extension on the north side, and on the south side, with an imaginary line running through Gansevoort Street, Woodlawn Avenue, and Cortland Street. When Arbor Hill, the former village of Colonie (1806–1815), was annexed as the city's fifth ward, it too gained a grid system, which, while allowing for some

Facing page
Right
In this 1913 view of Arbor Hill, the spire of St. Joseph's Church towers over the neighborhood.

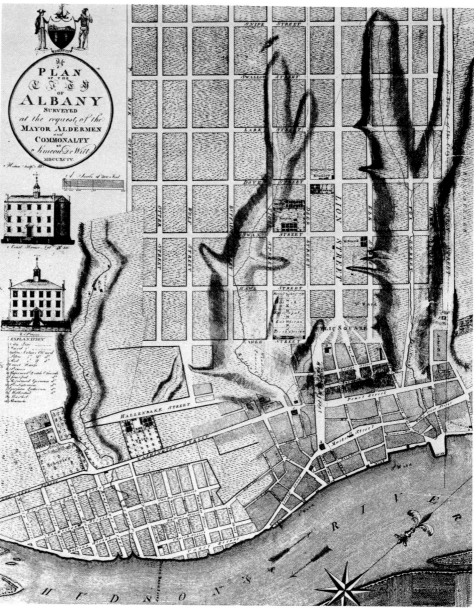

Above
Simeon De Witt was responsible for mapping Albany's grid pattern in the late 18th century. Ezra Ames painted this portrait of the cartographer.
Right
Simeon De Witt's 1794 map shows the grid-like organization of Albany's streets. Note the "bird" and "animal" street names.

longer blocks and narrow service alleys, remained equally as monotonous and inflexible as the street pattern of Capitol Hill and beyond. When West Hill, from Oak Street to beyond Quail Street, was annexed in 1870, the system was extended, even eliminating the back alleys. By the final quarter of the 19th century, Victorian Albany had expanded well into Pine Hills, where at Allen Street the old system would be completely abandoned.

One of the main reasons that the grid system had to be altered was that public and charitable institutions, as they moved out of older neighborhoods downtown, required more land to carry out their functions. These institutions frequently absorbed paper streets and land not yet developed or poorly developed into their campuses. In effect, by closing streets they created "superblocks."

Ringing the older neighborhoods of the city are several such superblocks that have been created over the past century or so. Albany High School, La Salle School, the Armed Forces Reserve Building, the Brady Building, and St. Catherine's Home share one such block, which once included St. Mary's Cemetery. These blocks unwittingly play a significant role in the lives of the city's people. In many cases they serve as preservers of open spaces or "greenbelts," marking the end of one neighborhood and the beginning of another, and helping to break up the pattern of the city into a network of intimate neighborhoods rather than one large, impersonal urban sprawl.

The largest of the superblocks, University Heights, had its roots in the original street pattern as Alms House Square, which extended from Lark Street to Perry Sttreet (now Lake Avenue) and from West Ferry Street (Myrtle Avenue) south to the city line.

Dennis Holzman

Originally the square was devoted exclusively to public institutions: the county poor farm, which remained there until the 1920s; the county pest house, a rather unattractively named quarantine hospital for people with communicable diseases; and the county jail, located approximately where the Hackett Middle School is today. During the Civil War the jail was used as a prison camp for Confederate soldiers, and for many years after the jail paid for itself by taking in federal prisoners from as far away as the Carolinas. Most of these functions have now been moved to the old Shaker farms in Colonie, and in their place three hospitals, two nursing homes, a home for children, three private schools, several colleges and graduate schools, a regional psychiatric center, and the National Guard armory all share a common location in the very heart of the city they serve.

Creating the Parks
Just to the north of the old Alms House Square is Washington Park. Designated as a park in 1869 and preserved from residential or commercial development, this 98-acre expanse of land in the heart of downtown Albany has proved one of the great legacies of 19th-century Albanians to their 20th-century descendants.

Following the Civil War the North began to prosper again, and the tide of immigration resumed into Northern cities such as Albany. Industry, which had expanded greatly because of the war effort, now attracted more and more workers who crowded into neighborhoods already short of land and open space. Washington Park, then on the outskirts of the settled city, was intended as a place where people of all classes could spend their Sunday afternoons.

The city appointed a board of park commissioners, consisting of representatives of the better educated and wealthier families of Albany society. The commissioners then embarked on an ambitious project to expand the relatively small parade grounds, a legacy of colonial times, that extended from Madison Avenue to State Street below Knox Street (Northern Boulevard), which at that time extended in a straight line through Washington Park. A pedestrian walkway today marks where the original Knox Street formed the western boundary of the park.

In the northern part of present-day Washington Park were the State Street Burial Grounds. These burial grounds had been laid out at the time of the American Revolution and by the mid-19th century were almost completely occupied. Psychologically they retarded development in the area—as was also the case with the Van Rensselaer burying ground next to St. Joseph's Church on Ten Broeck Street—because few prospective home buyers were willing to settle in a neighborhood where they could sit on their front stoop and watch the daily burial of their fellow citizens. In the 19th century, with infant mortality so much higher than it is today, funerals were a much more constant factor than they are in present-day life. A city law, in fact, banned the pealing of church bells at funerals because of their inordinate frequency.

The State Street Burial Grounds also presented a problem of vandalism. Street gangs, predominantly German and Irish, were active in Albany in the 1860s, and rival gangs would battle one another in isolated, undeveloped areas of the city, including the cemetery. At the same time, the concept of the rural cemetery was beginning to take hold. Albany Rural Cemetery was established in nearby Menands in 1841, and the adjoining St. Agnes Cemetery in 1866. These cemeteries, and that of Jewish Beth Emeth, would eventually service several generations of Albanians; in fact, more people are buried in these cemeteries than live today in all of Albany County.

The State Street Burial Grounds, already filled to capacity, had little future in the city's grand scheme. The bodies were exhumed at Common Council expense and their remains moved to the newer, more suburban cemeteries to the north, outside the city limits.

The burial grounds coupled with the parade grounds now provided a substantial expanse of land in the very heart of the city. Meanwhile the railroad tracks, originally located to the south of Madison Avenue, were relocated in the 1840s to Tivoli Hollow, far north of this section of the city. All that remained was to expand the western part of the park southward to Madison Avenue, then all the way west to Perry Street (Lake Avenue).

Below
After the Civil War enterprising real-estate speculators constructed Martinville on the site of an old brickyard. The neighborhood, shown in this 1892 photo, was built on land not well suited for residential construction. It was obliterated around 1910 for the development of Lincoln Park.
Facing page
In 1866 geologist and paleontologist James Hall was appointed director of the Museum of Natural History in Albany. In 1893 he was made state geologist of New York.

Morris Gerber

The park commissioners completely displaced a new housing development known as Lakeview, replacing it with gardens and the famous statue of Moses that is so dear to the hearts of most Albanians. The lake was formed by damming up a natural stream, a branch of the Beaver Kill that ran down today's Elberon Place which was once the site of a cotton mill. What the commissioners were not able to do was to displace the millionaires who had built their homes on Englewood Place and Thurlow Terrace; a number of these mansions can still be seen today. The fact that several residents of these two streets were also members of the park commission may have had some direct bearing on the fact that the park was never expanded to its "natural boundaries" of Lake and Western avenues.

At one point the park commissioners were able to buy out the rights of the old Great Western Turnpike Company, and in so doing they gained title to all the land on both sides of Western Avenue from Washington Park up to Manning Boulevard. Even today, it is a responsibility of the city of Albany to plow the sidewalks on Western Avenue from Manning Boulevard to Washington Park because of this long-forgotten purchase by the park commissioners.

The city's other major park, Lincoln Park, was originally known as Beaver Park—the name of an estate situated near present-day Morton and Delaware avenues, where the tennis courts are today. The workshop or studio of James Hall, the noted geologist and paleontologist who trained a generation of scholars in the field, was built there in 1848 and still remains in the park.

At the beginning of this century, the upper end of today's Lincoln Park was known as Delaware Square. It included a stream, barely visible today at the bottom of the great ravine to the south of Park Avenue, with a pond at the bottom known as Rock Ledge. The adjoining Hinckel (later Dobler) Brewery dumped its effluent suds into the water supply, thus giving the area its more common descriptive name of Buttermilk Falls.

The eastern part of Lincoln Park, which today serves as an athletic field in a bowl, was once a community known as Martinville—an extremely poorly planned ghetto of wooden row houses built upon the ruins of an abandoned brickyard. A predominantly Irish neighborhood paralleling the now-defunct ways of Martin Street and Johnson Alley, it was mercifully destroyed about 1910 to create the present Lincoln Park. The park shrank in size in the 1960s when, as part of urban renewal, the extreme lower end of the park was converted into Lincoln Park Homes, a high-rise public housing development.

Lincoln and Washington parks were overwhelmingly popular and are still successful additions to the urban environment. A less successful experiment occurred on the north side of town, where abandoned Water Department property was turned into Tivoli Park. The area proved to be just too much land for the city to develop and maintain, and in recent years Tivoli Park has been relegated to the status of a nature preserve.

Swinburne Park, named after a popular Albany doctor and Republican mayor, also comes from the the conversion of the old water system into a more usable facility. Two large reservoirs had previously been utilized— one above and one below Manning Boulevard. In the 1930s, the lower body of water, known as Bleecker Reservoir, was cut through in four places by WPA workers and then turned into the stadium that it is today.

Albany High School and Bishop Maginn High School use it for their athletic contests. The stadium has also served a variety of uses for Twilight League baseball, and at one time it was the principal parade ground for Christian Brothers Academy.

Turnpikes and Growth

The first major assault on the grid pattern came, however, not from institutions or parks but rather from the development of turnpikes which, like arteries carrying the economic lifeblood of the region, radiated out from the city and ultimately determined how and where the original settlement would grow to form new neighborhoods.

From the close of the Revolution to the opening of the Erie and Champlain canals, the state government placed great emphasis on the development of the vast expanse of western lands seized after the war from the Iroquois, who along with their Johnson family allies had remained loyal to the Crown. Land companies and land speculators abounded, with the full blessing of the state, as Yankee emigrants from the declining farms of New England, Revolutionary veterans, and immigrants from abroad turned their sights westward.

"By 1795," according to Albany historian Codman Hislop, "the tide of migration through Albany to the West was so great that in one day a citizen counted over five hundred sleighs crowding up the State Street hill. . . .Twelve hundred sleighs went through Albany in three days during that winter, loaded with whatever their owners thought was necessary to begin life on their new land." Albany soon found itself adapting to a new role as banker, teamster, and general store for the tens of thousands of pioneers who made the journey west.

The lack of adequate roads was sorely felt by the emigrés from Yankee New England. Narrow, decaying military roads from the colonial wars, with their "corduroy" paving of logs thrown across muddy stretches,

placed travelers completely at the mercy of the weather. Lengthy travel
had to be deferred until the winter months when the ground was frozen.

The solution to the problem proved to be the turnpike—a vastly improved
type of road built and maintained by a private company that charged a
toll for the use of its facility. A far cry from the washed out, rutted roads
of colonial New York, the turnpikes were, by early 19th-century standards,
broad and well graded; they were surfaced with dirt, crushed stone, or
heavy wooden planks. Tollgates, or "turnpikes," placed at intervals of
approximately 10 miles, were used to collect the fees, which varied greatly
according to whether the traveler was on horseback, in a stagecoach, or
driving cattle, sheep, or hogs to market.

The popularity of the turnpikes was immediate. By 1815, every major
valley in the state had one, and virtually all of them eventually fed into a
turnpike leading to Albany.

Albany soon became the turnpike center of the state. Central Avenue
(Route 5) was started in 1797 as the Albany-Schenectady turnpike, linking
the commerce of the Hudson and Mohawk rivers while providing safe
portage around the Cohoes Falls. As a direct result of this development,
the old Kings Highway—which had been strategically placed in the city's
Pine Bush to keep the Albany fur trade out of the jurisdiction of the
surrounding manor of Rensselaerswyck—now became all but obsolete,
condemning the area to the status of an obscure backwater for the next
century and a half.

Western Avenue (Route 20), the Great Western Turnpike, was started two
years later and eventually carried the bulk of stage and freight traffic
through the heart of the state to Buffalo. Great, lumbering stagecoaches
were developed that could transport a dozen passengers from Albany to
Buffalo in the breakneck speed of six days.

The Albany-Lebanon Turnpike (Routes 9 and 20), which dates from 1798,
carried travelers from New England to the village of Greenbush, where for
the next half-century a ferry franchised by the city brought traffic across
the Hudson to Albany. Other major roads dating from this period were the
Bethlehem Turnpike (now Route 144), the Delaware Turnpike (now
Delaware Avenue), and the Schoharie Turnpike (now New Scotland
Avenue).

The significance of this lively travel to Albany cannot be overstated. All
roads led to Albany, not just in a geographic sense but in an economic
sense as well. The typical Yankee settler moving with his family from
Massachusetts to the fertile valley of the Genesee would not only traverse
toll roads owned in part by Albany investors but would often purchase
land held by Albany speculators and mortgaged to Albany bankers. Once
settled, he would clear his land with Albany tools and supply his farm with
provisions ordered from Albany merchants and factories.

The turnpike and stagecoach companies enjoyed a symbiotic relationship
with numerous other industries that sprang up along the routes they
followed. Livery stables dotted the roadways, providing frequent changes
of horses, and roadside inns offered welcome shelter and refreshment to
weary travelers tired of sitting three abreast on a wooden plank seat for
upwards of 60 dusty miles a day. For sustenance, financial backing, and
even newspapers, innkeepers and tradesmen, like the travelers and
farmers they served, looked in only one direction—Albany.

Great fortunes were made by the Dutch and Yankee merchant princes of old Beverwyck. By the mid-1790s Dutch had ceased to be the majority language of the populace. The city was growing, and as it expanded it became more and more Yankee and less and less Dutch. The population tripled from 3,506 in 1790 to 10,762 in 1810, almost entirely as a result of the Yankee invasion; by 1830 the figure had more than doubled to 24,238.

Entire neighborhoods had to be developed to accommodate the city's growing population. Narrow streets were laid out paralleling the new Albany-Schenectady turnpike, the principal source of the new prosperity; the formal grid pattern was largely ignored. The lower part of present-day Central Avenue was known as the Bowery because it led to the "bouweries," or farms, of the Dutch. Present-day Sherman, Elk, West, and Bradford streets served as working-class neighborhoods for the people who earned their living along the turnpike and in its related industries.

In 19th-century Albany, as in all of urban America at the time, the typical citizen commonly worked a 10 to 14-hour day for six days of every week. Public transportation was rare, and if a man wished to spend any time with his family it was an absolute necessity that he live close to his place of work. This was true not only for the least skilled worker but for the senior manager as well. In the case of women, common household chores were difficult and time consuming, and the days left little time to be wasted in traveling long distances for everyday goods and services.

Albany's street patterns were designed to respond to this common need.

Wide sidewalks and streets characterize Madison Avenue east of Dove Street in this photograph taken circa 1915.

That portion of the lot not occupied by the building is set apart for recreation purposes, and has been properly graded and paved with the "Scrimshaw pavement," a patent concrete pavement, and presents a very clean appearance.

The girls' portion, which is on Herkimer street, contains about three thousand square feet. The boys' playground is on Franklin street and contains 4,830 feet, and is separated from the girls' ground by a strong fence nine feet high.

In each of these playgrounds are the necessary privies, urinals, etc., all of brick, with floors of flag-stone, and proper screens in front to secure privacy.

The exterior of the building, which is both imposing and pleasing, is constructed of the following materials: The water-table and lintel course of the basement is Grawacke stone; the trimmings and belt course to first and second story windows are of cast iron; the main cornice and dormer windows are of wood and are very ornamental. The French roof is covered with slate banded in two colors, while the roof is surmounted with a neat cornice and ornamental iron cresting. The wood and iron work is painted and sanded to imitate the stone.

Albany Argus, August 29, 1871.

Each neighborhood, as it was laid out, provided appropriate housing for all of its requisite personnel. Worker and manager, servant and master, immigrant and Brahmin, all lived within a few yards of one another.

Each neighborhood met this challenge by utilizing essentially the same solution—the creation of an alternating rich street/poor street residential pattern, interspersed with corner shops, groceries, drugstores, and saloons. In some cases the centermost building of a block also contained a store at ground level. This pattern is readily apparent in the neighborhoods established in Albany prior to 1850.

A prime example is the north Pastures District, that part of the South End closest to downtown. It extended from Madison Avenue to South Ferry Street and from South Pearl Street to the river. From 1794 on, the Dutch Church, by much dredging and filling in of what had been oft-flooded common pastureland, developed the land into a neighborhood that still contains nearly 90 buildings listed in the National Register of Historic Sites. It is completely depopulated now, with the goal of rebuilding the neighborhood through restoration and in-fill housing.

The Pastures is typical of the rich street/poor street pattern. The wide street of Madison still contains the Sanders Mansion (built in 1808), the executive mansion of Governor Joseph Yates (built in 1812), and the classic Federal row houses built by the prominent Dublin-born merchant Dudley Walsh between 1817 and 1821. To the south, Herkimer Street has the remains of a prominent Jewish synagogue and the city's first modern public school, built in 1871. Westerlo Street boasts an unbroken row of Federal homes designed by architect Henry Rector, of the New York State Court of Appeals. South Ferry Street contains the pretentious homes of the Boyd family, whose large brewery once provided employment to scores of men in the South End. A Schuyler family mansion also still stands on South Ferry Street—a building considered so elegant that it sold for $28,000 in 1865 at a time when $7 a week was considered a living wage. Around the corner on Green Street, Philip Hooker, Albany's foremost architect of the time, maintained an office from which the city's most prominent buildings were designed.

But these silent surviving examples of Federal architecture, with their wrought-iron railings, multipaneled doors, leaded-glass sidelights, pillared dormers, and sandstone or marble trim portray only half the story of the neighborhood. Gone from today's Pastures are the "poor" streets. John, South Lansing, and Bleecker streets, and even little Franklin Street—whose narrow passage, like Green and South Pearl streets, once extended

The Schuyler Mansion was completed in 1762 under the supervision of Mrs. Philip Schuyler while her husband was in Europe. In 1818 Philip Hooker painted this water-color for one of the mansion's subsequent owners. It depicts the octagonal entrance way designed by him in that year.

across both the North and South Pastures from Madison Avenue to the old city line at Gansevoort Street—were lined with homes that are no more. Scores of buildings have been demolished on these narrow alleys. Gone, too, are the profusion of carpenters' shops, garages, immigrants' hovels, and servants' quarters that typified the back streets.

In the course of its inhabited existence, the area was never exclusively poor or rich, nor did it ever exist exclusively as a ghetto for any one ethnic group. School No. 15 once held 1,000 students; its churches and synagogues were among the city's best attended. Its residents have included Governor Joseph Yates; Rabbi Isaac Mayer Wise, the founder of Reform Judaism in America; Anthony N. Brady, the multimillionaire; William S. Hackett, the O'Connell organization's first Democratic mayor; and a host of prominent Irish, Jewish, Italian, and black families representing most of the city's businesses, trades, and professions.

By 1969, the Pastures had run its full course from new housing to abandoned slum. Within a century and a half, it had evolved from a Yankee-Dutch neighborhood to a haven for Irish and German Jewish immigrants, to a community of Italians and Eastern European Jews, to a magnet for Southern blacks, to ultimate depopulation.

St. John's Church, empty since 1979, dominates the Pastures now. The mansard-roofed PS 15, long vacant, is scheduled to be torn down; extensive fire damage has made its restoration economically unfeasible. To the south, next to PS 15's underutilized replacement, five nearly vacant high-rise apartment buildings dominate the sky of what was once the South Pastures—a neighborhood totally obliterated by the old-style urban renewal of the 1950s and 1960s. Now a decade of planning, property acquisition, relocation, demolition, and emergency stabilization is coming to an end, and the area awaits repopulation and revitalization.

Expansion of Neighborhoods

In 1890 a city directory was published for advertising purposes by a company calling itself the Pine Hills Land Development Corporation. At the top of each page was an advertisement extolling the virtues of the new neighborhood of Pine Hills; these advertisements suggest some of the problems of the city as it existed in 1890.

"Architectural Covenants in Deeds," reads one of the advertisements. Other areas of the city had no zoning—no control on porches, alleys, garages, or outbuildings, which could be put up and taken down almost at will with little or no consideration of the effect on health and safety, let alone aesthetics.

Another advertisement promises "No Saloons in Pine Hills." The old immigrant city had a saloon on almost every corner—considered a public nuisance by some. When Pine Hills was built, there was a guarantee of no saloons, enforced by covenants in the deeds. As a consequence, to this day there are few bars in the city west of Allen Street.

Downtown Albany in the late 19th century was characterized by block after block of row houses with very, very few alleys put in to separate one house from another. Land was expensive, and in an age of inadequate mass transportation—and for the average worker certainly, no individual transportation at all—it was essential that homes be built as close as possible to the factories, shops, and other places of business where people earned their living. By the same token, homes had to be close to the grocery store, the pharmacy, and other essential services (including the corner saloon).

By 1890, however, streetcars were finally moving not only crosstown—it was relatively easy to go from North Albany to the South End, with no hills to climb—but up the hill into what was then the Pine Bush, beginning roughly at Allen Street. Another ad in the 1890 directory tells us that Pine Hills was just a few blocks from the streetcar line, which, it was pointed out with considerable pride, now came up as far as Quail Street. Thus it was no longer necessary to walk to one's place of business; one need walk only as far as the trolley line.

The homes in Pine Hills were described in the directory as villas. Certainly their architecture was more individual than that of the row houses. The lots on which they stood were at least 50 feet across and sometimes 150 feet deep, providing a degree of open space unheard of in the row-house districts to the east. There were trees, lilacs, and grass in Pine Hills, and to many people the new development represented the epitome of urban living. Those who settled during this period along Madison Avenue, Pine Avenue, and Manning Boulevard were predominately nonimmigrants—Protestant and older Jewish populations—and Pine Hills was seen as a rejection of the immigrant city farther to the east.

By the 1890s the row house was considered passé, and builders developed a new type of housing known as the flat—a two-family home, originally with a flat roof, later peaked, with an alley on either side. The alley was considered to be a major reform. Not only did it help prevent the spread of fire, but it let light into the middle of the building by permitting windows on all four sides. The alley also provided access to a private backyard.

Great rows of flats were built from the late 1890s up until the 1920s along Delaware Avenue, off New Scotland Avenue, throughout Pine Hills, in the uptown sections of the city, and along Second Avenue. New churches—St. Vincent de Paul, St. Andrew's Episcopal, Madison Avenue Baptist, and Madison Avenue Presbyterian—were built to serve new congregations on the edge of the older city.

The flat appealed far more to the working class than the turreted villas of Pine Hills because the flat provided an income apartment. The two apartments each ran the full length of the structure; the owner could live in one and rent out the other to help pay for the house. Until comparatively recent times, the second apartment frequently housed other relatives. Thus the extended family, by pooling its resources, was able to move up to a better neighborhood and greatly improved living conditions.

The key to neighborhood expansion lay not in architecture, however, but in the development of mass transportation—the extension of trolley and bus service farther and farther up the hill—and, ultimately, the development of the automobile.

Around 1915, in the very early years of the automobile, the Albany Automobile Club sponsored a building program for bungalows—modest, free-standing, single-family homes (a new idea at the time)—to be located on Academy Road and Lawnridge, Glendale, and Forest avenues off New Scotland Avenue, which started as a yellow brick road. This type of development caught on immediately, and from that day forth New Scotland Avenue pressed farther and farther out in its development, eventually taking over and obliterating all the farms that had once lined the old Schoharie plank road.

The identification of developments in Albany becomes obvious even to the casual observer. Pinewood, Sycamore, and Glenwood, for example, all "tree" streets, show a common theme in development. Yet interspersed among these theme names are the names of the old owners of the farms that once occupied the neighborhood—Weis Road, Ramsey Place, Harris Avenue, and Kakely Street.

Today the city has more than 20 neighborhood associations—a phenomenon that most people assume to have originated only in the 1960s and '70s. In fact the Pine Hills Association was formed at the time of neighborhood expansion just after the turn of the century, primarily to lobby for additional city services in the then semirural area west of Partridge Street. One of its major concerns prior to World War I was to ban the dumping of dead horses near 19th Street (now Winthrop Avenue), where a slaughterhouse was located. The Delaware Avenue Association was a similar institution geared toward ensuring proper city services to the then outlying areas.

Dennis Holzman

In this photograph, circa 1880, the Union Pacific Tea Company on North Pearl Street displays patriotic finery. Albany's merchants traditionally decorated their shops for celebrations and parades.

Flats such as these on Delaware Avenue were considered an improvement in housing over the row house. These were two-family homes with a peaked roof, alley, and private backyard. Fire danger was lessened and light was let in by spacing the houses farther apart from one another.

The designation of neighborhoods in Albany today is much less clear than it once was. Pine Hills is probably the best example. The realty company that coined the name considered it to be the neighborhood around the point where Western Avenue and Madison Avenue came together. It was very simple to know where Pine Hills ended and other neighborhoods began. Starting at Alex's Pond by Homestead Avenue, a stream proceeded to the south blocking off most development and forming the brook line (from which we get the name Brookline Avenue), which meandered down into Hawkins Pond at the foot of the hill and South Manning Boulevard. That same stream then proceeded down past the Little League and the bowling alleys, by the Knights of Columbus, until finally it went underground. There was no difficulty a generation ago in determining where Pine Hills left off and the New Scotland Avenue neighborhood began because a series of swamps and ice ponds clearly separated one neighborhood from another. One reason for the opening of St. Teresa's parish in 1920 was that the people off New Scotland Avenue felt isolated from the older parish of St. Vincent's across the swampy fields that separated the two neighborhoods.

Modern-day Albany has put its streams underground and run viaducts over them, and the problem of urban sprawl within the city makes it difficult to distinguish one neighborhood from another. Today the Pine Hills Neighborhood Association has had to use specific streets to define its location, and those street boundaries have excluded some traditional Pine Hills residents such as those on Lenox, Euclid, Marion, and Brookline avenues who for years identified with no other neighborhood because there was no other neighborhood around them.

Two neighborhoods that were clearly separated from each other until comparatively recent times were the developments off Whitehall Road and those off New Scotland Avenue. The streams and swamps that had existed since the time of the Mohawks remained until Hackett Boulevard covered them over and tamed them by means of storm sewers.

Little is left of the stream system of ancient Albany. One of the last places where the sound of these streams can be heard is down in the ravine that once was Buttermilk Falls, at the northwest corner of Lincoln Park, where the roar of the storm sewer is so great it drowns out common speech and the rustic wooded thicket is but a memory of a time long gone.

CHAPTER 4
HUDSON RIVER PORT

The original motive for settlement at present-day Albany—and one that remained dominant throughout the colonial period—was the lucrative trade in beaver pelts and other furs. Control of the fur trade lay at the heart of the conflict between the Dutch West India Company and the manor of Rensselaerswyck and was a major motivating factor in the British takeover of 1664.

Even as the fur traders reaped their profits, however, other settlers were beginning to establish farms, build sawmills and gristmills, and trade their humble products alongside the more glamorous cargoes of pelts and furs. For the same reason that Albany had become the focal point of the fur trade—its situation at the headwaters of the Hudson River estuary, then the greatest waterway in British North America—it soon became a center of trade in other commodities as well. With the coming of independence and the influx of new settlers, the commercial life of Albany blossomed.

The Age of Sail

Probably the most accurate picture of economic life in colonial Albany comes, once again, from Peter Kalm, writing in 1749.

The location of Albany is very advantageous in regard to trade. The Hudson River which flows close by it is from twelve to twenty feet deep. There is not yet any quay made for the better landing of boats, because the people fear it will suffer greatly or be entirely carried away in spring by the ice which then comes down the river. The vessels which are in use here may come pretty near the shore in order to be loaded, and heavy goods are brought to them upon canoes tied together. Albany carries on a considerable commerce with New York, chiefly in furs, boards, wheat, flour, peas, several kinds of timber, etc. There is not a place in all the British colonies, the Hudson's Bay settlements excepted, where such quantities of furs and skins are bought of the Indians as at Albany.

The two principal exports in addition to furs were wheat flour and lumber. As early as 1686, at the time of the Dongan Charter, Albany was known as a wheat-producing and -milling area; Governor Dongan, in fact, granted a monopoly on bolting flour for export to the two cities of New York and

Facing page
The winter after the Clermont *made its historic trip on the Hudson, the vessel was enlarged, its wheels were covered, its fly wheels were placed within the hull, and it was renamed the* North River of Clermont. *This boat was 150 feet long and 18 feet wide.*
Right
In the late 17th century Albany became a leader in the production of wheat and wheat flour.

Book of Commerce

The Fur Trade

The European of the 17th century lived a cold and damp existence, particularly in the northern cities of aging masonry buildings, devoid of central heat, whose fireplaces were supplied by what little firewood could be gathered from nearly vanished forests. Dutch and English merchants were well aware that a cold Europe provided a rich market for warm pelts from Russia and North America.

The fur rush was on. Competition was keen, and profits for the fortunate were enormous. For generations the Europeans' demand for beaver hats and coats kept the good Dutch beer flowing in trading posts and taverns across the northern globe and gave the pioneer settlers a compelling reason to stay.

It was for such a mercenary motive that Fort Nassau and its successor, Fort Orange, were located at the headwaters of the Hudson River estuary, a point where the Atlantic tides were still felt and the Indians knew the Hudson as "the river that flows both ways." It was here, a few miles below the impassable falls of Cohoes, that the merchants who followed the *Half Moon* established the northernmost outpost of European settlement in 1614. Luxurious pelts of mink, otter, fisher, ermine, and, above all, beaver—an abundant wilderness commodity as treasured in the homeland as the gems, spices, and precious metals of more exotic lands—provided the original Albany community with its first solid economic base. It was no small coincidence that the settlement's first official name was Beverwyck or that the city's coat of arms displayed a beaver—as it does to the present day.

Throughout more than a century and a half of colonial history, whether governed by the Dutch West India Company or the British Empire, the merchants of Albany struggled to control the fur trade, guarding it jealously from all competitors. All traders were licensed either by the officials of Fort Orange or by the patroon of Rensselaerswyck, who profited enormously from the receipt of the proceeds of one of every six pelts

Book of Commerce

sold. The Dutch fur traders and merchants ensured their success by constantly currying favor with the Indians, especially the Iroquois, many of whom traveled hundreds of miles with their families in canoes laden with bundles of furs that came from places as far away as Lake Superior and the Upper Mississippi Valley. An insatiable market had been created among the fascinated forest people for a myriad of European manufactured goods, including muskets, powder, shot, scissors, brandy, silks, looking glasses, and beads, which were shipped from the mother country for their satisfaction. In return, the storehouses of Albany were filled with tons of pelts whose price in Europe was many times higher than that of the goods for which they were exchanged.

The flourishing trade brought safety as well as prosperity to the settlement, for it neutralized the Iroquois Confederacy as a hostile force and allowed the shrewd Dutch entrepreneurs to use the tribes' power and diplomacy to maintain a buffer between the competing French and British colonial empires.

A constant threat to the economic well-being of both the city merchants and the patroon throughout the history of the fur trade were the unauthorized traders and smugglers who ventured into the woods beyond the reach of local officials and plied isolated Indians with Dutch gin and counterfeit wampum in order to gain a fast profit from bandit sales.

It was in the hope of just such an opportunity to deal directly with Indians before they reached the palisaded trading center at Albany that one enterprising Dutchman, Arent Van Curler, gained permission to establish a "farming community" at Schenectady. Outside the domain of both Fort Orange and the Van Rensselaers, the Schenectady "farmers" no doubt found the tilling of the soil an occupation secondary to the more lucrative, illicit traffic with fur-laden Indians intercepted on their eastward journey to the trading center on the Hudson.

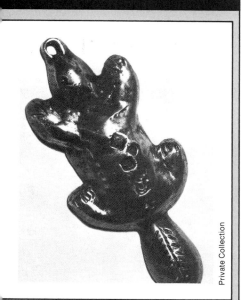

Above
Items such as this early 19th-century silver beaver trinket were traded to the Indians who used them for personal adornment and as displays of wealth.

The British takeover of the province in 1664 and again in 1674 brought little change in Albany's dominance of the fur trade. The Dongan Charter obtained by Albany citizens in 1686 explicitly granted to the mayor, aldermen, and commonality exclusive domain over commercial relations with the Indians—a monopoly they continued to enjoy for the next 60 years.

The fur trade dwindled after the Revolution, and future fur traders—including John Jacob Astor, who stayed on occasion in the city's Quackenbush House—were forced to pursue the raw market as it moved westward. The industry that had once been synonymous with Albany now left Albany behind, as westward expansion forced the source of the pelts farther and farther from what was evolving into a civilized "eastern" city. By the end of the 18th century, Albany's commerce had lost its wilderness roughness and diversified into the production of wheat, corn, lumber, and other consumer goods. The fur trade, like the wilderness, was gone.

Albany. The resulting clamor from other parts of the colony forced repeal of the monopoly in the 1690s, and with lowered standards the flourishing export trade in wheat slackened somewhat. Demand and prices for wheat elsewhere in the British Empire fluctuated widely over the next several decades in response to political and military factors over which colonial farmers and millers had little control. In 1749, however, Kalm was able to report:

The inhabitants of the country around Albany . . . sow great quantities of wheat which is brought to Albany, whence they send many boats laden with flour to New York. The wheat flour from Albany is reckoned the best in all North America, except that from Sopus (Esopus) or King's Town (Kingston), a place between Albany and New York. All the bread in Albany is made of wheat. At New York they pay for the Albany flour with a few shillings more per hundred weight than for that from other places.

The wheat arrived in Albany most commonly by sleigh, as farmers waited for winter weather to solidify the mire of primitive roadways and provide a firm, reliable surface of snow. The coming of the turnpikes facilitated overland transport, stimulating production for export, and a growing number of farmers throughout central New York State found a ready market for their wheat at Albany. There the grain was stored until the spring thaw brought the dormant river to life once again, when the huge stores of wheat were loaded aboard sailing vessels and shipped downriver to New York.

In similar fashion, Albany soon became an important market for livestock. Cattle, rounded up by New York's own cowboys, were driven on the hoof to Hudson River ports such as Albany, where they were slaughtered and the meat processed for immediate export downriver.

The other principal export throughout the 18th and much of the 19th century was lumber. "The white pine is found in abundance here," reported naturalist Kalm. "A vast quantity of lumber from the white pine is prepared annually on this side of Albany, which is brought down to New York and exported." A century later, in 1865, there were nearly 4,000 sawmills in operation in the vicinity of Albany.

In exchange for all these exports—furs, wheat, meat, and lumber—Albany's merchants imported British manufactured goods, tropical products such as sugar and tea, and rum from the West Indies. "This is absolutely necessary to the inhabitants of Albany," alleged Kalm, as a means of intoxicating the Indians in order to cheat them on the price of furs.

"All the boats which ply between Albany and New York," reported Kalm, "belong to Albany. They go up and down the Hudson River as long as it is open and free from ice." These were sailing vessels, of course, generally single-masted sloops of relatively shallow draft designed to clear the shoals and sandbars that were all too numerous along the upper part of the river. Most notorious was the area known as the Overslaugh, a few miles below Albany, where cargo often had to be offloaded onto smaller vessels to clear the bar, and ships' captains waited for full high tide before proceeding. Not until after the Civil War was the problem finally overcome with a series of dikes and dams designed by engineers of the federal government.

By 1810 there were more than 200 sloops on the Hudson; by 1850, despite the advent of steam, there were 400 to 500 sloops in regular service between Albany and New York. The average size was about 60 tons; one of the largest, at 220 tons, was the *Utica,* built at Albany in 1833. After 1850 the number of sloops decreased, and by the time of the Civil War no new sailing vessels were being built. Even so, in 1900 there were still about 200 sloops in service along the Hudson; the last one was reportedly destroyed by a hurricane in 1938.

Development of Industry
Early industry in Albany was generally oriented toward meeting the demands of local consumers and the export market through the processing

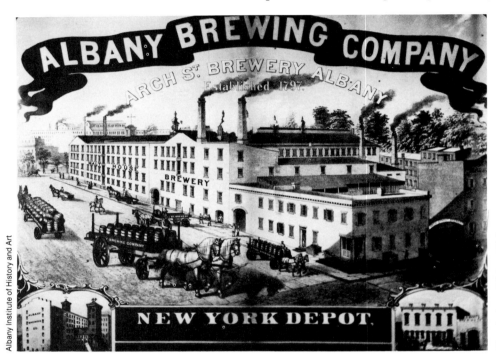

Albany Institute of History and Art

Albany Institute of History and Art

Albany Institute of History and Art

Book of Commerce

of primary products: the milling of flour and of lumber, the processing of meat, and—from earliest colonial times—the conversion of grain into beer and spirits. Brewing in particular, thanks initially to the Dutch and German presence, was a significant local industry up until quite recent times.

Among the more prominent breweries of the 19th century was the Dobler Brewery, originally the Hinckel Brewery, located in a complex of shops and industrial buildings that extended from Elm Street to Park Avenue along both sides of present-day Swan Street. Part of the old Hinckel Brewery still stands overlooking Lincoln Park and is considered one of the finer examples of 19th-century industrial architecture remaining in the city.

George Amsdell's great brewery still stands, too, although few Albanians would recognize it today. During Prohibition it was converted into the Knickerbocker Apartments, which occupy the block between Lancaster and Jay on Dove Street.

The Hedrick Brewery, started in 1852, was famous for its ownership by the late Daniel P. O'Connell, longtime political patriarch of the city's Democratic organization. The brewery was located at 400 Central Avenue, the present site of the high-rise apartment building known as Central Towers.

Another of Albany's political figures, Michael Nolan, the city's first Irish Catholic mayor, initially achieved fame and fortune as the president of

Facing page

Top left
Breweries provided jobs for hundreds of Albany residents throughout the 19th century. The Albany Brewing Company was established in 1797.

Top right
The building on State Street that housed the Albany Hardware and Iron Company gives a good indication of the size and diversity of the company's inventory.

Bottom
The West Albany cattleyards, established in 1850, were of great importance during the latter part of the 19th century. Until refrigerated boxcars made it unnecessary to transport live animals, cattle were driven down Central Avenue to the yards. The cattleyards were later replaced by the West Albany shops and the West Albany Industrial Park.

Below
Albany merchants imported tea from China. Agents were sent to the Orient to purchase the tea from merchants. Once purchased, the tea would be shipped to Albany.

Below right
Albany's lumberyards, established in 1850, were located between the Erie Canal and the Hudson River, extending northward from the entrance of the canal into North Albany. From this location, Adirondack timber was sent to points throughout the United States and Europe. At the turn of the century, the lumber district's business declined due to the scarcity of Adirondack lumber from exploitation and a major fire in the lumber district in 1908.

Quinn and Nolan, later known as the Beverwyck Brewery, in North Albany. Purchased by The F & M Schaefer Brewing Company, it was the city's last remaining brewery until the early 1970s, when it was closed down and the buildings demolished.

For many years The F & M Schaefer Brewing Company was known for its all-night Beer Fountain, where many a late-returning worker or city newspaper reporter would stop in for a final toast to the evening, and also for the great statue of King Ganbrinus that stood with foaming stein aloft looking down on the hundreds of North Albany workers who daily produced the sudsy brew.

Like many of the breweries, a number of 19th-century distilleries were associated with the names of politicians—among them, city aldermen Evers, Tracy, and Boyd. Their distilleries, in the days prior to modern zoning, stood in the midst of residential neighborhoods in Sheridan Hollow and in the city's South End.

Just as the city's hardware stores and bankers supplied and financed the westward expansion of the American people, so too did the distillers and brewers earn their fortunes by sending uncountable barrels and hogsheads of porter, ale, whiskey, and beer to the thirsty farmers and other settlers in the western part of the state.

A smaller but nonetheless interesting local industry, which survived until the 1930s, was tobacco rolling. In the 19th century it was not uncommon for Albanians to buy their tobacco by the leaf and to have bunches of tobacco leaves hanging in the attics of stores such as Coulson's on Broadway, where entire floors were maintained as great humidors. As the need arose, the discriminating tobacco smoker would order that a leaf be taken off and given to a tobacco roller, who would then make hand-rolled cigars for his use—an art that is virtually unknown in the United States today.

Another long-standing Albany industry, and one that survives to this day, is publishing. For much of the 19th century, Albany was second only to Boston in the number of books produced, particularly in the fields of law and religion. The first steam-driven printing press in the United States was installed at Albany in 1828. City directories of the mid- and late 1800s list large numbers of morocco workers in and around the central downtown area—the number of morocco workers, of course, reflecting the use of leather binding in the books produced at that time. The printing industry survives today on a greatly reduced scale in the northern part of the city, oriented primarily toward the production of government reports and other documents related to the role of Albany as the state capital.

The 19th-century industry most closely associated with Albany and its sister city of Troy was iron casting—most notably, the fabrication of cast-iron stoves. The Albany Institute of History and Art recently exhibited a major collection of stoves gathered from all over the country, almost all of which were manufactured in Albany.

The iron industry had its foundation in the city of Troy and was controlled by men with interests in both cities, including Henry Burden and Erastus Corning, Sr. The Upper Hudson Valley was an ideal location. Limestone from the banks of the Hudson served as flux; coal was brought in by the Delaware Canal from eastern Pennsylvania; and iron ore, mined in the Adirondacks, was transported down the Champlain Canal.

Below
Joel Munsell (1808-1880), printer, publisher, antiquarian, collector, and author of books about printing, was a native of Northfield, Massachusetts, but quickly developed a personal devotion to the history of Albany. His 10-volume Annals of Albany *and a 4-volume* Collections on the History of Albany *are considered invaluable historical reference works. His 58 State Street firm became a nationally prominent printing and genealogical publishing house.*

Albany Institute of History and Art

Right
At the reins of their delivery wagon, employees of the Beverwyck Brewing Company stop in front of the office. Formerly the Quinn and Nolan Brewery, the Beverwyck Company later became the Schaeffer Brewery.
Below
The Quinn Ale Brewery was operated by James Quinn from 1845 until 1866 when Terrance J. Quinn and Michael N. Nolan succeeded him. Their partnership lasted until Quinn's death in 1878. The business was operated by Michael Nolan until 1917. This 1902 watercolor of the brewery was painted by J. MacGregor.
Below right
Joel Munsell, one of the nation's leading genealogical publishers in the 19th century, printed this Albany bicentennial broadside. Local historians still use his Annals of Albany.

Cast-Iron Stoves

When the Albany Institute of History and Art recently exhibited a major collection of cast-iron stoves, nearly all of them manufactured in the Albany area, it made a timely display. Today's energy crisis has caused Americans to rediscover, and reconsider, the wisdom and craftsmanship of past generations in this fuel-efficient heating and cooking technique. The coal-burning cast-iron stove—initially, Albany's response to a serious wood shortage in the 1820s brought on by overconsumption of local timber by steamboats and factories—impresses present-day observers as a model of sound technology, usefulness, and careful design.

In 1833 the editor of the Albany *Daily Advertiser* stated that the "manufacture of iron castings was brought to a greater perfection in Albany than any other place in the country, or even Europe." Cast iron, a moldable and durable metallic material that could both accept and radiate high temperatures, proved the ideal

replacement in the 19th century for the fireplace as a domestic heating and cooking device. Raw materials basic to the production of cast iron were plentiful in Albany. Iron ore, limestone, charcoal, and silicon (sand) were either available locally or easily acquired from nearby counties in the Hudson Valley and the Adirondacks. Because of its high percentage of pure iron, the ore was of exceptional quality. Charcoal, produced locally, was used as fuel for the air blast furnaces; coke, serving the same function later for the cupola furnaces developed in Albany, came from Pennsylvania via the Delaware and Hudson Canal to the Hudson River. The excellence of the castings themselves was chiefly due to the fine-quality molding sand available in the region.

In the early 19th century new ideas were rife in the burgeoning industrial revolution, and inevitably the cast-iron stove challenged American innovators. Rensselaer Polytechnic Institute, founded in Troy in 1824 as the nation's first school of engineering, concentrated on practical applications of the physical sciences. Undoubtedly RPI supplied technical knowledge to the cast-iron stove designers and manufacturers in Troy and Albany, who were making the region the center of the industry.

Artisans in Albany and its sister city Troy contributed their own special talents to the development of the cast-iron stove as a parlor heater or kitchen range. Especially important were the patternmakers, whose designs molded into the iron were trademarks as well as decorations. The stoves of mid-19th century America simulated the Victorian Age's taste. Ornate decorations were possible in both flask casting (in which imbedded flasks received molten iron to form stove parts) and the new cupola furnace. Thus, stoves featured stylistic niceties found in castles, cathedrals, and Italian villas. There were elaborate floral and patriotic motifs; details from Greek, Roman, Gothic, Egyptian, and rococo revival architecture; Gothic and Palladian windows and columns shaped like dolphins; grapes and grapevines, leaves, acorns, and fruit baskets adorning the cast-iron stoves. After 1850 most stoves were given romantic names, such as "Venetian Parlor,"

1,800 workers, and grossed about a half-million dollars a year from its production of some 40,000 parlor stoves, kitchen ranges, and furnaces. Ransom and Rathbone was another major manufacturer during this period when Albany's cast-iron stoves were achieving worldwide recognition. Indeed, the area had proved a perfect breeding spot for the industry, not only because of the availability of materials and artisans, but also because of the transportation facilities by both ship and rail. The completion of the Erie Canal in 1825 gave access to the fast-growing settlements in the Great Lakes area. And the port of Albany along the Hudson River made it possible to ship stoves to New York City and thence to other American cities and to Europe. No wonder Albany was called the "Crossroads of the Northeast and the Gateway to the West." The introduction to the Perry Stove Company's catalog of 1876 was written in English, French, and German, indicating the far-flung recognition accorded the Albany craftsmen and manufacturers.

"Castle," and "Temple Parlor," which enhanced their allure while helping the buyer identify the stove of his choice when ordering from a catalog.

By 1875 there were 15 stove foundries in Albany. The Perry Stove Company, one of the largest in the U.S., covered five acres of ground, employed almost

Ultimately, however, after many productive years, the combination of unionization with tough competition from the Midwestern stove industry—which was partly launched as branches of Albany and Troy companies—brought an end to the lucrative operation. The Mesabi Range in Minnesota, too, offered a high-quality, low-cost source for iron ore that was depleted now along the Hudson. By 1900 most of the Albany area foundries had shut down or moved to the Midwest. Albany's last foundry, Rathbone, Sard and Company, closed in 1925.

Today the renewed popularity of cast-iron stoves, antique or newly made, is much in evidence. Appreciation of this uniquely American invention encompasses both its practical value and superior design with decorative appeal.

(Special credit to Tammis Kane Groft of the Albany Institute of History and Art and photographer William Knorr.)

The prosperity of the iron industry in both Albany and Troy was legendary. Iron foundries in Albany were located in the city's north and south ends, where generations of immigrants and their descendants served as ironmongers, puddlers, and molders of stoves that were sent all over the United States and Europe. Production flourished until the 1890s, when a combination of unionization and the opening up of the great Mesabi Range in Minnesota started its gradual decline.

The older neighborhoods of the city reflect this once great industry—from the earliest Federal buildings, with their iron acorn railings, to the square, boxy ironwork of the Greek Revival period, to the post-Civil War cast-iron lintels over windows and doors. The city's builders seldom had to look far for these cast-iron fixtures; most of them were fabricated right in Albany by Albany craftsmen.

These industries, plus the port, the canals, and later the railroads, begot other industries, including wholesale and retail trade, services of all kinds, and construction. Continuing expansion of the city required new housing, indeed whole new neighborhoods, with their corner stores, churches, and schools. Public and private buildings alike sprang up where once Dutch cattle and hogs had grazed, providing more employment for the Albanians they were destined to house and serve.

Steamboat and Canal

The key to economic prosperity in 19th-century Albany, however, lay not in industry but in transportation. The city that began its existence as a trading post and inland port flourished as the Hudson River traffic moved from sail to steam and the Erie Canal funneled raw materials from the great western hinterland out through the thriving port of Albany.

The first commercially successful steamboat, Robert Fulton's *Clermont*, ventured forth from New York harbor on the afternoon of August 17, 1807, reaching Albany two days later. The 133-foot vessel, powered by a pair of boiler-fired 12-paddle sidewheels, achieved the upriver passage in 32 hours and the return in 30 hours—compared with the three days to a week by sloop, depending on the wind and tides.

On September 4, 1807, the *Clermont* began regular passenger service between Albany and New York. The venture, like the development of the steamboat itself, was financed by Robert R. Livingston, who had first become acquainted with Fulton in the 1790s in Paris, where Livingston was serving as minister to France and Fulton was earning his living as a portrait and landscape artist while tinkering with new applications of the developing steam engine. The *Clermont*, in fact, was named for Livingston's country estate along the Hudson River in southern Columbia County.

The Fulton-Livingston service, granted a monopoly by the state, proved to be a huge success. In 1808 there were three steamboats in regular service between Albany and New York, and by 1811 there were eight. In 1824 a Supreme Court decision broke the Fulton-Livingston monopoly, and steamboat service mushroomed—from a total of 12 vessels in 1825 to more than 100 in 1840. By this time, travel time between Albany and New York had been reduced to 10 hours or less; by the 1860s it was down to seven hours. At the same time, the size of steamboats was increasing. The *New World*, built in 1848, was 352 feet long, and with overnight berths no longer a requisite, carrying capacity was vastly increased. In 1851 more than one million passengers traveled by steamer from Albany to New York; in 1884, despite the competition of the railroads, the figure was 1.5 million.

Clockwise from top left
The steamboat Rip Van Winkle, *owned by the Albany Line, ran nonstop between Albany and New York City. According to this 1847 broadside, the boat was "fitted up with staterooms in superior style." Thomas Schuyler, an agent for the line, was one of several family members who earned his livelihood from the river traffic.*

Hudson River sloops and steamboats as well as packet boats destined for the Erie or Champlain canals abound in this mid-19th-century lithograph of the Albany Basin.

Few people are aware that John Wesley Hyatt of Albany first fabricated celluloid as a substitute for ivory in the production of billiard balls in 1866. Hyatt and his friend Peter Kinnear formed the Hyatt Billiard Ball Company, which became the Albany Billiard Ball Company, shown above in this circa 1913 photograph.

Rathbone, Sard & Company factory workers catch iron from a cupola with hand ladles in 1911.

This Rathbone, Sard & Company employee is seen ramming up a mold by hand.

Robert Fulton, who designed the steamboat Clermont *for service on the Hudson River, painted this self-portrait from a miniature by Benjamin West.*

Steam travel on the river was not without its perils. In 1825 the boilers of the *Constitution* exploded, and for a time after that passengers were towed in "safety barges" strung a safe distance behind the mother vessel.

In April 1845 one of the fastest boats on the river, the *Swallow,* owned by Cornelius Vanderbilt's People's Line, sailed from Albany with 250 passengers. Blinded by a snow squall in the treacherous Athens channel just above Catskill, the captain ran the boat into a rocky islet. The hull split, and 15 people were drowned.

At its height, travel by steamboat was pleasant and luxurious, with plushly appointed gaslit parlors, lavish dining rooms, and airy staterooms high above the water line. Competition and the press for ever greater speeds, however, sometimes resulted in tragedy. In July 1852 the *Henry Clay,* racing southbound against the *Armenia,* erupted in flames and ran ashore at Riverdale, with the loss of 70 lives. Soon afterward racing was outlawed, and an outraged Congress imposed strict regulations on operation of the steamers.

The steamship and the sloop continued to operate side by side throughout most of the 19th century, with the steamship carrying the bulk of the passenger trade and, by midcentury, much of the waterborne freight as well. By the beginning of the 20th century, both had clearly lost out to the speed and all-weather efficiency of the railroad, and steamboats were used primarily for recreational cruises, as civic groups, churches, and schools hired the dwindling number of vessels for excursions and outings.

In 1910 the Hudson River Day Line built its ornate headquarters at the foot of today's Hamilton Street, where a liberty pole adorned what was then known as Steamboat Square; today the building houses L'Auberge restaurant, luncheon meeting spot of the prestigious Hudson River Club. The last regularly scheduled steamboat, appropriately named the *Robert Fulton,* cast off from Albany on September 3, 1948—the last of the "white flyers" that had brought such elegance to Albany's waterway transportation.

Of greater commercial importance to Albany even than the steamboat was the completion in 1825 of the Erie Canal, with its eastern terminus at

Bottom left
Hudson River steamboats, many of them owned by and named after their original investors, attracted the elite, who traveled the Hudson to and from New York. This illustration depicts the interior of the 244-foot-long steamer Daniel Drew. During its first six months of operation in 1863 the steamer completed 54 trips. The run from Albany to New York took just under eight hours.

Albany Institute of History and Art

Albany Institute of History and Art

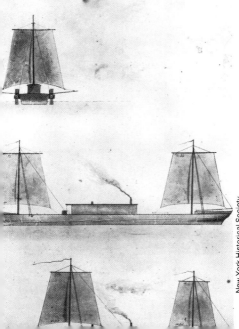

New York Historical Society

Albany. The Champlain Canal, completed in 1822, carried a much smaller volume of trade, though it did bring high-quality iron ore to the foundries of Albany and Troy.

To handle the anticipated volume of traffic, the city built a huge pier, 4,300 feet long and 80 feet wide, extending from the canal outlet at Lawrence Street south all the way to the foot of today's Hamilton Street, then known as Steamboat Square. The pier, at a distance of approximately 250 feet from the shore, enclosed a basin of 32 acres that could provide moorings for up to 1,000 canal boats and 50 steamboats. The pier itself offered eight acres of storage area as well as dry-dock facilities. Columbia and State streets were extended across the water to the pier; in later years the railroad ferry between Albany and Rensselaer shuttled from its Maiden Lane landing through a wide cut in the pier.

The predictions of good times ahead were amply fulfilled. In the canal's first year, 12,856 boats passed through the basin, and the toll collectors on the Lawrence Street parapet registered receipt of more than $120,000 in fees. Within two years Albany merchants reported that wholesale business had quadrupled, much to the covetous dismay of the Troy businessmen upriver who were stung by the commercial success of their entrepreneurial rivals on the western bank.

More varied forms of enterprise thrived at the notorious Watervliet Side Cut, a secondary entrance to the canal across from Troy, where a bawdy and brawling batch of saloons and brothels earned the area the sobriquet "Barbary Coast of the East." It was estimated that two out of three homicides occurring along the route of the canal took place at the Watervliet Side Cut.

Completion of the canal reduced transportation costs between Buffalo and Albany by as much as 90 percent. The result was a tremendous stimulation of agricultural output in western New York and the Great Lakes region, to the detriment of farmers on exhausted eastern soil but to the immense benefit of the merchant and shipping interests of Albany. In 1831 as many as 15,000 canal boats unloaded their cargoes at the Albany basin, while thousands of pioneers traveled westward from New England and New York by canal packet on their way to settle the frontiers of Ohio, Indiana, Michigan, and Illinois. Like earlier generations of pioneers, they found Albany a convenient place to provision themselves for the long journey and inevitable hardships that lay ahead.

A rapidly expanding commercial life required a sizable infrastructure of financial institutions. As of 1840, Albany had a total of six commercial banks—the Bank of Albany, founded in 1792; New York State Bank, 1803; Mechanics and Farmers Bank, 1811; Commercial Bank, 1825; Canal Bank, 1829; and Albany City Bank, 1834—as well as the Albany Savings Bank, incorporated in 1820. The American Express Company had its origins in Albany in 1841.

Albany was also in the forefront of telecommunications. The second telegraph instrument in the United States—designed by Samuel F.B. Morse but based on the pioneering work of Albany's Joseph Henry—was installed here in 1845. The following year Ezra Cornell of Ithaca built a telegraph line from New York to Albany, and soon Hiram Sibley of Rochester controlled a connecting line from Albany to Buffalo. In 1856 the two men merged their interests to form the Western Union Company, and by the end of the Civil War both Sibley and Cornell were millionaires.

Building the Canal

From Livingston Avenue to North Ferry Street, in what today is a heavily commercialized district of warehouses and truck terminals, the narrow streets of De Witt, Centre, Lansing, and Colonie housed a neighborhood teeming with Irish immigrants and their families. The neighborhood, which flourished from the 1820s until the 1940s, was known as The Basin, taking its name from Albany's four-foot-deep port of entry to the 360-mile-long Erie Canal, completed in 1825, which joined the waters of the Great Lakes to the lucrative trading routes of the Atlantic.

The notion of a navigable waterway through the western wilderness had been bandied about by colonial dreamers and engineers for at least a half century before becoming a reality. George Washington commented on the feasibility of a New York State canal in correspondence discovered in the papers of the Van Rensselaer family of Cherry Hill. In the 1780s a New England poet wrote of a canal "from Fair Albania" joining the Hudson with the Ohio. In 1791 an enthusiastic Albany engineer, Elkanah Watson, laid out a survey of a possible route between Schenectady and Geneva, awakening the interest of such early Albany investors as Stephen Van Rensselaer III, Philip Livingston (a signer of the Declaration of Independence), Abraham Ten Broeck, and Colonel Henry Quackenbush. In 1810 Stephen Van Rensselaer, accompanied by an engineer named Geddes, traveled over a proposed course to Lake Erie and brought jubilation to the tiny frontier village of Buffalo when he resolved that Lake Erie would be the western terminus.

The legislature, however, was reluctant to underwrite the cost of the vast and speculative public-works project. The War of 1812 intervened, and planning for the canal was disrupted. After the war a group of Albanians, including Harmanus Bleecker and Rensselaer Westerlo, revived the plan and on February 7, 1816, after a meeting at the Tontine Coffee House on lower State Street, mounted the first organized citizens' campaign in support of the canal. The issue remained controversial, however, and the proposal was not approved until the closing hours of the final day of the legislative session, on April 15, 1816.

Ground was broken at Utica the following year, and crews began working simultaneously westward toward Buffalo and eastward to Albany. Seasonal laborers from the sparsely settled farmlands along the canal's route originally were hired for the job, but they were found lacking in skill, motivation, and, above all, resistance to the mosquito-borne malaria that infested the wetlands along the right-of-way.

The labor problem was solved by recruiting thousands of Irishmen, many of whom had worked on the construction of the canal system in England before making the crossing to America, and whose resistance to bog fever appeared to be greater. Even so, construction in swampy areas had to be limited to the semifrozen early spring and late fall when the mosquitoes were dormant, and hundreds of young workers still fell victim to disease.

At last, in late autumn 1825, the *Benjamin Wright* headed west from Albany at the same time as the *Seneca Chief* left Buffalo. Scores of cannon, spaced at intervals of several miles but within earshot of one another, in a succession of volleys heralded the arrival of the *Chief*, which entered the Albany basin at 10:57 A.M. on November 2, 1825. "The thunder of

cannon proclaimed that the work was done," reported the *Albany Daily Advertiser*, "and the assembled multitude made the welkin ring with shouts of gladness. It was not a monarch which they hailed, but it was the majesty of genius, supported by a free people that rode in triumph and commanded the admiration of men stout of heart and firm of purpose."

Many of those who had helped to dig the canal later found work as teamsters, checkers, and laborers, earning their wages from the trade in furniture, dry goods, and tools that flowed through Albany's canal basin in exchange for corn, wheat, potash, and Syracuse salt from the west. Adjacent to the canal was the lumber district, extending for a distance of nearly two miles with docks 1,000 feet long, where broad-shouldered men could find steady jobs stacking the millions of board feet of timber annually cut into planks and hauled out of the rugged Adirondacks by Albany's legendary Lumber Baronage.

The physical mark of the canal is gone from Albany today, but the city and its environs are peopled by descendants of the visionary investors, courageous politicians, and hard-working immigrant families who gave to the city the spirit of their stout hearts and the firmness of their purpose.

The commercial life of the Hudson River at mid-19th century was described by an English visitor, Isabella Bird Bishop, the first female Fellow of the Royal Geographical Society, who passed through Albany late in 1854. By this time the railroad was competing with the steamboat for the passenger trade—Mrs. Bishop herself traveled by train—but barges and canal boats towed by steamboats still carried the bulk of farm produce down the Hudson during the summer months.

The Erie and Champlain canals here meet the Hudson, and through the former the produce of the teeming West pours to the Atlantic. The traffic is carried on in small sailing sloops and steamers. Sometimes a little screw-vessel of fifteen or twenty tons may be seen to hurry, puffing and panting, up to a large vessel and drag it down to the sea; but generally one paddle-tug takes six vessels down, four being towed behind and one or two lashed on either side. As both steamers and sloops are painted white, and the sails are perfectly dazzling in their purity, and twenty, thirty, and forty of these flotillas may be seen in the course of a morning, the Hudson river presents a very animated and unique appearance.

The Railroad Era
NEAR HERE MOHAWK AND HUDSON FIRST RAILROAD CHARTERED IN THIS COUNTRY, 1826, BEGAN ITS RUN ALBANY TO SCHENECTADY.

The familiar blue and gold cast-iron sign, located near Police Division One at the juncture of Madison and Western avenues in Pine Hills, is one of the few lasting reminders of the age of modern rail transportation, which began in Albany on August 9, 1831.

In 1812, five years before thousands of Irish laborers would begin carving the path of the Erie Canal through the forests and swamps of the Mohawk Valley, a farsighted pamphleteer predicted that future "Rail Ways and Steam Carriages" would prove to be vastly superior to canal navigation. A decade later a shrewd Schenectady investor, George W. Featherstonhaugh, persuaded the patroon, Stephen Van Rensselaer, to commit the prestige of his family's venerable name and a portion of its wealth to the development of a rail line to run westward from Albany through the desolate Sand Plains to the brow of the State Street hill in Schenectady.

Below
The last patroon, Stephen Van Rensselaer was instrumental in the development of a rail line between Albany and Schenectady in 1831. He was one of New York State's wealthiest residents at the time of his death in 1839. This portrait of Van Rensselaer was engraved by George Parker from a painting by Charles Fraser.
Bottom left
Various commercial buildings, including that of M.G. Stoneman and Murrays Line, lined the riverfront when this photograph was taken in 1913. Notice the "fireproof" Hampton in the center.
Bottom right
This turn-of-the-century lantern slide shows the upper deck of the steamer Albany, one of several ships by that name that plied the Hudson between New York and the capital city.

Dictionary of American Portraits

City Engineer's Office

Dennis Holzman

Van Rensselaer, at first skeptical of the proposal and wary of the criticism of his wealthy peers, nevertheless succumbed to Featherstonhaugh's blandishments and, in 1830, wielded a silver spade to break ground for the laying of 16 miles of wooden rails, reinforced on top by strips of iron. Melrose Avenue, which breaks the pattern of streets in Westland Hills, precisely follows the track of this original railroad bed, which was abandoned in the 1850s for a better route along the Patroon Creek valley.

One year later, on August 9, 1831, the world's first steam passenger train made its inaugural trip between Albany and Schenectady in one hour and 45 minutes, burning foul Lackawanna coal and showering the flammable brush of the pine barrens with sparks. The engine, dubbed the *De Witt Clinton,* had been built at the West Point Foundry in New York and transported upriver by steamboat, reaching Albany at the end of June. Less than 12 feet long, with no whistle, bell, or brake, the brave little locomotive pulled three small cars with Albany-built Gould stagecoach bodies on its inaugural run.

More powerful engines and new railroad cars—patterned, oddly enough, along the lines of a parlor stove designed by Union College president Eliphalet Nott—soon provided improved service. The line was extended east from the Pine Hills Junction downtown, then southward to a terminus at Gansevoort Street. The Saratoga and Schenectady completed its line soon after, and by 1833 two trains left Albany each day with connections for Saratoga Springs.

A 39-year-old Albany iron merchant, financier, and alderman, Albany's first Erastus Corning, noted these developments with great interest, and in 1833, on the eve of his successful campaign for Albany's mayoralty, Corning began a lifelong association with railroads that would make him Albany's wealthiest citizen and establish him as one of the leading figures in American business.

Corning became a director of the Mohawk and Hudson in 1833 and later assumed the presidency of the 78-mile Utica and Schenectady, thereby gaining control over America's first intercity rail route. Over the next several years, rail service connecting central and western New York communities proliferated, as rail companies overcame the opposition of powerful canal, turnpike, and steamboat interests and legions of immigrant laborers, thrown out of work by completion of the Erie Canal, extended the rails from city to city.

Worth, Random Recollections

Top
The world's first steam passenger train, the De Witt Clinton, *reached Albany in June of 1831. The following month the 12-foot-long locomotive, pulling three cars, made the trip between Albany and Schenectady in one hour and 45 minutes. E.L. Henry depicted the momentous event.*
Above
The Reverend Eliphalet Nott, born in 1773, became president of Union College. He designed a parlor stove after which some railroad cars were patterned.

Albany Institute of History and Art

Arthur J. O'Keefe

Howell and Tenney

Above right
The abandonment of the West Albany shops a few years after this 1949 photo was taken ended the presence of the railroad in West Albany. The buildings remained as ghostly ruins for many years. Eventually they were removed and replaced by an industrial park.
Above
"Captain" Joseph Mather was named agent for the New York Central Railroad Company at West Albany. During his administration Albany grew tremendously in population and commercial importance.

In 1842 a number of lines agreed to cooperate in providing through train service between Albany and Buffalo. By this time another line, the Albany and West Stockbridge, had been completed eastward from Albany to the Massachusetts state line, where it connected with the Western Railroad to Boston. Just 11 years after the *De Witt Clinton* made its first run from Albany to Schenectady, it was possible to travel all the way from Buffalo to Boston by rail.

Passenger traffic between Albany and Buffalo switched almost immediately from the small, cramped canal packets to the more comfortable railcars, but the canal interests succeeded in prohibiting the haulage of freight between Buffalo and Albany by train. In 1847 the railroads were permitted to carry freight, but only if they paid the equivalent tolls to the canal fund, making rail freight rates prohibitively expensive. Finally, in 1851, the tolls were repealed and the railroads permitted to compete directly with the canal.

Two years later Erastus Corning oversaw the consolidation of eight short lines across the state to form the New York Central, which was to become the giant of American railways. Freight traffic largely abandoned the Erie Canal in favor of the New York Central, with two major exceptions—lumber and grain. For these bulky commodities water transportation remained the most economical, but most other items—including cattle on the hoof—now reached Albany by train.

The New York Central soon became one of Albany's principal employers, opening its massive engine houses, repair shops, and cattle yards on 350 acres in the hamlet of West Albany, two miles northwest of Capitol Hill. The cattle yards fell into disuse after the introduction in the 1880s of the refrigerated boxcar, which made it possible for cattle to be fattened and slaughtered in Chicago and shipped directly to market. The railroad shops took up the slack until they, too, became outmoded, eventually to be replaced by a modern industrial park. The part of today's North Manning Boulevard that dips down into the site of the old shops was known a century ago as New York Central Avenue, and the existence of Corning Street in West Albany memorializes the founder of the great line.

Meanwhile New York City merchants, anxious to keep a competitive edge over their Boston counterparts, gradually pushed two rail lines—the Hudson River Railroad and the New York and Harlem—northward to Greenbush, directly across the river from Albany. On October 8, 1851, the

*The problems of traffic continue to be of a major nature.
On a long range basis there are clear-cut indications of
relief. I am hopeful that the waterfront arterial highway
can be started this year. When completed it should
eliminate from our streets a tremendous amount of heavy
traffic, as well as make it possible for the City to provide in
connection with it more than one thousand parking spaces
between Madison Avenue and Columbia Streets. In the
meantime we must recognize that many of our streets are
narrow, that we have many hills, and that our main
business section is at the eastern limit of the City. We
must make every effort to maintain a balance between the
natural wish of people to drive their cars into this
congested area, and the need to keep our streets as clear
as we can so that public transportation may move as
smoothly, promptly, and efficiently as possible. . . .*

Message of Mayor Erastus Corning 2nd to the Common
Council of the City of Albany, January 1953.

first train of the Hudson River line, which followed the east bank of the
river, arrived from New York in the record time of three hours and 45
minutes, having achieved an average speed of 40 miles an hour. The New
York and Harlem, which followed an inland route, initiated service the
following year. Cornelius Vanderbilt later gained control of both railroads
and joined them to the New York Central system. The journey from New
York to Albany that had taken four days by sloop could now be
accomplished—summer or winter, fair weather or foul—in the space of
four hours.

In the 1850s several north-south lines were built connecting the New York
Central with the Erie Railroad, the most important of which was the
Albany and Susquehanna (later the Delaware and Hudson). In 1883 the
West Shore Railroad was completed between Albany and Jersey City, and
passengers and freight thundered along both banks of the mighty river,
even as sloops and steamboats—now doomed to extinction—continued to
ply its waters.

The railroads opened Albany to once seemingly inaccessible parts of the
country. The city of 50,000 took on a cosmopolitan air in the early 1850s as
the rich and famous, enjoying travel in increasingly comfortable railcars,
transferred at Albany for other destinations. Albanians delighted in
playing host to their transient guests, including President-elect Lincoln
and his wife, who arrived in Albany in February 1861 en route from
Illinois to the inaugural in Washington, D.C.

The convergence of rail lines also brought fame to several Albany hotels,
including Stanwix Hall at Maiden Lane and Broadway and the nearby
five-story Delavan House, whose owner, E.C. Delavan, scandalized his
fellow temperance workers by selling intoxicants to guests over the hotel's
elegant bar.

For a decade and a half after the completion of the Hudson River
Railroad- -two and a half decades after the Albany and West
Stockbridge—travelers still had to cross the Hudson at Albany by ferry.
This anomaly was the result of political pressure by the merchants of

Right
*The last of the Delaware and Hudson Rail-
road steam engines made their way to the
scrap yards on September 24, 1953. A
riverfront arterial highway system surrounding the city now covers the area pictured here.*
Far right
*Locomotive 999 of the NYC & HRRR
became famous for establishing a new
speed record. In 1959 the locomotive was
exhibited at the foot of Columbia Street.*
Below
*The bridging of the Hudson River in 1866
finally ended the race for commercial
dominance between Albany and Troy. Prior
to this, rail and foot traffic from the south
and east had to cross the river by ferry.*

Troy, who sought to maintain the commercial advantage afforded by the city-financed Troy-Schenectady Railroad which bridged the river at Waterford. Enlisting the support of the steamboat and canal interests, Troy politicians successfully blocked legislative approval of a bridge at Albany until 1856, when a charter was finally granted. The bridge—nearly 2,000 feet long and supported by 21 stone piers—was not completed until 1866, giving New England a direct rail link at last with the burgeoning American West.

The new bridge led to the construction in 1872 of Union Depot on Montgomery Street. By the mid-1800s more than 200 passenger trains passed through Albany every day; in the single month of May 1885, nearly 160,000 passenger tickets were sold at Albany.

The century of railroad growth climaxed with the opening, in December 1899, of the mammoth Union Station on Broadway. Occupying the site of the old Delavan House, it stood as an ornate, spacious symbol of Albany's gilded age of transportation. In 1968 the station was abandoned by the state of New York, its original function transferred to a more utilitarian prefabricated structure across the river in Rensselaer. Today this once magnificent edifice stands forlorn and half boarded up—its copper roof stripped by thieves, its fine plasterwork crumbling onto the floor some 60 feet below—awaiting a new role as the focal point of a rejuvenated historic Albany.

Arthur J. O'Keefe

Arthur J. O'Keefe

New York State Archives

CHAPTER 5
THE PEOPLE OF ALBANY

Dutch and Yankee, German and Irish, Polish and Italian, black and Chinese—over the centuries Albany's heritage has reflected a succession of immigrant nationalities. Its streets have echoed with a dozen languages, its neighborhoods adapting to the distinctive life-style and changing economic fortunes of each new group.

Dutch and English
From earliest colonial times Albany was peopled by a mix of nationalities. The first boatload of settlers to arrive in 1624 under the auspices of the Dutch West India Company, in fact, consisted of French-speaking

New York Historical Society

Walloons, Protestant refugees from the southern provinces then beleagured by Catholic Spain. Throughout the colonial period the Albany fur trade, as well as nearby farmland, attracted a range of European nationalities that included Germans, Scandinavians, English, Scots, Irish, Poles, and Italians, as well as Dutch.

The dominant nationality of colonial Albany, however, was clearly Dutch. Dutch dominance at first was by sheer numbers, but even with the later influx of New England Yankees, Dutch language and culture remained strong. Even today names ending with -*kill* (creek), -*bush* (woods), -*wyck* (district), and -*vliet* (stream)—not to mention Van Zandt, Ten Broeck, Gansevoort, and many more—remind modern Albanians of their Dutch heritage.

"The inhabitants of Albany and its environs are almost all Dutchmen," wrote Peter Kalm, with some slight exaggeration, nearly a century after the British takeover of New York. "They speak Dutch, have Dutch preachers, and the divine service is performed in that language. Their manners are likewise quite Dutch"—manners of which Kalm, a Swede, evidently did not approve.

In their homes the inhabitants of Albany are much more sparing than the English and are stingier with their food. Generally what they serve is just enough for the meal and sometimes hardly that. The punch bowl is much more rarely seen than among the English. The women are perfectly well acquainted with economy; they rise early, go to sleep very late, and are almost superstitiously clean in regard to the floor, which is frequently scoured several times in the week. Inside the homes the women are neatly but not lavishly dressed. The children are taught both English and Dutch. The servants in the town are chiefly negroes.

Negro slaves as well as free blacks were a part of life in Dutch Albany and throughout colonial New York, which in fact had a larger slave population than any other colony north of Maryland. A number of slaves worked as domestic servants and farmhands; others were skilled artisans enjoying varying degrees of freedom. In 1714 the population of Albany was approximately 10 percent black (113 out of 1,136), while that of the surrounding county was about 15 percent black.

The change of administration from the Dutch West India Company to the British Crown in 1664 had very little practical effect on the Dutch way of life at Albany. The terms of surrender, followed in 1686 by the Dongan Charter, guaranteed to the inhabitants their language, religion, material possessions, and even their Dutch laws. Beverwyck was renamed Albany, in honor of James II's Scottish title as Duke of Albany, but virtually all the Dutch settlers elected to stay and life went on pretty much as before.

A century later, however, the tide of westward migration that swept through New England following the American Revolution threatened to inundate the Dutch with new settlers of English descent. Great swarms of Yankees passed through Albany on their way west, and many settled in the environs, leasing their farms from patroon Stephen Van Rensselaer. It was a group of New Englanders who founded the city of Troy in 1787, promptly capturing much of the trade of the Upper Hudson Valley and initiating a deep-seated rivalry with Albany that would last for generations. Another contingent of New Englanders founded the city of Hudson, chosen as a safe inland port from which whaling ships embarked on regular voyages to the Antarctic.

Memoirs of An American Lady, Munsell edition

Facing page
Johannes Schuyler and his wife Elizabeth Staats Schuyler were among the many Dutch residents of Albany in the 17th and 18th centuries. This painting of the Schuylers is attributed to John Watson.
Above
Anne Grant (1755-1838) of Laggan, Scotland, visited Albany as a child in 1768. Her descriptions of the town at the twilight of the British Colonial period tell us much about social customs of the area's Dutch families.

Worst of all, from the point of view of many old Dutch families, was the invasion of Albany itself. The New Englanders were energetic, ingenious, enterprising—and frankly intolerant of all that was not. Elkanah Watson, who arrived in 1789 and later became one of Albany's leading entrepreneurs, clearly expressed the Yankee view of the Dutch city and its inhabitants. "I settled in Albany, an old traveler, in the midst of the most illiberal portion of the human race—sunk in ignorance—in mud—no lamps—water spouts projecting several feet into the streets—no pavements—no library—nor a public house—or a private boarding house deserving the name." By 1803 Yankees outnumbered the Dutch, and an ordinance was passed requiring that those famous Dutch rainspouts be cut off short—to many traditionalists, a terrible blow indeed.

The political influence of the New Englanders extended far beyond the question of rainspouts. They helped push through a liberalized state constitution that extended the vote to all adult white males (a property qualification was retained for blacks), and by the 1830s most of the state's prominent political leaders were of Yankee stock. Among the Democratic leadership known as the Albany Regency, only Martin Van Buren was descended from an early Dutch colonial family; the others—including Silas Wright, William L. Marcy, Azariah C. Flagg, and John A. Dix—were of Yankee descent. Similarly, the leadership of the Whig and later the Republican party—men such as William H. Seward, Thurlow Weed, Hamilton Fish, and Horace Greeley—represented the tide of immigration from New England.

Over time the obstreperous Yankees mellowed, the original Dutch, Germans, and Scandinavians lost their accents, and monied members of both groups tended to merge into a single economic and social aristocracy. By the 1840s a new wave of immigrants, primarily Irish, cemented the alliance, as good old "American" Protestants prepared to defend themselves against what they saw as the onslaught of Catholicism.

Immigrants of the 19th Century

Irish immigrants, in the city since colonial times, together with a number of French Catholics, built St. Mary's Church in 1797—the second Roman Catholic church in the state of New York. After the turn of the century, the Irish began to arrive in ever-increasing numbers, drawn by the work of building and maintaining the turnpikes, the canals, and later the railroads. In the 1840s, the stream of immigrants became a flood, as famine at home forced thousands upon thousands of families to flee Ireland in search of a better life. By the end of the century, the Irish were the most numerous immigrant group, and Irish neighborhoods were to be found in every ward of the city—most notably, in North Albany, Arbor Hill, Sheridan Hollow, Cathedral Hill, and the South End. Albany elected its first Irish Catholic mayor, Michael M. Nolan, in 1878—two years before Boston followed suit.

Germans had also been a part of Albany since colonial times, but their numbers increased substantially in the 19th century. At first they tended to concentrate downtown in the vicinity of Holy Cross Church (since torn down) at the corner of Hamilton and Philip streets. In the course of the 19th century, German-speaking Albanians established a number of other neighborhoods. One revolved around Central Avenue, where Our Lady of Angels German Catholic Church still stands opposite St. John's German Lutheran Church; the area from West Street to Livingston Avenue was commonly known as Cabbage Town—a name that remained in use when Poles came to the neighborhood toward the end of the century. Another German neighborhood was along Second Avenue in the South End, in the

Albany Institute of History and Art

Above
This cover illustration from Leslie's depicts the parade of bobbing clubs, one of many events that took place at the Midwinter Carnival at Albany in 1888.

Facing page
Top left
From 1800 to 1830 the city's population quadrupled, primarily because of an influx of Yankees from New England. Mercantile establishments like the Relyea & Wright clothing store transformed State, Pearl, and Broadway streets into a fashionable shopping center.
Top right
In the reenactment of a 1650s Dutch wedding pageant during Albany's tercentenary celebration in 1924, Anna Hamlin and Huybertie Hamlin were bride and mother, respectively.
Bottom
Also participating in the mock Dutch wedding were other representatives of the city's Yankee-Dutch first families.

former village of Groesbeckville, annexed to the city in 1870. German neighborhoods were typified by side-by-side Protestant and Catholic institutions—churches, Sunday schools, and fraternal halls.

The German community up until World War I produced a number of German-language newspapers, the most prominent of which was the *Freie Blaetter.* Of 7,000 copies of the *Albany City Record,* detailing the proceedings of the Common Council and city government, published every week at the turn of the century, 3,000 were printed in German. As recently as the late 1940s, one Sunday school of a Protestant church in the South End still conducted classes in German. The cemeteries on Krumkill Road and at Eagle Hill on Western Avenue are full of inscriptions in the German language.

World War I was a particular tragedy for the German-Americans of Albany, as it was for all Americans of German descent. Even though their contribution to the U.S. war effort was as great as that of any other group, the wave of anti-German feeling that swept the country forced many families and community organizations to suppress their German heritage. In a sense, an entire ethnic group went "underground." German was dropped from the curriculum of Albany High School, books were banned from the library, and the colorful German street bands were heard no more.

Capital Newspapers

Morris Gerber

Facing page
Top
In the 1920s the area of the South End, now known as the Pastures District, was teeming with first generation Italian and Jewish families. In this view of Green Street from Herkimer, it is clear that the lack of open space provided by the layout of a century earlier forced children to regard the streets as their playground.
Bottom
Employees pose outside the German Publishing and Printing Company building.
Above
Rabbi Isaac Mayer Wise was the first rabbi of Congregation Anshe Emeth, which was established on South Pearl Street opposite Herkimer Street in 1850. Wise, who interspersed the English and German languages into his services, was frequently at odds with older Orthodox Jews who had established their congregation on nearby Fulton Street in the 1830s. His attempts to accommodate more simplified Reform methods with those of traditionalists caused great strife in Albany's Jewish community. At one Passover service it was said that law enforcement officials had to be called in to calm the heated debate. In 1854 Wise and some of his Albany followers settled in Cincinnati, Ohio, where Reform Judaism flourished.

During the war many German families found it advisable to instruct their children to cite their heritage as Dutch rather than German—ironically imitating the long-practiced Anglicization of the German word *Deutsch* into *Dutch*. Thus our Lady of Angels school was referred to as "the Dutch college," and the Osborne Street/Delaware Street neighborhood as "Dutch Hollow." The Fifth Dutch Reformed Church of Albany was in fact a German-speaking congregation.

Germans and Irish lived in close proximity in Albany's South End; the two elements came together politically after the war in support of Daniel P. O'Connell, a fourth-generation South End Irishman. O'Connell's father, John, was the popular owner of a saloon at the corner of Fourth Avenue and South Pearl Street—a neighborhood in which a bartender had to speak fluent German if he wanted to stay in business. The intersection, popularly known as Beatitudes Corner, was in its way a microcosm of the city that existed before the automobile revolutionized the American lifestyle. On these four corners, O'Connell's bar gave drink to the thirsty, Machwirth's grocery fed the hungry, Belser's dry goods store clothed the naked, and the Barry Brothers Funeral Parlor buried the dead.

The Jewish community of Albany also dates back to colonial times, indeed probably to Dutch times when a number of Sephardic Jews settled in New Netherland (including one patroon, named Gomez, in the lower Hudson Valley). The Jewish population of the city became clearly identifiable in the early 1800s when German Jews established their synagogue on Fulton Street. A culturally rich Jewish community was well established by 1840 when Rabbi Isaac Mayer Wise tried unsuccessfully to plant the seeds of Reform Judaism at his temple on South Pearl Street. Meeting with almost total rejection—a Passover service erupted into a fistfight that had to be broken up by the Albany County Sheriff's Department—Rabbi Wise and a number of his followers retreated westward to Cincinnati, where the movement took hold and flourished, returning to Albany at a later date.

The tradition established by the German Jewish families who settled in the South End near the present Pastures Preservation District and along Broad and Clinton streets was continued by Eastern European Jews, who began arriving in substantial numbers in the 1890s and early 1900s—a tradition reinforced by the Orthodox Jewish requirement that families walk rather than ride to Sabbath services. Meanwhile the older German Jewish families became the founders of the Pine Hills neighborhood, where many of their homes still stand along Madison Avenue across from and just above Washington Park.

Numerous Jewish cultural and benevolent associations flourished, along with the prestigious Adelphi Club, the Colonie Country Club, and later the Shaker Ridge Country Club. Today's Jewish community is still found in Pine Hills and off Delaware Avenue but centers primarily along New Scotland Avenue and Whitehall Road.

Polish and Italian immigrants began arriving in the latter part of the 19th century. Their numbers were relatively small in Albany compared to many other eastern cities, probably because the employment opportunities offered by the General Electric Company, established at nearby Schenectady in 1875, attracted many immigrants there instead. A similar diversion occurred of French-speaking immigrants from Canada. Albany had one French-Canadian church on Hamilton Street (destroyed to create the approaches to the Empire State Plaza), but by and large the French-Canadians were detoured away from Albany by the managers of the Harmony Mills in Cohoes—a city where as recently as the 1960s one could still hear older residents speaking French in the streets and see French-language advertisements in the windows of insurance agents.

Settling at first in the downtown immigrant neighborhoods, the Poles in the 1890s built St. Casimir's Church on Sheridan Avenue just above Northern Boulevard, and thereafter most Polish families strove to live within its figurative shadow. When a split occurred within the Irish-dominated Roman Catholic church and the Polish National Church was formed, it too remained within the established Polish neighborhood, founding its new church on Clinton Avenue just two blocks from St. Casimir's.

Similarly the Italians, once numerous in lower Sheridan Hollow, established St. Anthony's Parish in 1908 with its church at the corner of Grand Street and Madison Avenue. From that day forth the neighborhood was known as Little Italy; its characteristic street festivals continued until the advent of the South Mall in the mid-1960s. Many Italian families displaced by the Mall have since moved into the adjoining parishes of St. James, St. Margaret Mary, and the most Italian neighborhood of all—West Albany, just at the edge of the city in the town of Colonie.

The Immigration Acts of 1922 and 1924 effectively closed off new immigration from abroad. For evidence of its impact, one need only drive up Livingston Avenue and look at St. George's Lithuanian Church—still confined to basement level as it has been since 1917, when the war and the change in immigration policy cut short what had started out as a significant influx of Lithuanians.

Another group that was once numerically significant, but whose growth was cut off by changing immigration policies, was the Chinese. Albany's Chinese community, dating from the late 19th and early 20th century, was concentrated in an area of downtown that included lower Hudson Avenue, Green Street, and Division Street, where it coexisted—as in Boston, New York, and elsewhere—in close proximity with the city's Little Italy. For years the Chinese characters could be seen on an old Federal-style building between Green and North Pearl on Hudson Avenue that housed a Chinese benevolent society.

Today the Chinese community is so widely scattered throughout the greater Albany area as to have only a fraction of the visibility it had earlier in this century. Nearly 1,000 Asians live within the city limits, including Filipinos and Taiwanese as well as more recent refugees from Southeast Asia, the majority of whom are Ethnic Chinese.

The Black Community

The story of Albany's black community is different from that of other ethnic groups. At first a substantial minority of the city's population, Albany's black population remained fairly stable throughout the 19th century, at a time when white immigration—first from New England and then from Europe—was increasing rapidly. As a result, the proportion of blacks fell to less than one percent of the city's population. Since World War II this trend has been reversed, and blacks have made up an ever-increasing proportion of the Albany community.

The percentage of blacks in the city during colonial times was much greater than most present-day Albanians realize. Slaveholding was quite common among the Dutch settlers of Albany and the surrounding area

Greater Albany Jewish Federation

City Engineer's Office

Top
South Pearl Street was a thriving commercial area that included numerous Jewish proprietors in the 1930s. H. Margulies owned this kosher restaurant and hotel. Note the discrepancy in the spelling of the owner's name on the signs.
Above
A Broadway shop window displayed these help wanted notices offering jobs to 1600 people circa 1915.
Facing page
Top
Following the opening of St. Anthony's Church on Grand Street and Madison Avenue in 1908, the area below Cathedral Hill became a mecca for Italian religious and cultural events. Celebrations in honor of Saint Anthony, the Blessed Mother, and Saint Rocco attracted thousands of residents, Catholic and non-Catholic alike.
Bottom
Albany residents displayed their enthusiastic interest in their European roots with an International Fair at the State Education Building.

DENMARK NORWAY UKRAINE RUSSIA RUSSIA BULGARIA

until after the Revolution. In 1785 the state legislature prohibited the importing of slaves for sale, and in 1799 it provided for gradual emancipation. Not until 1827, however, was slavery ended in the state of New York.

Emancipation did not bring equality of economic opportunity or even of political rights. Long after property qualifications had been eliminated for voting by whites, the restriction was retained for free blacks, who in fact did not attain full political equality even on paper until the passage of the Fifteenth Amendment. This historical distinction in political status enables the modern historian to trace some of the area's early black families, as their names were listed in italics in a number of 19th-century records.

City directories and census reports of the 19th century suggest that blacks were largely confined to lower-status laboring and service positions; whitewasher, barber, and waiter were among the more common job descriptions assigned to black families. Of 25 churches in Albany as of 1840, two were designated as "colored"—one Methodist Episcopal and one Baptist. In the 1920s, St. Mary's established a black Catholic church, St. Philip's on Sheridan Avenue, as well as a parochial school to serve the city's black population. Both were discontinued in the 1960s because they perpetuated segregation.

Despite the heavy yoke of discrimination, however, a number of blacks did succeed in elevating themselves to positions of influence within Albany society, particularly after the Civil War. One such person was Adam Blake, the son of a slave belonging to the Van Rensselaer family, who through diligence and hard work acquired the Congress Hotel, then situated on the site of the present state capitol. When the state of New York decided to build a new capitol behind the old one, the Congress Hotel was demolished and its owner compensated. Blake used the proceeds from the sale to build a new hotel, the Kenmore, which for many years was one of the city's finest hotels—and ironically a segregated one. The Kenmore still stands today at the corner of North Pearl and Columbia streets.

At the turn of the century, Albany had a black recorder—a judicial office first established by the Dongan Charter and one of the most prestigious in the state of New York—by the name of James C. Matthews.

St. Sophia Greek Orthodox Church Library

Above
St. Sophia Greek Orthodox Church was the scene of many religious ceremonies such as this christening in 1938. The church was located on Lancaster Street, now the site of "The Egg," which is part of the Nelson A. Rockefeller Empire State Plaza.
Below
South Pearl Street, shown here in 1915, was a favorite shopping place that was famous for its bargains during most of its 20th-century existence.

City Engineer's Office

Autobiography of Dr. William Henry Johnson

St. Sophia Greek Orthodox Church Library

Above
William Henry Johnson came to Albany about 1850 from Alexandria, Virginia. A barber and manufacturer of vegetable compounds by trade, he was active in the Underground Railroad movement. After the Civil War he devoted his efforts to the fight for civil rights. By 1900 he succeeded in bringing about the passage of laws in New York State outlawing segregation in public schools, surcharges on life insurance rates for Negro policy holders, and discrimination in public places. In addition, he was active in gaining acceptance of black men into labor unions. He died in obscurity in October 1918 at Little Sisters of the Poor on Central Avenue.

Above right
Members of the Greek American Association of Albany pose in front of St. Sophia Greek Orthodox Church in June 1924. The parade is part of the annual celebration of the Greek War of Independence (1821-1829) in which the Greeks won their freedom from the rule of the Ottoman Empire.

Black neighborhoods in the early part of this century consisted of isolated pockets in the South End, along Third Street in Arbor Hill, and—prior to the opening up of the land near the state capitol—along narrow Congress and Lafayette streets, both of which have now been obliterated (by west Capitol Park and Lafayette Park, respectively).

The first significant immigration of blacks into the city in this century occurred in connection with the buildup of industry during World War I. There was some further increase during the 1920s and '30s, but by 1940 the city's black population was still only 1.5 percent of the total.

Since then the black population of Albany has grown dramatically, reaching 3 percent of the total in 1950, more than 6 percent in 1960, and more than 12 percent in 1970. During the 1960s—a decade of civil-rights activism and large-scale outmigration of Southern blacks—busloads of black families were arriving in Albany at a rate of 500 new arrivals every weekend. Arbor Hill—a neighborhood that had been predominantly Irish, then Polish—was by 1970 predominantly black, as was much of the city's South End.

The percentage of blacks in Albany—only slightly greater than their proportion of the American community as a whole—nonetheless remains substantially lower than that of many other, more highly industrialized cities. The 1980 census reveals that the black population of Albany—after doubling in percentage each decade since 1930—has in fact stabilized in the face of increased economic opportunities for people of all races in the New South and the Sun Belt.

Albany's newest immigrants have included Vietnamese, currently numbering several hundred, and Hispanics, though again in much smaller numbers than in other, more industrialized cities. Immigration today is on a much smaller scale than in its 19th-century heyday, but even now refugees from economic and political oppression—whether Vietnamese, Cubans, or Russian Jews—can still find in Albany the religious tolerance and economic opportunity originally sought by that first boatload of Protestant Walloons more than 350 years ago.

CHAPTER 6
SOCIAL AND CULTURAL INSTITUTIONS

Albany's diverse ethnic background and strong political position, coupled with its economically strategic location, have made the city a logical home for innumerable cultural, educational, humanitarian, religious, and medical institutions. Albany is the capital of the Empire State, the county seat of a metropolitan county, and the regional headquarters for numerous nonprofit organizations. As such, it enjoys a cosmopolitan atmosphere beyond what might be expected in a city of its size.

Howell and Tenney

Worth, Random Recollections

Religion

Albany today has more than 100 houses of worship representing dozens of denominations. Despite its long history of religious toleration, however, the town of Beverwyck originally had only one official or "established" church—the Dutch Reformed.

The colony's first spiritual leader was Dominie Johannes Megapolensis, who arrived on August 13, 1642, aboard the *de Houltyn*, along with Abraham Staes (Staats), a surgeon, and brewmaster Evert Pels—all of whose services would soon be much appreciated by the residents of the fledgling settlement.

Dominie Megapolensis delivered his first sermon in the patroon's warehouse, next to the fort, which was later converted into the colony's first church. In 1649 he left to become pastor of the church in New Amsterdam, and in 1652 Dominie Gideon Schaets arrived as pastor, first as an official of the patroon and then under the jurisdiction of the newly created town of Beverwyck.

Dominie Schaets inherited a congregation of about 130 members, though Sunday services—still conducted in the patroon's remodeled trading house—were generally attended by 300 to 400 residents of the town and the patroon's domain. In 1655 it was agreed that a new and larger church should be built. The patroon subscribed 1,000 guilders, the town appropriated another 1,500 guilders out of court fines, and a new site was chosen in what is now the middle of State Street at its intersection with Broadway. On June 2, 1656, one of the town magistrates, Rutger Jacobsen, laid the cornerstone with all due ceremony before the assembled officials and inhabitants of Beverwyck and Rensselaerswyck. A temporary pulpit was installed but was soon replaced by a carved oaken pulpit sent over from Holland by the Dutch West India Company, which also provided a small bell for the steeple. The pulpit, now in the First Church in Albany (Reformed), survives today as the oldest pulpit in the United States.

In 1715 a new and larger church was built, using a rather ingenious method of construction. The old church was left standing and the new one built around it, with the shell of the old church not dismantled until the very last. By this means the old church was kept in active use almost up until the dedication of the new one; in fact, only two Sundays' services were missed in the transition. This new church on the old site served until 1806, when it was torn down and the stone and other materials used to build what was known as the South Dutch Church, between Hudson and Beaver streets. The North Dutch Church—today's First Church in Albany (Reformed)—on the west side of Pearl Street, was designed by architect Philip Hooker and constructed in 1798.

Even during the Dutch period, however, not all residents of Beverwyck belonged to the established church. Lutherans met for their worship services in private homes—despite the objections of the local authorities— as they had been permitted to do in liberal 17th-century Holland. After the English takeover in 1664, the Lutherans were able to build a church of their own, on the southwest corner of present-day Howard and Pearl streets. Their first minister was the Reverend Jacobus Fabricius, succeeded in 1671 by Bernardus Arensius. Lutherans, like everyone else, however, were still required to pay taxes for the support of the established Dutch Reformed Church.

The Reverend Thomas Barclay began preaching the Anglican service, in

Facing page
Enlargement of the Protestant Dutch Church in 1715 consisted of constructing the new addition around the shell of the old church
Top
The oaken pulpit of the First Dutch Reformed Church was brought from Holland to Albany in 1656. It is still in use more than three centuries later.
Above
The two-steepled North Dutch Church on North Pearl Street was erected in 1798. Architect Phillip Hooker designed the building that today houses Albany's First Church

both English and Dutch, in 1708. In 1714 work began on St. Peter's Church on upper State Street near the fort; it stood in the middle of present-day State Street opposite Chapel Street. A silver communion service sent by Queen Anne, originally intended for mission use, was retained for use in the new church. The original St. Peter's was torn down in 1802, and its replacement, designed by Philip Hooker, was built on the northwest corner of State and Lodge streets. Today's St. Peter's, designed by Richard Upjohn, was erected on the same site in 1859; the tower and chimes were added in 1875.

The first Roman Catholic church in upstate New York was St. Mary's, founded in 1797. The present St. Mary's was built on the same site in 1867 and incorporates the original stone foundation.

A *Gazeteer of the State of New York* published in 1813 reported a total of 10 houses of worship in Albany, including the two Dutch churches, one Lutheran, St. Peter's Episcopal, St. Mary's Roman Catholic, two Presbyterian churches, and a Methodist meetinghouse. By 1840 there were 25 churches representing nine different denominations, including Baptist, Quaker, and Universalist. The first meeting of American Congregationalism was held in Albany in 1852.

In the second half of the 19th century, Albany acquired its two great cathedrals: the spired gothic Roman Catholic Cathedral of the Immaculate Conception and the solid medieval Episcopal All Saints Cathedral—two houses of ecclesiastical splendor that today anchor either end of Albany's grand governmental concourse stretching from Elk Street to Lincoln Park.

Below
The first St. Peter's Church, also called the Old English Church, was torn down in 1802. It stood a short distance from Fort Frederick.
Facing page
Top left
Following a major renovation of St. Mary's Church in 1895, which gave it the distinction of being the first church in Albany to have electric lighting, Father Clarence A. Walworth had this weathervane affixed, having admired a similar weathervane on a European Church. As the Angel of Judgement, Gabriel appropriately looks over a myriad of state, county, and municipal courts on Capitol Hill.
Top right
St. Mary's Church, located at the corner of Pine and Chapel streets, was erected in 1798. It was Albany's first Catholic church. The 50-square-foot interior of the building proved too small for the congregation, and by 1829 the structure was demolished. Work began on St. Mary's second building in 1830.
Bottom
Erected on South Pearl Street in 1796, the second building of the First Presbyterian Church cost about $13,000. In 1850 the edifice was sold to the Congregationalists.

Albany Institute of History and Art

Photo by Bob Paley

Worth, *Random Recollections*

Howell and Tenney

Immaculate Conception came first, and was in fact one of the first cathedrals of any denomination in the United States. Modeled after the twin-spired Cathedral of Cologne, its cornerstone was dedicated before a throng of thousands of immigrant families during the great Irish potato famine of 1848. Financed by the pennies of servant girls—the first contribution came from the Irish communicants of St. Joseph's—the cathedral's first tower rose 210 feet over the next four years, aided by the volunteer labor of impoverished workingmen. Its first bishop, Brooklyn-born Bishop John McCloskey, was the first native New Yorker to have been ordained a priest.

McCloskey's Protestant counterpart, William Croswell Doane, was the cultured son of New Jersey's Episcopal bishop. He had visited the majestic cathedrals of England and in the early 1870s implored his well-to-do congregation of Albany's elite to underwrite a house of Anglican worship in the tradition of Canterbury. In 1888 Doane was rewarded by becoming the first American Episcopal bishop to have his high-backed, wooden "cathedra" housed in a true cathedral, rather than in a parish church.

In 1871 Erastus Corning, Sr., through the Corning Foundation for Christian Work, donated to the diocese part of the block of Elk Street between Hawk and Swan. The abandoned, barnlike machine shop of the Townsend Brothers Foundry, which occupied the site, was altered to serve as a new church and school. Here on All Saints Eve in 1872—five months after construction began on the new cathedral—Bishop Doane lit a fire in the hearth of St. Agnes School, beginning a tradition that has been followed every year by succeeding Albany bishops.

The grandeur of the original design for All Saints unfortunately was never fulfilled, for Bishop Doane's grand scheme exceeded the financial resources of his diocese, and seemingly endless deficits prohibited construction of the high-reaching towers envisioned by architect Robert Gibson of England. All Saints' era of creative construction ended in the early 1900s. The 90-foot long choir, encasing stalls for 153 clerics, was completed in 1904, thanks to an anonymous contribution of $200,000, long presumed to have come from J. Pierpont Morgan, Sr.

BILL OF FARE
FOR THE
Alms-House.

FOR BREAKFAST—Bohea tea and coaco shell alternately, with common brown sugar ; sapaan and milk occasionally ; good rye and indian meal bread, with a moderate portion of butter ; sometimes buckwheat or Indian or johny cake, warm, with butter or molasses ; together with the potatoes and the residue of the dinner of the preceding day, if any.

FOR DINNER—Soup, made of beef legs or shins and heads, or coarse meats, with rice.

2d, Codfish and potatoes.

3d, Pork and pease or beans ; also bean and pea soup.

4th, Common beef or mutton, occasionally.

5th, Fresh fish, viz. shad, herring and sturgeon, &c. in the season of it. Indian pudding, baked or boiled, with molasses. Vegetables produced from the garden, with the above, as shall be suitable, and as prudence and convenience shall dictate ; observing strict economy and regularity.

For Drink—Sometimes spruce beer, made of healthy ingredients and with economy.

FOR SUPPER—Bohea tea and coaco shell, or sapaan and milk—the bread as above, with a moderate portion of butter.

The above courses to be varied as shall be suitable and convenient for the house, and for the health of the paupers.

NOTE—Breakfast and supper for the children, sapaan and milk or bread and milk, generally.

By order of the Common Council,

CHAs. D. COOPER, *Clk.*

Albany, October 23, 1809.

Today, much of Immaculate Conception's parish has been overshadowed by the massive, marbled Empire State Plaza, and All Saints, swallowed up in the overwhelming embrace of the State Education Building, is all but hidden from view. The two cathedrals continue to serve their respective dioceses, however, and to stand as visible reminders of the strong spiritual foundations of the city.

Health

The first "comforter of the sick" assigned to the garrison at Fort Orange was Sebastian Jansen Krol (Crol), who arrived in 1626 and remained a respected and vital part of the community for the next 20 years. He was succeeded in 1646 by Harmanus Myndertse Van der Bogart, a former ship's surgeon aboard the *Eendraght*, which had arrived at the settlement in 1630. Another ship's surgeon, Abraham Staes (Staats), was sent over by the patroon to service the needs of his tenants, arriving on the same ship as Dominie Megapolensis in 1642.

The early records of Albany list several other physicians of the 17th century, including Johannes de la Montagne, a Huguenot of some prominence, who not only served as a surgeon but aided in the administration of Fort Orange; a Frenchman named De Hinse; and, toward the end of the century, a Scotsman named Lockhart. An outbreak of smallpox in August of 1663 killed 12 people in a single week at Beverwyck; the death toll among the Five Nations was placed at 1,000.

Owing to the military domination of Albany during the period of the French and Indian Wars, it is not surprising that many of the prominent physicians of the 18th century held ranks within the British Army. One of the most distinguished was Dr. Samuel Stringer, who was present at Abercrombie's defeat at Ticonderoga when the popular Lord George Augustus Howe was killed. Howe's remains are interred within St. Peter's Episcopal Church on State Street. Less than a block away is the land donated by Dr. Stringer for the founding of Albany's Masonic lodge. Another block to the north, on the open space in front of St. Mary's Church, was a colonial hospital that served generations of wounded soldiers—most of them teenage farm boys from the Hudson Valley and neighboring New England.

Dr. Stringer always dressed in a cocked hat and tight breeches, and his shoes bore huge buckles long after that style had passed out of vogue. During the Revolution he was appointed director-general of hospitals for the Northern Department by the Continental Congress and in his official capacity accompanied troops on the invasion of Canada with the ill-fated Montgomery expedition of 1776. After the war he settled down in Albany, married, and opened a local practice, becoming the close friend and family physician of General Philip Schuyler.

Also participating in the invasion of Canada was Dr. Hunloke Woodruff, who had settled in Albany before the Revolution and been appointed surgeon of one of the New York regiments. He served as medical officer to Colonel Peter Gansevoort during the siege of Fort Stanwix and in 1779 accompanied General John Sullivan in his attempt to combat the raids of Loyalist Indians against the settlers of the Schoharie and Cherry valleys and the lands to the west.

Several other veterans of the patriots' cause also settled in Albany and opened medical practices after the war. Some, including Dr. Nicholas Schuyler, were natives of the area, but others came in afresh to serve the

Clockwise from top left
Bishop William Croswell Doane sets down the cornerstone of the All Saints Cathedral in 1872.

St. Agnes School for women was founded in 1870 by the Right Reverend Doane. The building was first occupied in 1872 and accommodated 110 students with board and lodging.

While serving as rector of St. Peter's Church in Albany, William Croswell Doane was elected in a heated dispute as the first bishop of the Albany Diocese which was established in 1868. His father had served as Episcopal bishop of New Jersey. The younger Doane was a firm advocate of High Church principles. All Saints Cathedral, St. Agnes School, and Child's Hospital, once served by Episcopal nuns, all were started during his episcopacy. Doane numbered among his supporters some of the most prominent Albany families including the Pruyns, Cornings, and Huns. Many of his flock chose to live near him on Elk Street on its first block, nicknamed "Quality Row."

In the early 1800s Albany maintained an almshouse for impoverished citizens at the site of the present-day Christian Brothers' Academy in University Heights.

A steeplejack scales the south spire of the Cathedral of the Immaculate Conception circa 1905.

growing population. One of these was Dr. J. Cochoran, originally of Pennsylvania, who had served as surgeon-general of the Middle Department and, after 1781, as director-general of the hospitals of the United States. Dr. Elias Willard, who came to Albany in 1801 as part of the "Yankee invasion," was a veteran of the battle of Lexington.

In its strategic military position, Albany was regularly transformed—particularly during the summer months when armies were wont to do battle—into a great quartermaster store and supply depot for soldiers fighting on the frontier. The city also served as a medical center. Hospitals were hastily built within the city and even on the Schuyler property at the Flatts in nearby Watervliet; contemporary descriptions suggest that much of the city, particularly after the battle of Saratoga, was turned into a de facto hospital ward. Private homes, the Dutch church, and any other facilities that were available were all pressed into service nursing the sick and the wounded of both sides. For several months after the fighting was over, Albany continued to fulfill its role as a hospital town. Local doctors commented favorably on the British surgeons who tended their former countrymen, but expressed only contempt for the German surgeons tending Hessian wounded who "with little exceptions do no credit to their profession."

Ironically, except for the hospitals erected hastily during time of war, there seems to have been no regular hospital service available to the citizenry until well into the 19th century. Treatment of disease in the 18th century was crude at best, and the Common Council relied heavily on two time-honored methods for combating the spread of disease in the city: prayer, accompanied by dutiful fasting; and quarantine, particularly in the case of yellow fever, or spotted fever, as it was known at the time.

On September 21, 1793, Chancellor John Lansing wrote to the city advising the city fathers that a sloop was advancing upriver with two persons from Philadelphia, a city already cursed with yellow fever. The city's reaction was to bar the vessel from continuing northward to Albany. The ship remained at anchor near the Overslaugh at Darrow's Point while five Albany physicians examined the two travelers suspected of bringing in the dreaded disease. In time a clean bill of health was granted, allowing the suspected transients to continue their journey northward. The fact that these individuals were none other than Secretary of the Treasury Alexander Hamilton and his wife, daughter of the respected General Philip Schuyler, made no difference to a city that was in near panic over the possibility that the dread disease might be introduced into its neighborhoods.

The most serious epidemics of the 19th century were of cholera; the worst, in the summer of 1832, resulted in 422 deaths. Armed guards were placed at all approaches to the city in an attempt to hold back the influx of Irish immigrants, arriving on foot by way of the Champlain and Hudson valleys from Quebec and Montreal, who were suspected of carrying the disease. When the first cases were reported in July, an armed posse forced several hundred immigrants onto Green Island to be held in quarantine, and more than 700 others were ushered into a hastily built shantytown in today's Washington Park. These temporary quarters, inadequate as they were, were actually less crowded and therefore more healthful than the usual accommodations available to immigrants. Though nearly 1,500 immigrants were crowded into the two detention centers, almost all of the deaths occurred in the city's four emergency cholera hospitals, in the Alms House, or in people's own homes. Social and business gatherings were

Top
Death to early residents of Albany was a much more common phenomenon than to us today. In an era of high infant mortality and frequent epidemics, people were encouraged to express their feelings through the creation of objects of mourning. This embroidery on silk is dedicated to Julia Louis Gourlay, who died on April 25, 1813, at the age of two years, 10 months, and 29 days.
Bottom
In the 1800s Albany residents were in constant fear of cholera epidemics. Wealthier residents fled to country homes during the summer, while city officials fruitlessly burned tar in the streets and debated whether to limit the roaming of hogs through the city streets. The poor were particularly hard hit during these times. Following the cholera epidemics of 1832, 1834, and 1854, many private charities and orphanages were founded.

BOARD OF HEALTH!

WHEREAS the Governor of the State of New York has, by *Proclamation*, revived the Law passed **June 22, 1832**, for the Preservation of the Public Health,—

Notice is hereby given :

That a BOARD of HEALTH has been organized, agreeable to the provisions of said Act, in this Village; and is now engaged in the duties with which it is charged; and, to prevent unnecessary alarm, and to enable the Board and the citizens to judge more accurately of the state of the public health, it is ordered that all keepers of Hotels, Taverns and Boarding Houses give notice of all cases of Cholera at their respective houses, not attended by a physician, at the office of Dr. Burras, within twenty-four hours after such attack, under a penalty of twenty-five dollars; and all physicians in the village are required to report all cases of Cholera under their care, at the same place, within the same time, and subject to the same penalty for neglect.

The public may rest assured that no case of Cholera exists in the village at present; and that all proper exertions are being made by the Board and its Agents, to cleanse the Village from all infectious materials, and make every preparation in their power to prevent or mitigate the effects of that most fearful pestilence; and the Trustees of the Village are requested to enforce the Ordinances they have passed for paving and grading alleys and filling up lots, and to see that the Superintendent and Road Masters are diligent and faithful in the discharge of their several duties; and all the citizens are earnestly requested to assist the Board in their exertions.

WEST TROY, June 9, 1849.

AND THE CITIZENS WILL TAKE NOTICE

1.—That all Nuisances, of whatever nature, must be abated immediately.

2.—Whenever personal notice of the existence of any nuisance is served on the owner or occupant of any Lot, the requirements of said Notice must be complied with, within the time therein specified, or the penalty of the Law will be enforced, as follows:—

"*Every person who shall wilfully violate any Regulations as to be made and published by any Board of Health, shall be deemed guilty of a misdemeanor, and on conviction thereof, shall be subject to fine and imprisonment, or both, at the discretion of the Court; such fine not to exceed one thousand dollars, nor such imprisonment two years.*"

3.—It is required, that, after being properly cleansed, quick lime shall be liberally strewed in and about all wet or damp places, such as vaults, cess-pools, cellars, stables, hog-pens, alleys, gutters, &c. And that all may be provided with Lime, measures have been taken by this Board to procure an ample supply; and it can be procured at cost price at the following places, viz: at R. Dunlop's Lime House in the 1st ward, and at John Ferrioo's Lime House in the 3d ward.

Persons unable to pay for the Lime, will be supplied without cost, on application to either of the members of this Board.

S. S. WANDELL,
P. FITZGERALD,
JOHN HILLMAN,
SAM'L CRAWFORD,
JOHN HASTINGS,
DAN'L CARTHY,
JAMES KEILY.

W. HOLLANDS, PRINTER, (near the Upper Ferry,) WEST TROY.

sharply curtailed that summer, commerce came to a standstill, stages and steamers ran half empty, and the air was filled with the pungent odor of burning tar whose thick smoke was intended to purify the atmosphere.

By midcentury Albany still had no sewage system, its streets were notoriously ill paved, and its water system, privately owned until 1850, left much of the city's growing population dependent on wells. Albany's neighborhoods were jammed with nearly 51,000 inhabitants, nine-tenths of whom lived within one-half mile of State and Pearl streets. The famous description offered in 1830 by Nathaniel P. Willis remained all too true: "Albany, looking so well in the distance, that you half forgive it for its hogs, offals, broken pavements, and the score of other nuisances more Dutch than decent."

The question of hogs running loose was regarded with almost no humor whatever. Until the middle of the 19th century, there were always many more hogs in the city than people. Since the earliest days of Dutch settlement, these animals had been allowed to roam freely, fattening themselves on the ubiquitous garbage and refuse scattered throughout the streets, alleys, and backyards of their neighborhoods.

During the dread cholera years, the agitation to banish the portly scavengers to the private property of their owners grew more intense. Not until 1854 were the tens of thousands of hogs finally outlawed from roaming their traditional urban pasture, and then only because cholera had once again descended on the city's terrified populace. The establishment of zones or "swine lines" eventually limited hog-raising to the less settled areas of the city, and even today keeping hogs is a tradition in the Rapp Road area of the city's Pine Bush.

The year of the last great cholera epidemic, 1854, was also the year that Albany's first real hospital began accepting patients. Advocated since 1830 by Dr. Alden March, Albany Hospital—known today as the Albany Medical Center—has the commonly accepted founding date of 1849. Its first home was on the corner of Madison Avenue and Dove Street in a row house that is still standing. Then, in 1852, the former county jail on the southeast corner of Eagle and Howard streets was purchased and the prisoners moved to a new facility located in what is now the backyard of the city hall. By August of 1854, at the height of the epidemic, the old building had at last been refitted to the point where it could accept its first patients. The new hospital stood directly opposite the street where the Albany Medical College 15 years earlier had acquired the old Lancastrian School, and from that day forth the two institutions became virtually one in the minds of the Albany populace.

Education

Albany's first schoolmaster, in 1648, was a local tailor by the name of Evert Noldingh; evidently his efforts did not last very long. In 1650 a schoolhouse was built, a simple wooden structure 34 by 19 feet, and Adriaen Jansen Van Ilpendam was engaged as teacher. The curriculum consisted principally of reading, arithmetic, proper manners, and "the true Christian religion."

Albany Institute of History and Art

Albany Medical Center

Albany Medical Center

Shortly after Beverwyck became Albany, Governor Nicolls granted a license to the town's first English schoolmaster, Johan Shutte, as well as to Dutch schoolmaster Jan Jeurians Becker. The next schoolmaster of whom anything is known was Johannis Glandorf, engaged by the city in 1721 "for teaching and instructing the youth in speling, reading, writeing, and cyffering." A house was provided rent free, but his salary came from the fees paid by his pupils' parents. Free public education was still more than a century away.

The 19th century saw the creation of Albany's well-known private academies. Albany Academy, originally chartered in 1813, held classes at first in a frame house at the corner of Lodge and State streets, under the headmastership of the Reverend Benjamin Allen. Its own building, on the south side of present-day Elk Street, was started in 1815—the cornerstone was laid by Mayor Philip Van Rensselaer—and occupied in 1817. Like so many public buildings of its day, the school—now the headquarters of the Albany Board of Education—was the work of architect Philip Hooker.

Classes began at the new school in September of 1817 under a new headmaster, Dr. Theodric Romeyn Beck, and by 1830 it had 200 pupils. The curriculum included Latin, Greek, history, geography, English, geometry, "cyphering," and "natural philosophy"—what we would call general science. Joseph Henry, whose work in electromagnetics made possible the Morse telegraph, was a teacher at the Albany Academy.

The Albany Female Academy opened just a year after the boys' school in a small building on Montgomery Street, with Horace Goodrich as principal. In 1834 the school moved to a new building, complete with classic columns and portico, on the west side of North Pearl Street. The curriculum of the girls' school included reading, writing, music, and needlework; tuition ranged from $12 to $32 a year.

Clockwise from top
Dr. Albert Vander Veer received the degree of M.D. from the Albany Medical College in 1869 and settled in Albany. That same year he was made attending surgeon of Albany Hospital and elected professor of general and special anatomy in the Albany Medical College.

Improved conditions in the Albany Medical Hospital included such things as this private room with a brass bed, circa 1925.

A Shaker bentwood rocking chair and an ornate dressing screen furnished Room 2 of the Albany Hospital in 1896.

This 1865 advertisement from the Albany Directory *is an example of the sorry state of the medical profession at the time of the Civil War. Reliable doctors fought in earnest for increasing education and legitimate licensing. Their efforts improved the quality of medical care available to Albany citizens.*

My previous visit to Albany having been very brief, I now remained some time in the place, to see its state house, public libraries, and normal school establishment. The State House, situated on the top of the rising ground on which the city has been built, is a conspicuous and elegant structure, devoted to the meetings of the legislatures of the state of New York. In connection with it, I was shown a library of 30,000 volumes, for the use of members, and open to the public. A considerable number of the books are of the best English editions, no expense being spared to procure works of the highest class in general literature. Adjoining is an extensive law-library. Among the more interesting works shown to strangers, is a series of large volumes, embracing the printed legislative proceedings since the English organization of the colony. It is interesting to observe in the series, how at the Revolution, the British royal arms and styles of expression are quietly dropped, and followed by the republican forms, as if no break had taken place in the course of procedure.

William Chambers. *Things As They Are In America*, 1853. Reprinted in Joel Munsell's *The Annals of Albany*, Vol. VII, 1856.

Not everyone could afford to send his children to one of the academies. For the rest there was a common school run by the Lancastrian Society. Here a single teacher, aided by the older and more advanced pupils, supervised the education of as many as 500 children. In 1817 the Lancaster School moved into a building designed by Philip Hooker on the west side of Eagle Street between Lancaster and Jay. With the advent of public education in the 1830s, the school was discontinued and the building taken over a few years later by the Albany Medical College, which occupied the premises from 1839 until 1929.

The Albany Medical College, founded in 1838, began in a day when medical training still depended primarily on the apprenticeship system. Dr. Alden March, who had lectured on anatomy for many years, took over the premises of the old Lancaster School and raised the necessary funds for its conversion into a medical college. Later the college began receiving state grants, and in 1927 it moved to a new building on New Scotland Avenue near the Albany Hospital.

Albany Law School—oldest in the state and fourth oldest in the country— was started in 1851 as part of a projected University of Albany. Among its distinguished graduates have been numerous judges, senators, cabinet members, and one President, William McKinley.

Only one other unit of the proposed university was created—a department of astronomy. Land in the north of Albany was contributed for an observatory by Stephen Van Rensselaer, but the largest single contributor to the project was Blandina Dudley, wife of former mayor Charles E. Dudley, for whom the new observatory was named. The building was dedicated in 1856, in conjunction with the Albany meeting of the American Association for the Advancement of Science; Edward Everett, one of the great orators of the day, made a notable speech on that occasion. The Dudley Observatory was devoted mainly to the study of comets and planets until 1888, when it began cataloguing the stars in designated sectors of the sky. In 1893 the observatory was moved to a new building on Lake Avenue in the southwest part of the city, farther from the vibrations of the New York Central trains that had been found to affect observations at the old site.

On January 27, 1874, Albany Medical College, Albany Law School, Dudley Observatory, and Union College of Schenectady joined to form Union University. The Albany College of Pharmacy—the 15th pharmacy school in the nation and the second in New York State—was added in 1881. The pharmacy school, which began with 21 students using classroom and laboratory facilities of the medical college, moved into its own building on New Scotland Avenue in 1927.

One of the oldest state teachers' colleges in the United States was established at Albany in 1844. Known until 1905 as the New York State Normal School, its original premises were the old Mohawk and Hudson railroad station on the north side of State Street near Eagle. (Albany's first public high school—known at first as the Free Academy—was opened in the same building in 1866.) In 1849 the normal school moved into a building on the northwest corner of Howard and Lodge streets, later occupied by the Christian Brothers' Academy. New quarters on the east side of Willett Street between Madison and Hudson avenues, occupied in 1885, burned down in 1906. Finally in 1909, the renamed New York State College for Teachers moved into a group of brick buildings on the north side of Western Avenue, on the site of the old Albany Orphan Asylum.

Above
This athletics class of the New York State College for Teachers was held in the basement of the Hawley Library building.
Facing page
Top
The third building of the Albany Female Academy was located on North Pearl Street until traffic made the congested business streets unsafe for young pupils. This photograph shows the Class of 1864.
Bottom
These eight young women comprised the Albany Female Academy's Class of 1898.

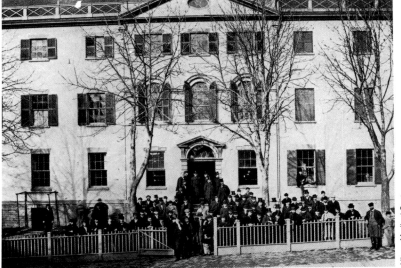

Today, as the State University of New York at Albany (SUNYA), the former State Teachers College still includes the old campus on Western and Washington avenues but is now headquartered in a massive uptown campus, designed by Edward Durell Stone and completed in 1970, whose white cement columns and familiar quartet of dormitory towers dominate the landscape. SUNYA is one of four university centers in the state system that award doctoral degrees. Over 14,000 students pursue more than 100 degree programs in the sciences, business, and the liberal arts.

Arts and Culture

When British officers staged Albany's first play in 1760, the event was looked upon as something of a scandal, evoking from the outraged Dutch Reformed Dominie, Theodorus Frielinghuysen, a scathing sermon on the sinfulness of the thespian art. The following morning a stick, a pair of old shoes, a crust of bread, and a dollar were left at his doorstep in hopes of sending the minister packing. Frielinghuysen did indeed leave the city soon after to return to his native Holland, only to drown on the voyage home.

The disapproval of theatrics was common throughout the northern colonies. A few professional acting companies did come to the city on occasion to play in the old colonial hospital, where the parking lot for the County Courthouse is now, but it was not until 1813 that a permanent theater was constructed on Green Street, under the management of John Bernard.

The new theater—a subject of much controversy—lasted only five years, after which it was sold and converted into a Baptist church. In 1852 it would be rededicated to the thespian art as the celebrated Green Street Theater.

Clockwise from top
The Yardboro Avenue School, shown here in 1922, was attended by well behaved, young students.

John Joseph Gaffie, a member of the Class of 1909 of the Christian Brothers Academy, poses during his sophomore year at the school. Established in 1859 as a private school to provide revenue for St. Vincent's Orphan Asylum, Christian Brothers Academy has maintained a military program since 1891, as has its secular equivalent, Albany Academy, since the 1880s.

Teacher, critic teacher, and superintendent of the primary department of the model school are pictured in 1896 with the first grade class. The school was part of the New York State Normal School at Albany.

The Albany Medical College Class of 1868 poses in front of the former Lancaster School building. Designed in 1812 by Philip Hooker, the building was occupied by the Albany Medical College from 1838 to 1927. It was the first schoolhouse to adhere to Joseph Lancaster's educational system, promulgated at the turn of the century, in which one teacher instructed scores of pupils.

Meanwhile the precedent had been established, and the Albany stage was destined to remain. In 1824–25 a new theater opened on South Pearl Street, where the old Leland Opera House would later be located. Because of the city's proximity to New York, stock companies readily made the journey upriver to test what was to become known as the "coldest audience" in the country. Until recent memory, it was said among theatrical circles that if a production was received well in Albany, it would do well anywhere.

Theaters were established throughout the 19th century. They survived with mixed economic success, degenerating occasionally, as in the case of the Gayety, into a saloon concert hall as part of a "Great White Way" already well established by the time of the Civil War. By the turn of the century, burlesque was in its heyday and Albanians would sneak into theaters like the Empire on State Street to see "Sliding Billy Watson" and other notables of risqué humor and merriment.

Attempts at establishing respectable theaters, often in converted churches whose congregations had moved out of downtown, generally failed until 1888, when the legacy of Harmanus Bleecker provided for construction of a new theater on the site of the present Albany Public Library on upper Capitol Hill. It was the first theater built outside the downtown theater district that centered around Green, Division, and South Pearl streets. Harmanus Bleecker Hall would survive as a respectable place for first-run plays and benefits into the mid-20th century.

Moving pictures, introduced before the First World War in nickelodeons like the Hellman's Fairyland on South Pearl Street, the first of a chain of such institutions, revolutionized the entertainment business. Movie theaters sprang up everywhere. In the city's South End, films were available in Yiddish and Italian. In some cases, the theaters were open air, utilizing courtyards, as was the case where the Lark Tavern is now located. In other experiments, the roof of the theater rolled back to expose the sky and let out the hot summer air from the crowded aisles below.

By the 1920s burlesque was dead and movies were no longer an experiment—they were big business. Large, elaborate theaters were built to accommodate 1,000 or 2,000 patrons. The Ritz, a converted municipal building on South Pearl and Howard streets, the Grand, the Strand, and, queen of them all, the Palace, all sprang up within a new theater district near Clinton Square. The only one left is the Palace, still 2,800 seats strong, complete with gilded baroque ornamentation, rising orchestra pit, and a mammoth crystal chandelier.

Neighborhoods had their local theaters, too. Some, like the Eagle and the Hudson, were converted from existing buildings. Others, including the Colonial, the Delaware, and the Madison, were new buildings constructed to accommodate large neighborhood crowds.

The 1950s and '60s were difficult times for the entertainment world. The movement to the suburbs and the advent of television took their toll of the old theaters. One legitimate house, Atterbury's, survived in the former Second Presbyterian Church on Chapel Street until the 1950s. The downtown movie houses, which had provided such affordable escapism to a Depression-ridden and war-weary public, saw their demise in the 1960s. Today, in a city that once knew the attraction of a score of movie houses, only three remain not including the Palace, which serves as a municipal auditorium. While movies today are making a noticeable comeback, it is in single-feature runs held at small cluster houses on the city's edge, accessible only by vehicle.

Within this void there has sprung up a welcome addition to the city's cultural wealth. As of this writing there are nearly two dozen theater companies in Albany County. The Albany Civic Theater, housed in an old firehouse on Second Avenue, is the city's oldest group, having been on the scene for 25 years. The Egg, located in the Empire State Plaza, is home to two professionally run full-time programs: the Empire State Youth Orchestra and Empire State Youth Theater, both of which have already earned international reputations.

Musical associations have long been a part of the city's cultural life. In the second half of the 19th century they tended to center around ethnic groups, especially German, and were often offshoots of church choirs. Indeed it was often the churches that hosted celebrated performers before the existence of a "proper" hall, as in 1851 when Jenny Lind sang at a concert in the Third Presbyterian Church, to the delight of the Harmonia Society, which had been formed in 1849.

The Singing Society Cecilia, formed in 1866, was predominantly German. It numbered about 150 members who participated in songfests and balls in Albany and throughout the state. The Union Musical Association, organized in 1858, was of similar size, as was the Albany Musical Association (1868), which performed in Tweddle Hall until it burned down. The Gesangverein Eintracht, the Mozart, the Apollo and the New Harmonic were other singing societies of 100 years ago. The Liederkranz

Top left
Born in the South End in 1890, Mel Wolfgang became the first Albanian to become a member of a world champion baseball club—the Chicago White Sox.
Top right
The Palace Theater opened in 1931 as one of the jewels in the RKO chain and is one of the grand survivors of an era of theater opulence. The Albany Symphony Orchestra and contemporary rock groups have been equally at home in the 2,800-seat theater. It has been owned by the City of Albany since the late 1960s.
Bottom
Marie-Emma Lajeunesse, born near Montreal in 1847, began her singing career in Albany as soloist and choirmistress at St. Joseph's Church on Ten Broeck Street. A distinguished operatic career followed her Paris debut in 1870, during which time she was affectionately known as "Madame Albani." This portrait was painted in 1877 by Albany artist Will H. Low.

Meldon Wolfgang 3rd

Beckman Associates Advertising Agency, Inc.

Musee du Quebec

Society and German street bands were typical of Albany at the turn of the century.

Modern-day musical Albany carries on the tradition of these earlier groups. The Albany Symphony Orchestra conducted by Julius Hegyi has replaced the earlier Albany Philharmonic Society, which had its origins in 1884 at the home of George Thacher, Jr. The Monday Musical Club is comprised of active artists and has met regularly since 1904 (though no longer on Mondays). The Mendelssohn Club, a men's singing society, is equally active, as is the Capitol Hill Choral Society, whose annual *Messiah* concert, long conducted by Judson Rand, has been an Albany tradition for a generation.

A unique musical institution is the Octavo School, which has been graduating students with Regents credits applied to their own high school since the idea was brought to fruition by its originator, Alice McEneny McCullen, in 1926—decades before the "university without walls" concept became popular. Originally the school consisted of several music teachers who had studied under a common mentor, Sr. Alphonsus de Rodrigues Ferland, at the old Academy of the Holy Names on Madison Avenue opposite Washington Park. The faculty still operates out of their own homes and studios, utilizing a common standard of excellence while avoiding the encumbrance of a common campus.

From earliest times, the visual artist has had an active part in the history of the city. In the 18th century, well-to-do Albany families immortalized themselves through portraiture. Although many of these formal oil paintings have come down to us, most of them are unsigned, according to the convention of the time, and many of the artists remain unknown.

Portraiture became increasingly popular after the Revolution, as great leaders sought to leave their image to posterity. The Albany Common Council made an extensive collection of such portraits, paid for from public monies. Many of them, including most of the early governors of the state, are now on permanent loan to the Albany Institute. The most prolific artist in this collection was Albany's Ezra Ames, who maintained a gallery of fine arts until his death in 1836.

Like many of his fellow artists, Ames started his career as a coach painter, painting scenes on carriages as a practical way of supporting himself. Albany was also a major printing center throughout this period, giving many an artist the opportunity to survive as an engraver. One of Albany's best known and most popular artists maintained a livelihood much further removed from his field of painting. Joseph Eights, who drew those wonderful scenes of Albany at the beginning of the 19th century, when the city was making the final transition from Dutch to Anglo-American ways, was a prominent practicing physician.

The Hudson River School was popular in the capital city, and although its great masters are generally associated with areas further south or more rural, Albany was the subject of many paintings. Scottish-born artists Harts, William, and James were raised in the city and had also been exposed to the traditional role of coach decorator. Walter Lunt Palmer, the Buycks, David Lithgow, and the Lathrop sisters carried on the tradition of fine painting into this century.

But it was in sculpture that Albany artists excelled. Erastus Dow Palmer and his student Will Low brought the city fame with their sensitive works in marble and bronze.

One of the area's most interesting artists was a potter, Bouck White, who for a short perod in the 1920s had a studio on Chestnut Street. Shortly thereafter he built a complex of stone buildings known as Heldeberg Castle, which still stands overlooking the road to Thacher Park. Originally from Schoharie County, White was a Harvard-educated minister who wore his hair shaved in the Mohawk style of his ancestors and held a dream of Albany as the center of a World League of Cities. The radical league never materialized and the "Hermit of the Heldebergs," his castle burned by vandals, retired to the Home for Aged Men in Menands, where he maintained an active flow of creative thought until his death a quarter-century ago.

Today's artists number literally in the hundreds, and the city is experiencing a growth of private galleries as part of its widespread renewal. Talented artists/teachers such as lithographer Thom O'Conner and metal sculptor Richard Stankiewicz at SUNYA enjoy reputations that extend well beyond this region. The much-sought-after works of David Coughtry, Alice Williamson, and Betty Warren present Albany in a warm and imaginative light that would have pleased Dr. Eights.

One of the city's most diversified artists, printmaker William Schade of the Junior College of Albany, has produced pieces as unique in their orginality as they are in their execution—among them the carved birdhouse in Washington Park, the cloth sculptured Indian at the Albany Institute, and the handmade-paper-making project.

Apart from the well-maintained libraries within the academic community, the city has three significant libraries. The largest is the State Library, now housed in the Cultural Building of the Empire State Plaza, which has its antecedents in a state law of 1818. From its inception the State Library has held many of the state's major historical documents. Under the

Albany Institute of History and Art

New York State Archives

Top
Dr. James Eights (1798-1882) is shown at the age of 40, approximately when he took up drawing—the activity for which he is best remembered. Eights, also a physician and natural scientist, is responsible for a series of drawings and water-colors that meticulously depict Albany's streets and houses at the turn of the 18th century.
Above
Albany native Charles Calverly, a student of Erastus Dow Palmer, the city's premier sculptor, fashioned the Robert Burns Monument and the bas reliefs around the base that depict scenes from Burns' works. Dedicated on August 30, 1888, in Washington Park, the statue was the gift of Miss Mary MacPherson. It stands on a pedestal of Scottish granite from Aberdeen. In 1979 the St. Andrew's Society cleaned the statue as a gift to the city in conjunction with its 175th anniversary in Albany.
Facing page
Prominent Albany sculptress and early suffragette Alice Morgan Wright is shown in her studio in the early part of the 20th century. Her estate contributed generously to the Humane Society as well as providing for the over 50 cats that were her constant companions.

guidance of longtime director Dr. E.B. O'Callaghan, a medical doctor who fled Canada after the political turmoil in that country in 1837, many of the state's important papers, including those of the Clintons, the Schuylers, and the Johnsons of Johnson Hall, were not only preserved but published.

In 1911, just months before the library was to move from its cramped quarters in the Capitol to the Education Building then under construction across the street, a tragic fire broke out, destroying innumerable priceless documents and artifacts that had been accumulated for nearly a century.

The library existed in its marble-columned home for more than 60 years, during which time its collections grew to include many municipal records, including the city of Albany's ancient Dongan Charter. The great vaulted ceiling of its reading room and the mosaic floors of its halls hid the fact that the library had once again outgrown its home. In its new location in the Empire State Plaza, it presently houses four million items, attracting tens of thousands of scholars each year.

The story of the State Museum is similar to that of the State Library, with which it has been housed since 1912. By the beginning of the 19th century Albanians could visit small museums at what is now the Albany Institute or at Trowbridge's, originally housed on the fourth floor of City Hall and later moved to a building at the corner of State and Broadway. In 1836 the state established the State Museum, and in 1870 the State Museum of Natural History, which occupied the Geological Hall opposite St. Peter's Church. This three-and-a-half story building, built in 1797–1799, was originally known as the Old State Hall. It was the first public building built in Albany by the state after the Revolution and, until construction of the old Capitol, it was the meeting place of the state legislature.

When the Empire State Plaza was completed, the museum was moved out of its massive top-floor exhibition galleries in the Education Building. Far more controversy surrounded this move than that of the library, as thousands of schoolchildren and former schoolchildren lamented favorite displays left behind. Many items made the move; others were put in storage; the whale skeleton and other artifacts were distributed to other

Below left
The prominent Scottish artist and portraitist David Cunningham Lithgow poses in his 57 North Pearl Street studio. During the early 20th century he was responsible for painting murals in such buildings as the State Bank of Albany, St. Andrew's Society, and Milne School. He also sculpted the bronze Spanish-American War Memorial in Townsend Park.
Below
Walter L. Palmer, son of sculptor Erastus Dow Palmer, painted the detailed Interior at Arbour Hill *in 1878. The painting depicts Thomas W. Olcott sitting across from a Shaker rocking chair, evidence of the Shaker presence in Albany.*

museums. The famed Cohoes Mastodon, found in a river pothole at the spindle city in 1863, was returned to Cohoes. After heated debate, the beloved Iroquois life scenes, with mural backgrounds by Albany's David Lithgow, were scheduled to move to the Cultural Bulding, which now attracts nearly one million visitors a year.

The Albany Institute of History and Art has roots extending back to 1791. Together with its McKinney Library and Harmanus Bleecker Center, its programs continue to preserve and enrich the cultural heritage of the city and the region.

Albany Institute of History and Art

New York State Archives

Above
A portrait of De Witt Clinton, the sixth governor of New York (1769-1828), by Ezra Ames (1786-1836) is seen on the wall above the main staircase of the Albany Institute. Many portraits of historically significant people are included in the Institute's outstanding collections of paintings, sculpture, and decorative arts objects related to the culture of Albany and the Upper Hudson region.
Above right
The Hall of Fossil Animals was part of the New York State Museum when it was housed in the State Education Building. The skeletons of the Cohoes Mastodon, found in 1866, and the Temple Hill Mastodon, recovered in 1921, are shown in this 1925 view of the Hall.
Right
The Albany Institute offers many events and activities designed to promote an appreciation of the cultural history of the region and the arts in general. This reception was held for the opening of a recent exhibition.

Albany Institute of History and Art

Albany Institute of History and Art

In the aftermath of the Revolution, a major concern of the young republic was the improvement of farming methods. In 1791, during the presidency of George Washington, "a respectable number of citizens" gathered at the New York State Senate Chamber in New York City to organize a Society for the Promotion of Agriculture, Arts and Manufactures. Of the 72 charter members, 25 were members of the legislature, suggesting a close tie with state government. An underlying motive expressed was to "supply the wants and relieve the necessities of mankind and thereby to render human life more comfortable," as well as "to excite a spirit of honest industry." The group chose Robert R. Livingston as president.

So oriented was this alliance to tillage of the soil that it called itself the Agricultural Society for short. The Society carried on correspondence with upstate rural counties relative to farming advances and made suggestions to the legislature. The "arts" part of its title was a vague dream for the future. From such parentage and through successive organizations, the Society was destined to flower into today's Albany Institute of History and Art, one of the oldest treasuries of regional heritage in the nation. Much of the Institute's great renown derives from the fact that its roots are deep in the early Dutch and English colonial life of the Upper Hudson Valley.

Centrally located at 125 Washington Avenue, not far from the State Capitol, the Albany Institute's facilities serve the city variously as art gallery, museum, school of the arts, social center, and library for historical research.

In the early years the parent Society was virtually an adjunct of the legislature, even timing its meeting periods to coincide with legislative sessions. The governor and legislators were ex-officio honorary members. At that time the legislature was alternating its sessions between New York and Albany. In 1797 the state government tacitly settled upon Albany as the capital by voting to erect "a public building" in this city for the storage of records and documents and to meet here annually in the old Dutch Stadt Huys. Predictably, the Society soon followed suit in order to maintain its contacts with the lawmakers

The Society's charter expired in 1804. The widening of its scope was indicated when the legislature reincorporated the group as the Society for the Promotion of Useful Arts—but agriculture was still the main "useful art." Robert Livingston, formerly chancellor of the state and temporarily abroad as mininster to France, was appointed president of the new Society. In Paris, Livingston became allied with Robert Fulton in a project to build a steamboat.

When the first State Capitol on the hill was completed in 1809, a special room was set aside for the Society for the Promotion of Useful Arts. According to Spafford's *Gazetteer of the State of New York* (1813 edition), this edifice contained "a room for the Society of Arts" in its "attic story." Because the Society was receiving donations of books, a second room was made available as a library. Some glass cases were added to display collections of minerals gathered by members, and the library began to take on the aspect of a museum.

In 1815 the State Board of Agriculture was created, reducing the Society's importance in that area. Soon thereafter the Albany Academy building was completed nearby, designed by the same local architect, Philip Hooker, who had planned the

Capitol. Space was provided in the Academy for the Society, which then vacated its rooms in the Capitol. By that time, chemistry, botany, mechanical arts, and "earthly fossils" had been added to its interests.

The lyceum idea was gaining popularity during this period—that i associations sponsoring lectures, concerts, and other entertainments. 1823 a group of eager young men organized the Albany Lyceum of Natural History, with Stephen Van Rensselaer, the last patroon, as president. With its legislative connections falling apart, the older Society was losing ground. It was revitalized in 1824 by merging with t Albany Lyceum under a new name— the Albany Institute.

A young teacher on the Academy faculty, Joseph Henry, became an Institute member and served as its curator-librarian, while embarking o experiments in electromagnetic induction that were to make him a scientific immortal. In 1827 Henry delivered his first paper on this work "On Some Modifications of the Electro-Magnetic Apparatus," at an Institute meeting. A fellow member, James Hall, in later years reminisced about watching Henry demonstrate t ringing of a bell at the end of a long wire by electrical impulse—the antecedent of the telegraph and telephone. Joseph Henry left Albany 1832 for a faculty post at Princeton a afterward won further renown as the first secretary of the Smithsonian Institution.

...ntless noteworthy papers were ...sented by Albany Institute ...mbers and published in its volumes ...*Transactions*. Many of these were ...Dr. James Hall, who became New ...k's first state paleontologist and ...logist. The Institute's example ...ped build up momentum for the ...neer Natural History Survey of New ...k State in the late 1830s. The ...titute spearheaded the movement ...t produced Washington Park, which ...s inspired by New York City's ...ntral Park.

...th much acclaim, in 1886, Albany ...ebrated the bicentennial of its ...rtering as a city. This occasion ...ught an outpouring of historic relics ...m the city's colorful past. As a ...todian for these heirlooms, the ...any Historical and Art Society was ...med. An Albany Gallery of Fine ...s, with a notable store of paintings, ...existed since 1846. In 1898 this ...llery of Arts was consolidated with ...Historical and Art Society to ...upy a building at 176 State Street.

...e mutational process came to a ...nax in 1900 when the venerable ...any Institute combined with the ...peting society to become the ...any Institute and Historical and ...Society. That unwieldy title was ...lly simplified to the Albany ...titute of History and Art in 1926. ...e two-story building that is still its ...tral facility was erected in 1907.

...e Albany Institute of History and ...houses, besides its many gallery ...ibition rooms, an auditorium much ...d for concerts, lectures, and other ...mmunity affairs. Among its priceless ...ections are portraits and scripture ...ntings by early Dutch and English ...ists known as limners; historical ...taits of prominent figures of the ...h and 19th centuries, many by the ...lific Albany artist, Ezra Ames; a ...erb collection of canvases by the ...dson River School of artists; and ...tuary by Erastus Dow Palmer, the ...ed 19th-century Albany sculptor.

Artifacts on exhibit include precious pieces of New York State furniture; Albany-made silver and pewter; and a wide range of ceramics, including Delft from Holland, Chinese export porcelain, and pictorially decorated Staffordshire china. The library holdings include some 500,000 manuscripts in addition to broadsides, maps, photographs, and books.

Having long since outgrown its quarters, the Institute was fortunately able to expand during the 1970s into an adjacent large brick mansion, formerly the residence of Mr. and Mrs. William Gorham Rice. Along with a variety of other functions, this annex contains the Laurence McKinney library, so named to honor a longtime former president of the Institute. For the past three years the Albany Institute has held curatorial responsibility for the contemporary art collections of the Empire State Plaza. More recently it has assumed custody of the nearby Harmanus Bleecker Center (former home of the Albany Public Library), now used to house the Bryn Mawr Bookshop, for teaching classes in art, crafts, and history, as headquarters of the Historical Society of Early American Decoration.

By such complicated steps has the Albany Institute evolved from a society primarily interested in tillage and husbandry to a position of cultural prestige and leadership in the capital city.

Albany Institute of History and Art

Above
In 1791 Robert Livingston was chosen president of the Society for the Promotion of Agriculture, Arts, and Manufactures, a predecessor to the Albany Institute of History and Art.
Below
Two of three buildings used by the Albany Institute are seen in the 1980 view along Washington Avenue—the Rice Building on the left, the main building set back on the right.

Albany Institute of History and Art

CHAPTER 7
POLITICS IN THE 19TH CENTURY

To say that Albany has taken politics seriously for a long time would be a gross understatement. Even if Albany had not been made the capital of New York State in 1797—beating out the city of Hudson in the state legislature—it would have been a political city. As a county seat at the crossroads of both commercial and political traffic between New York City and Montreal, Buffalo and Boston, whether by land or waterway, Albany played a vital role in the development of the state of New York. It has frequently taken an important part in national politics as well, having supplied many generations of congressmen, senators, cabinet secretaries, and other officials, in addition to sending four of its resident governors directly into the Presidency.

Albany itself rarely showed tendencies toward political agitations connected with reform. As the state capital, it was perhaps too closely committed to the status quo, the establishment that elected state legislators, the governor, and other representatives of the people through majority vote. Nevertheless, the physical presence of the state legislators during much of the year, as well as of the governor himself, guaranteed an incessant traffic, the comings and goings of committed and often colorful personalities with one or a whole host of proposals to be considered. During the 19th century's "age of reform," a stream of high-minded individuals and groups came in to address the legislators, and the governor if they could get to him, bombarding them with general or itemized protests and proposals: abolition of slavery; the establishment of married

Dictionary of American Portraits

Dictionary of American Portraits

Far left
Alexander Hamilton moved to Albany in 1781 to study law. There he married a daughter of General Philip Schuyler. In 1789 President Washington appointed him Secretary of the Treasury and Hamilton soon emerged as leader of the Federalists. This engraving by J.F.E. Prud'homme is from a painting by Archibald Robertson.
Left
In 1777 George Clinton was elected the first governor of the state of New York. Through reelection, he retained that office for 18 years. He resided at 66-68 State Street. In 1808 Clinton served as Vice President of the United States under James Madison.

women's property rights; the guarantee of humane treatment for the impoverished, the insane, or the criminal; the ending of the death penalty; the raising or lowering of tariffs on imports; the halt of military action against Mexico; the furtherance of voting rights for female citizens; the prohibition of the sale of alcoholic beverages; the prevention of unregulated immigration from Europe and Asia; the necessity of supporting the Union against Southern rebellion—or, contrarily, of letting the South depart in peace.

Albany provided residences, however temporary or permanent, for officeholders, office seekers, and lobbyists. Any Albanian with an interest in major and minor movements of a social or economic nature could simply take a visitor's seat in the Capitol and watch and listen through the years.

The Federalist Era

Even before the death of George Washington in 1799, American political thought was dividing into two main avenues of governmental philosophy. On one side were the followers of Secretary of the Treasury Alexander Hamilton, the brilliant son-in-law of Albany's Philip Schuyler and a frequent visitor to the city. Because of their belief in the need for a strong central (federal) government, they were known as Federalists; their advocacy of sound finances and of a government controlled by the well-educated and well-born appealed to many a Hudson Valley patrician.

The opposing group centered around another of Washington's former lieutenants, Thomas Jefferson of Virginia, whose followers looked toward French Revolutionary philosophy for inspiration, idealizing the small farmer and tradesman as the model American. Out of this group evolved a party known at first as Republican, then as Democratic-Republican, and ultimately as the Democratic Party of today.

In April 1801 New Yorkers ushered in the new century by electing the popular Democratic-Republican George Clinton to his seventh two-year term as governor. As the state's first chief executive, Clinton had helped guide New York through the difficult years of the Revolution and was governor in 1790 when the state grudgingly relinquished its claim to Vermont, once claimed as a part of Albany County. From his residence at 66–68 State Street, Clinton presided over a state whose conservative capital city staunchly supported a political philosophy at odds with that of his party.

His opponent, Stephen Van Rensselaer III, the aristocratic "last patroon," was only one of several Albanians to seek the governorship over the past 200 years. Despite the fact that Albany is the state capital, no Albanian has ever been elected governor, although two—John Tayler and Martin H. Glynn—rose from the position of lieutenant governor to governor when their running mates vacated the office. Three other Albanians served as lieutenant governor: the aforementioned Stephen Van Rensselaer, who later ran unsuccessfully against George Clinton; Clinton's running mate, Jeremiah Van Rensselaer, a kinsman to the patroon who, despite his name and residency, was elected by votes outside his home county; and Edwin Corning, who served as a Democrat under Alfred E. Smith.

From 1799 to 1816 and from 1819 to 1821, Albany's Federalist mayor was a Dutch patrician banker who, like the generations of mayors before him, still received his appointment from the governor of New York. Though an aristocrat by birth and marriage—he was the grandson of Philip

Livingston, a signer of the Declaration of Independence, and was married to Anne De Peyster Van Cortlandt—Philip Schuyler Van Rensselaer was tolerated by the Democratic-controlled Council of Appointment throughout an unbroken 17-year term of office. He was then removed and replaced by a Hudson-born Yankee, Colonel Elisha Jenkins, only to be restored to office three years later when his replacement resigned to return to his native city. As testimony to the personal prestige and popularity enjoyed by Van Rensselaer, his second appointment was granted by the Council of Appointment under Democratic governor De Witt Clinton, whose father had defeated the mayor's brother 18 years before.

During the 21 years of Van Rensselaer's stewardship, as well as the three-year interim under Jenkins, Albany survived the pressures of tremendous and unprecedented change. The Yankee invasion had not been repelled by the older Dutch elements, but it had most certainly been accommodated; the two groups had established a sharing of social, economic, and political power that still exists today. At the same time, the novelty of serving as the capital of the emerging Empire State had begun to wear off, as Albanians grew accustomed to the routine comings and goings of the officialdom of state government and those who would be their mentors—the great, the near-great, and the would-be-great. The ancient city of Thomas Dongan had not only tripled in population but had grown in area with the annexation of the former village of Colonie, the first of several annexations to follow.

During the years of Van Rensselaer's tenure as mayor, the position of the old Dutch oligarchy that had dominated the city's comings and goings since the 17th century was by no means extinguished. The names in the early 19th-century civil lists suggest that power was still largely monopolized by a succession of Dutch officeholders. From 1801 to 1829 Albany was represented by six congressmen: three of them were surnamed Van Rensselaer; two others, Harmanus Bleecker and Rensselaer Westerlo, were also Dutch; and only one, John Lovett (1813–1817), appears not to have shared—in his patronymic, at least—a common ancestry. In the state senatorial lists from 1800 to 1825, eight out of 10 names are Dutch. The assembly, too, maintained a Dutch-surnamed majority for most of the

Albany Institute of History and Art

Harmanus Bleecker (shown here in a 19th century daguerreotype), distinguished Albany attorney, assemblyman, and Federalist Congressman, served 12 years as a regent in the days when the regents visited every academy in the state annually. Although a fifth-generation Albany resident, Bleecker was fluent in Dutch, and through Martin Van Buren was chosen to serve as charge de affairs at the Hague. His estate was left to his Netherlands-born widow Sebastiana with the verbal understanding that after her death it would pass to the people of Albany in some benevolent manner. Influenced by John V.L. Pruyn, the final distribution of his wealth resulted in the building of Harmanus Bleecker Hall, and through the Young Men's Association, the Albany Public Library.

In the early 19th century many civic improvements, including the construction of the first State Capitol in 1809, were funded by lotteries. Albany, as well as many other cities, raffled off city building lots as a means of raising revenue. In the 1830s this practice was halted, as New Englanders of Puritan stock began to dominate New York State politics.

quarter-century, but by 1820 these seats, like those of the Common Council, would be dominated more and more by Yankees.

Some local offices such as sheriff, remained decidedly in Dutch hands, while others, such as county clerk and district attorney, alternated or were shared between Yankee and Dutch officeholders through the period. This pattern is far from unique in American politics. Older ethnic groups tend to hold onto higher offices long after they have passed into numerical inferiority, allowing newcomers to begin their ascent to power from the lower rungs of alderman and supervisor. Judgeships—particularly in the case of minor courts, with their limited power and patronage—can serve either of two purposes in ethnic politics. Because of their undeniable prestige, they can have great value in satisfying the political aspirations or pride of older groups whose support, though anxiously sought by party leaders, can no longer carry large electorates in which they are a decided minority. Newer groups, also not "electable," often measure success by the appointment of one of their own to a vacated judgeship.

By the 1820s Dutch and Yankee alike were making way for a substantial minority of Irish, whose migration to Albany as turnpike workers throughout the early years of the 19th century is too easily overlooked because of the more obvious and larger influx of New Englanders. The building of the Erie and Champlain canals, 1817–1825, attracted thousands more Irish, whose free-spirited political acumen would exercise substantial influence over Albany long before the Great Famine sent many thousands of their countrymen to join them nearly a generation later. Just as the Dutch accommodated the Yankees, collectively the two older groups absorbed the Irish, and to a lesser extent the Germans—and later the Poles, Jews, Italians, and others—in a political drama that plays without end in the clubrooms and election booths of cities across the Empire State.

Several signs that marked the end of the old order were apparent in the final days of Philip S. Van Rensselaer's administration. In 1821 the method of selecting the mayor of Albany was changed from gubernatorial appointment, a holdover from New York's days as a royal province, to indirect election by the city's aldermen.

On February 19, 1821, Democratic-Republican state senator and city alderman Charles Edward Dudley, a successful Albany merchant, was unanimously elected mayor by the Common Council. Dudley, a native of England educated in Newport, Rhode Island, had been in Albany for only two years. As was the custom at the time, he was allowed to retain his senate seat along with its legislative salary, which had just been lowered from $4 to $3 per day.

The 10 members of the Common Council elected on September 25 of that year—Theodore Sedgewick, John Stillwell, Chauncey Humphrey, John Cassidy, Nicholas Bleecker, Robert Davis, Philip Phelps, James L'Amoureaux, James Gibbons, and Richard Dusenbury—proved an all-time low for Dutch surnames.

In July of 1821 a constitutional convention was held in Albany with the aim of opening up New York's government to a greater number of its citizens. The Yankee-dominated convention—the liberal Bucktail wing of the Republican Party controlled 110 of the 126 seats—reduced the governor's term from four years to two, made more state offices elective, and pushed through several other Jeffersonian changes despite the outcry of the old landed aristocrats. Finally the worst fears of the old-line

The Capitol

New York State's imposing stone Capitol building, astride the old Public Square on the crest of the State Street hill, is a multiformed architectural monument to the gilded century in which a wilderness province matured into young America's Empire State. When Governor Frank S. Black, a tall, scholarly attorney from Troy, mounted the 77 steps of the "Eastern Approach" on Christmas Day in 1897 to proclaim the Capitol completed at long last, he opened the doors to the most expensive public building of its time. It had taken the administrations of 10 governors to finish and heavily drained the state's treasury while providing thousands of jobs to two generations of Scottish stonecutters, Irish laborers, and Albany contractors.

Howell and Tenney

The original architect was Thomas Fuller, a British Victorian renowned for his design of the Canadian Parliament building on a bluff above the Ottawa River. As early as 1863 he had submitted his plans for an elaborate Italian Renaissance capitol for Albany.

Work began in 1867, providing a patronage factory for local impoverished laborers. Excavation of the site's three acres altered the face of the city. A daily procession of 200 Albany Railway Company flatcars, pulled by draft horses, hauled away the deposits of glacial clay, returning laden with massive blocks of white Maine granite unloaded from wharves leased by the Capitol Commission.

The great undertaking consumed the next 30 years, spanning the decades between the Civil and Spanish-American wars. Above the six-foot-thick basement walls, the edifice rose through the first and second strata of Romanesque balustrades, vaults, and arches, through a transitional third story, flowing 100 feet upward finally to be peaked by the French Renaissance dormers and turrets fashioned by H.H. Richardson, master of the Capitol's third set of architects.

The original spending ceiling of $4 million was exceeded within nine years, beginning the Albany tradition of state construction-cost overruns that plagued the building of the Empire State Plaza 100 years later. By the time the Capitol was completed in 1897, the total cost was estimated to be around $25 million, an astronomical amount for that time.

During its inception stages it was declared that there had never been a building like it before. The effort to erect the Capitol drew the scorn of critics, who railed that the high-priced architects were trying to "out-Herod Herod" in raising a monstrosity which so lacked "repose and dignity" that it called for "the heroic remedy of dynamite." The extravagance of this "public calamity" so appalled Governor Lucius Robinson of Elmira in 1878 that he refused to deliver his annual address within the partially completed walls, staying home instead and telling reporters that the soaring interest on the cost of construction was sufficient to keep his native Chemung County supplied with chewing tobacco for all the days to come.

Ten thousand celebrants, however, ignored the governor's annoyance when they gathered in January 1879 to mark the dedication of the magnificent "North Center" enclosing the assembly's chamber. John Hay, once Lincoln's secretary, was among the throng standing 56 feet below the majestic three-ton Gothic central vault.

"What a great thing to have been done in this country!" he exclaimed to the hall's designer.

Yet the Capitol took a toll—measured in more than dollars. William Morris Hunt, a bearded philosopher-artist, was commissioned to execute, in oil pigment on bare sandstone, counterpoised allegorical murals high on the north and south walls of the assembly chamber. Pressured by the pecuniarily tight-stringed Governor Robinson, Hunt finished the murals in an astounding two months of labor on scaffolds 40 feet above the chamber floor. But Robinson cut off funds for further "internal ornamentation," breaking Hunt's commission and throwing the exhausted artist into a depression. He committed suicide a few months later. Alas, his murals survived him only 10 years, after leakage through a poorly constructed roof marred his work. Installation of a lowered ceiling shut the murals from public view; today, framed by steam pipes and ventilation ducts, they are seen only by Capitol maintenance crews.

Robinson was succeeded as governor by Alonzo B. Cornell, son of Cornell University's founder. He loosened the purse strings, retained Stanford White to complement Richardson's work, and directed the completion of the "South

Albany Institute of History and Art

Center's" senate chamber, described at the time as the most beautiful room in America, as well as of the "Red Room," the executive chamber a floor below.

The floors of the Capitol were linked by staircases with names proclaiming their grandeur. As state legislators ascended Leopold Eidlitz's "Senate Staircase," they passed arches bordered by arabesques; in carved relief, depictions of Darwin's theory of evolution moved from sea life at the lower levels to elephants and camels above. Richardson's "Great Western Staircase," rising 119 feet to the skylight, cost $1.5 million and took 10 years to complete. No wonder it was called the "Million Dollar Staircase."

Isaac Perry, a big, bearded man who looked more like a Southern farmer than the Binghamton architect he was, dominated the final years of the Capitol's construction. He indulged a devotion to stone carving and portraiture which made the Capitol one of the last grand repositories of a form of public-works ornamentation no longer undertaken. Armies of Scottish stonecutters and woodcarvers, drawn to the $5-per-day jobs, with mallet and chisel etched into the Capitol's soft

Corsehill freestone memorials to Lincoln, Whitman, Longfellow, Fulton, and the sculptors' own mothers and daughters. The severity of the granite was sometimes broken by the whimsy of winking men and sassy girls. As the suffragist movement rose late in the century, last-minute tributes to Susan B. Anthony, Mollie Pitcher, and a half-dozen other important women hastily found new niches.

When Governor Frank S. Black, one-third of a century after the laying of the Capitol cornerstone, declared a halt to any further work, the building had actually been open and functioning for 20 years. "The State needs the structure for its uses," he said, "but it needs still more to escape the scandal of a building of enormous cost and unparalleled extravagance undergoing at the same time the process of construction at one end and decay at the other."

So finally in 1897 the great Capitol was considered officially finished. The citizens of city and state would scarcely have envisioned its ever burning down, since it was carved from granite and seemingly indestructible. But early on the morning of Wednesday, March 28, 1911, after a bickering legislature, near the end of its work, called a late-meeting recess, two lingering messengers raised the cry of "Fire!" Wisps of smoke preceded an explosion of flame that erupted in the state library near the assembly and roared upward through the ceiling made not of stone but, scandalously, of papier-mâché.

Within 20 minutes the flames were leaping 200 feet into the air. Days later, charred remnants of state documents were found in the hills of Rensselaer County six miles away. Albany firefighters arrested the blaze's spread at the "Midway," confining the damage to the western section. After the fire, so much water remained in the assembly chamber that legislation jokingly was introduced to stock the well with fish.

The fire was the worst library disaster of its era, consuming 450,000 books and 270,000 manuscripts, including papers of early colonial statesmen and the journals of the state's 19th-century leaders. Missing in the rubble was a 78-year-old watchman named Abbott, assigned that night to the library. His charred body was found later near a cabinet in which valuable records were kept. He had started back into the office to save the papers and was overcome by the thick smoke.

Except for renovations and repair, the only change to affect the Capitol during this century has been the construction of the South Mall, which brought about the razing of brownstones and rowhouses huddled around the building, opening the hidden south front to the broad expanse of the sweeping marble plaza. The coming of the Mall opened the Capitol's interior as well, because the lavish Legislative Office Building across State Street provided office space for legislators and their employees, who previously had been jammed into cubicles installed over the years in every available corner of the Capitol.

Today the Capitol braces the Plaza's northern edge, its jumbled features surprisingly compatible with the sleek lines of the futuristic state office buildings nearby. A blue-ribbon commission is preparing the Capitol building for the future with plans for a restoration in the 1980s that would extend the building and its ornamental ancient gargoyles into the 21st century.

Federalists, led by Chancellor Kent, Stephen Van Rensselaer III, and Abraham Van Vechten, were realized—elimination of the property requirement for voting in favor of universal suffrage for white males.

At the conclusion of the convention, which met for 75 days in the old Capitol, the document was adopted by a vote of 98 to 8, with 18 absent. The final version lacked the signatures of 16 protesting Federalists. Despite a very close vote in the city of Albany and Albany County, it easily won approval statewide and became the law of the land on December 22, 1822.

The constitutional convention at Albany delivered a death blow to the all-but-vanquished Federalist Party. The last political strongholds of the conservative landholding class that had dominated New York State for more than 150 years were swept away. A bloodless revolution had been effected.

The Albany Regency

The most uniform statement that can be made about one-party democracies is that they are short-lived. The elimination of the Federalists and the inclusion of a great montage of widely varying political opinions under the eclectic banner of the Democratic-Republican Party was at best an artificial, confusing, and temporary situation.

Conservatives within the party began to seek a champion for their cause. In taste and temperament, as well as for his bold canal policy, De Witt Clinton—nephew of the state's first elected governor and father of the Erie Canal—seemed a likely standard bearer. He was elected governor by a landslide in 1817. Strongly opposed by the Van Buren faction, however, Clinton declined to run for reelection in 1822.

Joseph C. Yates of Schenectady, representing the more liberal Bucktail wing of the party, was elected to his only two-year term. The handsome federal townhouse in which he resided as the state's chief executive in 1823–24 still stands on the southwest corner of Madison Avenue and Franklin Street. During its brief period as the executive mansion, it was barely a decade old and was one of only a few houses then built in the city's North Pastures development.

De Witt Clinton, who served in both branches of the New York legislature, was the most notable promoter of the construction of the Erie Canal. He was governor of New York in 1817-1822 and 1824-1828.

During this transition period the personality politics of previous years were beginning to decline in importance. Groups formed around issues of considerable controversy—the chartering of the banks, the merits of tariffs, the cost of building canals, and the question of expanding slavery into the territories. The Democratic Party of Andrew Jackson and Martin Van Buren, in fact, remained badly divided for most of the next 35 years, especially over the issue of slavery. Northern Democrats were in a particularly awkward position because their party depended on Southern slaveholding states for much of its support.

In New York State the liberal wing of the party came under the control of several political giants led by Martin Van Buren, a Kinderhook attorney who practiced law in Albany from 1816 until 1829, when he moved to Washington to become Jackson's secretary of state. A bronze plaque on 90 State Street memorializes his residence; his office was moved in 1821 from 353 North Market Street to 109 State Street.

Van Buren joined with other New Yorkers of like political thought—Silas Wright, William L. Marcy, Azariah C. Flagg, Samuel A. Talcott, Benjamin

Columbia County Historical Society

Worth, Random Recollections

Top
A picture of Martin Van Buren decorates this childs' sled made circa 1841. Among the men who formed the "Albany Regency," Van Buren resided in Albany where he practiced law for over 10 years. He was chosen governor of New York in 1821, was Jackson's Secretary of State in 1829, and Vice President of the United States. In 1836 he was elected President. His Columbia County estate, Lindenwald, has recently been acquired by the federal government as a museum.

Above
While serving as governor, Martin Van Buren occupied this State Street house, which was erected in 1780 and demolished in 1841.

Knower, and Benjamin F. Butler (Van Buren's State Street law partner)— to form the Bucktail wing of the Democratic Party into a smoothly operating machine known throughout the country as the Albany Regency. Van Buren would be the only Dutchman in an otherwise exclusively Yankee association.

The term Regency was coined during the presidential election of 1824 by Van Buren's political rival Thurlow Weed from his base as publisher of the Rochester *Telegram.* Acting counter to their own professed political beliefs, Van Buren's supporters beat back efforts to remove the power of nominating presidential candidates from the legislative caucus, which they controlled. The Regency stubbornly backed William H. Crawford, candidate of the powerful Virginia dynasty, and feared that a convention, and the demand that presidential electors be directly elected by the voters, would bring out anti-Southern sentiments against their candidate. Van Buren's people not only lost the election that year but were substantially discredited by the pro-Adams forces of Thurlow Weed and newly reelected Governor De Witt Clinton, who replaced Governor Yates.

The Regency, though it never would shed its imperial-sounding name, made great efforts to avoid repeating the mistakes of 1824. By 1828, Van Buren, then a U.S. Senator, was espousing the cause of a new kind of candidate in the person of a backwoods war hero named Andrew Jackson.

Jackson, unlike most of the politicians with whom Van Buren associated in New York, brought the winds of change into the colorful and unpredictable world of 19th-century politics. Orphaned in early childhood, Jackson had migrated from his native North Carolina to the untamed land of Tennessee. Brawling, cockfighting, dueling, a minimum of schooling, and a maximum of Indian fighting were the principal forces that had created a national folk legend out of "Old Hickory," the hero of the Battle of New Orleans. Jackson was a product of the new rising West, while Van Buren was a reflection of the 200-year-old Dutch culture unique to the valley of the Hudson.

Somehow the two men were drawn to each other, each complementing the strengths and weaknesses of the other. In the critical election of 1828, one of the dirtiest and most bitterly contested elections in American history, Van Buren ran for governor of New York in a successful ploy to add strength to the national ticket.

A desperate effort by Thurlow Weed to unite the newly formed Anti-Masonic Party and the National Republicans behind President Adams and a single gubernatorial candidate failed, and Jackson and Van Buren won their respective executive offices. Fifty years later, Weed would reflect that this single victory engineered by the Albany Regency was responsible for a legacy of many years of Democratic rule in the state.

It is doubtful that Van Buren ever really intended to stay in the governor's chair. A mere 71 days after taking office he became Jackson's secretary of state, turning the reins of state government over to his handpicked and able running mate, Enos T. Throop. In his brief tenure as governor, Van Buren did manage to achieve two significant measures destined to have a lasting effect on his native state. His creation of a bankers' insurance fund to cover the losses of failing banks did much to create confidence in New York's financial institutions, and his implementation of "all or none" victories for presidential electors singled the state out as a "must" stop for every future presidential aspirant. Prior to the 1829 law, presidential electors were chosen by district, and the state's delegation could be selectively appealed to by candidates. The new system would make New York the greatest prize in America during a presidential election year.

Van Buren's successor, Enos T. Throop, who served as governor from 1829 to 1833, unwittingly started a quarter-century Albany tradition by selecting No. 1 Elk Street as his executive mansion. He was succeeded by fellow Albany Regency stalwart William L. Marcy, who resided at No. 2 Elk Street during his tenure from 1833 to 1839. This building is essentially still standing, incorporated into the headquarters of the New York State Bar Association. Several later governors also selected Elk Street for their official residences. Hamilton Fish (1849–1851) chose No. 15; Washington Hunt (1851–1853) rented No. 1, as did his successor, Horatio Seymour, during his first term (1853–1854). For years the long block of Elk between Eagle and Hawk streets boasted such a succession of prominent bankers, politicians, and merchant princes (as well as the bishop of the Episcopal diocese) that it became known as Quality Row; its elegant townhouses continued to attract the state's well-to-do until well into the 20th century. The present Governor's Mansion, at 138 Eagle Street, was purchased and remodeled by the state as its official executive mansion in 1874.

Just as the so-called Era of Good Feelings came crashing down in the national election of 1824, so too did Democratic Mayor Dudley's political honeymoon end in predictable dissension. Three times in nine weeks the Common Council declared the office of mayor vacant. In vain the names of Charles Dudley, John Quackenbush, and John Lansing were put to the council, exactly half of whose number stubbornly supported Ambrose Spencer. A blank vote by a Democratic-Republican member finally gave the election to Spencer, who took office as the city's 35th mayor.

Dudley was returned to office during the Jacksonian election year of 1828. When he left the office for the final time in 1829, it would be to replace Martin Van Buren as U. S. Senator.

Integral to the formation and maintenance of political parties at this time was the sponsorship of political journalists. In Albany, two giants of the newspaper world competed for the votes of their readers.

The *Argus* was founded in 1813 by Jesse Buel, whose large brick Federal-style home still stands on Western Avenue in Pine Hills. Edited from 1824

Below left
Elected governor of New York by a large majority in 1848, Hamilton Fish resided at No. 15 Elk Street in the block known as Quality Row. This engraving is by Alexander H. Ritchie.
Below
A decade after being elected mayor of Utica, Horatio Seymour was chosen governor of New York in 1852. He was re-elected in 1862. During his first term of office he lived at No. 1 Elk Street. Though Seymour was nominated for the Presidency in 1868, he was not elected. John C. Buttre engraved this portrait of Seymour from a Mathew Brady photograph.

Dictionary of American Portraits

Dictionary of American Portraits

TO THE
TENANTS
KNOX, BERNE, WESTERLO, AND
Rensselaerville.

GENTLEMEN:

Having intimated to you that no change of terms of Release would be made without notice, we take the trouble to inform those who do not make arrangements for a settlement of arrears of rent, before the 15th day of October next, and all who contest the payment of rents, that they will be charged for their soil, a sum, which at six per cent, interest, will produce the rent, estimating Wheat at *Ten Shillings* per bushel.

This change will make a difference of one quarter in our charge for Releases, but if the Tenants choose to delay to their own detriment, the fault is theirs, and they must pay for their folly.

Henceforth we shall immediately and indiscriminately Sue for the collection of all Rents in arrear; those who have settled must be prompt hereafter in their payments, as we will not allow the rent to accumulate. We have refrained from prosecuting all until every question which honest doubts or dishonest demagogues could raise concerning the Title and rights of the parties has been settled, even to the repeated failure of well paid lobby men, to get up the shallow pretence of an existing Indian claim. No further indulgence can reasonably be asked for, nor will it be given.

The Politicians will get through with you in November and they will probably then let the Indian Title rest until another Election. Now decide whether you will settle your rents without cost, and purchase your Releases at the lowest rate, or be fooled by politicians, pay heavy bills of cost, and 25 per cent addition for your soil.

ISAAC VAN LEUVEN, Esq., of Westerlo, is authorized to purchase stock, in payment for rent.

Dated Albany, September 14th, 1855.

STEPHEN VAN RENSSELAER,
CHURCH & TYLER.

Above
Upon the death of the "Good Patroon" in 1839, Stephen Van Rensselaer III and his two sons divided the Rensselaerswyck manor and were forced to collect nearly $500,000 in back rents to pay off debts on the estate. The civil unrest and violence that followed was known as the Anti-Rent War. Its outcome destroyed not only the archaic manor system, but also many small farms.
Below
Journalist Thurlow Weed became editor of the Albany Evening Journal *in 1830. Though prominent in the Whig and then the Republican Party, Weed would never accept a public office.*
Below right
Much to the disappointment of Thurlow Weed, Democrat William Learned Marcy was elected governor of New York in 1832 and reelected in 1834 and 1836. During his years as governor, Marcy commissioned the first geological survey of the state.

to 1854 by ardent Albany Regency supporter Edward Croswell, the *Argus* became the city's vocal Democratic newspaper.

Of no lesser status was the staunchly anti-Regency, anti-Jacksonian Albany *Evening Journal,* founded and edited by the indomitable Thurlow Weed, who in 1830 moved to the state capital, perhaps to get a closer shot at his enemies.

Like the evolving political thought of its founder, the *Journal* progressed from a National Republican and Anti-Masonic bias to Whig, and finally emerged as the city's Republican voice. Born in Cairo, New York, Weed had worked as a printer from the age of eight, and through tough journalistic partisanship, had created a seat of power in the northeast that was a major force of opposition to Van Buren's Albany Regency. With the collapse of the Anti-Masonic Party after 1830, a number of prominent voices—notably William H. Seward, Francis Granger, Millard Fillmore, and fellow journalist Horace Greeley—joined that of Weed. Together the oligarchy of future Whigs watched with chagrin the continued successes of Van Buren, the agile "Fox of Kinderhook."

In 1832 the Regency succeeded in getting William L. Marcy of Troy elected governor, despite heavy exploitation by the Weed-supported opposition of the issue of "Marcy's trousers"—a 50-cent pants repair job that Marcy, while a state judge, had foolishly and perhaps unthinkingly included in his state-reimbursed travel log. On the national scene Andrew Jackson, with the strong support of labor, won reelection easily. This time his running mate was Martin Van Buren, whose statewide political machine was now at the peak of its power. Marcy was reelected governor in 1834 and 1836.

During this period the Albany mayoralty seesawed back and forth between the National Republicans (soon to become the Whig Party) and the Democratic Republicans (who soon dropped the second half of their name). The impressive gains of the Albany Regency were largely offset in Albany by the city's traditional conservatism. Just outside the city limits the paternal influence of Stephen Van Rensselaer III, emanating from his North Albany manor house, still dominated the lives of thousands of tenants who held hereditary leaseholds on both sides of the Hudson River in Rensselaer and Albany counties. The physical presence of the popular Governor De Witt Clinton, whose canal had brought so much prosperity to Albanians, also did much to slow the trend to rally under the Regency.

The Neighborhood Saloon

The role of the neighborhood saloonkeeper at the turn of the century was an important one in the sociopolitical hierarchy of any city. In a society where the average man worked 10 or 12 hours a day, six days a week, the saloonkeeper was one of the privileged few among the working classes to have virtually continuous freedom to listen to, discuss, debate, and in rare instances even read the news of the day. If he lived in an immigrant neighborhood, he was of necessity bilingual, to some extent at least, and was looked upon as an interpreter of current events by many a trusting patron of foreign extraction.

A smart saloonkeeper allowed his establishment, generally located on a corner, to become a forum for debate on a wide variety of controversial issues, from politics to the rights of labor—with himself ever present to serve graciously as the recognized judge or referee of the day's discourse. The saloon, when properly managed, became the average man's "salon" or neighborhood club. From behind his magnificent mahogany symbol of office, the proprietor presided over an endless drama of debates and pleas concerning the true grass-roots issues of day-to-day life. No problem was too great or too small to merit his sympathetic attention or patient ear.

The saloon was the gathering place of the unemployed, and the last refuge of worried family heads struggling under the pressures and uncertainties of an economy fluctuating between boom and bust. At the same time it was the mecca of the successful, whose exploits at sports, gambling, and politics could only be properly celebrated over the cool refreshment served at the local "watering hole"—or, in lieu of a personal appearance, delivered to the patron by eager neighborhood boys, sent to the saloon with tin "growlers" to be filled to the brim with sudsy brew.

Promotions were celebrated and layoffs mourned as the workingman quaffed his nickel beer and devoured his free lunch. Occasionally a toast would be raised to a beloved sweetheart, a sainted mother, or a loving wife or daughter—with the unspoken understanding that any and all of them would be thrown out into the street if they so much as set foot across the threshold of this totally male world.

It was only logical that the progressive saloon should have a back room to accommodate the more serious conversations that required a degree of privacy. Back rooms offered seclusion for union meetings, political caucuses, and serious business deals—most of which the smart saloonkeeper would be privy to.

In time the brighter and more enterprising saloonkeepers turned their wealth of diversified contacts and grass-roots information to their own advantage and that of their families. Assuming that the saloonkeeper was prudent in his life-style, he could amass at least a modest fortune; in good times and in bad, his was a business that prospered steadily. If he had children, and most did, then the proceeds of the saloon would be used to obtain an education for his sons and daughters far in excess of his own. The next generation would be filled with insurance men and lawyers who, armed with a bartender's understanding and a gentleman's education, could aspire to and achieve high positions in politics, business, education, and the church that would have been closed to their fathers. Boston's Kennedy dynasty owes at least half its makeup to such a heritage; in Albany the phenomenon was epitomized by John Augustin McCall.

Born and raised above his father's saloon on the corner of Orange and Chapel streets in lower Gander Bay, McCall rose to become state superintendent of insurance, a trusted advisor to Governor (and later President) Grover Cleveland, and president of New York Life Insurance Company, building that corporation into the largest insurance company in the world. From a townhouse still standing at State Street and Sprague Place, he moved to New York and acquired his substantial fortune. Along with Anthony N. Brady, a native of the South End's Westerlo Street, and Tom Murray of Arbor Hill's Colonie Street, he was active in that city's Albany Society, composed of ex-Albanians who had moved to the metropolis to pursue great fortunes. A few years before his death in 1906, he donated a great carved pulpit to the Cathedral of the Immaculate Conception in memory of his Irish immigrant father—who continued to run the saloon until the day he died.

John O'Connell, the Irish-American who catered to a heavily German clientele in the South End, had his opposite number on the north side of town. Glatz's Hotel, at Broadway and North Ferry Street opposite old St. Peter's Hospital, catered to the Irish of the Basin and lumber district despite the German origin of its proprietor.

From north to south, on the hills and in the hollows, and "up on the hill" as well, each neighborhood boasted of (or lamented) one or more of these establishments, where a man could tarry awhile and claim sanctuary from the real world of family and work outside.

In North Albany there was Jennings's place on Broadway. In the West End, Horan's, on the point of Livingston and Third, and Murray's, at Allen and Central, did a lively business catering to the cattlemen and railroad workers of the West Albany yards; while further west at Colvin, Schaeffer's, with a recreational pond behind, catered to the lively traffic of the Schenectady Turnpike. In Pine Hills, Chris's Klondike Hotel, sitting opposite the juncture of Madison and Western, held a near monopoly over the newly developing neighborhood. Bulgaro's and Lombardo's, names still familiar today, catered to their countrymen in Little Italy, while DeBerry's at Elk and Northern and Yanas's on Lexington served the refreshment and social needs of the city's hardworking Poles.

Like the South End, Arbor Hill was densely populated and well supplied with saloons. Flynn's stood at First and North Swan, and Flanagan and Farrell's on North Lark. A half-block away, on the corner of Livingston, was Frank and Cyril Cassidy's, where horseshoe pitching in the backyard of the saloon was a Sunday afternoon ritual.

J.F. Toohey's at 39 South Pearl Street was among the city's well-frequented saloons.

Alward's at Livingston and Northern competed with Brennan's at the same intersection, the latter establishment achieving particular fame as the traditional first stop on the way home from funeral corteges choosing the high road from the cemeteries in nearby Menands. On such occasions the men of the party would enter the welcome way station, while the ladies would be brought lemonade or toddy as they waited in their carriages outside.

North Swan Street, along with Northern Boulevard, served as Arbor Hill's neighborhood shopping district. On the upper end of the street, below Livingston, Mike's Log Cabin, whose dimly lit booths and scarred tables boasted the initials of at least two generations of young love, had its origins in the pre-World War I era as Sheehan's Saloon.

McGarry's was at Clinton and Lark, while the Irish Lords, at Monroe and Sheridan Place, served the men of lower Sheridan Hollow. O'Connor's had its start on Washington above the

Capitol until development of Capitol Hill by the state forced it to move downtown to the Fireplace opposite the Albany Garage. At Central and Lark it was Bill Igo's, whose circa 1805 building is still standing, the last of a commercial row of Federal-style buildings that sprang up along the old Bowery when the Schenectady Turnpike opened. Farther up on Central, Pauley's Hotel, built on the site of the first St. John's German Lutheran Cemetery, was representative of several German-run establishments along the Avenue. It, like the present Three S's on West Hill, or the former Schramm's on Yates Street in lower Pine Hills, probably retains as much of the flavor of the early pre-Prohibition era as any establishment in the area.

The list of well-frequented saloons, as the temperance advocates were eager to point out, seemed endless. Swift Mead's White Elephant at Maiden Lane and James, and Dwyer's on Green Street near Division, offered first-class free lunches to compete with the city's better hotels and restaurants for the patronage of downtown businessmen

and politicians. Along South Pearl Street were many such saloons, such as Toohey's and Farley's below Madison, and one establishment on the corner of Van Zandt which succeeded in circumventing the ethnic question by calling itself the House of All Nations.

Closer to downtown, the ever-popular McNamara's on South Pearl below Beaver served as the gathering place for a regular city dwellers' harvest rite. Each fall Happy Conroy would recruit and organize large work crews who departed by the wagon load for the hill towns of Schoharie County as hop pickers, in order that the great breweries of the capital city, along with their many hundreds of prideful workers, might never cease to produce their foaming brew. In other neighborhoods the annual hop harvest was viewed as a family ritual, with whole families taking part in the annual trip to the country as a means of supplementing their income while at the same time experiencing a welcome break in the urban routine.

Howell and Tenney

Dictionary of American Portraits

In the election of 1836, Van Buren, as the handpicked successor to the legendary Andrew Jackson, won a slim victory over William Henry Harrison. The Kinderhook "fox" became the first President born under the American flag.

With Van Buren in the White House, Marcy reelected to the governorship, and Mayor Erastus Corning in Albany's City Hall, the stars shone brightly on the Democratic party and its indomitable Regency—just as the clouds of economic disaster began to gather on the horizon.

Early in his sole term of office as President, Van Buren's bubble burst. The Panic of 1837 was a product of the shaky financial climate of the times. Land speculation and overexpansion in canals, railroads, cotton, and slaves, all accomplished with borrowed money, contributed to the crash in which banks and merchants failed and factories closed, forcing workers out onto the streets at the same time as a major crop failure sent the price of wheat and flour to prohibitive heights.

Incumbent Presidents have traditionally paid the penalty for depressions during their terms. Since the Democrats had abolished the monopolistic Bank of the United States, there was in fact some justification for holding them responsible for the long series of bank failures that would destroy many a family's life savings—a recurring disaster until the banking reforms of the New Deal nearly a century later.

Van Buren's administration never really got off the ground. His entire four-year term was spent fighting the depression, to little effect. In 1840 the Whigs, in a spirited national campaign that would set the model for future media specialists, rolled over the Democrats with a campaign based on hard cider, huge hollow balls pushed from village to village (symbolizing the "gathering majority"), log cabins, and the catchy slogan "Tippecanoe and Tyler too." Bitterly the Democrats, who had lost both the Albany mayoralty and the state government in the early years of the depression, complained that they had been "shouted down, sung out, lied down, and drunk down."

Thurlow Weed was ecstatic over his victory. In William Seward, who was reelected to a second term as governor, he had found a capable vote getter and statesman. In 1840 Weed could not resist gloating in his Albany

Above left
Built with convict labor of white stone from the Sing Sing quarries in 1842, the State Hall on Eagle Street once housed the state records and was occupied by various state officials.
Above
Though known for the purchase of Alaska from Russia in 1867 for $7,200,000 in gold, William Henry Seward also served two terms as governor of New York in 1838 and 1840. The Whigs were extremely happy with his administration.
Facing page
Albany Regency leader Silas Wright replaced Democrat William Bouck as New York governor in 1844. He believed that the common-school system of New York should make children "American freemen and American citizens, and to qualify them to judge and choose for themselves in matters of politics, religion, and government."

Evening Journal: "To all those with whom we have bet—please call one at a time, approaching our office from Washington Street [now Avenue] and departing through Congress Street, keeping in line so as not to block up the highway." Weed, who had acquired the title of "Dictator," was relishing his new prominence with zest.

Martin Van Buren did not disappear from politics, and the famous Albany Regency remained a force in New York and national politics for several years to come. In 1842, with Seward refusing to run, the Democrats won the governorship with William Bouck. Two years later he was replaced by the capable Regency leader Silas Wright, while fellow Democrat James Polk was elected President.

The election of 1844 saw both parties flirting with nativism, foreshadowing the "Know Nothing" campaign of 1848 with its scurrilous campaigns against foreign and particularly Irish Catholic influences.

In that year Van Buren, still tainted by the memory of hard times, consented to run for President on the Free-Soil ticket, on a platform of "free soil, free speech, free labor, and free men." Although he did not win a single electoral vote, his campaign eroded New York's support for Democratic candidate Lewis Cass, throwing the state and the election to the Whig candidate, Zachary Taylor, a Mexican War hero who had never before held civil office. With the defection of Van Buren from the Democratic party, more split than ever over the slavery issue, the days of the famous Albany Regency were over.

Without question, Van Buren had shown many strong qualities during his career in New York and national politics. As secretary of state he had been recognized as the most capable member of Jackson's cabinet, and his loyalty to the President was unquestioned. Philosophically Van Buren had been inconsistent, changing his position on controversial issues to suit the times. His was the art of the politician; his ability to connive and manipulate people and issues to achieve his goals earned him the appellations of "Little Magician" and "Fox"—used as terms of endearment, admiration, derision, or rebuke, according to the occasion.

But above all the Jackson-Van Buren years brought about the first flowering of American democracy. The undereducated tenant farmers and hired hands of the patroon had never identified with the family-owned farms and great plantations of Jefferson's idealized bucolic republic. And to the teamsters, cartmen, and day laborers who earned their wages in the sweaty factories or along the crowded docks of Albany and Troy, Hamilton's urban world of high finance and industrial entrepreneurship was far removed from their daily existence. The government of the followers of these two great men seemed equally irrelevant to the great mass of the American people.

Prior to 1829, when Jackson took office, the civil service of the United States had grown remote and unresponsive; many federal offices remained in the hands of octogenarians who proudly displayed letters of appointment from George Washington a half-century before. Prior elections had brought new bureaucrats to power but rarely resulted in having many incumbents turned out.

Jacksonian democracy meant more than just the figurative and literal opening up of government to the masses, who on Inauguration Day invaded the White House by the thousands, causing considerable damage

until the thirsty mob could be lured out onto the lawn by the promise of free liquor and punch. Jackson truly believed that virtually no job in government should be so specialized as to exclude the average American, and he immediately set about eliminating or breaking down such positions so that citizens could "rotate" in and out of them. In some cases the system worked reasonably well; in others it was a predictable disaster.

By later 19th-century standards, the percentage of federal officeholders actually replaced over the course of Jackson's eight years—some 2,000 out of 11,000—does not seem excessively high. But the precedent set— summed up by Regency stalwart William Marcy, "To the victor belong the spoils of the enemy"—evolved into the infamous patronage or "spoils" system that affected every level of American government until well into the 20th century.

City Politics, 1840–1900

In 1840 the selection of Albany's mayor was taken out of the Common Council and, for the first time in its 154-year history, placed squarely in the hands of the city's voters.

Owing principally to the influence of Thurlow Weed and a succession of aristocratic Whig politicians, the city voted in the Whig column for 10 of 14 two-year elections; only one Democrat, Eli Perry, was able to succeed himself for more than one term. By the mid-1850s, however, the Whig Party, by trying to be all things to all people, had succeeded in standing for nothing, and its momentum was captured by the newly formed Republican Party. Thurlow Weed made the same graceful transition to that new party as he had in graduating from Anti-Masonic to Whig Party a quarter-century before. And as expected, he once again brought his influential newspaper with him, which he continued to edit as a pillar of the Republican Party and press until he moved to New York City in 1866.

The office of mayor, unlike that of governor, however, was not to be so politically portable. In the second half of the 19th century, the new Republican Party found little success in the immigrant-dominated city politics of Albany.

Albany Democrats took pains to identify with the newly arrived immigrants, particularly the Irish. Erastus Corning, Sr., a former mayor and great-grandfather of the present mayor, was a champion of the Irish cause and addressed rallies on the topic at the state Capitol. As a congressman during the Civil War, he was instrumental in leading the Copperhead (antiwar) movement and championing the rights of young immigrants, who were drafted as soon as they arrived in this country. At the outset of the war, he was a party to a lawsuit brought against President Lincoln in a civil-rights case that won him considerable notoriety.

In 1856 the incumbent Whig mayor, William Parmalee, died in office—the last Whig mayor the city would know. Starting with the election of May 1856, all future mayors would be either Democratic or Republican. In the hotly contested election of 1856, both mayoral candidates, Democrat Eli Perry and Republican John Quackenbush, were declared to be the winner. Both were paid full salaries for the two-year term of office, while the city recorder actually ran the affairs of the city. Perry was reelected in 1858, followed by fellow Democrat George H. Thacher in 1860. Perry won again in 1862 and 1864; Thacher again in 1866; another Democrat, Charles Bleecker, in 1868; and Thacher once again in 1870.

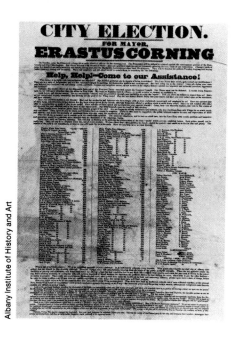

CITY ELECTION.
FOR MAYOR,
ERASTUS CORNING

Facing page
Erastus Corning, Sr., (1797-1872), the most prominent of the Yankee merchant princes that dominated the city after the New England "invasion" of the early 19th century, was a driving force in the formation of the New York Central Railroad in 1851. He served as its president. As a politically active Democrat, Corning became alderman, mayor, state senator, and Congressman. During the Civil War he successfully sued President Lincoln for civil rights violations. Though moderately educated, Corning, who was a lover of books, served as regent of the University for nearly four decades. On a farm just south of Albany, Corning resided with his wife (also shown here), the former Harriet Weld, and his children. The Corning offspring married into the most prominent Yankee families in the city. For four generations their descendants have followed in the senior Corning's footsteps, distinguishing themselves in many facets of Albany life.
Above
This election broadside of 1840 touts the reform platform of Mayor Erastus Corning, Sr., in his unsuccessful bid to become Albany's first popularly elected mayor. Corning was defeated by fellow Democrat Jared Louis Rathbone that year.

I came here October 8, 1870, when the foundation was being built, from Washington, D.C., where I had been employed as a stone-cutter on the United States Capitol and other public buildings. At that time the building was under the management of a commission, of which the Hon. Hamilton Harris was Chairman. The cornerstone was laid June 24, 1871, by the Masonic fraternity. After the laying of the corner-stone, measures were taken to push forward the construction with the greatest rapidity. I worked as a stone-cutter on the building until May 25, 1872, when I was appointed assistant foreman of stone-cutters, which position I held until 1876, when Mr. Reynolds, who had been principal foreman, died. I was appointed his successor. In 1883 I was further promoted to Superintendent of Granite Work by Commissioner Perry.

In my department are employed almost two-thirds of the whole force on the building, the total of which is about eight hundred and fifty men. In my office are two clerks, one messenger and one assistant.

The average number of men employed yearly since 1870, is 1,100. . . .

James J. Mitchell, quoted in George R. Howell and Jonathan Tenney, *Bi-Centennial History of Albany*, 1886.

In 1872 another hotly contested election divided the city. Thacher was at first declared reelected, but in January of 1873 Edmund L. Judson, the Republican, was declared to be the city's first Republican mayor since John Quackenbush. Judson held office for the balance of the term and was reelected in 1874. He was replaced in 1876 by A. Bleecker Banks, a Democrat.

In 1878 Michael N. Nolan became the city's first Irish Catholic mayor—three years after Troy elected its first Irish mayor, Edward Murphy, and two years before Boston followed suit. Nolan was returned to office in 1880 and again in 1882, but in June of 1883 the courts ruled that his Republican rival, John Swinburne, had actually won by 118 votes.

The election went to Banks in 1884; John Boyd Thacher, son of the earlier Mayor Thacher, in 1886; Edward Maher in 1888; and James Manning in 1890 and 1892. All of them were Democrats. In 1894 Oren Wilson, a Republican, was elected for a single two-year term. Thacher was returned to office in 1896 and was replaced in 1898 by fellow Democrat Thomas Van Alstine.

Of the 22 mayoral elections between 1856 and 1898, the Republican party won only four, not counting one that was declared a tie with neither candidate actually taking office. Of the four victories only two were clearcut—Judson's second term in 1874 and Wilson in 1894; the other two—Judson's first term and Swinburne's—were the result of court reversals of the initial outcome. Ironically, perhaps, these two men, who were related to one another, ended up immortalized in the name of a street and a park, respectively, on the west side of the city.

CHAPTER 8
POLITICS IN THE 20TH CENTURY

Something happened just at the start of the new century, within the staunchly Democratic atmosphere of Albany, to lay the groundwork for establishing one of the most powerful political "machines" ever to exist in New York State. In 1900 Mayor Thomas Van Alstine, a Democrat, announced his intention to step down; his position had been promised to a young man named Bowe, from Albany's South End. But the Democratic boss at the time, Judge D-Cady Herrick, decided that the incumbent mayor should run again, promises to Bowe notwithstanding. The resulting split in the party over this broken promise decidedly affected the voter turnout. It was also rumored that the powerful Patrick ("Packy") McCabe, the Herrick faction's opponent in the party, had made a deal with William Barnes, the "boy wonder" who ran the local Republican Party, agreeing to back the Republican candidate, James Blessing, to throw the mayoral victory to the Republican camp. It would take 20 years for the Democrats to recover from this political debacle.

Facing page
State Street, just below Eagle, was lined with spectators during a women's suffrage parade in June 1914.

Above
William "Billy" Barnes, Jr., sire of a prominent Yankee family and editor of the Albany Evening Journal, *took advantage of a split in the Democratic Party to dominate city and county politics during the first 20 years of the century. As a state and national committeeman, he wielded influence well beyond Albany, and was instrumental in costing Theodore Roosevelt the nomination for President in 1912. His statement that "labor is a commodity" eventually brought about his defeat by the O'Connell organization in 1921.*

The Barnes Era

For years William Barnes occupied the "boss" position common in political life throughout the 19th and early 20th centuries, when a nonpartisan press was virtually unknown in the nation. This potent figure, based in Albany, was the grandson of Thurlow Weed of national Republican fame; he had also inherited Weed's influential position as editor and publisher of the Albany *Evening Journal*. Like his grandfather before him, Barnes was a dyed-in-the-wool Republican, strongly in favor of business interests and active on three political fronts: local, statewide, and national. He never held public office himself, preferring to take important committee posts within the Republican Party. Barnes would not allow his political protegés to develop "cults of personality" around themselves, and he frequently shifted candidates about, allowing them two to six years in a particular office and then moving them elsewhere, or even having them retire from the ranks for a while.

Owing in large part to Barnes's manipulative skills and strong leadership, Albany's long tradition of Democratic rule was gradually eroded; by 1920 voter enrollment heavily favored the Republican Party. During the period of Barnes's reign, "Packy" McCabe remained chairman of the local Democratic Party, a position seized from D-Cady Herrick after the disastrous election of 1900. It was widely believed that McCabe held his position because he had arranged a convenient patronage setup with Barnes whereby loyal Democrats managed through him to get jobs—which in the early 1900s were essential for the survival of low-income, immigrant-stock Albany families.

The peak of "Billy" Barnes's power came between 1911 and 1914, when he served as Republican state chairman. From 1912 to 1916 he was also a Republican national committeeman. During the presidential nominating caucus in 1912, it is probable that Barnes actually cost Theodore Roosevelt the Republican nomination, which then propelled Roosevelt into his independent "Bull Moose" stance, splitting the Republican voters and consequently ensuring the election of Woodrow Wilson. During his campaign, T.R. referred to Barnes as a "corrupt boss"—an epithet that Barnes resented. He sued Roosevelt for slander, and although the court did not find Roosevelt guilty, he was held liable for the court costs.

As the Barnes reign continued, charges of widespread civic corruption were voiced by newspapers and rival political factions. In 1911 a New York State legislative investigation produced an extremely damaging report decrying the flagrant existence of gambling dens and brothels throughout Albany and calling for the removal of Barnes-backed Mayor James B. McEwan. Meanwhile, Barnes's reputation as the astute "boy wonder" politician was tarnishing. From both his newspaper and political posts he opposed Prohibition, which in some Republican circles was a popular cause, and he also protested the growing demand for women's suffrage. Preferring to leave the selection of candidates in the hands of party bosses, Barnes fought the direct primary. In 1918, as dissatisfaction mounted within the city, Barnes experienced a primary fight that displayed his vulnerability.

Into this boss-controlled political scene came young Daniel Peter O'Connell on his return in 1919 from Navy service aboard the U.S.S. *Prairie* during World War I. O'Connell and his three brothers, ironically enough, were the products of a Republican family, fourth-generation Irish, within Albany's South End—then a bustling neighborhood of immigrant families, primarily German—where their father, John, was the popular owner of a saloon at the corner of South Pearl Street and Fourth Avenue. John O'Connell was able to furnish his sons with ample contacts when they decided to move into the political arena.

Dan O'Connell was considered a "man's man." In his prominent position as a player and promoter of the Delphians, a spirited football team, Dan came into contact with other young athletes from the area, giving him name recognition beyond the South End. He also was a devotee of cockfighting, an avocation that brought him into association with the young male scions of the prestigious Corning family, who maintained a suburban farm at Kenwood. His brothers all took different paths. Pat became a leader of the First Ward and was widely known for his quiet charitable work. Edward went on to college and then law school, eventually proving invaluable to the Democratic Party because of his education and acumen in governmental affairs. John J. ("Solly") became a prizefight promoter, a gambler, and a frequenter of nightclubs, and for many years remained a registered Republican.

In 1919 the Democrats tapped a returning World War I captain, Reynolds King Townsend, grandson of a former mayor, to run for the top position on the city ticket. Dan O'Connell, virtually unknown and untried in politics, aimed for the lesser position of assessor. He was pitted against aging John Franey, a South End veteran politician who had held a variety of positions under the Republicans, including that of county clerk. Franey, who had problems with William Barnes, viewed this as a comeback attempt in politics; but unlike other Republicans that year, he unwisely accepted the backing of the less-than-popular Prohibition Party.

When the votes were counted, almost the entire Democratic slate had gone down to defeat, excepting, of course, the usual Democratic aldermen from North Albany, Cathedral Hill, and Sheridan Hollow (Gander Bay). But citywide the Democrats did have one winning candidate—Daniel P. O'Connell, who had campaigned in his wartime sailor's uniform.

O'Connell had made the first significant crack in the power structure of the Republican machine since 1899. Such a signal victory was not to be thrown away, and Boss Packy McCabe turned over the Democratic command post to young O'Connell. In the ensuing municipal elections— which at that time came every two years—the South End O'Connell brothers successfully aligned themselves with the powerful Yankee-patrician Corning family, men of a different stamp indeed, yet linked to them through interests in sports and politics.

For the Barnes-controlled city administration, 1920 and 1921 proved difficult years. The Republican boss had become increasingly remote. He seldom ventured into local politics now, choosing to rule from the background, and his image as a shadowy, behind-the-curtains puppeteer pulling political strings was scarcely alluring. His stands against women's suffrage and Prohibition were problems enough. Then, during the election of 1921, he made a fateful statement. "Labor is a commodity," he said, and like all commodities, it was to be exploited on the economic market. The building-trades unions were already disgruntled with the awarding of city construction jobs to out-of-town contractors who hired out-of-town workers. Organized labor turned against Barnes en masse.

Resentment against the Barnes coterie grew, exacerbated by newspaper campaigns, particularly by the Democratic *Times-Union,* which was headed by former Governor Martin H. Glynn (who, as lieutenant

Erastus Corning 2nd

Erastus Corning 2nd

Top
From his election as a city assessor in 1919 until his death in 1977, Daniel Peter O'Connell was the undisputed leader of the Albany County Democratic organization. His fedora hat became the symbol of the party patriarch whose advice, support, and consent were sought after by generations of politicians who regularly visited him at his Whitehall Road home or his camp that overlooked the city from the height of the Helderberg mountains.
Above
Here is a view of the mayor's office in Albany City Hall, prior to renovations in 1917.

Top
A former Democratic congressman and proprietor of the Albany Times-Union, *Martin H. Glynn became governor in 1910 after Governor Sulzer was impeached by Tammany legislators. He maintained a Spanish-style townhouse on Willett Street, as well as an elaborate country home, now the Bethlehem Elks Club. To this date, Glynn is the only Albanian ever to achieve the office of governor.*
Above
William Stormont Hackett, shown here in 1921, rose from a South End schoolboy to become an accomplished banker and a popular and effective mayor. His powerful administration conscientiously applied itself to many of the city's problems.

governor, had succeeded Governor William Sulzer after his impeachment by Tammany Hall forces in 1913). Various inflammatory city issues were served up on a daily basis to the voting population. A school-construction study known as the Watson Report was suppressed by Barnes, leading to widespread speculation of wrongdoing that did more harm than anything in the report itself—including significant cost overruns in the construction in the South End of Public School 14, which later became Philip Schuyler High School. Probably the worst scandal resulted from the bankruptcy of the Montgomery Coal Company. When its records were exposed in legal proceedings before respected Judge William Woolard, it was found that 79 carloads of coal, valued at $18,000, had never been delivered to city buildings; during the same period, the company had delivered numerous loads of free coal to the homes of city officials.

Meanwhile a prolonged and difficult transit strike, which occasionally erupted into violence, was widely supported by Albanians, who in many cases boycotted trolley cars manned by "scabs" and walked long distances to work. The Barnes-run administration was clearly identified with the owners of the United Traction Company, and the transit strike added to the Republicans' antilabor reputation.

For their part, the Democrats shrewdly recognized the ethnic diversity of the city's population. They chose once again to balance off Irish-Catholic political candidates with a frontrunner from the Yankee aristocracy that controlled the city's banks and most of its industries. Through friendship with Edwin Corning, the O'Connell brothers were introduced to William Stormont Hackett. Like them, he was a South Ender. Through hard work and initiative he had risen from his humble background to become a respected attorney; he was now president of the Albany Safe Deposit Company, as well as a bank director.

Hackett put on a vigorous mayoral campaign that was aided by the newspapers. He spoke, or debated, at every opportunity. The GOP candidate for mayor, William Van Rensselaer Erving, agreed at first to debate him at the Women's City Club but then went back on his word—a poor move indeed in view of the recent passage of the 19th Amendment. At one point, in an attempt to discredit the O'Connells, Erving inadvertently maligned the South End by saying they came from the wrong kind of upbringing to serve in high public office. His comments did not go unnoticed. More than anything else, this indirect attack on a large, politically astute and active section of Albany brought about the Republican defeat. In 1921 virtually all city and county offices were won by the Democratic Party, which to this day has never lost a firm hold on Albany city and county politics. After this blundering campaign, William Barnes left Albany forever—with the aid, Dan O'Connell later revealed, of $5,000 borrowed from him, the new Albany boss; the loan was promptly repaid.

The Democrats Come to Power

William S. Hackett's new administration, buoyed up by the Democratic landslide, was as welcome to the city as a rejuvenating springtime. Efficiently run, it addressed itself to many of the city's problems and citizens' complaints that had accumulated during the waning years of Barnes's rule. In his four years of office, Hackett completely reorganized the city's water department, which became a hallmark of positive Democratic accomplishment in the years ahead. Other deeds and attitudes that kept the Democrats in power included good water, preferential treatment of senior citizens in many low-paying jobs,

Erastus Corning 2nd

Erastus Corning 2nd

neighborhood contact through a well-organized committeemen's system, accessibility to government officials by the average citizen, and relatively low taxes for services delivered. During the Hackett administration, the new water department developed a fine source of water, with the Alcove Reservoir in the Helderberg Mountains, in the towns of Coeymans and Westerlo (where today the city of Albany is still the chief taxpayer). It also renovated all the city's schools and built four new schools—one of which would ultimately be named as a memorial to the first Democratic mayor of Albany in the 20th century, William S. Hackett.

The city government was reorganized and streamlined. The mayor's term was changed from two to four years. Ironically, the elected Board of Assessors, Dan O'Connell's steppingstone to power, was abolished in favor of a single Commissioner of Assessment and Taxation. O'Connell might have his imitators in later years, but none could duplicate his path to political hegemony.

Undisputed control of the local Democratic Party was now amicably shared among three O'Connell brothers (Dan, Pat, and Edward) and two Corning brothers—Edwin, elected as the party's New York State chairman in 1926, and Parker, who in 1922 had replaced Democrat Peter Ten Eyck as congressman.

Tragedy struck Albany on March 4, 1926, when Mayor Hackett, reelected and at the height of his popularity and civic power, and already mentioned as a potential candidate for governor, was killed in an automobile accident in Cuba.

John Boyd Thacher II, as president of the Common Council, succeeded Hackett as mayor of Albany—the third member of his family to hold the office. Thacher, who served during World War I as a YMCA director and later as an ambulance driver, had originally run for treasurer on the ill-fated Democratic ticket of 1919. His great interest in physical education and outdoor sports found expression in ambitious public programs initiated during his 14 years as mayor, including numerous playgrounds, swimming pools, and a municipal golf course.

The Thacher administration was the first Democratic regime in this century to experience a scandal; in this case it involved the boss himself; Daniel P. O'Connell. The Albany Baseball Pool, which had originated as an in-house company pool at the J.B. Lyons Printing Company in 1905, had expanded into a multimillion-dollar business which the O'Connells virtually controlled. In 1927 Dan pleaded guilty in a Boston federal court

Above left
Democrats Cornelius A. Casey, Jim Farley, Dan O'Connell, and Edward O'Connell (left to right) are seen during the Chicago Convention in 1928.

Above
Two of the three mayors elected to serve Albany citizens in the past 60 years are shown in this photograph. Edwin Corning (left), Albany attorney and grandson of a previous mayor, succeeded William Stormont Hackett (right) after his untimely death in Cuba in 1926. He served for 14 years and resigned to accept a position as Children's Court Judge. At the writing of this book, Thacher's successor has served for 40 years — the longest tenured mayor of any city in America. He is currently seeking his 11th term.

JOHN OLEY

*Alias John Joseph Oley,
John Walsh, John Kinstler,
John Blake.*

Description:
Age, 32; height, 5 ft. 10½;
weight, 164 lbs.; clean shav-
en; large build; medium
sandy complexion; brown
hair; brown eyes; two vac-
cinations on left arm.

F. P. C.
9 R 8 Ref 9 R 8
1 Rt   1 Rr

PERCY GEARY

*Alias Jack Edwards, John
Nolan, Frank Andrews,
Frank Edwards.*

Description:
Age, 32; height, 5 ft. 9 in.;
weight, 131 lbs.; clean shav-
en; medium build; medium
complexion; blue eyes; light
chestnut hair.

F. P. C.
9 A R 9 Ref 1 A R 9
2   Aa   2   Aa

FRANCIS OLEY

Description: Age, 27; height, 5 ft. 9 in.; weight, 150 lbs.; clean
shaven; medium build; hazel eyes; brown hair.

The above may be riding in the following cars:

1. Cadillac Sedan, Color Green, 1928 Model. License 1 A 64-08 N. Y. (1933).
2. Buick Sedan, Color Blue, 1931 Model. License 1 A 77-96 N. Y. (1933).
3. Buick Coupe, Color Maroon, 1931 Model. License 1 A 9712 N. Y. (1933).

Dennis Holzman

Erastus Corning 2nd

Above
This 1933 poster depicts three of the men involved in the kidnapping of John J. O'Connell, the nephew of Democratic Party Chairman Dan O'Connell.
Above right
Governor Alfred E. Smith (left) is posed with Lieutenant Governor Edwin Corning, who had previously served as New York State Democratic chairman. Due to poor health, Corning decided in 1928 to step down after one term as lieutenant governor. His decision paved the way for Franklin Delano Roosevelt to serve as the party's nominee.

to a minor violation of the antilottery laws and was forced to pay a fine of $750. In 1929–30 the gambling connection again surfaced, this time involving charges that the pool was crooked—rigged to favor the O'Connells' henchmen, who would either force winners to split the proceeds of the pool with fictitious tying ticket-holders or would fix the pool in various ways so that party loyalists were in a better position to win. In 1929 Dan O'Connell served two days in a New York City jail for contempt of court. The next year he spent 90 days in jail, in an extremely luxurious incarceration that allowed him occasionally to be escorted to Broadway shows.

In July 1933 the city was shocked by the kidnapping of John J. O'Connell, Jr., —Solly's son and Dan's nephew—who was seized outside his Putnam Street home by four men who later demanded a $250,000 ransom. At one point in this sensational case, a payment of $42,500 was made in Washington Park by the O'Connell family to representatives of the kidnappers. The money was never recovered; some say it still lies buried somewhere within the 98-acre park. Young John O'Connell was finally returned 23 days after the ordeal began, having been held first in a barn in the Helderberg Mountains and then in Hoboken, New Jersey. A number of people, including gangsters Manny Strewl and Johnny Oley, were rounded up and sentenced to long prison terms under the anti-kidnapping Lindbergh Law.

Generally, the Democratic Party in Albany was respected throughout the state. By 1931 there was not a single Republican alderman left in the Common Council, a situation that exists to the present day. The last ward to go Democratic was the old 16th Ward, which included the "silk-stocking district" on State Street opposite Washington Park.

During the 1930s, the Democratic organization run by the O'Connells experienced two notable defections. Reynolds King Townsend (nicknamed "Cap"), who had headed the ticket in 1919 when Dan O'Connell was elected assessor, became disenchanted with the political setup and in 1933 headed an unsuccessful fusion ticket against City Hall. He had previously served in the important post of city chairman of the Democratic Party—a position that now was abolished. The abolition of another party office eliminated William V. Cooke from public life. Cooke, a popular assemblyman from North Albany who was active in New York State gubernatorial conventions and had facilitated the nominations of Al Smith, had served as Commissioner of Public Safety since the Hackett administration. In 1936 the position was eliminated, to be replaced by two commissioners, respectively, for fire and police—offices that lasted for the next three decades.

Other party stalwarts, however, managed to progress throughout the various offices of government. A fascinating aside to the O'Connell story is that of Edwin Corning, father of the present mayor. Corning had served briefly as Albany County's Democratic chairman during the Barnes reign, then as New York State chairman. Governor Alfred E. Smith asked him to run as his lieutenant governor in 1926, believing that Corning would enhance his own chances for the Democratic presidential nomination in 1928.

At the end of this term, Corning resigned from public office, and indeed all public life, choosing not to run for governor as Smith had expected. In poor health, Corning died in 1934 at a relatively young age. The gubernatorial nomination was offered instead to a younger former state senator and Assistant Secretary of the Navy named Franklin Delano Roosevelt.

Erastus Corning 2nd

The Port of Albany Is! It stands like a colossus astride the world thoroughfare, at the crucial point where the Deeper Hudson, stretching straight from the sea, meets the only low-level corridor through the Appalachians and the natural, direct route to the north. One outstretched hand probes the marts of Europe, South America, the Atlantic coast, and, in a magnificent sweep through the Panama Canal, the rich Pacific ports. The other hand, stretching west, lays questing fingers in the treasure houses of the mid-West, the Great Lakes states, reaching out to the Dakotas and up into the granaries of Manitoba and Saskatchewan.

The Port of Albany: Its Destiny, Its Birth, Its Growth, Its Promise. Published by Albany Port District Commission, 1932.

In 1935, a year after the death of his father, Erastus Corning 2nd—recently graduated from Yale and newly embarked on his own insurance business—was elected assemblyman from Albany. A year later his uncle, Parker Corning, having become disenchanted with the liberal Roosevelt administration, did not run for Congress, giving his nephew Erastus the opportunity to move up the political ladder. Parker Corning was replaced by popular State Senator William Byrne, who was himself replaced by Erastus Corning 2nd. Byrne remained in Congress until 1950, when he was succeeded by newspaperman Leo W. O'Brien, who went on to sponsor Alaska and Hawaii for statehood. Erastus Corning remained a state legislator through the balance of the Thacher years, until Mayor Thacher chose in 1940 to run for the position of Judge of the Children's Court.

Facing page
The mayor's office is a regular stopping point for visiting politicians and celebrities. In this 1945 photo Greer Garson is shown calling on His Honor Erastus Corning 2nd.
Top
Governor Herbert Lehman (center) poses with predecessors Alfred E. Smith and Franklin Delano Roosevelt. The three men occupied the Eagle Street Executive Mansion for over two decades.
Bottom
Erastus Corning 2nd meets with John F. Kennedy.

For one brief year, Herman Hoogkamp, an obscure printer who had spent nearly two decades as an alderman, served as acting mayor. The position would ordinarily have gone to the president of the Common Council, Frank Harris, then age 72, but Harris held a full-time position, equivalent to that of state treasurer, which he would have had to resign if he became mayor. He resigned his presidency of the Common Council instead, making room for Hoogkamp, who was then selected as mayor by the other aldermen.

In 1941 Erastus Corning 2nd was elected mayor of the city of Albany—a position held by his great-grandfather from 1834 to 1836. Corning represented the epitome of the Democratic Yankee dynasty. In addition to his mayoral ancestor, his grandfather had been an alderman, his uncle a congressman, his father county and state Democratic chairman, and his brother would become an assemblyman. As of this writing, Erastus Corning has been reelected to 10 four-year terms as mayor, making him the longest-tenured mayor of a major city in United States history.

POLITICS IN THE 20TH CENTURY

"The Capitol As Seen From City Hall"
By Erastus Corning 2nd—March 15, 1981

The Capitol of the State of New York has been the dominating and central feature of the ancient city of Albany for a century. It is much more than a building, much more than a place or places where the governmental affairs of the state are carried out. It is a place where people react to the conditions in the world at large and to the wishes of their constituents. The Capitol at Albany has seen many changes in the way governors and legislators, department heads and politicians, and people generally have looked at government and how government should best serve the people. The Capitol has also seen great changes in people's ideas—what used to be acceptable then, and is not now.

As mayor of the city of Albany for close to 40 years, I have looked at the Capitol from across the street hundreds of times every week, and have dealt with its tenants thousands of times. Before that I look back another 20 years to the time when Governor Miller lost his bid for reelection, and he and his wife and seven beautiful daughters left Albany and my 12-year-old heart was terribly saddened, if not broken.

I remember the wonderful relationship that my father had with Al Smith as Democratic state chairman, and then as lieutenant governor, and the times I used to sit on the rostrum in the state senate with my father and watch Barney Downing, the minority leader with his great sense of humor, tweak the nose of the temporary president of the senate, John Knight, and have all the best of it in the debate—but that John Knight always prevailed because he had the votes, and that was what

counted then, and that is what counts now. There were oyster roasts put on by my father for the senate and staff in the early spring of 1927 and 1928, catered by Jack Rosenstein of Jack's Restaurant (he is still going strong)—with two kegs of beer, one marked near beer, supposedly for the Republican members, and the real stuff for the Democrats, both of them far above the alcoholic content permitted by the Volstead Act. There were many professional "drys" in those days who did not practice what they preached. My father used to tell me that he was the first lieutenant governor since Prohibition came in who had not had liquor in his office next to the senate chamber, and he was far from being a dry either professionally, politically, or personally.

A few years later I came back to the Capitol as a freshman assemblyman, elected, as all the members were, for a one-year term at a salary of $2,500 a year plus round-trip travel expenses once a session between home and Albany. There were real advantages—no state or federal income tax on the legislative salary—and disadvantages such as just a desk and no office staff. Other advantages were a legislative index much less than an inch across, at least a 50–50 chance of adjournment by April 1st, and a state budget of under $300 million.

After that year I spent five years as a state senator, with part of the time as chairman of the Hudson Valley Survey Commission, and then came the start of my real Capitol watching—taking office as mayor of Albany just three weeks after the Japanese attack on Pearl Harbor.

Seven governors—Lehman, Poletti, Dewey, Harriman, Rockefeller, Wilson and now Carey—have come on the scene, a majority of them having thoughts of being President. Two of them, both gone from our midst now, came very close: Dewey, the best administrator of all; and Rockefeller, the one with the greatest vision.

The war years were exciting, new, with no one in state or local government having any real knowledge as to what to do—a time of experimentation, a time when all the goals of peacetime were shoved far back on the top shelf. Order eventually came out of confusion so that, after a year or so, both state and local governments were able to feel more or less comfortable in their new roles, and life went on.

Then came the end of the war and the years of catching up again: the Thruway, one of the earliest of the great modern highways; the vast expansion of peacetime government; new forms of federal and state assistance for social programs, public housing, urban renewal, federal aid to education; vast increases in federal, state, and local budgets. Up until the end of World War II, the various levels of government had kept pretty much to themselves. The city had little contact with federal programs and little more with the state, except for its support of education—education in this state being a state purpose by direction of the Constitution, and not a local purpose, except for the privilege of paying the largest share of the cost.

With the tremendous flow of federal dollars to state and local governments, it was inevitable that the home-rule powers of this and all other states became badly eroded. The erosion suffered locally grew even worse, being worn down on one side by the state and on the other by the federal government. This change in home rule and loss of state and local autonomy is the greatest difference that I have seen in almost four decades of Capitol watching. It is one of those features of government that is not easy for individuals to understand, but it has provided a fascinating study in change and a challenge to keep up with the change. While state and local authority has been reduced, local government has also become more complex, with many different and entirely new problems.

One thing that doesn't change is human nature—governors, legislators, department heads. Yes, the problems are different, but the people are the same, with the same desires and ambitions, the same abilities and faults. Capitol watching has been a lot of fun, always interesting, most of the time exciting, whether it was the most exhaustive state investigation of local government and politics in the history of our country in the war years under Governor Dewey, or the 15-year vision and construction of the fabulous Empire State Plaza under Governor Rockefeller.

History always needs to be looked at anew. Much that is forgotten is more interesting than what has been written down. As a Capitol watcher, I have had a good time. I have learned some of the things that change and some of those that do not. I do know for sure that we are always discovering new things in old history. I do know that we have here in Albany a great building with a century of existence that is always changing as new facts are discovered, always changing as government changes in its responsibility to the people, always changing as new actors come on the stage.

Mayor Erastus Corning 2nd and Congressman Samuel Stratton (former mayor of Schenectady) have collectively served as Democratic elected public officials for over 75 years.

Erastus Corning 2nd

One year after Erastus Corning's election, the national career of another prominent politician affected the city of Albany. Thomas E. Dewey, who had won a reputation as a crusading, crime-busting district attorney in the city of New York, had unsuccessfully sought the governorship against Herbert Lehman four years previously. Now, in 1942, he ran his new campaign with the promise that he would make an example of the O'Connell machine in Albany. Once elected, Dewey went to work almost immediately by investigating the election process that had taken place that fall. The "Dewey Investigations," which dominated city politics for more than three years, resulted in only 38 minor convictions for subverting the election laws. These tense years saw the regular district attorney supplanted, accusations brought against the Albany County jury system, and state troopers placed at the polls at election time.

But for all his bad relations with the city of Albany, Dewey's record as governor was good. Ever since Al Smith modernized the government in the 1920s, no one had done more to streamline the bureaucracy, reform the civil service, and open up opportunities to the minorities. Yet the one thing that Dewey had aspired to achieve—a well-publicized destruction of the Albany machine—remained beyond his grasp. Unquestionably, achieving it would have greatly helped his presidential campaign of 1948.

The Democratic Party leaders in Albany have generally been conservative. They backed Al Smith instead of Franklin Roosevelt in the 1932 presidential convention, and they never quite got along with James A. Farley, Roosevelt's strong associate (who eventually broke with the President over the third-term issue). The politicos also argued with a series of New York State Democratic chairmen throughout the 1950s and

1960s. But opposition to the party in Albany during the 1950s was, by today's standards, dull and unimaginative. Probably the Party had grown complacent.

The sociopolitical turbulence of the 1960s, coupled with the aggressive governorship of Nelson A. Rockefeller, brought new challenges to the Democratic Party, and the aging Democratic organization showed a surprising degree of resilience. In 1961 the State Investigation Committee (SIC) conducted a probe of the city's purchasing operations. As with the Dewey investigation more than a decade before, the end result was negligible in terms of actions taken for long-due improvement; but the publicity was sensational and gave heart to those who sought to eliminate the domination of Chairman Dan O'Connell's organization in Albany County politics.

A series of reform movements grew up during the 1960s, spearheaded by opponents of the Democratic machine identified primarily with an independent "reform movement" and only secondarily and incidentally with the Albany Republican Party. The revolt began in 1961 with Citizens' United Reform Effort (CURE), headed by 27-year-old the Reverend Robert Hudnut, a Presbyterian minister originally from Cincinnati, and his running mate, Charles M. Liddle of Albany. Four years later the campaign was less sensational, but in 1969, and again in 1973, the efforts to take over City Hall were well organized and well financed. In each case it was a third party that took the lead, with the Republican Party endorsing the effort.

By 1966 most of the ward leaders were men who had risen to power with O'Connell decades before. Now mostly in their sixties and seventies, they chose candidates for alderman and county supervisor to represent neighborhoods that no longer existed as they had in the 1920s—modern-

In 1964 former Attorney General Robert F. Kennedy campaigned in Albany for the position of United States Senator, an office he subsequently won and held until his death in June 1968. As the brother of the late President, who had also campaigned in the city six years earlier, Kennedy's popularity was at an unprecedented high and he attracted tremendous crowds. Local law enforcement officials struggled with security problems in crowds such as this one.

day "rotten boroughs," many of whose voters had long since migrated to uptown and suburban neighborhoods. As a result of population shifts, nearly one-third of the city was represented by a single ward (the 13th), while other wards such as the 4th (Dutch Hollow) and the 12th (Sheridan Hollow) held only a fraction of their former population. The election of 1966, however, was based on an entirely new structure of wards, endorsed by the League of Women Voters and imposed by the courts upon the city and county governments. From the Republican and third-party points of view, the new wards had distinct advantages. Rather than being drawn by neighborhoods, they created wide economic belts across the city that cut across traditional neighborhood lines. People living near the Crestwood Shopping Center, for example, voted in the same ward as those who lived across from the Madison Theater in Pine Hills. The people who lived across from Beverwyck Park on Washington Avenue were to vote for the same candidates as those living in the Loudon Arms Apartments far across the Tivoli hollow.

A massive shifting of candidates naturally occurred. The new county legislature that took office in 1967 included numerous new faces—young attorneys such as Thomas Brown, later assemblyman; E. David Duncan; Joseph Harris, later county judge; Paul Devane; Robert Leyden; and Harold Joyce, who alone among the group had also served on the old board of supervisors. Two years later, when aldermen were selected, they too included names and faces that were sometimes new to Albany politics, and almost invariably decades younger than their predecessors from the downtown wards that had dominated city politics for two previous generations.

During the 1960s, under Governor Rockefeller, efforts were made not only in the negative sense to bring pressure on the city's Democratic organization, but also with the positive intention of putting life into the generally disheartened Republican Party. The first major Republican candidate to be elected to office was Daniel E. Button, executive editor of the Albany *Times-Union,* which in the early 1960s had merged in general management with the *Knickerbocker News,* creating a newspaper monopoly under the Hearst Corporation while maintaining separate editorial boards. Button served two terms as congressman, defeating the popular president of the Common Council, Richard J. Conners, and Jacob Herzog, respectively. In 1970 he lost his job to neighboring Congressman Samuel S. Stratton, a former mayor of Schenectady, whose district was redrawn to include Albany County.

In 1968 the race for legislative and county offices became a debacle for the once seemingly invincible Democratic organization. The New York State senate seat was lost to Walter Langley, who had been active in the Albany Independent Movement (AIM); two years previously he had unsuccessfully sought a seat on the new Albany County legislature. Both assembly seats were lost—to Raymond Skuse, who replaced the aging Frank P. Cox, and to Fred Field, now supervisor of the town of Colonie, who replaced Albany attorney Harvey Lifset. Another Republican victory in the 1968 election went to Arnold W. Proskin, who was elected district attorney; during his career he conducted several investigations of the city administration, with few tangible results.

The State senate seat was held by the late Walter Langley, who stepped down in poor health in 1974; he was succeeded by Democrat Howard Nolan, who now holds the seat. Nolan had occasionally opposed Mayor Corning; he mounted a vigorous, if unsuccessful, primary challenge in

Top
The Nelson A. Rockefeller administration was marked by style and enthusiasm, as the energetic Republican governor literally changed the face of Albany. He is shown here with his wife "Happy," Lieutenant Governor Malcolm Wilson (left), who later succeeded him, and Mayor Corning (right), at one of his many receptions at the Executive Mansion.
Above
Governor Carey gives an address at the Port of Albany in 1976. Renewed interest in the economic potential of the port brought substantial state aid during the late 1970s.

1977. Ray Skuse held his assembly seat for only one term, losing in 1970 to Democrat Thomas W. Brown, but Field's seat, now held by Michael Hoblock, has remained in Republican hands ever since. (Both Field and Hoblock are from Colonie, which, like all three of the large suburban towns surrounding Albany, has been exclusively Republican for well over a century.)

City politics in the 1980s revolves to a considerable extent around neighborhood and citizens' group issues; at this writing, there are 23 neighborhood associations in the city. The Republican Party—undermined by deliberate efforts to recreate an independent third-party opposition that seeks only endorsement rather than leadership from the Republicans—has dwindled to slightly more than 2,400 registered voters, compared with more than 42,000 registered Democrats. The Republican Party itself is virtually dormant except in the towns surrounding the city, where it remains dominant.

Erastus Corning 2nd

In retrospect, the most difficult year in recent memory for the Democratic Party in Albany was 1973—probably the worst possible year for an incumbent mayor to run for office. The city's downtown area was virtually a ghost town. The new Ten Eyck Project—including a hotel, bank, office building, and parking garage—was little more than a barren landscape on the city's most prominent corner of State and Pearl. Taxes had increased more than 83 percent in one year because of the separation of the school board from the city's taxing authority. In the course of a decade the city had lost more than $10 million in revenue from areas now encompassed by the South Mall—still under construction at the time and not yet an asset to the city. The Mall, moreover, though not yet open to the public, was sufficiently completed that it no longer provided the large number of construction jobs that had been readily available throughout the previous decade.

Under these less-than-auspicious circumstances for an incumbent, a well-organized, well-financed, positive opposition campaign was launched by a prominent businessman, Carl Touhey, and citizen-activist Teresa Barber Cooke, a relative newcomer to Albany. A strong advocate of an independent, elected school board, Cooke had also been actively involved in economic criticism of the city's purchasing and assessment practices, creating, along with Robert Stein, the Albany Taxpayers' Association. Throughout 1972, through publicity and press conferences attacking one issue or another in city government, Cooke had succeeded in maintaining a high profile.

Touhey conducted an excellent campaign, coming within slightly more than 3,200 votes of defeating the then eight-term mayor. The following year Teresa Cooke was elected Albany County treasurer for the last year that the office existed; she went on to run unsuccessfully for county executive in 1975 when the new county charter of government took effect.

With Governor Rockefeller's resignation to become Vice-President of the United States under Gerald Ford, followed by the defeat of former Lieutenant Governor Malcolm Wilson in his bid for the governorship, the situation for the city's Republicans has grown progressively worse. Whether this condition will improve with the new Republican national administration remains to be seen. It seems clear, in any case, that any effort to change the status quo enjoyed by the Democratic Party in Albany for so many years would have to be coupled with a very strong independent movement.

CHAPTER 9

THE 20TH CENTURY CITY

The turn of the century in Albany was marked by the roar of cannon, the peal of church bells—and the opening of Union Station. The mammoth Beaux Arts railroad station stood as a symbol and reflection of the gilded age of industrialization, of robber barons and labor unrest and the uniting of a great country by rail from coast to coast. That era was now drawing to a close, but in the course of the new century, Union Station would take on a patina of personal meaning for generations of Albanians. Countless journeys and adventures would have their beginnings here. Families would be separated and reunited in its cavernous waiting room. And two generations of Albany mothers would see their sons off to war, many of them never to return.

Between the opening of Union Station in 1900 and its closing in 1968, Albany's physical appearance changed only gradually—except for the intrusion of several 1920s office buildings, still standing. An Albanian of the early 1960s, when construction began on the Mall, would have felt pretty much at home in Albany of the 1910s or 1920s.

The first major change in the downtown shopping district occurred in

Dennis Holzman

Above
Just after the turn of the century this Albany baseball team posed in front of a broadside advertising Harmanus Bleecker Hall.
Left
This view of the riverfront along Hudson Avenue and Quay Street, shows the buildings as they looked before the Delaware and Hudson Plaza was built.

Albany Public Library

Beer Driver's Union No. 88 marched in this 1910 Labor Day parade. During this time Beverwyck, Dobler, Hedrick, and Amsdell brewery workers were an especially important part of the city's work force.

1906, when the old John G. Myers Company store on North Pearl Street was replaced. While construction was underway, the building collapsed; floor upon floor came crashing down, all the way to the basement. In one of the great tragedies of Albany history, 80 people were trapped in the wreckage and 13 lost their lives.

The new Myers building was ultimately completed, and soon after a number of Albany banks began to expand, tearing down older buildings that had served as theaters and hotels and putting up new skyscrapers. The resulting skyline of the city, with its great bank buildings near State and Pearl and its two big hotels, the De Witt Clinton at the head of State Street and the Ten Eyck on the corner of State and Pearl, was a skyline as familiar to people of the early '60s as it was to those of the '20s.

The turn of the century was a time of considerable labor unrest in Albany. Motormen and conductors of the United Traction Company went on strike in 1900 and again in 1901, when the National Guard was brought in to patrol the trolley routes and the city was placed under martial law. The 23rd Regiment, called in from Brooklyn as reinforcements, were greeted by a rock-throwing crowd along Broadway; they opened fire on the crowd, killing two. Other strikes involved painters and decorators, carpenters, plumbers, stonemasons, printers, and even vaudeville performers—the so-called White Rats strike that spread from New York to Albany, darkening theaters in both cities.

In April of 1917, the United States entered the war in Europe. Albany's National Guard units were called up in July, and 10,000 Albany men registered for the draft. The city responded to one Liberty Loan drive after another, as well as appeals for Armenian Relief, the Salvation Army, the Red Cross. A medical unit raised by Albany Hospital served in England as Base Hospital 33. Albanian Henry Johnson, serving with the 15th New York (Colored) Infantry Regiment, was awarded the French Croix de Guerre. Three hundred Albany men in all lost their lives in "the war to end all wars."

Prohibition

On January 16, 1920, the Eighteenth Amendment went into effect, making America the land of the dry. The Noble Experiment had begun, leaving in its wake a host of unemployed urban brewery workers, shuttered saloons, and their once-prestigious proprietors, who would now have to seek out a new life among the righteous and the saved. Or would they?

The abrupt disappearance of the saloon and inauguration of the Prohibition era were at best ill-timed, and at worst set the stage for one of the most lawless periods in American history—a period in which the average citizen became involved for the first time.in wholesale disregard for the law. Many saloonkeepers did, in fact, close their establishments, seeing their premises turned into grocery stores, hops, or colorless storage facilities. Others, pursuing the only trade they new, opened speakeasies.

The illicit "gin mills" were to be found in every neighborhood. Prohibition was held in ridicule not only by immigrant stock Albanians, who considered alcohol a centuries-old part of their culture, integral to the family dinner table, to fellowship, mourning, and celebration, but by returning servicemen who, having seen their comrades decimated by trench warfare, mustard gas, and finally the Spanish flu, were not about to be told they could not drink to the country they loved. And drink they did—smuggled scotch from Canada, applejack from nearby farms in Albany County and the rural areas beyond, and bathtub gin made by local people in exactly the way the name implies.

Law-enforcement officials at all levels were quick to read the temper of the times, and their selective enforcement of the unpopular law was a reflection of their willing corruption. One incident, still told in West Hill, involved several barrels of whiskey confiscated from a "closed down saloon" on Judson Street and sent to the nearby 5th Precinct on Central Avenue. The following morning, a miracle was discovered:

overnight, inside the police station, every barrel's contents had turned to water. Less humorous to one North Country farmer was the discovery that his cows' drinking supply had been polluted by bootleggers being pursued by Prohibition agents on their way down from Canada to Albany. The cows were intoxicated by the abandoned evidence, and their milk was unfit to drink for some time.

The most insidious aspect of the new morality, old-time saloonkeepers were quick to point out, was that Prohibition had introduced women to the bars. Unlike their predecessors, the speakeasies were used for courtship and dating. As the purveyors of forbidden fruit, with their secret buttons, signals, and passwords by which those in the know might gain entry, they provided a mystique unparalleled except by the sultry charms of Rudolf Valentino. The introduction of the automobile, the rise of movie theaters all over town, the short-bobbed hair of the flapper, the ubiquitous hip flask, and the widespread corruption of officials gave rise to the saying that America's innocent years were over. No wonder women now voted, the older generation lamented—they had sunk to the level of men.

Unlike the saloons, speakeasies are more difficult to document. Often they moved, sometimes functioning in more than one place simultaneously, and they most certainly cannot be found in the City Directory. Galogly's was in lower Sheridan Hollow. Ames O'Brien's Parody Club was on Hudson, next to the firehouse, not far from Foggy Farrell's on Green Street and the famous "Big Charley" Van Zandt at Green and Division. O'Connor's was not only on Beaver Street but also had a place in Havana, Cuba—ironically the city where Mayor Hackett died. "Mother," an Italian woman, ran her place on Market Street, while a few blocks north, Polly Pleat, ran two establishments, on Norton below Pearl and on Broadway near the railroad station, where he competed with Brockley's, Swift Mead's White Elephant, and Johnny Mack, the gambler. Most of the downtown places had nickel

slot machines, introducing a new illegal device for the patrons' amusement and the proprietor's profit.

But Albany's neighborhoods were not to see such revelry confined to downtown. Brownie Mullen and Jim O'Malley ran a speakeasy at Northern and First. Eddie Cahill's was at 6 New Scotland Avenue, George Linter's was at Sherman and Quail, and Pauley's, Jennings's, and Schramm's were still doing business at their old haunts. King Brady, of baseball fame, opened a place at North Street and Broadway not far from where Ray Curley made beer in the South Street Garage. North Albany was particularly wet, not only because of the support of the neighborhood, but also because of the convenient position of its main street, Broadway, which was the main route to Troy, Watervliet, and Cohoes. Jennings's services were augmented by those of Tom Prime on Genesee and Hugh Diamond's on Erie, as well as Jennings's son's speakeasy on South Street and Champlain, discreetly situated a block off the main road.

Illegal breweries and distilleries cropped up everywhere. Allen's was at Clinton and Quail, and Joe O'Hagan's made Black Horse Ale where the Westgate Shopping Center is today. Worst among the offenders were the druggists of the city, who dispensed "medicinal alcohol" at an alarming rate, both over the counter and out the back door. Alcohol was the marijuana of its day, symbol of a liberated counterculture firmly entrenched against the official law of the land and openly endorsed by many classes of society.

By the time Franklin Roosevelt ended the Noble Experiment in 1933, it had left in its wake an America forever different from that which existed prior to World War I. The Prohibition-based fortunes accumulated by the Dutch Schultzes, Legs Diamonds, and similar rum runners of the Roaring Twenties would found even greater crime enterprises in the years to come. It is a legacy that, while generally bypassing Albany, has plagued the nation ever since.

By the 1920s people were ready to relax and enjoy themselves—in nightclubs, speakeasies, and big-band ballrooms. Once again Albany was a crossroads of trade, this time in bootleg liquor produced in the north country and the Catskills or smuggled in from Canada. "Dutch" Schultz achieved a fame and following generally reserved for movie stars or sports heroes; "Legs" Diamond was shot to death in a Dove Street rooming house.

Albany's red-light district, notorious in the earlier days of the century, continued to thrive with its never-ending nightlife along Green, Dallius, and Liberty streets. Actually, red lights were seldom used; instead, an awning was kept out in all kinds of weather to signal the nature of the establishment. Big Charley's was only one of a whole series of establishments that offered music, booze, gambling, and women to those who sought them, catering as much to the carriage trade from up on the hill as it did to the transient, the soldier, and the gangster.

As the city moved in the early part of the century across Madison Avenue, local residents had the name Dallius Street changed to Dongan Avenue, ostensibly in the name of Irish pride. The real reason was probably to

Right
In 1918 Henry Johnson, a black resident from Sheridan Hollow, became the first American to win the Croix de Guerre in World War I. The local importance of the event is evident by the sign on this trolley car promoting the war stamp drive.
Below
Jack "Legs" Diamond is shown leaving the Rensselaer County Courthouse in Troy, New York, in this 1931 photograph. "Legs," one of the more notorious gangsters of the bootlegging era, was shot to death two years later in a Dove Street rooming house.
Below right
Albany women, such as the marchers in this 1916 War Chest parade, were very much involved in fund raising and Red Cross activities during World War I.

differentiate it from the "Sin City" of Dallius Street closer to downtown. Two generations earlier the residents of Trinity Place in the South End had asked that two blocks of their street be changed to disassociate it from Broad Street and some of the goings-on there in antebellum Albany. One of the great ironies of the Pastures District is that in the end, when the area had fallen upon sad times, it was along the streets named after early ministers of the Dutch Reformed Church that many of the houses of prostitution carried on their business.

The 1920s also saw the expansion of state government under Governor Alfred E. Smith, who modernized the state bureaucracy and created a larger number of full-time jobs than had ever existed before. As a result, when the Depression hit in the 1930s, Albany was in a much better position than some of its sister cities with their aging factories and heavy dependence on industry. Not only was the Depression felt later in Albany than in cities such as Schenectady, but its effects were less severe, thanks to the "cushion" of government employment.

Efforts to combat the Depression included the Man-a-Block Program designed to employ one man on every block to do odd jobs as a means of creating work. At the same time there was a conscious effort on the part of churches to dip into their endowment funds to build church halls, schools, and other semipublic projects as a means of putting people back to work. In the long run, all of these things were in vain. The best that could be done for most families was to give them free land near the present University Heights to enable them to grow their own food.

With the election of Franklin D. Roosevelt and the advent of the New Deal, the WPA came to Albany—federally funded and federally controlled. The O'Connell organization, while welcoming the concept of job creation, was less than enthusiastic about the method. Among the WPA projects completed during this period was the building on Broadway that most Albanians still refer to as the New Post Office, which stands today as a magnificent example of Depression art. The old Bleecker Reservoir, rendered obsolete by a new system that extracted water from the foothills of the Helderbergs, was turned by WPA workers into the present Bleecker Stadium. Streets were repaved, schools were refurbished, and—of more questionable social value—most of the firehouses in the city of Albany were covered with bright yellow brick, all in an effort to put people back to work.

Above left
Albany does not appear to be too hard-hit by the Depression in this 1936 view of Hudson Avenue between Grand and Philip streets.
Above
Johnny Evers was a local baseball hero who played in several World Series with the Chicago Cubs. He also played with the Boston Braves, and later served as superintendent of Bleeker Stadium. Baseball fans may remember Evers, shown here in 1939, as pivot for the famous double play combination termed "Tinker to Evers to Chance."
Below
Temporary barrack-type homes were provided by the State of New York for returning World War II veterans and their families. The American housing market was brought to a virtual standstill by the Depression and the war.

The coming of World War II ended the massive public-works projects, as the country moved into a new era—one in which Albany would participate fully. Among the city's best-known wartime causes was a naval vessel, the U.S.S. *Albany*, the fourth ship of its kind to be subsidized by the city and to bear that name. Albany's mayor, Erastus Corning, requested that he be drafted and in fact served one year in a combat infantry regiment in Europe. Of the thousands of Albany men and women who served in Europe and the Pacific, 556 lost their lives.

The large number of veterans returning to the city in the 1940s presented new challenges, and temporary, barrackslike housing was built near St. Mary's Park where the present Albany High School is located. After the hardships of the Depression, when many couples put off having children, and the disruption of families by World War II, the post-1945 period witnessed a "baby boom" and a corresponding boom in construction. A number of factors conspired, however, to orient this new development away from the central cities into a rapidly emerging suburban society. State funds were used to subsidize suburban schools, while the Federal Highway Act extended roads—wide and safe and federally paid for—far into areas previously thought of only as farmland. Even more important, national policy on the part of those who approved mortgages and insurance for housing clearly favored suburban development.

The automobile, whose growth and spread had been checked to some degree by the Great Depression and by wartime shortages, now burst forth in abundance. The New York State Thruway was completed in the 1950s, followed by the Adirondack Northway, rendering obsolete and impractical an interurban trolley system that up until the late 1940s enabled Albany residents to take a trolley car from downtown Albany to the Adirondacks or to Chatham in Columbia County. Trolley service within the city was discontinued in favor of buses in the 1950s, and the suburbanization of America was well on its way.

By 1959, when Nelson A. Rockefeller took office as governor, the city of Albany looked on the surface much as it had looked generations before. Downtown was still a place of prestige, dominated by banks interspersed with numerous stores and service industries—everything from clothing and furniture emporiums to hat-blocking shops and shoe-shine parlors. Grand names such as Van Heusen Charles and Lansing's offered

Below
In April of 1944 Mayor Erastus Corning 2nd, still in his first term of office, left for service as a P.F.C. with the United States Army in Germany.
Below right
In June of 1952 buses from London were seen on Albany streets as part of a British travel promotion.

Erastus Corning 2nd

Arthur J. O'Keefe

Arthur J. O'Keefe

fashionable gifts, while an entire "cheap side" along lower South Pearl Street enabled families to buy shoes for growing children at Swartz and Levison's or floor coverings for the kitchen at Leonard's. Downtown was still a place where all young ladies wore gloves, a place where you "always saw someone." Mothers could be seen dragging tired children from store to store, rewarding them afterward with a trip to Peter's for a soda. The city's first shopping center, Westgate, opened in the late 1950s, followed by Stuyvesant Plaza, just outside the city limits, but the impact of the shopping center on downtown merchants had barely been felt.

The 1960s were a different story. These were long and difficult years for the city, for reasons that were common to every Northeastern city of the period—the flight to the suburbs, the ultimate red-lining by banks and insurance companies, the subsidization of suburban schools by state governments, increasing racial tension.

Arthur J. O'Keefe

Federally subsidized urban-renewal programs of the 1960s were oriented toward demolition first and new housing second; no attempt was made to rehabilitate existing neighborhoods. The first urban-renewal project in the nation took place in the area where Boardman's is located today. The historic neighborhood that had surrounded the Erie Canal basin was completely demolished in blitzlike fashion and replaced with a large shopping center and commercial properties, none of which provided a home for a single person. In the South End, under the federally funded Green Street and Morton Avenue projects, hundreds of small row houses were torn down and replaced with tall high-rises, hitherto unknown in the city of Albany. Of the 2,300 units of public housing in Albany today, the only ones that can be termed successful are those in buildings of three stories or less—as in North Albany, on Colonie Street, and along the lower end of South Pearl Street—and in the high-rises reserved for senior citizens.

Timothy Leonard

Only within the last five or six years has it become possible for cities to obtain federal aid to rehabilitate existing housing in neighborhoods built on a more human and personal scale. Under the Community Block Grant program, more than 1,000 housing units have been restored and neighborhoods have been brought back to such an extent that a major problem now, instead of abandonment and disinvestment, appears to be "gentrification"—the displacement of lower- and middle-income residents by young, educated, higher-income people seeking to move back into the city from the suburbs.

Nelson Rockefeller was a man of great vision and a man of single purpose when he put his mind to achieving a goal. Many of his accomplishments will benefit Albany and the state of New York for many years to come. Under his administration the state university system was totally revamped and the Albany State Teachers College expanded into the State University of New York at Albany. The college was moved from its modest facility in the center of the city to a huge new campus far to the west in the city's Pine Bush area, adjacent to the state office-building complex begun in the mid-1950s by Governor Thomas E. Dewey.

When it came to the question of state offices in downtown Albany, Rockefeller felt, as he had in the case of the university, that the present facilities were inadequate. The State Office Building, described in 1928 as Al Smith's folly because it would never be fully needed or utilized, was now totally inadequate, and the state had become the largest tenant in downtown Albany. Local legend has it that on the occasion of the visit of

Morris Gerber

Facing page

Top
The White Elephant Grill on Maiden Lane and James Street was once a landmark in downtown Albany. This photograph was taken in 1952.

Middle
The 119 Club opened on Dana Avenue after the repeal of Prohibition. It was owned by Eddie Cahill and former boxer John Leonard, whose brothers, Paul and Charlie, also ran the neighborhood grill. The club was popular with a generation of law school and medical students.

Bottom
The Normanskill Farm Dairy, whose route-man is shown above, had its headquarters at the Steven's Farm adjoining Normanskill. Until the 1960s Albany neighborhoods were regularly serviced by a variety of route salesmen who relied upon a lively traffic with housewives who found it convenient to patronize their street trade.

Right
The Roman Catholic Cathedral can be seen through a partially demolished building during the construction of the Nelson Rockefeller Empire State Plaza. The office building in the foreground of the cathedral was among the last buildings to be razed.

Princess Beatrix of the Netherlands, Rockefeller, who acted as host for much of her visit, found it embarrassing to drive with his royal guest from the Governor's Mansion on Eagle Street up to the New York State Capitol. The city appeared to be in a state of decay, many of its downtown neighborhoods were slums, and all in all the governor considered it an unfit capital for the state of New York.

In March of 1963, with less than a week's notice for a consultation with the mayor of the city—something that would not be possible today— Albanians read in their local newspapers that the state, by its power of eminent domain, was seizing all the land between Lincoln Park and State Street and between Swan Street and Eagle. In addition to this parcel of nearly 100 acres, additional property would be seized for arterial highways leading into the proposed South Mall.

The Mall started slowly. There was talk in the initial stages that certain churches and other prominent buildings, such as the chancery of the Roman Catholic diocese, could be left standing and accommodated within the Mall. As time went on, however, it became apparent that a 21st-century office complex was to be imposed upon a 19th-century city and nothing could be accommodated beyond the Roman Catholic Cathedral and the Governor's Mansion itself. Everything else would have to go.

The Mall was to be placed upon a huge platform of cement with layers of parking underneath for thousands of cars. Before it was finished, it would employ thousands of workers imported from union locals stretching into neighboring states, and in one case employing artisans who only spoke French. It would utilize more than 500,000 cubic feet of marble, backing up marble orders in the states of Vermont and Georgia by more than a year. The original cost of the Mall was estimated to be in the neighborhood of $400 million; by the time it was finished, it had exceeded $2 billion in construction costs and debt service.

The Port of Albany

The Port of Albany, about to celebrate its 50th year, has a history as old as the city itself. On Albany's riverbanks the furs acquired by the early Dutch traders were gathered and shipped down the mighty Hudson by the Dutch West India Company.

The first stone docks were built at Albany in 1766—three docks 80 feet long and 30 to 40 feet wide; four more docks were added in 1770. In November of that year, the sloop *Olive Branch* cleared Albany for the West Indies; many more followed, carrying flour, lumber, and fish and returning with sugar and rum from the islands. In 1785, tradition relates, the sloop *Experiment* under Captain Stewart Dean cleared Albany for Canton—the second American ship to make the voyage. For the newly independent nation, no longer a part of the British imperial trading network, establishing commercial relations with China was an important first step toward economic independence.

Sloops, barges, and steamboats plied the Hudson throughout the 19th century, but by the end of the century oceangoing vessels were no longer reaching Albany. Silting, shoals, and sandbars rendered the last 30 miles, above the city of Hudson, too hazardous and uncertain. A particularly massive build-up located three miles south of Albany and known as the "Overslaugh" had impeded river traffic since colonial times. Unless a channel of sufficient depth could be created and maintained, Albany's days as an international port were gone forever.

On December 8, 1913, Albany Representative Peter G. Ten Eyck introduced a bill in Congress "to provide for a survey and estimate of cost of a deep water channel in the Hudson River, New York between the City of Hudson and the dam at Troy." The bill was ultimately passed as part of the Rivers and Harbors Act of 1915. Surveys, estimates, and feasibility studies followed, and at last, on March 3, 1925, President Calvin Coolidge signed a bill authorizing the expenditure of $11 million to dredge a channel 27 feet deep—deep enough to accommodate 85 percent of the world's oceangoing vessels. The cities of Albany and Rensselaer were required to commit another $10 million to provide suitable port facilities.

On March 25, 1925, New York Governor Alfred E. Smith signed a bill creating the Albany Port District—comprising about 200 acres within the city of Albany and another 35 acres across the river in Rensselaer—and a five-member Port Commission to oversee development and operation of the port. Construction of the new port was formally initiated in March 1926, and in April 1927 the process of dredging the Hudson River began. The channel was completed in June of 1931, and one year later the Port of Albany was officially dedicated.

Today the port plays an active part in the city's economy and the nation's international trade. Huge quantities of wheat and corn—stored in one of the world's largest grain elevators—are exported annually, recalling on a far grander scale the cargoes of colonial times. Once again molasses flows into Albany—not only from the West Indies, but from as far away as Brazil, Australia, and South Africa. Bananas by the ton arrive from Central America, wood pulp from Sweden, and steel products from Italy. Volkswagen of America, which recently consolidated its East Coast import operations at Albany, brings in tens of thousands of Volkswagen, Porsche, and Audi cars annually for distribution throughout New England and the Midwest. The Hudson River channel has been deepened to 32 feet and, thanks to icebreaking operations by the U.S. Coast Guard, the Port of Albany is now a thriving year-round facility.

Facing page
Top
An Albany Port District Commission vehicle loads lumber onto a freight car.
Bottom
Under construction from 1926 to 1932, the Port of Albany increased river traffic at a time when the city could boast of having the largest single-unit grain elevator in the world.

HUDSON RIVER
STEAMBOATS.

The following list embraces all the PASSAGE BOATS built and running on the Hudson River, between New-York, Albany and Troy, since their first introduction by Robert Fulton, in the fall of 1807:

When Built.	Names.	Tons.	Remarks.
1807.	CLERMONT.		Name changed to North River.
1808.	NORTH RIVER.	166.	Broken up.
1809.	CAR OF NEPTUNE.	295.	" "
1811.	HOPE.	280.	" "
1811.	PERSEVERANCE.	200.	" "
1811.	PARAGON.	331.	Sunk, 1925.
1813.	RICHMOND.	370.	Broken up.
1815.	OLIVE BRANCH.	249	" "
1816.	CHANCELLOR LIVINGSTON.	495.	" "
1823.	JAMES KENT.	364.	Coal Barge.
1824.	HUDSON.	170.	Broken up.
1825.	SANDUSKY.	220.	Tow Boat.
1825.	CONSTITUTION.	376.	Now Indiana.
1825.	CONSTELLATION.	376.	Tow Barge.
1825.	CHIEF JUSTICE MARSHALL.	300.	Lost in Long Island Sound.
1826.	SARATOGA.	250.	Tow Barge.
1826.	N. Y.	200.	Burnt, 1861.
1826.	NEW PHILADELPHIA	360.	Runs on Delaware River.
1827.	ALBANY.	350.	Runs to Troy.
1827.	INDEPENDENCE.	366.	On Philadelphia Route
1827.	NORTH AMERICA.	497.	Destroyed by Ice, 1836.
1827.	VICTORY.	390.	Sunk in 1845.
1828.	DE WITT CLINTON.	371.	Engine in Knickerbocker.
1829.	OHIO.	419.	Tow Barge.
1830.	NOVELTY.	477.	Broken up.
1832.	CHAMPLAIN.	471.	Tow Barge.
1832.	ERIE.	473.	" "
1833.	HELEN.		Destroyed 1834.
1835.	ROBERT L. STEVENS.	296.	Runs to Saugerties.
1836.	ROCHESTER.	491.	Runs to Albany.
1836.	SWALLOW.	420.	Destroyed April 7th, 1845.
1837.	UTICA.	340.	Runs to Albany.
1838.	DIAMOND.	205.	Laid up.
1839.	BALLOON.	204.	Runs to Newark.
1839.	NORTH AMERICA.	494.	Runs to Albany.
1840.	SOUTH AMERICA.	626.	" "
1840.	TROY.	724.	Runs to Troy.
1841.	COLUMBIA.	391.	Runs to Albany.
1841.	RAINBOW.	230.	On Delaware River.
1842.	CURTIS PECK.	316.	On James' River, Va.
1843.	EMPIRE.	936.	Runs to Troy.
1843.	KNICKERBOCKER.	858.	Runs to Albany.
1843.	BELLE.	436.	" "
1843.	EXPRESS.	296.	" "
1845.	NIAGARA.	730.	Runs to Troy.
1845.	RIP VAN WINKLE.	516.	Runs to Albany.
1845.	HENDRICK HUDSON.	1170.	" "

[*Extract from the Picturesque Tourist, published by J. Disturnell, in 1844.*]

"PASSENGER BARGES—In 1826 the steamboat Commerce, Capt. George E. Seymour, towed the passenger barge Lady Clinton, and the steamboat Swiftsure, Capt. Cowden, towed the passenger barge Lady Van Rensselaer."

[*Copy of an Advertisement taken from the Albany Gazette, dated September, 1807.*]

"The North River Steamboat will leave Pauler's Hook Ferry (now Jersey City) on Friday, the 4th of September, at 9 in the morning, and arrive at Albany on Saturday, at 9 in the afternoon. Provisions, good berths and accommodations are provided.

"The charge to each passenger is as follows :

To Newburg, dols. 3, time 14 hours.
" Poughkeepsie, " 4, " 17 "
" Esopus, " 5, " 20 "
" Hudson, " 5½, " 30 "
" Albany, " 7, " 36 "

"For places, apply to Wm. Vandervoort, No. 48 Courtlandt street, on the corner of Greenwich street.

"Sept. 2, 1807."

[*Extract from the N. Y. Evening Post, dated Oct. 2, 1807.*]

"Mr. Fulton's new-invented Steamboat, which is fitted up in a neat style for passengers, and is intended to run from New-York to Albany as a Packet, left here this morning with ninety passengers against a strong head wind. Notwithstanding which, it was judged she moved through the waters at the rate of six miles an hour."

[*Extract from the Albany Gazette, dated Oct. 5, 1807.*]

"Friday, Oct. 2, 1807, the steamboat (Clermont) left New-York at 10 o'clock, A. M., against a stormy tide, very rough water, and a violent gale from the north. She made a headway beyond the most sanguine expectations, and without being rocked by the waves.

"Arrived at Albany, Oct. 4, at 10 o'clock, P. M., being detained by being obliged to come to anchor, owing to a gale, and having one of her paddle-wheels torn away by running foul of a sloop."

NOTICE.—It is stated, on the authority of Capt. E. S. Bunker, that the CLERMONT, or experiment boat, as sometimes called, the first steamboat constructed under the direction and superintendence of Robert Fulton, in 1807, was 100 feet long, 12 feet wide, and 7 feet deep. In 1808, she was lengthened to 150 feet, widened to 18 feet, and had her name changed to NORTH RIVER. The engine was constructed in England, by Watt & Bolton, and brought to New York in Dec., 1806, by Mr. Fulton. The hull of the boat was constructed by Charles Brown, an eminent ship builder in New York. In August, 1807, the boat was propelled by steam from the East River to the Jersey shore, and on the 2d of October following she started on her first trip to Albany.

☞ The above was taken from the SCRAP BOOK of Mr. ALEXANDER MATTHEWS, No. 164 Greenwich street, corner of Cortlandt, (directly opposite the site of the first established Steamboat Office,) where the Book, containing this, together with many other interesting reminiscences, can be seen.

New York PRINTORIUM, 29 Ann Street, cor. Nassau, N. Y.

Albany Institute of History and Art

Albany Public Library

New York State Library

By all accounts the Mall is a magnificent structure. Efforts have been made, at the urging of local officials including the mayor, to make it more than a 9-to-5 facility. The "I Love New York Festival," held every other fall, attracts tens of thousands of people. A grand fireworks display on the Fourth of July revives a custom of a generation ago, when such festivities were held in Lincoln Park.

Visitors to the city are almost always impressed by the Mall, but most Albanians maintain a peculiar love-hate relationship with what is known today as the Governor Nelson A. Rockefeller Empire State Plaza—and with good reason.

When Governor Rockefeller appeared before the Senate committee for confirmation as Vice President of the United States, he was challenged with the fact that more than 7,000 people had lost their homes to an office-building complex in the capital city. Rockefeller proudly answered that the area cited had been one of the worst slums in the United States, with one of the highest infant-mortality rates. The fact of the matter was that the governor was not familiar with the neighborhood at all; his knowledge of Albany was a straight line along Eagle Street from where he lived to where he worked. The area in question was a working-class neighborhood whose residents included blue-collar workers on Cathedral Hill and even some legislators who lived in rooming houses and rental properties on Capitol Hill. The infant-mortality rate for the three years prior to the Rockefeller testimony was among the lowest in the city, with a grand total of two deaths per year prior to demolition. Ironically enough, the highest infant-mortality rate in the city was in Pine Hills—a relatively well-to-do middle-class neighborhood.

To assess what really happened, one has to understand what was there originally. A time frame that goes back 10 or 15 years, when the entire city was a mass of dust and construction materials and equipment, suggests that nothing but improvement has occurred in the area. But the creation of the Mall entailed destruction of some very positive things. There was, of course, the obvious loss of buildings that had stood for more than 100 years, some of them representing the finest in 19th-century craftsmanship. Also lost to the area were four beautiful church buildings. St. Paul's Episcopal and St. Sofia's Greek Orthodox were both relocated from Lancaster Street; First Methodist and the Church of the Assumption were never replaced.

The approaches to the Mall did further damage, wiping out two small neighborhoods of particular interest. One was a street of French-Canadians opposite a French-Canadian church built shortly after the Civil War. It was an elderly community and one not known to too many people. More obvious, more flamboyant, and better known was Little Italy, centered around St. Anthony's Church. People from all over the city came to Grand Street and Madison Avenue to enjoy the annual festivals and street fairs. The residents of Little Italy were not only elderly people, as was the case with the French section, but included many younger families—many of them still speaking Italian in their homes and in the streets.

The Mall also had an effect on other urban neighborhoods. The streets that surrounded it suddenly became prey to speculators who purchased family homes at inflated prices, immediately cut them up into small apartments, and rented them out to workers at above-average prices.

On the approach to the Mall, now partially covered by the Arterial Highway, was an open-air market that had its antecedent back in Dutch times. It had been moved several times, from the center of Broadway to the center of State Street, and finally, in this century, to larger quarters in the vicinity of Hudson Avenue, Philip Street, Grand, and Market. The Market Square, as it was known, attracted farmers from truck farms outside the city who sold their produce in the early years from horse-drawn wagons, and in later years from the back of pick-up trucks. Twenty years ago it was possible for any Albanian to go to the Market Square six days a week and buy anything from live rabbits and chickens to flowers, fruits, and vegetables in season. It was a lively and wonderful place and rivaled, in many ways, Boston's Quincy Market—thought of by many people today as something new in urban development.

Perhaps the most damaging result of all, however, was the effect on downtown. Myers and Whitney's were by this time great dinosaurs in an age when only chain stores survived—and then only with difficulty—in downtown areas. They probably would have gone anyway. To the hundreds of local shopkeepers, downtown was looked upon not as a central shopping area, but primarily as a neighborhood shopping center for the 7,000 to 14,000 people who lived within the Mall area and its environs and were eventually displaced. People from Arbor Hill, Sheridan Hollow, Little Italy, the South End, and the so-called Mansions District, as well as the neighborhoods above the Mall, used downtown for everything from grocery shopping to routine clothing purchases, providing a cushion for the downtown merchants when the normal cycle of boom and bust affected the business community. Without these people, and with other families being replaced by transient workers in row houses and brownstones surrounding the construction sites, little by little downtown began to die. In time, the theaters closed—as many as five or six in the immediate downtown area. Stores closed one by one. Suburbanization continued, and downtown no longer had its local neighborhood population to support it in times of stress.

What is left is magnificent and almost unrivaled in the United States, but it is important to remember that it was built at a cost—a cost measured both in material and in human terms.

Below
Generations of coal heat and city traffic have necessitated the cleaning of many landmark buildings in downtown Albany, especially during the preservation-conscious, post-South Mall era. Construction and cleaning on the facade of the New York State Education Building, shown here, took place in the 1960s.
Below right
The Van Heusen Charles and Company, established in 1843, was once a landmark in downtown Albany. During the building of the Rockefeller Empire State Plaza, there was a decline in large retail store business in the downtown area and the company established a smaller store in a renovated 19th-century commercial building on Howard Street.

Albany D.H.R.   Photo by Lindsey Watson

Albany D.H.R.   Photo by Lindsey Watson

Photo by Rich Frutchey

Facing page
The Colleoni II, *sculpted by Jason Seley out of welded steel automobile bumpers, stands in the Tower Building of the Rockefeller Empire State Plaza.*
Top left
One may view bronze sculptures of children on the 1912 State Education Building around the lamps at the head of the stairs.
Top right
These World War I soldiers sculpted by G.K. Lathlop in 1933 appear on an Albany monument. Do you know where it stands? See the inset on the next page for the answer.
Above
The Englewood Place gardens display their colorful beauty. The Guilded Age mansions of Albany's elite held Washington Park from further expansion to Western Avenue.
Right
A panoramic view from the Tower Building looking northwest shows the Governor Nelson A. Rockefeller Empire State Plaza.

Photo by Rich Frutchey

Facing page, inset
The World War I Memorial Flagpole in Memorial Grove at New Scotland and South Lake avenues is flanked by bronze beavers, the city's emblem, and depicts soldiers and sailors of the "Great War" who are accompanied by horse, dog, and carrier pigeon allies.
Facing page and top left
The Normanskill Farm, recently purchased by the city, is one of several pastoral reserves that make up Albany's "green belts," separating the city from the neighboring town of Bethlehem.
Above
Can you guess which municipal building this fierce-looking stone lion appears on? See the next page, top, to find out.
Left
This view of Albany was taken from the Heldebergh escarpment at Thacher Park, a popular state facility known for its fossils, "Bear Path," and former "Indian Ladder."

Albany D.H.R.   Photo by Lindsey Watson

Albany League of the Arts

Photo by Rich Frutchey

Facing page, top

Albany City Hall, designed by H.H. Richardson, boasts elaborate stone carvings in natural, imaginary, and Classical themes on its south and west fronts as if to rival the State Capitol across the street.

Facing page, bottom

Pinksterfest, a spring festivity held in Washington Park in conjunction with the popular Tulip Festival, is a recreation of an early slave celebration held on Capitol Hill. The city fathers outlawed the original Pinksterfest in 1811 and it has been revived only since the early 1970s.

Left

Lark Street, developed in the last half of the 19th century, serves as a key residential and shopping street within the "brownstone revival" neighborhoods of Center Square, Hudson Park, and Washington Park.

Right

"The Lady Window" of the Cathedral of the Immaculate Conception was designed by H.W. Akeroyd and made in Newcastle-on-Tyne, England by the studio of William Wailes. It is original to the Cathedral's dedication in 1852. When the building was enlarged in 1891-92, the great window was relocated from its original place above the main altar to its present location fronting Madison Avenue, and a bottom row of female saints was added to the composition. Originally commissioned by Albany's first bishop, John (later Cardinal) McCloskey, the magnificent work of stained glass was restored by his successor Howard Hubbard, ninth Bishop of Albany, in anticipation of the commemoration of the 150th anniversary of the founding of the Roman Diocese of Albany in 1997.

Bottom

The skyline of Albany captured in this 1995 photo by Lindsey Watson, reveals a city containing the architectural styles of three centuries. The gleaming marble towers of the of the Empire State Plaza compete amiably with the bricks and brownstone of federal row houses of the Pastures neighborhood and the gothic spires of the 150 year old Cathedral of the Immaculate Conception on Mansion Hill.

Cathedral of the Immaculate Conception. Photo by Dave Oxford

Albany D.H.R.   Photo by Lindsey Watson

Albany League of the Arts

New York State Department of Commerce

Windsor Publications, Inc.

Albany D.H.R.   Photo by Lindsey Watson

Photo by Rich Frutchey

Photo by Rich Frutchey

Facing page

Top left
The Madison Avenue window of the Cathedral of the Immaculate Conception, created in England, was originally located behind the altar when the building was constructed in 1848-1852.

Top right
Skating at the Plaza, coupled with regular festivals and fairs, demonstrates the favorable evolution of the Empire State Plaza from its original purpose as a "9 to 5" office complex into a vibrant regional attraction.

Bottom
Thomas Olcott built the Executive Mansion on Eagle Street circa 1850. It was first leased to the state in 1874 for the residence of Governor Tilden. Three years later the state purchased the building and thoroughly "Victorianized" it with trim and gingerbread decorations.

Above
The Port of Albany, relocated to the city's far South End in 1925 to 1932, bolsters the region's economy through extensive international shipping.

Top
Albany is a city of contrasts. Here the peaked roofs and dormers of Albany's early 19th-century Pastures district are overshadowed by the gleaming marble of the Empire State Plaza.

Middle
In addition to serving traffic in grain, scrap iron, oil, bananas, and paper products, the Port of Albany has several industrial firms located within its district.

Bottom
The State University of New York at Albany was transformed during the Rockefeller years into a major university center, and its main campus was relocated to the site of the Albany Country Club on the city's western edge.

CHAPTER 10
ALBANY IN THE POST-CORNING ERA

Times Union-Lindsey Watson

On Saturday, May 28th, 1983 Albanians were to hear on the noontime news that Erastus Corning, 2nd, the longest tenured mayor in the nation, a trusted advisor of presidents and governors, and the only mayor that most of them had ever known, had died earlier that day in a Boston Hospital.

Observers unfamiliar with the peculiarities of Albany's history must have thought it a bit strange that so many people expressed such a strong reaction to the news. After all, the 73 year old mayor had not been in City Hall since being stricken at work nearly a year before. Initially, he had attempted with considerable

"The People Say Good-bye," photo by Lindsey Watson captures the funeral cortege of Mayor Erastus Corning 2nd as it pauses to hear a last concert played by Joey Emma, City Carilloneer, on the bells of the famed Peace Carillon in the tower of City Hall.

In 1981, from the steps of City Hall, Mayor Erastus Corning 2nd, declared his candidacy for an eleventh four-year term as the city's chief executive.

Times Union-Willie Ross.

"The Changing of the Guard," May 31, 1983. City officials, led by Mayor Whalen leave City Hall, which is draped in mourning, to attend Mayor Corning's funeral at All Saints Cathedral.

Times Union-Dickstein

success to run the city government from his hospital room in Albany Medical Center. He had appointed a "regency" of five attorneys to be available if necessary to handle any crisis that might occur in his illness.

Vincent McArdle and Robert Lyman represented, respectively, the city and county governments whose legal affairs they directed; Douglas Rutnik represented the Democratic Party's interests, and former city Recorder, John Holt-Harris, protected the mayor's personal and business interests and those of the Corning family. The advisory group had been headed by retired State Court of Appeals Judge Francis Bergan, a highly respected senior jurist whose career had its beginnings in the founding years of the O'Connell organization more than a half century before. "This way," Corning confided to intimates, "if two or more of the lawyers find themselves in disagreement, they'll listen to Bergan and he'll keep them in line." The "Big Five," as they came to be known, had unofficial jurisdiction over all but two city commissioners who were told they were "on their own," and a bizarre chapter in the city's administrative history commenced.

At first Corning, an unabashed workaholic, continued to govern City Hall and Democratic Party affairs from his sick bed in Albany Med. Commissioners, politicians, well wishers and supplicants streamed in and out of the large medical institution on a daily basis. At the mayor's insistence, the daily volume of mail, now greatly augmented by get well cards and well wishes, was sent daily to his room each day for his personal perusal. All were answered personally in what had become the familiar Corning style—promptly and briefly.

For three and a half months the system seemed to be working, visitations were curtailed to a reasonable flow and most city bureaucrats did their best not to bother the mayor more than absolutely necessary. But years of cigarette smoking had taken their toll. His emphysema worsened, and nothing seemed to help. On October 6th 1982, the day before his 73rd birthday, Corning left the city by ambulance to enter an ambitious therapy regimen in Boston University Hospital.

The absence of a city's mayor from his office while he was still in the city was one thing; the absence of a mayor from his state was quite another. The "Big Five" became the "Big Six" with the addition of Thomas M. Whalen, III, a former City Court Judge and Corning's running mate for his election to an eleventh four year term. As President of the Common Council with right of succession, Whalen added much needed legitimacy to the regency of Corning appointed lawyers who, at best, had only advisory authority in city affairs.

For eight months the familiar black Buick with its distinctive "A" license plate, made a well traveled journey to Boston carrying the correspondence, bureaucrats and selected citizens who were now more important than ever to the man who had made his city and public office synonymous with his very being.

When in January Corning's health took a turn for the worse, Whalen began to spend more and more time in the mayor's office in City Hall. Rather than send a message, however subtle, that a shifting of power was taking place, he ordered a temporary folding table to be set up in the office on which he could do his paperwork. Mayor Corning's plain metal desk and chair, so incongruous with the elegant décor of the room, remained unused lest anyone forget the Mayor was still the Mayor.

In March, the newly elected governor, Mario Cuomo, signed a legislative resolution naming the imposing office building which dominates the Governor Nelson A. Rockefeller Empire State Plaza the Mayor Erastus Corning 2nd Tower.

The naming of the massive marble and glass tower in Corning's lifetime was not only a great honor to give the mayor, it had an appropriateness and irony that was overlooked by many. The Tower had 42 stories; Corning was in his 42nd year as mayor. Prior to the governor's signing, the resolution had been passed by the Senate and Assembly, where Corning had served in the early years of his career. Prime sponsor in the Assembly was his old friend Dick Conners, who had also entered city service on the same 1941 ticket that had elected Corning mayor. The Senate sponsor was Howard Nolan who had unsuccessfully opposed the mayor in a Democratic Primary in 1977. But the irony that undoubtedly was most appreciated by the ailing chief executive was that the massive former South Mall, now renamed as a memorial to Nelson Rockefeller, that same controversial project that had been so insensitively imposed on the city by the ambitions and ego of his sometime friend and adversary Nelson Rockefeller, would for all its existence, be dominated and literally overshadowed by the 589 foot presence of the CORNING Tower.

The funeral of Erastus Corning marked the end of an era. It also marked an end of a longstanding tradition of having members of

Times Union-Al Jessen

The announcement By Governor Hugh Carey in 1979 that the state would invest one million dollars to stabilize the derelict Union Station on Broadway paved the way for its renovation as Kiernan Plaza by Norstar (now Fleet) Bank four years later. The 1899 railroad station had been rendered obsolete in 1969 when arterial highway construction connecting the riverfront traffic to the Empire State Plaza forced the relocation of the station facilities across the river to Rensselaer. In the photo are, left to right; Mayor Erastus Corning, City Historian Norman Rice (partially obscured), Assemblyman Richard Conners, City D.H.R. Commissioner and Historic Sites Chairman, John McEneny, Governor Carey, and County Executive James Coyne.

In 1986 the city joined the New York State Urban Cultural Parks Program. With Enviromental Quality Bond Act assistance, an exciting new Visitors Center and planetarium were built in a century-old former Water Department facility at Quackenbush Square

City of Albany-Urban Cultural Park

Visitors pause in the courtyard of the Urban Cultural Park Visitors Center. The Quackenbush House, the city's oldest existing house, ca.1683, serves as a popular up-scale restaurant, adjacent to the Visitors Center.

City of Albany-Urban Cultural Park

the Corning family playing key rolls in the destiny of the city of Albany. Since 1814, when the first Erastus Corning arrived in the city, its economy, its politics and its cultural life had felt the influence of the family. The 1983 eulogy preached to 1,300 mourners by Dean (later Bishop) David Ball in the Episcopal Cathedral echoed to gothic columns and arches erected on donated Corning land and subsidized by the legacies of numerous Corning family benefices and legacies. Even the needlepoint cushions on the sanctuary kneelers were crafted by three generations of Corning women especially Albany's First Lady, Elizabeth Platt Corning, his wife of half a century. It was she, using flowers from the couple's own garden, who had arranged the sole flower arrangement permitted in the ceremony.

City Hall officials had taken care of publicity, honor guards, and the seating of hundreds of current and former officials from the governor on down; but it was the family, forgotten in the mind of so many of people, who chose the liturgy, acted as pallbearers and accompanied the remains to the expansive family plat in Albany Rural Cemetery for a private commitment service. It was as though the family which had given Erastus Corning to the people for so many years were at last taking him back.

THE WHALEN YEARS

Thomas M. Whalen, III became mayor by succession at Corning's death. He served out the remainder of his predecessors's term, and subsequently went on to be easily elected to two four year terms in his own right. Give or take a little internal bickering in Democratic political circles, Whalen never experienced serious opposition from the voting booth. His more than ten and a half years as the city's chief executive would constitute the fourth longest mayorality in the more than 300 years of Albany's history as a chartered city.

Comparisons between Mayors Corning and Whalen are difficult to make with any degree of objectivity. Not only was each man a

Times Union–Luanne M. Ferris

The annual Empire State Regatta was started by Mayor Whalen and several local business leaders in 1985. The city's Hudson River waterfront is now a location for sculling, competitive rowing, and even an Irish Curragh Club.

The blooming of tulips in Washington Park each spring has been an important part of Albany tradition since 1948, when thousands of bulbs were given to the city by our Dutch sister city of Nimijen, in gratitude for post war recovery assistance that had been arranged as part of the Marshall Plan. The Albany Tulip Festival, now a half century old, dates from that time, and celebrates the city's nearly four century old heritage of Dutch and African traditions.

City of Albany–Department of Economic Development—Photo by Tim Raab

product of his own background and generation, but just as importantly, each mayor was responding to the challenges of his own time. Corning's abilities and personal style became most obvious in the last decade of his life, after the passing of his old mentor and party boss, Daniel O'Connell. The 1970s were a period of an optimistic and long overdue rediscovery of cities by the federal government. As part of the newly embraced policy of Revenue Sharing, millions of dollars of federal money were earmarked for locally run programs in the Community Development and in the Comprehensive Employment and Training Act (CETA) programs. All over the country, the political fortunes of mayors rose and fell on the voter's judgment of how effectively they had applied for and utilized federal money, money which had already begun to dry up by the time Thomas Whalen had succeeded to the mayor's office.

By necessity Whalen's administration had to respond to the world of "Reaganomics," in which private business would become a fully participating partner in municipal affairs. In this new environment, Albany's new mayor was more than ably suited for the job. Whalen had not just been a lawyer in private life, he had been a corporate lawyer. His familiarity with the city's businesses, and especially its important banking community, brought private sector participation into the city government such as had not been seen in generations.

Times Union-McKinney

Mayor Thomas M. Whalen, III and his Golden Retriever, Finn MacCool, march in the St. Patrick's Day Parade, 1988. There were many days when Finn was a regular fixture in the Mayor's office in City Hall.

A strong believer in a regional approach to solving the problems of urban America, Whalen enlisted business leaders from throughout the Capital District to sit on city boards and blue ribbon study groups. Strong ties to the University at Albany, where he had served as chairman of the University Council, enabled him to enlist key minds in academia, including popular University President Vincent O'Leary and faculty members from the Rockefeller Institute. In an effort to address those challenges unique to Albany, a major effort was started to reach out to other capital cities across the country, to learn what experiences might be appropriate to help Albany improve its quality of life. In these exchanges Whalen tapped citizens from government, academia, business and neighborhood associations to insure that a good cross section of the people had a voice in determining the future of their city.

Whalen's enthusiasm for Albany seemed almost unlimited. Corning had saved the riverfront for public use, but it was an isolated area used by few and separated from the city's downtown by the formidable multi-laned highway of concrete and barriers which led to Rockefeller's Mall. Whalen rediscovered it. Within two years the passive recreation area, appropriately named the Corning Preserve, echoed to the sounds of not just joggers and bird watchers, but to the thousands of boating enthusiasts from surrounding communities who came to partake in the revived sculling and rowing once so familiar to generations past. With the help of enthusiasts who had learned to row in their college years, the Empire State Regatta, a tradition which had disappeared from the city's life nearly a century before, was restored to the people of Albany.

By the end of his term, Whalen would also totally reshape the Albany Municipal Golf Course. The New Course, as it is now known, boasts a new clubhouse and welcome replacement of a "back nine" that had become legendary for its challenge to coronary patients. The introduction of a cross-country ski trail helped expand the golf course into a diversified year-round facility.

Perhaps Tom Whalen's greatest accomplishment was his most subtly executed. Not unlike many of our nation's older cities, Albany's problems were significant. Albany's aging housing stock presented formidable challenges; the city contained not hundreds, but thousands of occupied homes built in the nineteenth century. Years of middle class out-migration to suburban towns and school districts, subsidized by short sighted government policies, had reduced the population to just over 100,000. The aging downtown seemed to be fighting a losing battle trying to compete with the free parking and glitter of ever expanding suburban shopping malls. By the 1980s thousands of local residents, both uptown and suburban, had gotten out of the habit of frequenting Albany's downtown, except when such a visit was totally unavoidable.

In his efforts to break down the urban-suburban wall which had grown up since the 1960s, Mayor Whalen utilized a very old tool—the three hundred year old Dongan Charter. Within a month of taking office he started planning for a mammoth Tricentennial Celebration. This would not be the first time a celebration had been planned in honor of an anniversary of the ancient charter, but this time there was to be a major difference.

Times Union-Ray Hoy

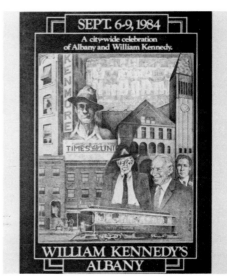

Times Union-LeFevre

Above
As evidenced from the September 6-9, 1984 date on the poster advertising a celebration of William Kennedy's literary accomplishments, Albanians already recognized the accomplishments of their native son, even before he would receive the Pulitzer Prize in Literature, the Book Circle Award or MacArthur Foundation recognition.

Above left
Albany author Bill Kennedy at the opening of "Ironweed," starring Jack Nicholson and Meryl Streep, filmed in the city and based on his Pulitzer Prize winning book of the same name, about a homeless alcoholic living in 1930s Albany.

While previous celebrations had concentrated on one day, Whalen's celebration would concentrate on an entire year.

Nineteen eighty-six Albany can be best described as a city in celebration of itself. With considerable community support and substantial financial aid from the State of New York and a host of corporate sponsors, the city celebrated from January to December with everything from lectures, concerts and exhibitry. A grand parade and hot air balloon race were held on Dongan Charter Day, July 22nd. Street festivals and block parties were held throughout the summer. A gala was held in the concourse of the Empire State Plaza in which 4,863 people were wined and dined. By New Year's Eve Albanians celebrated their first "First Nite" Celebration in the streets and public spaces of their ancient downtown. They and their visitors from across the region entered 1987 feeling optimistic about themselves and their Capital City.

More than a decade later, there are the physical legacies of the great celebration. A group of investors constructed a new office building on North Pearl Street and named it after the Tricentennial. As a lasting monument to the city government's 300th birthday, Tricentennial Park was created opposite the former railroad station on Broadway. The park was graced with a life sized bronze rendition of the 1797 Seal of the City, stylized by Albany artist and award-winning *Times Union* cartoonist Hy Rosen with the trappings of trade and commerce in honor of the city's important historical role as a center of free enterprise. The statue was underwritten by Fleet Bank whose dramatic new headquarters Plaza had created a spectacular 17 million dollar phoenix from the ashes of the architectural wreck which had been Union Station. The former railroad station was renamed Kiernan Plaza in honor of Albany native, Peter D. Kiernan, whose willingness to have his corporation invest in the landmark, saved one of the city's most beloved structures for future generations to enjoy. The city's "Alive at Five" free Thursday evening concerts to keep office workers downtown after work, also initiated under Whalen, have become a summer tradition in front of the reborn railroad station.

Unlike the sixties and early seventies, the late 1970s and most of the 80s were good years for historic preservation. The earlier loss of several familiar landmarks; the Hun House and Governor Tompkins house on upper Capitol Hill, the massive cast iron dome and classic pillars of the Albany Savings Bank, and the elegantly ornamented stepped roofed Pruyn Library at Clinton Square had saddened and shocked city residents. These individual losses, coupled with the collective loss of more than three thousand buildings which had once comprised the South Mall, saw a reaction in the activism of the Historic Albany Foundation and a rapidly increasing number of neighborhood groups protective of their quality of life. City government, determined to join in saving the unique character of the city, and now took a belated leadership role.

In the twilight years of the Rockefeller era, the great gothic Delaware and Hudson/Albany Evening Journal Building, was in desperate need of a new tenant. Thanks to the brokering of Mayor Corning, the complex was joined to the old Federal Building to become University Plaza, the new state headquarters of the State University of New York. Following City Hall's cleaning in 1975, in preparation for the Nation's Bicentennial, several architecturally significant downtown bank buildings followed suit, and landscaped traffic islands were placed in the middle of State Street. As part of the 1986 Celebration, a clock was placed in the traffic island at the top of State Street hill, and a still visible quarter mile outline of the 1675 British stockade was outlined on the streets and sidewalks of downtown using the orange, white and blue colors of the city's tricolor flag.

From the mid seventies to the late eighties, Albany became a state and national leader in utilizing community development funds and historic preservation tax credits to rehabilitate its historic structures. The state economy began to enter the recession in the 1990s, causing prices and development to decrease. The Whalen administration responded by using new state housing monies to fill in the 'missing teeth' in old urban townhouse streets, creating much

Since 1614 with the establishment of Ft. Nassau on an island in the Hudson until the British takeover in 1664, Albany was under Dutch control. The Dutch regained the colony briefly in 1672-74 only to lose possession forever at the treaty table. Dutch culture and even language dominated Albany County until after the American Revolution when the "Yankee Invasion" of New England emigrants reduced them to minority status. The traditions of Nieu Nederlandt are celebrated each May during the Tulip Festival and Pinxterfest. An annual St. Nicholas Day Dinner is hosted each year on December 6th by the Dutch Settlers Society, composed of descendents of the original colonists.

Albany County Convention and Visitors Center.–Photo by Tim Raab

Under Mayor Jennings, the annual Hudson River regatta held at the Corning Preserve has been augmented by a "Riverfest" including craft vendors and a carnival.

City of Albany–J.M.Elario

needed two unit owner occupied housing which blended into, rather than clashed with the character of existing historic neighborhoods.

One hallmark of the Whalen years was an extensive increase in activity in the city's cultural life. Old stand-bys like Capital Repertory Theater, the Albany Symphony Orchestra, The Albany Institute of History and Art and the State Museum, coupled with grassroots organizations like the Musicmobile, Center Galleries, Electronic Body Arts and City Arts Office, which had had their beginnings during the CETA era, continued and were now joined by the Berkshire Ballet, The Irish-American Heritage Museum, Shakespeare in the Park and Live at the Lakehouse, which later evolved into Park Playhouse. A new Mayor's Office of Special Events was established to encourage more festivals and arts programs. Corporate sponsorship greatly increased the number of business people and suburban residents involved in the city's cultural life. Whalen's plan to marshal the people and resources of the region to the mutual benefit of the city was working. When the 1990 Census results were announced the population had stabilized at 100,000, ending a long decline that had begun 30 years before.

Less successful was an attempt by Whalen to expand the city's international horizons through the twinning with foreign cities. Albany had been twinned with Nimijen in the Netherlands since the Marshall Plan years after the Second World War. Under Thomas Whalen new twinning delegations were exchanged with Verona, Italy, Tula in Russia, Quebec City, Canada, the Province of Extramadura in Spain, Ghent, Belguim and even Grand Bahama Island. Of the several twinnings, the most recent, Tula, and the first, Nimijen, in the Netherlands, have been the most productive. In fact, it is the association with Nimijen, who in gratitude for post war assistance sent the city 50,000 tulip bulbs in 1948, which led to the establishment of the Albany Tulip Festival. The festival is now a fifty year old tradition which celebrates the city's Dutch, and in more recent years, African American heritage.

In an age of decreasing aid from the state and federal governments, city governments had to become leaner and more efficient. To that end, Whalen sold off underused structures to the private

Below left
Albany award-winning actor William Devane, known to millions for his numerous movie roles and starring role as "Greg Sumner" in television's Knot's Landing, is shown here as John F. Kennedy in the acclaimed TV special "The Missiles of October," a portrayal of the Cuban Missile Crisis. Devane regularly returns to his hometown to perform in benefit productions on behalf of local charitable and cultural causes. His sister, C. Patricia Devane is the former director of the Albany City Arts Office. Another well known Albany actor, is Harold Gould ("Rhoda"'s father, "The Golden Girls," "The Sting", and over sixty other film projects) whose support of the theater department of the University at Albany has been substantial.

Below
Broadway and Hollywood actor Charlayne Woodard began her acting career in student productions at the Albany High School. Among her many acclaimed film roles are "Cindy," "Ain't Misbehavin,'" "The Crucible," "Hair," "Buffalo Girls," and "Chicago Hope." In her a acclaimed solo performances in "Pretty Fire" and "Neat," she depicts auto-biographical experiences from her childhood growing up in Albany's Arbor Hill neighborhood and memories of spending summers with grandparents down South. The popular actor and playwrite regularly returns to her family in Albany, where she has also performed for Capital Repertory Company.

Times Union

Times Union

Thomas Rocco

The life size bronze statue of Lewis A. Swyer, a successful and affable developer and patron of the arts, was crafted by Richard Kislov, M.D. a Michigan sculptor and plastic surgeon. The strikingly life-like statue is positioned in Academy Park facing the City Hall he advised for many years.

sector in the hopes that they might better serve the people and enrich the tax rolls at the same time. Several nineteenth century schools converted into condominiums exist today as a testimony to that policy. In the interest of efficiency a new Public Works garage to house DPW and the newly independent Water Authority was built in North Albany. The building's new access road off Erie Blvd. was named in honor of long time Alderman, Common Council President and Assemblyman Richard J. Conners.

In the boom years of the 1980s Albany could boast that it had two Fortune 500 companies, Key Bank and Fleet Bank. Changes in the overly protective, state "home-town banking law" in the late 70s encouraged competition and mergers. But the national economy and contemporary banking trends continued with the trend of consolidation and merging, so that by the late 1990s virtually every bank in Albany was part of a large financial institution headquartered in another city or state. Along with government, education and medicine, the "FIRE" industries – i.e. finance, insurance and real estate, continue to be a vital force of the city's economy. The prosperity of Key Bank under the energetic leadership of Victor Riley also changed the city skyline with the addition of two new office towers on the east side of South Pearl Street, near the Knickerbocker Arena.

Politics in the post Corning era changed radically. Long term office holders and household names like Erastus Corning and Congressman Sam Stratton, passed on in the natural progression of time. Michael McNulty, scion of an almost legendary and popular Green Island political family, was elected Congressman to replace Stratton in 1988. Democrat Hugh Carey, the Brooklyn Congressman who had become governor after the four term Republican regime of Nelson Rockefeller and Malcom Wilson, was in turn succeeded after completing two terms, by his Lieutenant Governor Mario Cuomo.

As the local political calendar moved into the 1990s, events were anything but ordinary. The decline and fall of James J. Coyne, Jr., Albany County's first and, up to that time, only County Executive was a painful drawn out process for Albanians, and especially Democratic Albanians, to watch.

Jim Coyne, of Colonie, a former schoolteacher, in his second year as County Clerk, had been selected by the Albany Democrats as a compromise candidate to run in 1975 for the newly created and comparatively weak position of County Executive. Coyne's general election against Republican former Rockefeller Commissioner, General Almerin C. O'Hara, and Independent Democratic Reformer, Theresa Cooke, the County Treasurer, was grueling. Between the general Election and the Democratic primary with Cooke, Coyne had participated in fifty-four debates before being elected!

Early in his tenure Coyne proved himself to be independent of the Democratic organization, and did not hesitate to sue the County Legislature, to affirm his powers under the untested new county charter. Needless to say, his relationship with Mayor Corning chilled considerably, with the mayor strengthening his considerable influence in the County Legislature.

Despite the fact that Coyne was frequently at odds with the Legis-

James J. Coyne, Jr. on January 31, 1991, at the Frank Sinatra concert and grand opening of the $68 million 18,000 seat Knickerbocker Arena in downtown Albany.

Times Union-Skip Dickstein

lature, he was still able, by force of personality and very effective public relations to accomplish a number of his initiatives. The early years of Coyne's sixteen-year tenure were marked by a considerable amount of progressive government. Delinquent property taxes, once a plague on the county budget, were greatly reduced, and foreclosed properties sold off. New social programs were started and new blood and ideas brought in to the county government.

But by 1983, following the death of Mayor Corning, the political climate began to change. Newspaper coverage of city politics, which had been so intense under Corning, began to shift to the County government. Coyne, often viewed by the press as the "fair haired boy' in the Corning years, now seemed to have inherited the black hat in the drama of Albany politics. There was no longer a septuagenarian political boss and city chief executive to contrast him with. His rivalry and chilly relationship with the Legislative majority did not lessen, nor was his relationship with the new mayor of Albany any better than it had been with the previous mayor.

Coyne's casual image and active social life was initially a political asset. In time it would become a source of controversy. Coyne had been a three-letter athlete in both high school and college. In his post college years he had even earned a try out in minor league baseball. His enthusiasm for virtually all sports had led him into an unofficial manager's position with the Patroons, a new basketball team that packed the old Washington Avenue Armory.

His interest in baseball was the moving force in the county's building Heritage Park in Colonie, home of the Albany-Colonie Yankees. Bolstered by these popular successes, Coyne began to expand his vision for Albany County. Following his reelection in 1983, the drive to build an Albany County Civic Center was begun in earnest.

The building of the Civic Center was torturous. From 1984 through its opening in 1990, the process of building the enormous multi-block hulk of aluminum and glass was highly controversial. Originally, Coyne wanted to build the facility in Latham, where land was cheap and parking would be plentiful. The city politicians wanted no part of it. They insisted that if this large public project were to be built at all, it would have to be an urban structure whose vitality would bring life to the Capital City's struggling downtown.

A site fronting on South Pearl Street and covering several city blocks which in "pre-Mall" days had been the old Market Square, was selected for development. Downtown land prices, building demolition costs, and infrastructure relocation costs, all combined to increase the construction price of the great colossus, which would become known as the Knickerbocker Arena.

As more players had their hand in the works, more amenities were demanded. Upholstered seats replaced the plastic. A million-dollar cube-like electronic scoreboard, suspended from the ceiling to accommodate scorers and advertisers alike, was added to the plans. Another last minute decision to expand the hockey capacity to Olympic size in the hopes of attracting the winter Olympics, further escalated the costs of the project. Finally private "sky boxes," the ultimate in corporate luxury and exclusiveness, topped off the plan, which had risen from an anticipated 35 million dollars to 78 million dollars in seven years.

Of the total cost, less that 10 million dollars came to the county in state or federal aid. Such aid offset the cost of the covered sidewalk, elevators, bridge over Eagle Street and ramps which now made it possible for a person to travel in a wheelchair from South Pearl Street to the Empire State Plaza, regardless of the weather. All other costs were born by the county taxpayers.

Albany owes its prosperity and its importance in history to its strategic location at the head of the navigable waters of the Hudson. The city is actually built along an estuary—an arm of the sea. The Hudson is tidal at Albany and remains so as far as the Troy dam.

Times Union-Skip Dickstein

The highlight of Jim Coyne's career was surely the opening of the Knickerbocker Arena with a gala concert by Frank Sinatra on January 31, 1990. It was also, for Coyne, the beginning of the end. In the midst of the excitement over the new facility which would attract sellout crowds to see groups ranging from Billy Graham to the Grateful Dead, Coyne's personal life and finances began to unravel. In January 1989 the FBI had informed him that he was a target of a criminal investigation regarding his business activities and income tax. Ironically, an exhaustive audit of several years of income tax records resulted in a refund rather than additional liabilities. But the investigations had led to other areas in the County Executive's personal and public life. For over a decade, Coyne's personal lifestyle had exceeded the means provided by his public salary. To supplement his income he had invested in so-called "gray market" cars imported from Europe and a number of racehorses at Saratoga. Both endeavors were accomplished by involving partners, many partners, some of whom had diverse business interests of their own, and in some cases a high riding lifestyle incompatible with local politics.

In time, Coyne's public image began to clash with the preferred low key middle class model civil servant image preferred by the old O'Connell organization. His regular presence at the Saratoga social scene was faithfully followed in the media, and to most observers was more reminiscent of a Jimmy Walker than an Erastus Corning.

When in 1986, the federal tax code was revamped to take the profit out of such speculative investments, Coyne faced a financial disaster. Finding himself with few options, he stalled off the inevitable by gambling and borrowing beyond his capacity to repay. He was finally indicted by the federal government in July of 1991 on nearly a score of charges primarily relating to his failure to report his true debt to lending institutions. As bad as the situation was for Coyne personally, there were at least two charges that related to his conduct as an elected official. His acceptance of a used car from a county vendor and receipt of a loan of several thousand dollars through a go-between from the architect of the Knickerbocker Arena, brought his problems squarely into the political area.

The County executive's scandal, occurring in the last year of his term, could not have come at a worse time or had worse results for the Albany County Democrats. The party selected former County Attorney, Robert Lyman, to run for the office. The Republicans, seeing an opening to offset the Democrats better than two to one enrollment advantage, ran one of their best vote-getters, attorney Michael Hoblock, a popular Colonie town councilman and former Assemblyman, to run for the office. Hoblock waged a spirited and vigorous campaign to become the first Republican elected countywide in nearly 20 years.

While the make-up of the County Legislature changed little, three anti-machine candidates upset incumbent regular Democrats. Michael Conners and E. Nancy Wiley replaced incumbents in the primary, while John J. McEneny, following a disputed tied primary vote, defeated the Legislature's 18 year incumbent majority leader in an unprecedented " write-in" election. Albany politics would never be the same again.

Jim Coyne was able to finish the last year of his fourth term as County Executive. He refused to plead guilty to any charge related to his office, refused a plea bargain offer, and was prosecuted in federal court. His first trial in the spring of 1992 ended in a hung jury on all counts. His second trial, held in the summer of the same year and just a few weeks after he was forced to declare personal bankruptcy, resulted in a conviction on several charges and a sentence of 46 months in federal custody. To this day, Coyne has never admitted his guilt on any charge related to his public office. He wrote two books while in prison, one a work of fiction, and another describing his downfall at the hands of the federal government. Following his release, in 1997 he made a last attempt at a political comeback by running as an independent against an incumbent for his old job of County Clerk. He was resoundingly defeated, and so far has returned to private life.

Like the South Mall project of nearly a generation before, the Knickerbocker Arena has always had vocal devotees and detractors. Prior to its existence, the largest single indoor gathering place in the capital city was a 1931 movie theatre or a century old armory, both capable of holding just 3000 patrons, and then only under very crowded conditions. Since the Arena is used mainly in the evenings and on weekends, the insurmountable parking problems that were predicted never materialized. By the end of the decade, the facility now known as the Pepsi Arena, is finally paying for itself each year and is at least partially meeting its original goal of breathing new life into the city's three-centuries-old down-

College of St. Rose

Students on the porch of Wellworth Hall

Times Union-Paul Buckowski

Above
Students at the College of Saint Rose are an integral part of their neighborhood. The four year liberal arts college, founded in 1920 by the Sisters of Saint Joseph, has blended into the residential character of its century old community by mixing modern classroom, library and athletic facilities with the original Victorian and early twentieth century architecture so typical of Pine Hills. Well-used porches, as evidenced by this photo, are appreciated by students and passers-by alike.

Above right
Archeologist Karen Hartgen holds up a portion of seventeenth century Chinese export porcelain used by the early settlers who lived on the block developed in 1996-7 for the new Empire State Development Corporation on Broadway. Development in Albany's four century old downtown Albany must, by state law be preceded by thorough archeological exploration.

town. Regardless of the controversy and skepticism surrounding its birth, Jim Coyne's imposing vision outlived his political career and remains today as the legacy of a very controversial and complex man.

The administration of Mayor Thomas Whalen was to end on a much happier note. After ten and a half years as the city's chief executive, Tom Whalen felt it was time to move on. The partnership in a downtown law firm that he had given up shortly after becoming mayor could be resumed, and in fact, U.S. Senator Daniel Patrick Moynihan had nominated him to a lifetime appointment to the federal bench. Two years before leaving office, Whalen, in the Rose Garden of the White House, received from President George Bush the crowning affirmation that his efforts on behalf of his city had not gone unrecognized. The City of Albany was designated by the National Civic League as an "All America City," a well-earned laurel still celebrated on city entrance signs today, a reminder of a good time in the city's history when Albanians consciously rediscovered who they were and felt good about their heritage.

THE JENNINGS ADMINISTRATION

The 1993 primary election for mayor in the still overwhelmingly Democratic city pitted two well established office holders against one another. County Legislature Chairman and Electrical Workers

Times Union-Michael P. Farrell

Since 1995 The University at Albany has become the Summer Training Camp of the New York Giants team. The camp, which has been subsidized by New York State, the City and the University, brings thousands of sports enthusiasts each summer to the campus athletic fields located on the Albany-Guilderland boundary.

Business Agent Harold Joyce, scion of a large and respected West End family long prominent in Democratic circles, stepped down from the party chairmanship to run for mayor as the party nominee. His challenger, Alderman Gerald D. Jennings, was vice-principal of Albany High School and had served as a rare dissident voice in the Common Council during the Whalen years. Both candidates ran vigorous and expensive campaigns collectively spending more than a half million dollars. Jennings won by 843 votes as 25,021 Albany Democrats voted for their choice. The general election resulted in a predictable Democratic landslide with Jennings winning nearly 74% of the 31,803 votes cast.

The administration of Jerry Jennings was ushered in by a colorful inauguration at Albany High School, and would set a different style from that of his predecessors. The 1993 election would produce the first time inclusion of two women in top city-wide elected positions, former Alderman Nancy Burton as comptroller and former Arbor Hill Community Center Director Betty Barnette as re-elected treasurer. When both women were re-elected four years later, they would be joined by University at Albany professor, Dr. Helen DesFosses, as President of the Common Council. As Albany's municipal government enters the next century, three of its four top elected officials will be female, a far cry from former years. Additionally, with the election of Betty Barnette, the city saw not only its first female city treasurer, but also its first African American elected city-wide to a non-judicial position.

Principle programs of the Jennings administration included the consolidation and reduction in the number of city departments, the hiring of additional police, especially through the use of federal grants, reestablishment of decentralized neighborhood policing and continued development of downtown and, more recently, Central Avenue corridor. In 1996 local sports enthusiasts got a boost when the University at Albany became the summer training

Alderman Gerald D. Jennings (left) and County Legislative Chairman Harold L. Joyce. Photo taken in February, 1993, three months before the two Democrats would oppose one another in a heated, costly and close primary election.

Times Union-Steve Jacobs

camp for the New York Giants football team. In 1998, the City's efforts in working for neighborhood improvement won the U.S. Conference of Mayors coveted Livability Award.

Political observers have found much to study in the close relationship that the city enjoyed with the governorship, then in its twentieth year of Democratic occupancy at the time Mayor Jennings took office. Governor Mario Cuomo, running for his fourth four year term, demonstrated his support for the city by purchasing and closing the polluting Sheridan Avenue recycling plant from the city, thus solving a controversial political problem for the new mayor and injecting the city's coffers with millions in welcome state dollars.

In addition, Cuomo had conducted an extensive survey of state office buildings at the Harriman Campus on the western edge of the city. The results of the Cuomo study concluded that the deteriorating 1950s and 60s architecture was too costly to renovate, and might be better off being sold, with the agencies and their workers being relocated elsewhere to reinvigorate the urban economy. Pursuant to this end, Cuomo released architectural renderings of a towering new state office building which he proposed to be built on the site of a vacant lot and a non-functioning parking garage next to the County Office Building on State Street. At the same time fellow Democrat, State Comptroller Carl McCall, announced that he too would be constructing a substantial new home for the Comptroller's Office and the State Retirement system at another downtown location not yet selected. The future appeared to bode well for the city…, and then the bottom dropped out.

New York State, which had been late drifting into the national recession, was late getting out. Layoffs and corporate downsizing had destroyed fully half of the million new jobs created during the Cuomo years. State Senator George E. Pataki of Peekskill, a relative unknown, campaigned across the state on the Republican and Conservative tickets. His anti-Cuomo platform was in sync with the national Republicans calling for smaller government, less taxes and a more business friendly environment. Perhaps just as important as his exploitation of economic issues, Pataki's pledge to restore the death penalty in New York brought the Republicans back to the Eagle Street Governor's Mansion in full force.

The USS Slater, now permanently docked on the Albany waterfront, is the last floating survivor of the World War II fleet of over 500 Destroyer Escorts. One reason for its miraculous survival was its more than two decades of active duty in the Greek Navy. In 1993 it was brought back to the United States for restoration as a memorial and museum by the Destroyer Escort Historic Foundation.

Times Union-Skip Dickstein

Almost immediately, the new administration citing a multi-billion dollar deficit sharply curtailed state spending. The State Street office building was scrapped, the McCall building put on hold, and a comprehensive reevaluation of the State workforce was begun. For two years relations between the Pataki administration and the Capital District remained tense. Rumored and actual downsizing of the state workforce through attrition, hiring freezes, early retirements, and attrition dominated the media and depressed consumer confidence. Most controversial of all Pataki actions was the unsuccessful attempt to move 4,000 state worker tax processing jobs south to Kingston and other parts of the state. This proposal was coupled with a vague and controversial plan to consolidate scores of state data centers "somewhere" in the state.

While many of the Pataki proposals most threatening to the status of Albany as the state's capital never came to pass, the rancor and tension between local politicians, the Democratically controlled State Assembly, County Executive Michael Breslin and the public employee unions made for a considerable lack of harmony in a city which had taken state government for granted for far too many years.

This view of Albany from the hills of Rensselaer taken in 1997 by Albany photographer, Lindsey Watson, shows the unique topography of the Hudson Valley. Before the glaciers of the Great Ice Age had left the valley, a natural dam backed up water covering the valley floor of today's Albany County and beyond. The resulting body of water which geologists call Lake Albany had its shoreline at the Helderberg escarpment seen in the background of the photo. This long forgotten prehistoric lake is the reason why petrified shells and fossils are found in such abundance along the limestone cliffs of John Boyd Thacher State Park, now 1100 feet above the valley floor.

Prior to World War I, the Market Square relieved congestion on State Street, where farmers had peddled their goods for generations. Many Albany housewives made daily visits to the market.

CHAPTER 11

CHRONICLES OF LEADERSHIP

In one respect or another it may be said that Albany has always been the capital city on the Hudson. Its often-mentioned strategic value at the head of an estuary, near the confluence of the Hudson River with the Mohawk, made the small, palisaded community important out of proportion to its size. That location, too, was important in bringing commerce to Albany.

Albany was a natural funnel for the flow of Americans moving westward, for the produce of the Old West moving east. The funnel opened wider with the building of the Erie Canal, the markets of the Great Lakes opening to Albany's manufacturers, financiers, and merchants. The people and the institutions of Albany were generally equal to the challenges of the virtually unregulated economy of 19th-century America; where they were not, the factories, banks, and companies they created were swept away.

If anything is illustrated by the business biographies in this book, it is that the business community of Albany is as adaptable, as pragmatic, and yet remains as human now as were the fur traders who started it all, on a lost island in the Hudson River, long ago. The older firms included demonstrate a great continuity, a special sort of creative endurance, the newer ones enterprise and imagination. Family-owned businesses, many of them several generations in a single family, possess a rich folklore relating to their firms and founders; a sense of familial responsibility seems to come with the obligations of management. In other corporations, without exception, the strong, the colorful, the omnicompetent, and the idiosyncratic managers, employees, and officers linger on like shades, occasional reminders of halcyon, salad days, both inspiration and example for the hectic present, the unformed future.

Albany was a center for river and canal traffic, open since its beginnings to the sea, connected by rail for nearly a century and a half to other parts of the continent, for decades by air. This city has seen all sorts of pioneers, from Dutch *boslopers* to technological and financial innovators; tradition continues in a city grown old but no less independent, vital still in ways perhaps unintelligible to the Albany of the past, in other ways most familiar. In business, as in so much else, Albanians did not lose sight of the past, kept solid grip on the present, and did not dread the future. The motto under the city's crest reads "Assiduity," which has in our case not been passive observation. In all the institutions of Albany presented here, diligence has been the key to endurance and the passage to success when coupled with vision. Because of this, Albany has been, and remains, the capital city on the Hudson.

ADAM ROSS CUT STONE CO., INC.

Adam Ross, the founder, was born in 1839 in Prestonpons, Dunbartonshire, Scotland. In 1854, at the age of 15, he left Scotland on a sailing ship and after a six-week voyage arrived in New York City with scarcely a dollar in his pocket. His desire was to become a stonecutter and master carver. Traveling up the Hudson River, he began to ply his trade and went into business for a time with Robert Connell, brother of his wife-to-be. Many markers in Oakwood Cemetery in Troy, New York say "Connell and Ross" in small carved letters on the base. Several years later, Robert Connell left for Iowa.

In 1865 Adam married Agnes Connell and after their marriage Agnes saved up so Adam could go into business for himself. At first he worked by himself accepting only very small jobs. As time went by he hired two or three stonecutters to help him. At that time the principal tools of the trade were hammers and chisels and cut stone was delivered by horse-drawn wagons. A stonecutter worked ten

First year in Albany, 1906.

hours a day for five days and eight hours on Saturday allowing some time for family shopping on Saturday evening. His pay might reach as much as $12.00 per week.

In 1889 Adam's sons, John, Adam, Jr. and Charles, began working for their father and as a result the business began to expand and Adam Ross & Son was founded on Sixth Avenue in Troy, New York. From here the business grew and moved to its present location at 999-1003 Broadway in Albany, New York in 1906 and an office was still maintained in Troy.

In 1911 Adam Ross & Son in Troy merged with the Albany business and became incorporated as Adam Ross Cut Stone Company, Inc. Adam Ross, the founder, died prior to World War I and his son, Charles Ross, Sr. took control and continued to operate the business until the time of his death in 1951 with the help of his three sons, Donald, Kenneth, Charles, Jr. and one daughter, Bertha. In the years following, sons Donald, Charles, Jr. and then grandson, Robert E. Ross and great-grandson, David C. Ross have headed the business. Currently, David C. Ross and Randall R. Ross (sons of Robert E. Ross), George E. Mallette (grandson of Charles Ross, Sr.) and June B. Ross (wife of David C. Ross) are running the business. Thus, five generations of the Ross family have continued to operate the stone business since its inception in 1889.

There have been some difficult times over the years in the stone industry. During World War I (1917-18) there was no demand for stone. However, Charles Ross, Sr. was aware that stone planers could be used to roughly plane iron and steel for which there was a demand. Through his contacts with others in the stone industry, he was able to buy stone planers that were then idle and sell them to

Albany parade, 1924.

those in the iron finishing industry and thus were able to survive during the lean war years. Then, of course, the Depression years from 1929-36 were extremely difficult. During World War II (1940-45) the stone business came to a screeching halt. At this time they went into warehousing in transit mainly for General Electric products (transformers, motors, etc.). These items awaited the availability of a ship leaving from New York City. When a ship became available items from the Ross warehousing operation would be loaded on railroad cars and shipped to New York City.

Over the years there have been many changes in the tools and machinery used at Adam Ross Cut Stone. Some of the major changes were:

• Trucks replaced horse-drawn wagons

• Using shot instead of sand on the gang saw making cutting of stone much easier

• Wooden leanto buildings were replaced by brick buildings in 1927

• Introduction of overhead crane instead of hand-operated derricks

• Compressed air which made pneumatic tools possible instead of hammer and chisel

• Introduction of diamond saw blades to replace the old carborundum blades

• Introduction of diamonds for finishing and polishing

• Use of thinner pieces of stone (panels) for exterior of commercial buildings

• Use of stone for interior use in homes and businesses

• Introduction of computer controlled saws and routers

Over the years the business has increased from less than $5,000 to over $2,000,000 a year in sales and, at the same time, the territory served has grown from the Tri-City

Inside new mill, 1927.

area to the entire eastern United States. Cut stone is supplied for commercial and institutional use as well as interior and exterior applications to meet every need of homeowners. Shapes and finishes are contingent upon owner's specifications and variety is almost unlimited except for availability and practical consideration of cost. Modern transportation facilities on land, water and air have bridged the gap from most anywhere in the

world to their shop or to the jobsite.

Adam Ross Cut Stone Company, Inc. has produced a product which is long-lasting and practically indestructible. Their basic philosophy has been long hours of hard work to produce a quality product. Guiding principles for over 100 years have centered on quality and service.

New mill and office, 1927.

ALBANY INTERNATIONAL CORP.

In 1895, three Albany businessmen, with a capital investment of $40,000, formed the Albany Felt Company to manufacture papermakers' felts, large woven textile fabrics used to dewater paper stock and impart a finish to the paper sheet. In 1902, Albany Felt moved from its beginning at 19 Thatcher St. to the site that would be its principal home—a site which today remains a major manufacturing center, as well as the Company's corporate headquarters—1373 Broadway, located on the boundary line between the City of Albany and the Village of Menands.

All operations were conducted at the Broadway location from 1902 until 1947, when the first venture outside of Albany was established. Over the next twenty years, Albany Felt constructed mills in Canada and the Southeastern United States; developed overseas markets with acquisitions and joint ventures that brought it into Scandinavia, Latin America, The Netherlands, France, and Australia; and expanded into industrial fabrics and plastics.

In 1969, the most significant milestone in the Company's development took place. Albany Felt merged with Appleton Wire Works, the largest U.S. manufacturer of forming fabrics, and Nordiska Maskinfilt, the leading European clothing supplier to the Scandinavian paper industry as well as a major exporter to other countries, to form Albany International Corp. Each of the companies that joined together to become Albany International was privately owned and all held positions of leadership in their respective markets and communities.

During the 1970s, Albany International acquired paper machine clothing companies in England, Brazil, and Norway, as well as overseas and domestic capabilities in paper machine auxiliary equipment. The Company continued to expand and modernize existing paper machine clothing manufacturing

Today, the Broadway site houses Albany International's corporate headquarters and remains a major manufacturing center.

operations, as well as investing in its growing plastic products and industrial fabrics businesses and ventures. In the United States, it acquired a leading textile research firm near Boston, Massachusetts, now the home of Albany International Research Co.

Albany International offered its stock to the public in 1972, and listed on the New York Stock Exchange in July 1974. In 1976, the Company moved its corporate headquarters from the location on Broadway to the newly renovated Sage Estate, about a mile away. In 1983, in order to accommodate one of the Company's largest shareholder groups, who wished to diversify their holdings, management took the Company private in a leveraged buyout. Then, to reduce its newly acquired debt, all operations not primarily serving the paper industry were sold, and the Company again focused its resources on paper machine clothing and auxiliary equipment.

The shareholders voted in 1987 to make Albany International a public company once more. Class A Common Stock was offered to the public in September 1987, and in 1988, the

Company returned to a listing on the New York State Exchange.

With the completion of the new Press Fabrics division plant and offices across the Hudson River in East Greenbush, the former corporate offices in Menands became available. After extensive renovation, corporate headquarters returned to 1373 Broadway in April 1989.

Since 1987, Albany International has consolidated its global leadership position through acquisition, technological innovation, and investment in additional manufacturing facilities, including plants in China and Korea. By utilizing its core technologies and competencies, the Company has expanded to other industrial process growth applications in the High Performance Products markets. Today, Albany International is the world's largest manufacturer of paper machine clothing and high performance industrial doors, with 39 plants in 14 countries and approximately 6,000 employees. Net sales in 1997 were $710.1 million.

ALBANY LADDER

An entrepreneurial spark ignited by L.J. Heath, Sr. in 1932 burns bright today, over three generations later. From humble beginnings in a small Central Avenue building selling wood ladders, the company grew to one of the largest construction and industrial equipment rental companies in the northeast with eight locations in four states, 200 employees and also one of the largest rental fleets of aerial work platforms and contractors' equipment in the northeast.

Wood scaffolding was soon added to the ladder business. L.J. Heath (Papa) traveled with his crew to install the scaffolding for artists, painters and contractors. In 1945, Lester J. Heath, Jr. (Jack) joined the family business, after serving as an Air Force pilot. Jack was instrumental in adding sectional steel scaffolding,

Jack Heath, and his son Les with a sample ladder used by company founder L.J. Heath when he traveled the northeast selling ladders in the earliest days of the company.

and cable swing scaffolds to the company that was now beginning to specialize in equipment to get workers off the ground. Their destiny was in motion.

Scaffolding has remained important to Albany Ladder. In 1994, Albany Ladder successfully brought to market SWC sectional steel scaffolding. SWC represented the first significant design change in this product in over four decades.

Another Heath son was on the scene in 1970. Lester J. Heath III (Les), President from 1986 until his death in 1998, led the company's tremendous growth and geographic expansion into Vermont, Massachusetts and Pennsylvania. He grew the business from three locations to the eight it has today.

New technology and products to make the contractor's job easier, safer and more efficient were continually sought. In 1975 the first aerial work platform lift arrived. It was a 27 foot boom lift. Albany Ladder now has everything necessary, from ladders to scaffolding to 150 foot aerial work platform lifts, to solve construction or industrial needs for an elevated working platform. Aerial work platforms are now found everywhere on construction and industrial jobsites.

Albany Ladder has been a part of many high profile projects including the Empire State Plaza, Lake Placid Winter Olympics, Walmart Distribution Centers, Pyramid Malls, Carousel Malls, *Woodstock*, Watkins Glen NASCAR Races, ESPN Golf Tournaments, Ryder Cup Matches, the Buffalo Bills practice dome, Albany International Airport, major motion pictures, most recently "The Horse Whisperer," many church restorations, and the creation of the Leonardo daVinci bronze horse which will soon be shipped home to Milan, Italy. Albany Ladder provided aerial work platforms, contractors equipment, scaffolding and scaffolding installation.

Les wanted more. He had a vision for the company and every one of the employees who worked to make Albany Ladder succeed. "Business is a part of life, and I have a real interest in restoring spirit to the workplace and meaning to work," Les said. His fundamental beliefs and philosophies were put to the test in the running of his company. He

Drivers and scaffold crew taking a break before loading the next truck in the fifties.

instituted company wide training programs to foster employee involvement. Believing that "the core of our business is people," his programs emphasized integrating work life with other aspects outside of employment. Many of his programs received national recognition.

The Heath family created and grew their business from 1932 until 1998. In 1998 "the ladder company" changed hands. After the untimely death of Les Heath, grandson of the founder, the family sold the business to National Equipment Services. Now a national, public corporation it continues to grow and prosper, still using the Albany Ladder name.

Platforms designed and installed by Albany Ladder sit atop the Lake Placid ski jump. In the foreground sits an early scissor lift work platform where ABC Sports cameramen were positioned to televise the 1980 Winter Olympics.

ALBANY LAW SCHOOL

In 1945 the world held its breath as humanity asserted its right to condemn the most horrific acts the world has ever witnessed. A gavel slammed, a final breath was taken, a chair screeched back and the stately gentleman began to speak. The scene was Nuremberg at the start of the Nazi war crimes trials. The stately gentleman, who tempered the collective anger of the world with his quiet sense of justice was U.S. Supreme Court Justice Robert H. Jackson, chief U.S. prosecutor. This small country lawyer had risen beyond national prominence to garner the attention of a world stage.

Justice Robert H. Jackson's educational roots can be traced to December 16, 1851, the opening of Albany Law School. On that day, 23 men climbed three flights of stairs in the Exchange Building on State Street in downtown Albany. For them, it was the first day of their professional lives. For the institution, it was to be the first

---

Albany Law School follows a traditional approach to the study of law—learning through doing—that gives students a greater educational experience through direct involvement in actual or simulated lawyering situations.

lecture of nearly 150 years of legal education.

Albany Law School is one of the oldest continuously operating law schools in the nation and the oldest within the State of New York. The School's founding fathers, Ira Harris, Amasa J. Parker, and Amos Dean, were visionaries who realized the practical importance of a formal legal education. These gentlemen provided a cutting-edge and revolutionary education for the

Since making its permanent home at 80 New Scotland Avenue in 1929, Albany Law School has grown into a haven of legal scholarship within the heart of New York's Capital City.

cost of $40 per term and $10 for a diploma. While the tuition has increased over the years, a diploma still costs $10.

She refused to accept that she had been told "no." She refused to accept the notion that no place existed for her at the bar. She refused to accept the fact that the law itself, excluded her from practicing what the law demanded. She refused to accept and she forced them to change. Kate Stoneman, after being denied the ability to practice law because she was a woman, petitioned the New York Legislature to allow women to be admitted to the practice of law. Stoneman graduated from Albany Law in 1898 and proceeded to become a fixture in the movement to gain equal rights for women.

Stoneman ushered in a new era for the New York Bar, but Albany Law School also has helped form the legal minds of such distinguished individuals as President William McKinley, Supreme Court Justice David J. Brewer, New York State Court of Appeals Chief

Judges Lawrence H. Cooke and Alton B. Parker, former Secretaries of War Redfield Proctor and William F. Vilas, and Secretary of Housing and Urban Development Andrew M. Cuomo. James C. Mathews, class of 1868, the first African-American judge in New York state, set an example for many of today's leaders, such as Time Warner's first African-American president, Richard D. Parsons.

Since making its permanent home at 80 New Scotland Avenue in 1929, the law school has expanded to include a library housing more than half a million volumes, a modern moot courtroom for 280 spectators, and cutting-edge

In 1936, the law school's library accomodated 205 students. Today, the remodeled Schaffer Law Library offers training and electronic services for 732 future lawyers and houses a media center and more than half a million volumes and microfilms.

computer facilities. By focusing on the complexities of New York law, the School has earned a reputation as one of the state's foremost law schools. Albany Law School was one of the first institutions to develop a curriculum that effectively trained students for the practice of law. Its graduates have consistently performed well on the New York Bar examination and have distinguished themselves in the legal profession.

Its location in the capital city has fostered a strong emphasis on the lawyer's role in the realm of government. This led Albany Law School to establish the Government Law Center in 1978, which has become a national model for other law schools. The Moot Court program, in the spirit and tradition begun by Amos Dean, won a national competition in 1995.

She killed her husband, yet society paused, to say that while we do not condone your actions, we do not condemn them either. This woman made national headlines when she was granted clemency from her murder conviction because her now dead husband

had beaten and abused her. She was free thanks to the efforts of students who refused to let injustice lie. The Clinical Legal Studies Program at Albany Law is designed to teach students how to practice law. In the case of Charline Brundidge, the students learned that the law is about people: real people with real life problems, not merely faceless names reprinted in textbooks. The students fought for justice, and they won.

Since the earliest days when a single year of lectures combined with a two-year clerkship constituted an Albany Law School

education, practical experience has played a vital role in legal education. Albany Law's Clinical Legal Studies Program places students into the world of working law. Practicing under New York Student Practice Rules, law students started their own *pro bono* projects in areas such as disabilities law, AIDS law, domestic violence law, and litigation law. These projects have freed wrongfully imprisoned individuals, secured the rights of the physically handicapped, and assisted the elderly in preparing for the future.

In marking its sesquicentennial in 2001, Albany Law School affirms its commitment to providing a top legal education. Under the leadership of its dean, Thomas H. Sponsler, along with a distinguished faculty, Albany Law School is working to extend its scholarship. The School has recently endowed three professorships in international commercial law, law and democracy, and law and technology. Along with its partners Albany Medical Center, the Sage College and Albany College of Pharmacy, Albany Law is expanding its presence in and service to the community through the University Heights Association. The aim of the University Heights Association is to create a world-class learning center that will provide the faculty and students with the necessary resources to go beyond the traditional realm of studies.

Three years of graduate school come down to this one test. With nervous apprehension she opens her exam booklet. Pausing, she takes a deep breath, reminding herself of the quality professors and challenging courses she has behind her. She thinks of the history, of those before her, and with confidence, the Albany Law graduate enters the legal profession.

ALBANY MEDICAL CENTER

Albany Medical Center, one of the nation's select academic health sciences centers, has been providing leadership in patient care, medical education and biomedical research for more than 150 years.

The institution consists of the 651-bed Albany Medical Center Hospital, one of the nation's oldest medical schools, Albany Medical College, 16 off-site primary care sites and the Albany Medical Center Foundation, Inc., one of northeastern New York's most active fund-raising organizations.

The non-profit institution has a staff of 6,500, including 350 members of the physicians' group practice, more than 1,200 nurses and a basic science faculty of 100. Each year, more than 600 medical students and 400 residents train at the center under some of the most outstanding physicians in the nation.

Albany Med serves as the region's institution of choice for a wide variety of care, including trauma, transplantation, cardiovascular, neurological, oncology

and geriatric. Albany Med also includes the region's only comprehensive pediatric treatment center, the Children's Hospital of Albany Med, which includes pediatric and neonatal intensive care units, as well as physicians from more than two dozen sub-specialties.

The institution serves as the designated trauma center for 25

Albany Medical College opened its doors on Jan. 2, 1839. The city of Albany donated the vacant Lancaster School building to house the fledgling college.

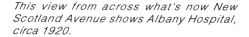

This view from across what's now New Scotland Avenue shows Albany Hospital, circa 1920.

counties of northeastern New York and western New England. Helping them get to Albany, in many cases, is Albany Med Flight, a BK-117 helicopter that is known as a flying intensive care unit. It was put into service in February, 1996.

In addition to providing leadership in all aspects of health care, Albany Med is an important regional economic resource. According to a recent economic impact study, Albany Med generates more than $600 million in economic activity annually. Of that, more than $350 million is directly felt in the four-county Capital Region. The study took into account medical center spending, including sales tax paid, charitable contributions and spin-off employment, as well as employee and student spending.

The college, which was founded in 1839, and hospital, founded 10 years later, took a major step forward in 1984 when the umbrella organization, the Albany Medical Center, was formed. This was done to ensure that the missions of the college and hospital were complementary and mutually reinforcing. While the two institutions were affiliated since the 19th century, the unified approach has helped strengthen both institutions.

In 1820, Alden March, M.D., arrived in Albany after graduating from Brown University. Within a year, he began teaching anatomy in a tiny school while trying to establish a more formal school of medicine. Assisting Dr. March was his brother-in-law, James Armsby, M.D. The idea was not well received by the community or the state legislature, which rejected the proposal because it felt the state had enough medical schools.

However, bolstered by the 1832 and 1834 cholera epidemics, the legislature approved Dr. March's plan and the people accepted it. So in the vacant Lancaster schoolhouse donated by the city, Albany Medical College opened Jan. 2, 1839 with 57 students. It moved to New Scotland Avenue in 1899.

Dr. March became the first medical college president and professor of surgery. Dr. Armsby was professor of anatomy and physiology. In 1849, Drs. March and Armsby led a group of supporters in establishing Albany Hospital at Lydius and Dove streets. This initiated the clinical affiliation between the hospital and college that exists today.

Distinguished alumni include John Swinburne, 1846, port of New York health officer and congressman, who was memorialized with Albany's Swinburne Park; James Salisbury, 1850, nutritionist for whom the Salisbury Steak is named; Theobald Smith, 1883, bacteriologist and discoverer of disease transmission by insects; Thomas Salmon, 1899, director of the National Committee for Mental

Hygiene and senior consultant in neuropsychiatry to Pershing's American expeditionary forces; Kenneth D. Blackfan, Harvard Medical School professor of pediatrics from 1923 to 1941; and ABC News Medical Editor Timothy Johnson.

Albany Hospital was the first private hospital in upstate New York. A fund drive raised $9,000 for the purchase of the former Albany County Jail at Eagle and Daniels streets. The hospital moved there from its location at Lydius and Dove streets and opened in 1854. The Civil War necessitated the construction of barracks for wounded soldiers and other activity prompted expansions. By 1872 the hospital had 131 beds and 21 physicians.

The hospital suffered continued financial difficulties and in June 1877 the sheriff padlocked the doors for unpaid debts. The hospital opened again six months later when the debts, except for a $24,000 mortgage, were paid by physicians and other professionals connected with the hospital.

This aerial view of Albany Medical Center shows Albany Medical College, left, and new additions such as the parking garage, right foreground, and the nine-story patient tower on the right.

Moving to New Scotland Avenue in 1899 was costly, despite the gift of land from the city Park Commission and $230,000 raised by residents. The new hospital included a wing for the nursing school, which was established in 1896 and closed in 1989. Other buildings were erected soon after. Mosher Memorial Pavilion, the first psychiatric unit attached to an American general hospital, went up in 1902. A year later, the Hun Memorial Tuberculosis Pavilion, was completed.

In 1928 came a fundamental step in the creation of Albany Medical Center—an agreement with the medical college that allowed for the construction of a new college building at the hospital's west end. A new hospital wing also was created. Today, Albany Med's main campus includes more than 20 buildings, many of which are now connected, and multiple off-site properties.

212

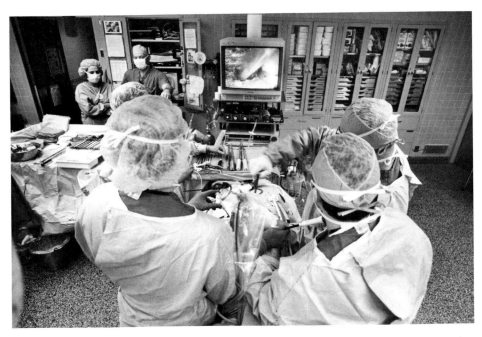

Advances in patient care include the new Minimally Invasive Surgery Center for Training and Education.

In recent years, major renovations and additions have included a new patient tower, a central services support facility, a cancer center, new research laboratories and a parking garage.

Affiliations also have expanded Albany Med's reach into the community. To date, some of the affiliations include the Albany Visiting Nurses Home Care Group, Child's Geriatric Organization, Capital Cardiology Associates, Capital District Pediatric Cardiology Associates and Capital District Metropolitan Medical Associates, P.C. In the summer of 1998, Albany Med announced plans to buy nearby The Child's Hospital in an effort to expand surgical capabilities.

In recent years, Albany Med researchers have achieved a number of breakthroughs, including:

• A new method for testing drugs that could lead to individualized dosing guidelines for antibiotics to make them more effective, less likely to cause side effects and far less prone to create resistant strains of infectious microbacteria.

• The use of lidocaine, an inexpensive anesthetic, during and after prostate surgery speeds recovery and reduces pain in patients.

• Camouflaging the surface of red blood cells that could create a universal blood type.

Additionally, Albany Med became one of the first hospitals in the country to offer a test that detects the presence of the abnormal gene associated with breast cancer, and an experimental laser procedure known as trans-myocardial revascularization to relieve angina pain. It also has established a minimally invasive surgery center, funded in part by $1 million from U.S. Surgical Corp. of Norwalk, Conn.

In the half century since World War II, the college and hospital, under the umbrella of Albany Medical Center, have emerged as the premiere medical facility in northeastern New York and western New England. .

For example, Albany Med was honored three times in recent independent national surveys for its level of care. In 1994, *Modern Healthcare* magazine named Albany Med one of the top 100 hospitals in the country, one of 15 academic health sciences centers to make the list. In 1996, *U.S. News and World Report* ranked the hospital among the 42 best for cardiology and urology. Then in 1998, *Modern Healthcare* again selected Albany Med as a top 100 hospital.

From its humble beginnings, Albany Medical Center has become renowned for its excellence in patient care, medical education and biomedical research. The medical center continues to identify underserved segments of the northeastern New York and western New England in an ongoing attempt to ensure that residents have access to the highest quality of care.

An Albany Hospital nursing class, circa 1922.

ALBANY MEMORIAL HOSPITAL

Early in 1868, a group of civic-minded individuals opened the Albany City Free Dispensary, in a store-front at 39 Green Street. This would be the city's only public institution providing gratuitous medical service and medicines at that time. Expenses that first year were approximately $1,000, of which $30 per month paid the resident physician on duty. In 1869 the 24-hour dispensary treated 5,296 patients. Within five years, the dispensary outgrew its original site and two additional locations downtown.

In 1875, a large building at 123 North Pearl Street became the fourth location for what now was called the Albany City Homeopathic Hospital and Dispensary. The first president of this institution was Erastus Corning, grandfather of Albany mayor Erastus Corning II. The structure was remodeled to include operating rooms, clinic rooms and beds for 30 patients; it would serve as the hospital's home for 34 years.

By 1901, the board of trustees realized that a larger facility was needed. Land was purchased at 161 North Pearl Street, and, eventually, nearby buildings were acquired as a home for nurses. In this same year, the School of Nursing became the first in the state to be registered by the New York State Board of Regents.

In 1906, the cornerstone for the new hospital was laid with great fanfare at a ceremony officiated by James Ten Eyck. Following two years of construction, the new hospital opened with facilities for 87 patients. Land acquisition, building, and equipment cost $195,000. Another name change occurred, to Homeopathic Hospital of Albany.

In the years following, improvements such as asphalt paving on the streets in front of the hospital were made in consideration of patients' comfort. In 1931, the first Tumor Clinic between New York City and

Ambulance at the Homeopathic Hospital, 161 North Pearl Street, Albany.

Buffalo was established at the Homeopathic Hospital.

The hospital quickly outgrew the North Pearl Street facility, with the daily census reaching as high as 167 at times. After much deliberation, new land–13 acres–was purchased in 1946 at the north end of the city, between Shaker and Loudonville Roads.

Nine years later, ground was broken for the new hospital, with Mayor Erastus Corning II turning over the first shovelful of earth at a ceremony attended by more than 1,000 people. Following breakfast one morning in September 1957, using motorcycle police, ambulances, and convalescent coaches, patients were moved, and settled in to the new hospital in time for lunch.

Since then, Albany Memorial Hospital has continued along the path of growth and service improvements. The School of Nursing building was constructed in 1960 to accommodate the growing program. In 1974, another major addition was begun, resulting in expanded coronary, intensive, and emergency care; radiology; and new operating rooms. In addition to bricks and mortar, service improvements including centers for diabetes, pain manage-

ment, lithotripsy, and fertility, were introduced to keep pace with the diverse needs of the community. A professional office building and dialysis service were established on the hospital's campus under separate ownership. To provide the latest in comfort and convenience for patients, staff and physicians, all nursing floors and several clinical areas were renovated in 1997.

Today's healthcare market encourages partnership among providers to make the most effective use of a region's financial, technological, and human resources. In keeping with this trend, Albany Memorial Hospital merged with Northeast Health in 1997, to become part of a regional, comprehensive, healthcare continuum. Northeast Health consists of Albany Memorial and Samaritan Hospital as well as The Eddy, a network of services for seniors and those with special medical needs. Northeast Health provides primary, outpatient, acute, chronic, long-term, residential, rehabilitation, retirement housing, community-based, and homecare services in 15 counties.

ALBANY STEEL INC.

In the early 1920s, F. Arthur Hunsdorfer worked as regional sales manager for Carnegie Steel Corporation. Hunsdorfer was responsible for covering all of upstate New York, from Newburgh to the Canadian border, on both sides of the Hudson River. Due to the lack of bridges across the Hudson in the 1920s, Hunsdorfer usually only made sales calls on the eastern side of the river in the winter when he could drive across the ice. He would put the car in neutral and place a weight on the accelerator to hold it down. Then exiting the vehicle, he would stand on the running board outside the car, reach in and jam the shifting lever into gear. The car would start its slow progress across the river with Hunsdorfer ready to jump off at the first sign that the ice was cracking. He had a few close calls but never got wet.

It may have been this early experience that made him decide to start his own business; building a warehouse in one place and letting most of his customers come to him.

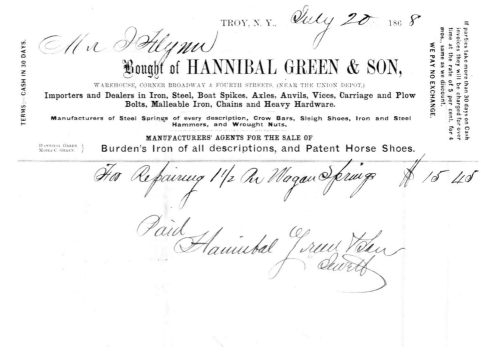

A July 20, 1868 invoice from Hannibal Green.

In 1922, Hunsdorfer joined forces with two of his business associates, Ben Gifford, president of Gifford-Wood Company of Hudson and Walter Strope, purchasing agent for McKinney Steel of Albany. Gifford provided funding; Hunsdorfer and Strope were to run the business. The first business, named General Mill

and Contractors Supply Company was located in a vacant flower and vegetable stand at 899 Broadway, near the corner of Ferry Street, the current location of the Miss Albany Diner. It also had a small warehouse behind it that ran back to McGowan Street behind Broadway. Next door was the Boardman and Gray Piano Company.

After one year, Strope split off and started a competing business, Strope Steel, on Terminal Street in Albany. Hunsdorfer, with Gifford's financial support, moved across the street to much larger quarters at 892 Broadway (now called 900 Broadway, housing Universal Auto Parts) and incorporated the new company as Albany Steel and Iron Supply Company.

The main product of Albany Steel and Iron Supply Company in 1922 was reinforcing bar. The City of Albany was slowly converting from cobblestone to concrete streets. Large blankets of steel reinforcing bars were fabricated to strengthen

Albany Steel's first location in 1922. Current site of Miss Albany Diner.

the concrete. Other products fabricated and warehoused by Albany Steel included hot and cold rolled steel bars, rolled bands and hoops (for making barrels), beams, angles, plate, sheet, tin plate and rail track.

Since Strope stored most of his inventory outside in an open yard, Hunsdorfer would drive up to Terminal Street whenever a large rebar bid was requested to see if Strope had enough inventory to bid the job. Hunsdorfer adjusted his bid accordingly.

In 1929, Albany Steel moved to new, much larger quarters at 45 Broadway, Menands. This location, currently Cranesville Block, was located across the street from Albany's Hawkins Stadium, home of the Eastern Baseball League's Albany Senators. Each season Albany Steel could count on about a dozen broken windows from baseballs fouled straight back over the roof. When this plant was first opened, Hunsdorfer worried that he had built it too far out of the city. Broadway was unpaved at that time and early photographs show a trolley track running along a dirt road flanked by weeds.

In the 20s and 30s, Albany Steel started to build one of the area's first trucking fleets to deliver steel. The stake trucks and flatbed trucks of the day were about the size of a pickup truck today. These trucks were used to deliver reinforcing bar and steel beams up to 40 feet long. This was accomplished by running the beam up along the side of the truck and securing it to the side of the truck and front bumper. It was not unusual to have beams running along both sides of the truck making it impossible to open either door. The driver climbed in through the window.

The 1920s were a time of great prosperity in the Albany Area and the country as a whole, and Albany Steel prospered and grew rapidly. The stock market crash and depression in 1929 and the 1930s slowed

growth but Albany Steel was always prosperous. In the early 1940s, the preparations for war and the later outbreak of war brought a large increase in government contracts, many originating through the Watervliet Arsenal. At the same time, steel shortages reached epidemic proportions. Albany Steel had many more orders than they could fill. Steel mills went into production 24 hours a day, 7 days a week trying to meet demand for raw material. Albany Steel's military contracts, including one to fabricate escape hatches to be mounted to the bottom of tanks, got priority over other work. Albany Steel grew and expanded.

Albany Steel's expansion included the purchase of Hannibal Green's Sons of Troy. Hannibal Green had been originally formed in 1809, by Henry Nazro and Jacob Hart on 6 Lane's Row, east of River Street. It was completely gutted by the great fire in downtown Troy in 1820, but rebuilt at 3 Lane's Row shortly thereafter. In the earliest days, Hannibal Green sold hardware,

nails, iron bars, anvils, vices, Smith's bellows, mill saws, cutlery, horseshoe iron, and manufactured "steel springs of every description." They were also listed as distributors of Fairbanks Celebrated Scales.

Nazro and Hart (1809) became Nazro and Green (1834), Green and Cramer (1838), Hannibal Green (1852) and later, Hannibal Green's Sons (1875). In 1855, they moved from 231–233 River Street to the corner of Albany (later Broadway) and Fourth Street, that at the time, was called "the old Corning lot."

Ads from the 1870s listed Hannibal Green as "importers and dealers in iron, steel, and heavy hardware, Agents for Burden's Iron, horseshoes and boiler rivets." An early 1800s Troy newspaper said that Hannibal Green was "...the direct representative of the Burden Iron Company for its iron, a product which has a worldwide reputation." On their hundredth anniversary in

Second location of Albany Steel 1923. Currently Universal Auto Parts.

Albany Steel after 1929.   Currently Cranesville Block.

1909, Hannibal Green received congratulatory letters from steel companies from Maine and Boston to Buffalo and Chicago, from Watertown to New York City, Pennsylvania and Louisville, Kentucky (probably a purchaser of Burden's patented horseshoes). Some of the letters came from the New York Central and Hudson River Railroad, Delaware and Hudson Railroad, Boston and Maine Railroad, Carnegie Steel of Illinois, Townsend Furnace of Albany, and Robert Cluett of Troy.

Remarkably, one of the congratulatory letters came from the Lake George Steamboat Company and sent along a copy of an order sent to Hannibal Green in 1826. Lake George Steamboat is still in operation today operating tour boats including the Lac Du Saint Sacrement, Mohican and Minne-ha-ha on Lake George. (Lake George Steamboat has been buying steel from Albany Steel for over 170 years!)

When Hannibal Green was purchased by Albany Steel, they were housed in one of the Burden Iron Buildings at the foot of Monroe Street. The purchase of Hannibal Green expanded Albany Steel's products into hardware and fasteners, as well as specialty steels.

Albany Steel expanded into the fabrication of structural steel for buildings and bridges through the purchase of the Clausen Iron Company of Tivoli Street in Albany. Clausen was comprised of three buildings and a large warehouse and structural yard on the south side of Tivoli St. just west of Pearl St. One of Albany's most historic and beautiful buildings, the D&H Building, now State University Plaza, was fabricated here. The building was designed by Marcus T. Reynolds and construction started in 1916. Also part of this project was the fabrication of the adjacent Albany Evening Journal Building, thought by most people to be part of the D&H, but actually a separate building.

In 1946, Albany Steel purchased a building in Glenmont and developed a machining division at that location.

In January 1965, Richard Hunsdorfer succeeded his father as president of Albany Steel. Charles Straney, Marvin Hinkelman, and Walter Fredenburgh continued as

Clausen Iron circa 1917.   Purchased by Albany Steel.

MARCH 21, 1917

Steel Erection on the D&H Building and the Albany Evening Journal.

department managers. The top priority of Albany Steel continued to be expansion.

On July 10, 1976, Albany Steel officially moved into a newly constructed modern facility at 566 Broadway in Menands. This facility, approximately 200,000 square feet, comprises four divisions in eight contiguous buildings:

Service Center – warehousing and cutting plate, sheet, bar, structural and specialty steel with the area's largest stacker crane system housing 10,000 tons of bar stock.

Fabrication – since the Clausen Iron days, Albany Steel fabricates and erects buildings, bridges, towers, stairs, railings, and almost any steel

structure. A computer controlled drill line drills structural steel and plate. The Fab Department also does shotblasting and painting, as well as bending and rolling of shapes.

Reinforcing Bar Fabrication – Rebar was Albany Steel's largest product at their formation 75 years ago, and continues to be a large factor today. They bend, roll and cut rebar for use in concrete structures.

Fasteners – inherited from Hannibal Green days, fasteners of all types and descriptions are sold. Some large sizes are fabricated in-house.

Machining is still done in Glenmont.

In June 1985, Peter Hess, former vice president and general manager of Albany Steel bought the company

from Richard Hunsdorfer, who retired.

Today, Albany Steel is Albany's largest and oldest Steel Center. Their history goes back almost 200 years to 1809. They have survived major fires, the War of 1812, the Civil War, two world wars, major depressions, five major strikes, and many periods of iron and steel shortages and rationing. As the elder Mr. Hunsdorfer demonstrated by crossing the river on the ice, the ability to survive lies in the ability to adapt to constant challenges.

ALBANY REGIONAL CANCER CENTER

In the mid-1970s, two doctors on the faculty of Albany Medical College formed a private practice to provide oncology services at St. Peter's Hospital in Albany, a modest beginning for a practice that has grown into one of the leading-edge cancer research operations in the United States—Capitol District Oncology PC, better known as the Albany Regional Cancer Center.

At the time of the Center's inception, oncology was a new medical specialty sparsely practiced outside major university hospital centers. However, as the national dedication to finding a cure for cancer has intensified, so has the commitment of the research staff of the Cancer Center, which over the years has consistently followed the underlying philosophy of striving to deliver the best possible medical oncology care in convenient locations. As a consequence of that focus, the practice has expanded from a central office in Albany adjacent to St. Peter's to outreach clinics elsewhere in the Capital District Area of Upstate New York, with branch offices in Amsterdam, Catskill, Hudson, Troy, Canajoharie, and Gloversville. The Center also maintains an affiliation with two medical oncologists in Schenectady who provide services at Ellis and St. Clare's hospitals as well as in their private offices.

Currently, nine physicians are on staff and plans call for that number to grow to 15 or more. Drs. Tom Cunningham, Michael Kolodziej and James Arseneau head the staff in Albany; Dr. Carolyn Mook is the senior physician in Amsterdam, assisted by Dr. Regina Resta (who moonlights as Mrs. Kolodziej); Dr. John Caracandas directs the Hudson Cancer Center, where Dr. Charles Collier is the radiation oncologist; Dr. Cora Bonatsos is the senior physician in Catskill/Hudson; Dr. Edwin Taft is the Center's chief hematologist.

All branches of the Cancer Center participate extensively in cancer research.

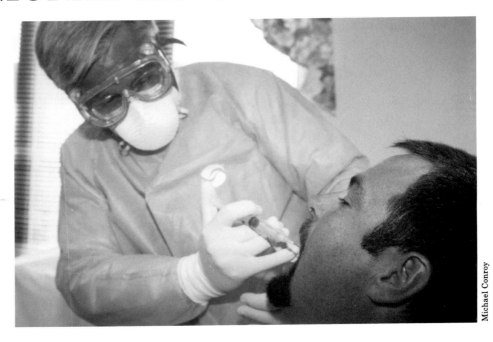

Dr. James Arseneau gives gene therapy to a head and neck cancer patient.

"We conduct as good a research program as any found even in the largest cancer centers," asserts Dr. Arseneau. "We are one of only a half-dozen sites on this planet doing gene therapy, and maybe the only site on this planet outside of large university cancer centers that is doing that."

The Center assigns between six and ten patients per month to gene therapy protocols in national-cooperative group clinical trials, a number in fact corresponding to the patients assigned on average by a major university center. Center research-physicians function primarily in association with organizations such as the National Surgical Adjuvant Breast and Bowel Program, the

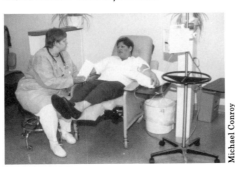

A nurse discusses chemotherapy treatment issues with a patient.

Radiation Therapy Oncology Group, the Gynocologic Oncology Group, and most importantly with PRN Research, Inc., through which it is highly involved in the testing of innovative treatments. Staff scientists routinely participate in state-of-the-science studies such as those involving new treatments for melanoma and head and neck cancers, and in recent years they have been heavily involved in angiogenesis cancer trials with drugs such as Marimistat and Recombinant Monoclonal VEGF. Other trials involve a large number of conventional but exciting new chemo-therapy drugs as well as preventative protocols that go well beyond the standard eat-a-good-breakfast-and-don't smoke prescription.

Dr. Arseneau sums up the Center's mission: "We endeavor to provide the best services we can, and we hope that they're as good as anything you could get at Dana Farber or Sloan Kettering, and I think that they probably are, but to provide them in a convenient fashion so people don't have to travel hundreds of miles."

ARMORY AUTOMOTIVE

"If I can think it, I know we can do it," says Donald Metzner the energetic young president of the Armory Automotive Family in Albany.

In 1997, he conceived the idea of an "automotive theme park" linking a new state-of-the-art service department and car wash with an entertainment-oriented complex. Now the 85,000 square foot Armory Center is a breathtaking reality that includes a cafe, accessory boutiques, Ticket-Master, a television studio operated by NBC affiliate WNYT, and a NASCAR superstore. It's the latest chapter in the distinguished and innovative 80-year history of Armory.

Metzner's grandfather, Anthony Metzner, founded the automotive business on Sherman Street in Albany in 1918. It was close to the Washington Ave. Armory, so he named his company Armory Garage. But Anthony Metzner was a visionary who anticipated the population shift toward the "suburbs." In 1928 he bought property at Central and Colvin and moved his business to the area then known as Shaeffer's Grove. Ironically, the parcel where Metzner's grandson has now built the fun-filled Armory Center was then home to an amusement park with rides and picnic tables.

In the mid-30s, local businessman James A. Clark Sr. joined Anthony Metzner to form an Armory dual family management team which continues today. After World War II,

Armory Garage, open for business on Sherman Street circa 1918.

Armory Center (rear) under construction at the Armory Central and Colvin complex.

Metzner's sons, Stanley and Robert, and James Clark Jr. joined the business. In 1985 Stanley's son Donald became a third generation member of the Armory team, as did Jim Clark's daughter Betsy in 1993.

Armory became a Chrysler dealer in 1931, and is recognized as Chrysler's most honored dealership, winning their prestigious Award for Excellence every year since its inception 41 years ago. Armory added Chrysler's Jeep-Eagle line in 1993, and is now home to Suzuki and Nissan vehicles as well.

Armory's chairman, Stanley Metzner, says "our company has always put the customer first. We offer amenities that make car shopping more pleasant and more comfortable." Indeed, in 1957 Armory built an unprecedented all-weather indoor home for the display of up to 250 new cars. "The World's Largest Auto Showroom" was given a 1997 nod by "Ripley's Believe It or Not," when the famous illustrated panel honored Armory in newspapers around America and in 38 other countries.

With sales of over $117 million in 1998, Armory is often asked for its "sales secrets." Jim Clark Jr., executive vice president of Armory, claims that there are none. "We have no sales systems," he says. "We just try to make buying a car a pleasure."

Donald Metzner points to one important factor behind Armory's success—the stability of its staff. "We employ over 200 people, and the average employee has been with us about 15 years. I think our customers appreciate that the Armory Automotive Family is really a family."

A new breed of customer is coming Armory's way on the Internet. "We were the first auto dealer in the Capital Region to go on line," says Metzner. "Now people are shopping with us at Armoryauto.com. But our customers can't get their cars washed on the Internet, and they can't get their cars serviced on the Internet. So Armory Center is here to give them that and much, much more. I know many in the auto industry are looking at our new facility as a prototype of things to come. I'm proud that, once again, Armory is ahead of the curve."

BELTRONE CONSTRUCTION COMPANY, INC.

Salvatore R. Beltrone was born in Stignano, Calabria, Italy, on 19th of October 1924, the son of Bensiero Beltrone and Angelina Squillace Beltrone. At the age of two he and his sister Mary accompanied their parents to the United States, where the family settled in Schenectady, New York. At the age of eighteen Mr. Beltrone entered the U.S. Navy where he served a three year term, receiving his honorable discharge in 1946.

Before the year ended, he had started a small masonry concrete construction business in Albany, N.Y. He married Anna E. Campagna in 1947. Following a successful decade of steadily increasing contracts, in 1956 Salvatore incorporated his business as S.R. Beltrone, Inc. His clientele continued to grow to include major governmental offices and well financed private investors. With success and steady growth Beltrone Construction Co. Inc., was organized in 1961 to perform general construction work on a large scale.

Operating out of offices in Latham since 1968, Mr. Beltrone has developed his company into an innovative enterprise, employing a quality-con-

scious and highly mobile workforce numbering as many as 350 employees dedicated to meeting the highest standards of the construction industry. Indeed, Beltrone Construction has participated in some of the most prominent construction projects in the Tri-Cities region, including but far from limited to the Empire State Plaza; the Teresian House Nursing Home; Our Lady of Hope Nursing Home; the Blue Cross, Blue Shield in Corporate Woods, Key Corp. Tower; the New York State Dormitory Corporate Headquarters; Wolf Road Shoppers' Park; Capital Plaza Office Park I, II, and III; the Omni Financial Center; the Forensic Investigation Laboratory; and the Latham Farm Shopping Center.

In recent years Beltrone Construction has expanded its operation into the construction management field, overseeing the construction of the Albany County Civic Center, the Town of Colonie Municipal Building, the Albany International Airport expansion, the Teresian House expansion, South Colonie Central schools, the New York State Office of General Services and Correctional facilities.

Always desirous to advance activities that benefit the area, Mr. Beltrone takes particular pride in his responsibility in such conspicuous projects as Wolf Road Shoppers' Park, Capital Plaza Association, Capital Plaza Association III and AYCO Plaza. Beltrone Construction

Blue Shield of Northeastern New York, 187 Wolf Road, Albany, N.Y.

also includes a real estate division that, individually and with partners, controls a portfolio listing more than two-million square feet of office, retail and warehouse properties. Now well into his eighth decade, Mr. Beltrone continues to develop and manage those retail properties as well as to innovate productive and progressive business practices for his firm as a whole.

Throughout his business career, Mr. Beltrone has taken an active interest in serving the community of the Tri-Cities area, a service that has won him renown as a distinguished citizen whose keen interest in civic affairs has left an imprint on the human spirit and the structural landmarks of his locale. He has been a member of the board of trustees at the St. Peters Hospital, is an active member of the board of directors of Capital Bank & Trust, and has also served on the Chamber of Commerce Traffic Study Task force charged with solving the traffic problems of the town of Colonie.

Salvatore and Anna Beltrone are the parents of four daughters, two granddaughters and a grandson. Two of the daughters are active in the firm: Tonia heads the property management accounting division, and Angela is a licensed real estate broker and public relations director of the real estate division.

N.Y.S. Dormitory Authority Corporate Headquarters, Albany, N.Y.

MATTHEW BENDER & COMPANY

A two room walk-up office at the corner of State Street and Broadway was the location of Matthew Bender, "law bookseller," in 1887. At that time, Bender sold other firms' publications but quickly emerged as a publisher of quality New York State lawbooks. Matthew Jr. ("Max") was already working for his father when younger brother John joined the business. The family concern soon moved around the corner, to 36 State Street, and then to a Broadway storefront in 1892, when the city directory first listed Bender as "law bookseller and publisher." That year, Matthew Bender began issuing an annual "Lawyers' Diary," a desk book successful for the next 56 years. Issuance of William M. Collier's treatise on bankruptcy in 1898 marked the advent of Bender's most long-lived series. Abreast of the times, Bender published early books on streetcar and automobile laws.

Matthew Bender became partners with his sons, Max and John T. Bender, in 1905, and within a year they had three salesmen on the road. In 1910 the firm consumed 108 tons of paper and employed seven salesmen, with gross sales exceeding $188,000. By 1915 Bender had nationwide clientele, with additional customers in Paris, London, Havana, and Berlin; the company established a New York City office at that time.

Matthew Bender, Sr. died in 1920; his son Max succeeded him as president of the company, a position he held for 21 years. During his tenure, Matthew Bender & Company prospered in the 1920s and successfully weathered the Great Depression. His son, Matthew Bender III, and his nephew, John T. Bender, Jr., entered the firm during the '30s. Nephew John took charge of the New York City operation, displaying considerable ability in recruiting writers. It was John Jr. who pioneered loose-leaf binders for ease in updating Bender publications, a system employed thereafter.

Although World War II inhibited the growth of Matthew Bender & Company, the postwar years were ones of continual growth. If as late as 1950 the State Street offices were "straight out of Dickens," the company was seeking improved facilities; the firm relocated in 1952 to modern offices at 255 Orange Street. In 1963 Matthew Bender & Company became a subsidiary of The Times Mirror Company and shortly thereafter occupied its 1275 Broadway headquarters. By 1980, Bender employed 1,000 persons, 300 of them at it Albany operation, and had offices in San Francisco, New York and Washington, D.C. Printing its first international catalogue in 1980 to service customers throughout the world, Matthew Bender & Company has continually increased its international market. In 1998, Matthew Bender & Co., Inc. was acquired by Reed-Elsevier, a British-Dutch leader in the U.S. legal information industry. This move provided even greater opportunities to expand the reach of Matthew Bender's unique content around the globe and in all media (i.e., print, CD-ROM, on-line and over the internet). The company has offices in New York City, San Francisco (CA), Binghamton (NY), Minneapolis (MN), and Provo (UT), in addition to Albany where operations now employ 380 people. The overall picture of this old Albany firm is one of dynamic growth in a highly competitive and specialized field.

In 1892, the Benders—Matthew, Matthew Jr., John, and Melvin—were photographed standing in front of their store at 511-513 Broadway. Fred Bender, far right, was no relation.

CAPITAL DISTRICT TRANSPORTATION AUTHORITY

The Capital District Transportation Authority (CDTA) has played an integral part in the City of Albany's history. It was created by the New York State Legislature in 1970, but its roots, through its predecessor companies date back to the 1940s and beyond. The State Legislature created CDTA on August 1, 1970 for "the continuance, further development and improvement of transportation and other services related thereto within the Capital District Transportation District...." CDTA's mission statement is "To transport customers safely and reliably at reasonable cost." Currently, CDTA's service area includes Albany, Schenectady, Rensselaer and Saratoga Counties. It is governed by a nine-member Board of Directors who are appointed by the Governor, approved by the State Senate and represent the four county service area.

When first formed in 1970, CDTA was headquartered at its current location on Watervliet Avenue in West Albany, with an additional facility on Quail Street near the downtown area. The Watervliet Avenue location at one time also housed the United Traction Company (UTC), and has since seen many modifications. The most recent of these was completed in 1990. In 1973, a satellite facility in the City of Schenectady was dedicated, and the following year, the Quail Street and Watervliet Avenue operations were consolidated to Watervliet Avenue. In 1981, CDTA dedicated a satellite facility in the City of Troy.

Much of CDTA's history is attributed to the many transportation organizations it has acquired. In 1971, CDTA assumed responsibility for the routes operated by the Albany-Nassau Bus Company, and acquired the Schenectady Transit System from Schenectady County. In 1972, CDTA acquired the assets of the United Traction Company and assumed the local service of the Troy-5th Avenue Bus Company. In addition to these milestones, CDTA has since marked

CDTA buses line the streets of downtown Albany—June 1973.

several more highlights including: bus service in Saratoga County (1976), the introduction of paratransit service called STAR (Special Transit Available on Request) (1982); the start of service using wheelchair lift-equipped buses (1988); the debut of Clean Air buses (1992); the installation of electronic fareboxes on buses (1992); the

celebration of its 25th anniversary (1995); and the unveiling of low-floor, accessible buses (1996).

The historical importance of public transportation to the Albany area is evidenced by the fact that during World War II, bus and trolley operators were excused from the draft because their work was considered necessary to the war

CDTA's headquarters, in 1990.

effort. Gasoline was rationed, so many people were forced to rely on public transportation. At that time, 16 tokens could be purchased for $1.00. Today, $1.00 will buy you one token. During the 1940s when trolley service was at its heyday in Albany, trolley motormen working for the UTC gave a boost to the area's businesses by acting as tour guides. They would call out the names of some of the smaller downtown establishments on their routes such as The New York Deli on South Pearl Street and Goldfarb's Fruit and Vegetable Store on Second Avenue. A former trolley motorman for the UTC recalls coming across a stranded car on Second Avenue and Broadway on a winter night in 1943. He offered the driver, a priest from a nearby church, a push up the Second Avenue hill. The trolley slowly pushed the car to the top of the hill at which point the priest told the motorman that he had said three Hail Mary's that they would make it!

Although the popular mode of public transportation locally has changed from trolley to buses, the importance of the service to the

CDTA's 110 Watervliet Avenue headquarters, Albany—June, 1981.

Albany area remains the same. It provides residents with access to jobs, shopping, appointments, school, and anywhere else they need to go. For many, it is the only means of transportation available to them, providing them with a link to the community and vice versa.

As CDTA looks to the future, its focus has expanded from only a "bus company" to the role of the region's mobility manager. CDTA is the lead agency in projects such as the re-vamping of Amtrak stations in Rensselaer and Saratoga Counties, demonstration commuter rail

service, the construction of park and ride lots, local land-use studies designed to improve the transit market, and the implementation of improved transportation technology such as traffic signal priority for buses, to name a few. Despite this expanded role, the core of CDTA's service will always be moving people safely and reliably.

CDTA has been an integral part of the City of Albany's history. Although the love affair with the automobile has caused ridership over the years to decline, CDTA is committed to restoring public transit's role as an attractive mode of transportation.

CDTA mechanics pose next to a bus at the Watervliet Avenue location—June 1982.

CDTA FACTS
Service Area: *Albany, Rensselaer, Schenectady, Saratoga Counties*
Population of Service Area: *769,000*
Fleet size:
   Regular Route Vehicles: 225
   Paratransit Vehicles: 25
Annual Bus Mileage: *6 million*
Annual Bus Hours: *590,000*
Annual Customer Boardings: *11 million*

DODGE CHAMBERLIN LUZINE WEBER ASSOCIATES, ARCHITECTS

Dodge Chamberlin Luzine Weber Associates, Architects, an Architectural firm located in Rensselaer, New York since the mid 1950s, has its roots in the City of Albany with its founding as the firm of Loth & White in 1915. In 1927 J. Russell White became the sole proprietor of the firm and was joined soon thereafter by W. Parker Dodge. The Washington Park Lakehouse today stands as J. Russell White's signature piece for the residents of the City of Albany and the Capital District. Upon the death of Mr. White in 1949, W. Parker Dodge became the principal of the firm and remains today as the firm's standard bearer for the quality of design and concern for clients' needs that continue to be intrinsic to all projects commissioned to the present firm of Dodge Chamberlin Luzine Weber Associates. In 1970 Mr. Dodge formed a partnership with Bernon P. Chamberlin and was subsequently joined in 1974 by Edmund L. Luzine and in 1988 by Martin Weber. Mr. Luzine and Mr. Weber today continue as the active partners in the firm.

With over eight decades of experience in designing facilities for educational, health related, municipal, commercial and recreational entities and utilizing the latest computer-aided design, the firm completes projects with aesthetic taste and traditional concern for

The Teresian House is a 300 bed skilled nursing facility operated by the Carmelite Sisters for the Aged & Infirmed under the auspices of the Albany Catholic Diocese.

functional and efficient design, and has developed a tradition for completing its projects to the satisfaction of its clients on time and within budget.

Educational clients have been and continue to be the mainstay of the firm's commissions. Long-standing relationships are maintained with many school districts throughout the suburban areas of the City of Albany and throughout the State of New York. The New York State School Board's Association, headquartered in Albany, recently renamed their building The Dodge Building to reflect W. Parker Dodge's lifelong dedication to the field of education.

The firm is proud of its continuing work within the City of Albany and lists among its clients Albany Medical Center, the Main Post Office for the City of Albany, The Freihofer

W. Parker Dodge, seated; Bernon P. Chamberlin, seated to his left; Edmund L. Luzine, standing in rear and Martin Weber to his right. Mr. Luzine and Mr. Weber are the current active members of the firm.

Baking Company, The Teresian House Nursing Home, Hope House, Siena College, and the restoration of the Wilborn Temple.

Architectural awards of distinction have been conferred upon the firm including *American School and University's* "Architectural Portfolio for Education Design Excellence," *American School and University's* "Educational Interiors Showcase," and The Northeastern Subcontractors Association's "Outstanding Architectural/Engineering Firm" award.

Dodge Chamberlin Luzine Weber Associates, Architects is large enough to offer specialized services by experienced licensed architects with the capabilities of handling multiple concurrent projects without sacrificing the individual attention of the firm's principal members.

With the advent of the twenty-first century, Dodge Chamberlin Luzine Weber Associates looks forward to continuing its tradition of quality in architectural design for clients in the City of Albany, throughout the Capital District and New York State.

EMPIRE CORPORATE FEDERAL CREDIT UNION

Empire Corporate Federal Credit Union was founded in Albany in 1977 with $123 and a dream. Today, still headquartered in Albany, Empire Corporate has nearly $3 billion in assets and provides financial services to over 1,000 credit unions in the Northeast.

Since Empire Corporate's inception in 1977—when the early years had only a handful of employees—Empire Corporate has grown to become the nation's third largest corporate credit union in asset size, and currently employs over 160 people. Whereas Empire originally served credit unions in New York State only, two mergers in as many years have allowed Empire to substantially grow and serve credit unions in the contiguous New England states. Headquartered in Albany, New York, Empire Corporate also has branch offices located in Warwick, Rhode Island and Hightstown, New Jersey.

To understand their story, it is important to first understand the key difference of credit unions. It is truly an untold American success story—one that continues to play a pivotal role in the nation's financial industry.

Credit unions behave differently because they are different—they think differently. Driving everything they do is a set of powerful ideas that make up the credit union philosophy. These ideas are enduring, universal, whole-hearted, and have been virtually unchanged for the past century and a half. Yet the ideas that form the core of their philosophy are also

Joseph P. Herbst, president/CEO.

Empire Corporate Federal Credit Union's new headquarters. (www.empirecorp.org)

simple. They are based on one strong belief—people are more important than dollars.

Unlike any other financial institution, a credit union is owned and controlled by the people it serves. They are called members, not customers. The members are the owners. Owners have equal voting power, regardless of their balance; there are no stockholders, just member/owners. Most important, a credit union returns profits directly back to its member/owners.

Credit Unions believe in the philosophy of "people helping people." Part of this cooperative spirit is the tradition of social responsibility. They have pride in their hometowns and the people who live there. They share their history...they're connected. Not everyone's a member, but everyone's a neighbor. Credit unions are locally owned, locally controlled, and have offices in

the community providing affordable financial services to those that may need it most.

Corporate credit unions emerged from the same cooperative spirit that gave rise to the American credit union movement in the 1930s. As the credit union industry grew, so did the urgency for central credit unions—or credit unions for credit unions. Corporate credit unions were born of that need.

Corporates became an important source of low cost liquidity for credit unions within the credit union network, thus eliminating reliance on other financial institutions. Soon, many corporates expanded to a full line of products and services designed to assist and ensure credit unions' independence. Today, over 99 percent of the nation's nearly 12,000 credit unions use a corporate credit union for one or more services. These credit unions serve more than 74 million American consumers.

A corporate credit union, such as Empire Corporate, is also a not-for-profit cooperative that serves natural-person credit unions within its field-of-membership. Like natural-person credit unions, Empire Corporate is guided by a volunteer board of directors and is totally owned and directed by its nearly 1,100 member credit unions.

Credit unions demand, and deserve, financial services from their corporate that keep pace with emerging technology, offer the utmost in flexibility, and rival investment vehicles available in the financial marketplace. Empire Corporate Federal Credit Union is a full service financial institution offering everything from investment to payment services designed specifically by and for credit unions' unique needs and business philosophy.

Empire Corporate is proud to part of the credit union network and proud to help Albany's credit unions remain competitive, continue to flourish, and be the primary financial institution of choice for their members.

FIRST ALBANY COMPANIES INC.

First Albany, a securities broker-age and investment banking firm, was founded in February of 1953. The firm's founder, Daniel V. McNamee, started by acquiring the brokerage business of George R. Cooley & Co., Inc. The firm had seven employees and a single office at 100 State Street, in downtown Albany. In that first month, First Albany had revenues of just over $1,700. By 1954, First Albany had consummated its first corporate finance transaction, and in 1956 acquired a seat on the New York Stock Exchange.

Ever since its founding, the firm has maintained its corporate head-quarters in downtown Albany within a few blocks of its first offices. During its initial period of growth, First Albany focused on developing branch offices for its brokerage business in upstate New York and New England, including an additional office in Albany.

In 1975, the securities industry saw the advent of competitive commissions, and First Albany was among the first firms in the nation to provide competitive rates to non-institutional customers. In this same year, the board of directors named George McNamee its new president. At the end of 1975, the firm had offices in Albany, Binghamton, Elmira, Kingston, Norwich, Pawling, Syracuse, Waterbury and Pittsfield, Massachusetts, employed 150 people, of which 60 were private client account executives, and had revenues of $2.4 million.

In 1977, George McNamee tapped Hugh Johnson to join the firm as chief investment officer. Hugh Johnson was formerly a principal of Hugh Johnson & Co., a regional brokerage firm based in Buffalo, New York. Today, Mr. Johnson is also Chairman of First Albany Asset Management Corporation, with over $400 million under management.

In 1980, Alan P. Goldberg, formerly president of Hawthorne Securities, a Boston-based securities firm, joined the firm as executive vice president. Mr. Goldberg was named president in 1990 and later co-chief executive officer with Mr. McNamee, who is also chairman of the firm. During the 1980s the firm expanded significantly into both the municipal capital markets and the corporate fixed income capital markets, becoming a national trading and finance presence, which complemented its strong regional brokerage activities.

Today, First Albany is a nationally recognized research driven investment bank, offering the full panoply of financial services. As investment bankers to corporations, First Albany focuses particularly on the needs of emerging growth companies through the underwriting of initial and secondary offerings, the provision of advisory services for mergers and acquisitions, and the private placement of equity and debt. As investment

bankers to municipalities, First Albany is a leading underwriter and financial advisor to a broad range of state and local governments and governmental agencies throughout the country in connection with public and private offerings or refundings of municipal securities. First Albany also provides a complete array of investment capabilities of value to the institutional investor, including proprietary research and the trading and market-making of a broad spectrum of corporate, governmental and municipal securities. In addition, over the last forty-five years First Albany has remained committed to assisting discriminating individual investors preserve and enhance their wealth through its full-service Private Client Group.

As of December 31, 1997, First Albany had total revenues of $192 million, customer assets of over $10 billion, over 840 employees and 27 offices in 10 states, from Boston to Silicon Valley. Despite this new national focus, First Albany remains steadfastly committed to serving the financial needs of the Capital region and strongly supportive of its continued vitality.

Timothy Raab, Northern Photo

George McNamee, chairman & co-chief executive officer.

Timothy Raab, Northern Photo

Alan P. Goldberg, president & co-chief executive officer.

HUDSON RIVER CONSTRUCTION CO., INC.

Hudson River Construction Co.,Inc. is a full service municipal highway contractor. Employing approximately 150 laborers, teamsters and operating engineers during the construction season, the company specializes in all manner of road construction, particularly asphalt and concrete paving. Over sixty years of experience in providing the finest in both materials and craftsmanship has positioned the company well as it enters the new millennium.

Hudson River Construction Co., Inc. was founded in Buffalo, New York, in 1937 by Eugene D. Hallock, Jr. and Frederic H. Stutzman. The company opened in the Capital District as the first company specializing in bituminous concrete paving. Stutzman was 24 then, a recent Amherst College graduate, and Hallock at 20 had already been involved with the construction trade. With six employees and the front wheel of an old steamroller as a hand roller, they did a total of $8,000 of business that first year.

The start of the fledgling company was interrupted by World War II, when the partners joined the U.S. Navy, Stutzman as a line officer and Hallock as a Seabee. After returning from active service, the partners

resumed their construction activities. In 1947, Hudson River Construction was a low bidder on its first municipal contract for the paving of Dove and Swan Streets in the city of Albany. In 1948, the firm was awarded its first New York State Highway contract in Rensselaer County.

To secure a source for excellent paving materials, a subsidiary company, Albany Asphalt & Aggregates was formed in 1948. Erected in the Port of Albany, the asphalt plant has been renewed and updated over the years, and continues to supply the Capital District with the finest paving materials while at the same time exceeding all environmental standards and quality assurance-quality control guidelines.

As construction industry leaders, both Hallock and Stutzman were very active in the New York State Chapter of the Associated General Contractors. Stutzman served as president of that group in 1961, and Hallock served as president in 1985. Continuing that tradition, Eugene D. Hallock, III served as president in 1996.

In 1981, Stutzman and Hallock began the process of succeeding the business to the second generation of sons. Their work and forethought guaranteed the continued success of the business. Fred Stutzman died in 1982. Gene Hallock is still active in the business, and has celebrated

his 60th anniversary as a member of the operating engineers.

Current management of the firm is provided by Fred and John Stutzman and Eugene and Peter Hallock, the sons of the company's founders. This group brings over 115 collective years of experience to the enterprise. Some recent projects successfully completed include: the landslide terminal improvements at the Albany International Airport, major asphalt resurfacing of the mainline and ramps of the New York State Thruway between exits 23 and 24, and the municipal street paving programs for the cities of Albany, Schenectady and Troy.

Hudson River Construction Company is a joint family enterprise. The company has provided employment to second and third generation members of employee families. In an industry increasingly dominated by the acquisition of smaller closely-held companies by regional construction conglomerates, Hudson River Construction Company is steadfastly committed to remaining local in every way.

In June 1952 Hudson River Construction Company crews lay blacktop on Broadway at Steuben Street, near union Station.

Flanked by crew and equipment in this 1949 photograph are company founders Eugene D. Hallock, Jr. and Frederic H. Stutzman (standing fourth and third from right, respectively). They are cutting the ribbon to open a Department of Transportation job—the paving of 6.31 miles of Route 66 in Columbia County

THE HUM GROUP

Healthcare Underwriters Mutual Insurance Company (HUM), the flagship of The HUM Group, was formed in 1976 as Hospital Underwriters Mutual, in response to an extreme tightening of the medical malpractice market in New York state. From its founding until 1996, HUM remained a single-state underwriter, almost exclusively of hospitals in suburban and rural areas. However, HUM and its Board of Directors recognized that to ensure the company's survival and growth, it would be necessary to diversify its product offerings and market, and to become a solution provider for those it insures. The company slogan "A Policy of Partnership" was created to reflect this culture.

HUM first began seeking licenses in surrounding states, while at the same time pursuing potential mergers and alliances with other insurers. In the late 1990s, the markets HUM served expanded dramatically to include physicians, surgeons, allied health care providers, nursing homes, adult homes, managed care organizations, physician hospital organizations and more. In addition to underwriting professional liability, HUM developed employer and provider excess, Errors & Omissions and Directors & Officers coverage. HUM's territory expanded as well to include Connecticut, Maine, Massachusetts, New Hampshire, New Jersey, Ohio, Pennsylvania, Rhode Island, Vermont and Wisconsin, with licenses pending in other states.

The development in 1995 of The HUM Marketing Group as HUM's own insurance agency and new business unit met with great success. In addition to efficiently distributing HUM's products, the Marketing Group enables HUM to offer products it doesn't directly underwrite, such as property, business owner's and auto coverages.

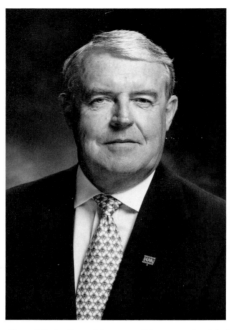

Gerald J. Cassidy, president and chief executive officer.

HUM's commitment to understanding the health care market is further evidenced by the creation in 1996 of its own HMO, called HUM HealthCare Systems, Inc. (HHS), based in Glens Falls, NY. Known commercially as Partners Health Plans, it offers enrollment in more than a dozen counties in New York. HHS also has a third party administration division called Partners Administrative Services, which handles self-insured health and Workers' Compensation funds.

In 1997, HUM acquired The OHIC Insurance Company, based in Columbus, Ohio. Like HUM, OHIC offers medical malpractice coverage and other types of insurance to health care facilities and providers. With the addition of OHIC's territory in the Midwest, South and West, The HUM Group's geographic reach extended to nearly 40 states.

In addition to a wide range of insurance products, HUM also offers substantial risk management resources, such as software products, extensive library, regional seminars and network meetings, on-site risk management consultations and more.

In the event a claim is filed against one of its insureds, HUM is dedicated to seeking prompt and just resolution by aggressively managing the litigation process. Their corporate claim and litigation management philosophy is to vigorously defend their clients from non-meritorious claims. Meritorious claims are resolved promptly and equitably. HUM also has a full array of claims management programs and services aimed at providing the best defense possible while minimizing expense.

The offices for HUM and the headquarters for The HUM Group are located in Airport Park, at 8 British American Boulevard in the Albany suburb of Latham. These new offices were built in 1998 to accommodate a growing number of employees and enhanced operations resulting from The HUM Group's dramatic growth.

KEYBANK N.A.

KeyCorp, a financial services holding company, has a rich history woven from the archives of more than 100 financial institutions around the country. The 1825 founding of one of the earliest predecessor banks stemmed from the opening of the Erie Canal and the resulting vast markets made available for Albany's merchants. Four banks then existed in Albany, and the increase in commerce caused by the Erie Canal forced the realization of a need for a "people's bank" for Albany; in 1826 the state legislature chartered the Commercial Bank. Because this was the first such bill to legally define the functions of a bank, it became a national model for subsequent bank chartering legislation.

By 1830 the bank was circulating $413,700 in its bank notes, and by the following year it had become a legal depository for New York State funds, which it remains to this day. Its officers were early investors in railroads and provided economic leadership; during the financial panic of 1837 the bank was the first in the state to resume specie payments.

In 1862, when the state of New York found itself with no money to support the Union Army's recruiting drive, Commercial Bank advanced $3.5 million, enabling the army to raise required military units. At the end of the Civil War the bank was chartered as National Commercial Bank of Albany.

KeyBank was a pioneer in establishing branch banks. In 1945 the bank was a forerunner in international banking and in the 1950s it was the first commercial bank in the United States to use an online teller terminal. During the 1970s Key premiered the first automated teller machines (ATMs) and cards in the Midwest and point-of-sale electronic debit services in upstate New York.

Key has successfully pursued growth through mergers and

Derived from classical Greek architecture, the stately bank was erected in 1920. Keeler's Restaurant is on the left; Boyce and Milwain, Clothiers, on the right.

acquisitions. In 1979 the corporation adopted the "Key" name to develop a consistent identity among the holding company and its subsidiaries. In 1983, KeyCorp's common stock was listed on the New York Stock Exchange under the symbol KEY.

Key's first interstate acquisition occurred in 1984 when Key entered the state of Maine. Over the years, Key broadened its base through entries into the states of Alaska, Colorado, Florida, Idaho, Indiana, Michigan, New Hampshire, Ohio, Oregon, Utah, Vermont, and Washington.

An important milestone in the company's history took place on March 1, 1994, when KeyCorp in

Albany, New York, and Society Corporation in Cleveland, Ohio, merged to form a "new" KeyCorp. The resulting company, with assets of $76 billion, is the nation's 14th largest bank-holding company. KeyCorp maintains a strong presence in, and commitment to, the Albany area. Headquartered in the Capital District, the Albany District has the second-largest contingent of Key employees, behind the corporation's headquarters in Cleveland.

On August 11, 1997, KeyBank became the first bank in the United States to offer nationwide banking services to its customers, which allows a consistency of products, services, and accessibility to customers throughout the country. A cornerstone in the organization's ability to support nationwide banking is the state-of-the-art data center located in Albany.

LATHAM MEDICAL GROUP

Latham Medical Group has been an integral part of the Albany community since 1955. Founder Howard J. Westney, M.D. started the practice of Family Medicine on Herbert Drive in Latham, where the Latham Circle Mall now stands. He had the vision to combine the trusted values of the Family Physician with the idea of group practice to help provide better care for patients and reasonable call schedules for the physicians. In the old days, house calls were common, the office was busy and hospital rounds were part of the daily routine. Most of the patients were from the Town of Colonie. The addition of new partners allowed the group to grow and provide service to a wider area including Albany, Troy, Schenectady and southern Saratoga County.

Dr. Westney was again an innovator when he saw the need for an organized approach to community emergency medical services. Working with leaders in the Town of Colonie he developed training programs for emergency medical technicians and organized Medico which brought all of the ambulance services in the Town of Colonie

Medical Dental Center at 694 Troy-Schenectady Road, Latham, N.Y.

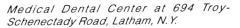

together with common standards of training and a central dispatching function. In 1976, in cooperation with the Federal Emergency Management Agency (FEMA), Dr. Westney helped to procure a grant which allowed the Capital Region to fund the start up of what is now the Regional Emergency Medical Organization (REMO). Local hospitals were reluctant to provide backup for the ambulance crews by radio when they were at the scene of an emergency in the early days. For more than two years the physicians at Latham Medical Group provided medical backup and advice for the REMO ambulance crews twenty four hours a day seven days a week, using two way radios and radio transmitted EKG information.

The physicians at Latham Medical Group have continued this proud tradition of innovation over the years. In the 1980s, as special-

Latham Medical Group building as it looked 30 years ago.

ization became more important in medical care, the Family Physicians at LMG teamed up with prominent area subspecialists to provide most needed specialty consultations on-site at their offices in Latham. The addition of X-Ray, and laboratory facilities made LMG the "one stop" place for health care in the area. Families could find personal, continuing care for children, adults and seniors. Women's health and maternity care have been an integral part of the practice since the beginning. Over the years the physicians at Latham Medical have delivered hundreds of babies at Bellevue Maternity Hospital in Niskayuna and St. Clare's Hospital in Schenectady.

In recent years, managed care has become the predominant mode of health care delivery in the Nation. Once again, Latham Medical Group took a leadership role by working in partnership with local managed care organizations to provide quality care for patients in a cost effective way. Throughout the change to managed care LMG remained committed to patient advocacy, working to ensure that every patient gets the care she or he needs. Their mission statement says it all; "Our Family Caring for Your Family."

The Latham Medical Group is proud to be a part of the Albany heritage. Family Physicians serving the community with professionalism and creativity.

LORETEX CORPORATION

The Loretex Corporation has been located in the Northeastern Industrial Park in Guilderland Center, NY for 25 years.

On July 21, 1974 orders were placed for equipment to manufacture a woven polyethylene fabric. Production of the woven fabric began on December 6, 1974.

Test marketing started three years prior to the opening of the plant in the United States based on a product developed by an affiliated Norwegian company, which had produced the polyethylene fabric since 1969.

The Loretex fabric started with strips of high-density polyethylene approximately .002 inches thick and .100 inches wide, woven into a scrim and coated with low density polyethylene. Because of substantial amounts of ultra violet and thermal stabilizers, Loretex fabrics are resistant to sunlight and degradation.

Loretex fabric is made in a variety of colors and is available in fire retardant and ultra violet grades. Loretex can also be corona treated to create a printable surface.

The Loretex Corporation also has the capabilities of extrusion lamination to foam, paper, and films.

Among the current uses of Loretex fabrics are winter pool covers, boat covers, constructive tarps, agricultural covers, ditch

Beaming machines.

Extrusion line.

liners, poultry curtains, industrial covers and bags, vinyl banners, field covers, patio and grill covers, and tent walls and floors as well as other customer requirements.

Originally started by Ovind Lorentzen Activities Inc. of Norway, Loretex began operations using 36,000 square feet of warehouse space with 30 employees. In 1984, the company expanded to 58,000 square feet and in 1985 expanded again to 66,000 square feet.

In 1997, Polymer Group Inc. acquired Loretex. Loretex has since been in the process of expanding once again. Upon the completion of this expansion, Loretex will have a total of 82,000 square feet, and will employ over 100 people by year 2000. The completion of this expansion is scheduled for October 1998.

After 25 years of growth and development, the company's proud to have some of their original employees still working with them.

The Loretex Corporation over the past 25 years has not only continued to expand on their building but has also continued to add new equipment to keep up with its ever growing sales market. Everyday, new uses are being found for the application of woven polyethylene.

New quality control systems and testing equipment have been added to the quality controls laboratory to ensure that every customers'

product meets or exceeds their standards. Every lot of product is sampled by quality control and tested to ensure that they meet product specifications.

Loretex Corporation has in-house capability for testing materials for strength, weight, thickness, elongation, thermal shrinkage, tensile and tear strength, flame resistance, and accelerated weathering testing.

The company is proud to print materials at their customer's request "Manufactured With Pride In The U.S.A." They also take pride in the fact that they have produced thousands of covers for

Weaving loom.

the United States Government that are in use around the world to help other nations in the event of natural disasters. The firm has also made protective covers for the Federal Emergency Management Agency (FEMA) for disaster relief from severe storms, floods, and hurricanes in the United States.

The Loretex Corporation has grown to a 24 hour a day, 7 day a week operation to meet its customer requirements.

The company's goal is not only to provide a quality product for customers, but to also maintain a safe working environment for employees and to ensure job security. Employees are their greatest assets.

MOHAWK PAPER MILLS

Mohawk Paper Mills, Inc. is one of North America's leading producers of premium printing papers. Their product line includes coated, uncoated, and a complete line of papers for the new digital presses, such as ink jet, color copy, and laser. Small by paper industry standards, this highly successful company has grown from 900 tons per year on three paper machines (in 1878) to 90,000 tons per year—on the same three machines. The company has thrived through its competitive spirit and its ability to interweave the craft of traditional papermaking with cutting-edge technology.

The story began with the Mohawk and Hudson Paper Company, which was established soon after the Civil War at a former ax-handle factory on Kings Canal in Waterford. The enterprise was purchased soon thereafter by Frank Gilbert, one of the founders, and renamed the Frank Gilbert Paper Company. Nathaniel Sylvester, in his 1878 *History of Saratoga County*, describes the operation as employing 40 people who produced three tons of printing paper a day, using rags, wood and straw as raw materials. The mill building was purchased in 1881 from Uri Gilbert, a prominent manufacturer of railroad cars.

Frank Gilbert constructed a second paper mill in 1917 in Cohoes, just south of the junction of the Erie and Champlain canals. It manufactured groundwood, bond, mimeo, and wallpaper base stock, until the firm went into bankruptcy in 1930 and was reorganized as Mohawk Papermakers, Inc. George E. O'Connor, a Waterford lawyer, and father of current president and CEO, Thomas D. O'Connor, was appointed receiver and eventually bought the mill.

At the time the product mix was 80-90% converting base stock, box liner and box covering (with very little printing papers). In 1946, Mohawk began to develop its first cover and text line, called Mohawk Superfine. The paper ultimately gave

George O'Connor, founder and original president of Mohawk Paper Mills.

a whole new identity to Mohawk, which began to focus on commercial printing papers. During the 1950s and 60s Mohawk built a strong presence in the large northeast advertising and printing markets that developed in New York, Boston, Philadelphia, and Washington, DC. It was known for its quality papers and excellent service.

In 1969, the company was sold to Riegel Paper Co., which was subsequently taken over by Federal Paperboard. Then in 1972, the company was bought back by Tom O'Connor, Sr. and other family members. Thus began the current history of Mohawk Paper Mills, Inc.

In the 1970s and 80s, under Tom O'Connor's direction, Mohawk grew

with a series of major capital investments totaling more than 90 million dollars. A new paper machine was installed in Waterford, replacing an old one; the Cohoes machine was essentially rebuilt, with the addition of high-speed metering technology, an on-the-machine coater, calendaring equipment, and a state-of-the-art electric drive. The result of these investments was a 20,000 ton capacity boost to 75,000 tons per year; entry into the coated market; and the ability to produce a much wider range of grades.

Mohawk also upgraded its environmental systems to meet the 1972 Federal clean air and clean water standards. One of the outcomes of this upgrade was a shift to cationic dyes. New to the US paper industry, these dyes were safer for employees to handle. They also allowed for the production of acid-free colored papers, which are more permanent than traditional acid-based papers. In fact, Mohawk was an innovator in the manufacture of alkaline papers (which has made it a favorite of fine book publishers around the world). In 1990 Mohawk also pioneered the first post-consumer

Carton-packing line, 1954.

Cohoes machine room, 1954.

recycled coated paper—Mohawk 50/10—and in 1993 the company received its first Green Seal certification.

Thomas D. O'Connor, Sr., president and chief executive officer, has been with the company for over fifty years, starting with summer employment while in school and interrupted only by a tour in the military. In an interview in the early nineties, he took time to survey the company's accomplishments and look forward to some of the future challenges. "We have spent millions on new technology and equipment in recent years, but have not provided management and employees with the training and business tools they need to efficiently manage and operate with our new technology." With this in mind, his vision for the nineties was to build the "people" side of Mohawk, by investing heavily in training and systems that would allow the company to anticipate customer needs and provide them more efficiently.

The decade that followed was a challenging one for Mohawk, as it was for many enterprises. A major recession, combined with technology-driven shifts in the graphic arts industry, completely changed Mohawk's marketing environment. Production of printed materials, once highly concentrated in major industrial markets had become decentralized, with the largest growth in areas where Mohawk had little representation: the South, Midwest, West, and Asia. Plus, a wave of industry consolidations was creating billion-dollar competitors—offering a dizzying array of new products for this small, but lucrative, premium paper market.

Mohawk responded aggressively, and by 1995 had essentially re-invented itself. The company turned its small size to an advantage, moving quickly to capitalize on new opportunities. In 1995 the mill introduced the first of its revolutionary Inxwell® papers, Mohawk Options. Inxwell is a proprietary new paper treatment developed by Mohawk. It provides uncoated papers with demonstrably better print quality and much higher opacity than was previously possible. Mohawk's Inxwell papers gained immediate market acceptance and have been chosen for many Fortune 500 annual reports. But the pace of change did not stop there. In 1998 Mohawk introduced a new line of Digital Papers, designed to make the most of new digital printing presses just being launched by Xerox, Agfa, Heidelberg and Xeikon. Also in 1998 the company began shipping paper from its Western Regional Distribution Center in Reno, Nevada— dramatically improving service and deliveries to its western customers.

Today, a third generation of the O'Connor family is closely identified with the business. Tom O'Connor, Jr. is v.p./general manager. Joe O'Connor is director, sales administration, and John O'Connor is director, international sales and customer service. Together they oversee a highly successful operation. With over 350 employees, manufacturing over 275 tons of premium printing paper per day, Mohawk papers are now distributed across North America and in all major international markets, including Australia, Japan, China, Indonesia, Europe and South America.

View of the Waterford mill from the Mohawk River, 1954.

MCVEIGH FUNERAL HOME, INC.

The McVeigh Funeral Home began in business as John Harrigan, General Furnishing Undertaker in 1852 at the corner of Sheridan Avenue and Chapel Street. The Harrigan family was well-known and prosperous, owning considerable Albany property. John's sons, Harvey, Daniel and Joseph F. Harrigan, lived at 22 Sheridan Avenue until 1936 when the last, Joseph, died like his brothers a bachelor.

Upon the death of ex-President Ulysses S. Grant at Mount McGregor in 1885, the Harrigans handled the arrangements, in which the president, one of the first modern embalmings, was laid out in the Albany State Capitol.

William C. McVeigh.

As the Harrigan brothers aged, they cast about for trustworthy help. William C. McVeigh was a young man from Saratoga who in 1901 passed the state embalming exam in Albany's City Hall. He was recruited by the Harrigans and in addition to working as a funeral director, he helped manage their real estate holdings; McVeigh subsequently earned a real estate license as well.

In 1938, after the death of the Harrigan brothers, McVeigh changed the name of the business and moved the funeral home to 208 North Allen Street, off Central Avenue. He lived upstairs from his business and by this time had been joined at work by his son, William J. McVeigh, licensed in 1938. William C. McVeigh survived Joseph Harrigan by just 11 years and died in 1947.

Left to right: William E. McVeigh, Laurel A. McVeigh, Kristin McVeigh Parente and David A. Parente.

McVeigh's son William J. then succeeded to operate the family firm. He was aided in turn by his son, William E. McVeigh, who entered the business in 1958. During this era father and son oversaw two major expansions to the funeral home to better serve the needs of the business.

The 1980s saw momentous changes for the McVeigh funeral home and family. William E. McVeigh's daughters, Kristin and Laurel, were licensed and entered the family business in 1984 and 1989 respectively. In 1986, just 8 months after his father's death, William E. was elected president of the New York State Funeral Directors Association. He would later go on to serve as a District Governor of the National Funeral Directors Association. In 1988 the funeral home completed a construction project that would double the size of the facility to accommodate the ever increasing demand for services.

The McVeigh family and business continue to grow. Kristin's husband David A. Parente joined the firm in 1993. Expanded parking facilities and a 4 bay garage were completed in 1998.

At the turn of the century, there was practically a funeral home on every corner. Today, many of those businesses have either dissolved or been acquired by the multi-national funeral conglomerates. The McVeigh's have chosen to maintain their independence and deep commitment to their community. The McVeigh Funeral Home has grown to be one of the largest independently owned funeral homes in the Capital district. It is to the family's credit that they have managed tremendous growth over the years without jeopardizing the personal service that is so essential to their profession.

Original funeral home, circa 1872.

NEW YORK STATE THRUWAY AUTHORITY

The 641-mile New York State Thruway has been the Empire State's economic lifeline since it opened in 1954. Known as New York's Main Street, the superhighway system links major cities and provides safe and reliable travel for millions of people each year.

The 426-mile mainline connects New York City and Buffalo, the state's two largest cities, and runs through Albany, the state capital. A majority of New York's 62 cities, including the nine largest, are located within the Thruway corridor.

Named for Governor Thomas E. Dewey, the driving force behind its construction, the Thruway is the longest toll superhighway system in the United States.

In 1992, the Authority was also given stewardship of the 524-mile New York State Canal System, the

More than 40 years after it opened, the 641-mile Thruway system remains the primary north-south and east-west route for accessing Albany, New York's capital city. More than 235 million vehicles travel in excess of 8.5 billion miles on the Thruway each year.

historic 173-year-old waterway that provides seasonal navigation between the major state water bodies. The Erie Canal, the oldest and longest of the state's four canals, opened in 1825. The Erie was critical to westward expansion in the U.S. as it provided a way to move people, goods and services quickly and efficiently from the eastern seaboard to western states.

The cross-state superhighway and canal systems are operated and

maintained by the New York State Thruway Authority, an independent public corporation created in 1950 by the New York State Legislature. A three-member Board appointed by the Governor and Legislature oversees the Authority.

The Authority was established to build, operate and maintain the Thruway system as a self-supporting project financed through bonds being retired from proceeds of tolls and other income. State tax dollars are not used to operate and maintain the system, which is user-fee supported.

The Thruway Authority is headquartered in Albany, just off the Thruway's Downtown Albany interchange. Signs along the Thruway in this area alert travelers to Albany's national designation as an All-America City.

The New York State Thruway mainline as it looked when under construction in the early 1950s. The first Thruway tolls were collected on June 24, 1954.

Today, the Thruway is recognized as a national leader in safety and technology. Statistically one of the safest superhighways in the nation, the Thruway pioneered the use of electronic toll collection in the Northeast when it implemented E-ZPass in 1993.

Current New York State Governor George E. Pataki appointed Howard E. Steinberg Chairman and Chief Executive Officer of the Authority in January 1996. The other board members are Nancy E. Carey and William C. Warren III. The Executive Director is John Platt.

NIAGARA MOHAWK

The story of Niagara Mohawk begins not in the 19th century as you might expect, but in the 18th century as colonists settled by the streams and rivers of upstate New York. Along with providing a means of transportation and communication, the natural waterways also gave the settlers routes for developing commerce and industry.

Early traders followed these navigable streams, up the Hudson River, west along the Mohawk River, across a two-mile portage to a creek flowing into Oneida Lake, down the Oswego River to Lake Ontario, west across the lake to the narrow land strip separating Lakes Ontario and Erie, the gateway to the west. Pioneers formed settlements by the cascading waterfalls and used hyropower to run their grist mills and sawmills.

Early in the 19th century, 175 years of corporate history for Niagara Mohawk began with the organization of the Oswego Canal Company in 1823. At Cohoes, Canvass White, an Erie Canal engineer, harnessed the power of the 100-foot fall of the Mohawk River to establish Niagara Mohawk's second pioneer predecessor, the Cohoes Company, in 1826.

The pioneers kept moving west as the Erie Canal was completed in 1825, opening a more direct water route to Buffalo and Lake Erie. Railways later followed the waterways which nourished the Great Corridor crossing New York State. When power transmission came of age, power lines followed those same paths forged by the pioneers.

As settlements became villages and cities, the demand for industrial power grew along with an increased need for lighting in streets, stores and homes. Gas lighting provided a safer and cleaner alternative to oil lamps, and grew rapidly in popularity before the Civil War. Niagara Mohawk's earliest predecessor in the gas industry was The Albany Gas Light Company, incorporated in 1841. It piped manufactured gas,

Cohoes Company Dam erected in 1865.

providing lighting to the Capitol and many other Albany buildings.

With Thomas Edison's invention of the incandescent lamp in 1879, electric lighting began to replace gas lighting. Although gas companies still provided power for cooking and heating, most of the gas operations joined with the developing electric companies for financial support, thus initiating the trend toward the integrated interconnected systems that provide power today. Most of the gas lighting companies became combination gas and electric companies with the development of electric power in the last decades of the 19th century.

The industrial revolution that began in the 19th century was driven by electrical inventions such as Edison's light bulb and it fueled demand for electricity in factories as well as homes. Despite the challenges that the use of electricity presented, engineers and inventors solved the problems with pioneering efforts and methods at Niagara and elsewhere. The year 1896, when long-distance transmission of electricity generated at Niagara Falls was used to light streets in Buffalo, heralded a new phase of development.

Successful development on the Niagara brought renewed interest in converting the tumbling waters of the Adirondack streams into electric power. Generating stations sprouted on East Canada Creek at St. Johnsville, on the Hudson River at Mechanicville, on the Raquette River at Hannawa Falls, on the Beaver River at Belfort and on the West Canada, which flows into the Mohawk.

As the electric power industry developed, large steam-driven generating plants were built requiring substantial investment and highly efficient business organizations. By the turn of the century, the needs of industry, commerce and homes for mechanical power, gas and finally electric power far outgrew the ability of small enterprises to produce. The family-owned and other small generating companies disappeared as the larger electric and gas companies grew into "public utilities."

Before 1929, three large groups served most of the Great Corridor across New York State. Although these groups had interconnections for interchange and purchase of power supply they were not an integrated system. One group brought power from the upper Hudson River system and the eastern and southeastern Adirondack slopes. Another delivered power from the northern and southwestern Adirondack slopes and the Mohawk River system. The third gathered power from Niagara and other western New York waterways.

With the formation of the Niagara Hudson Power Corporation in 1929 to acquire these properties along with their holdings, the new corporation began the long and painstaking task of organizing these 59 companies into an integrated system. By 1937, the number of companies was down to 20, including five principal operating companies and only one intermediate holding company.

In 1950, with the formation of Niagara Mohawk Power Corporation, the long- sought goal of a single operating company serving most of upstate New York was realized. The new corporation emerged from the three principal operating companies: Buffalo Niagara Electric Corporation, Central New York Power Corporation and New York Power and Light Corporation.

Throughout the 20th century Niagara Mohawk and its predecessors faced numerous challenges as the industry grew and changed, including expanding facilities, increased customer and service demands, changes to natural gas, extensive financing requirements, vital inter-

Cohoes Hydro, circa 1910.

connections with other systems, programs for continued economy and efficiency, war production challenges, regulatory problems and public power competition.

Niagara Mohawk perservered through additional adversities such as: the loss of its largest hydro plant in 1956; the substitution of governmental-agency development for additional Niagara power; shortages of natural gas, oil and coal; environmental problems, large-scale financing demands, inflationary costs

Expanding the needs of Albany, circa 1950s.

and multiple government controls.

Thirty-eight years after creating a single operating company, Niagara Mohawk announced a new corporate structure, pending regulatory approval, in 1998. To position itself better in the market and grow in value, Niagara Mohawk is forming a holding company, Niagara Mohawk Holdings, Inc., with two subsidiaries: Niagara Mohawk and Opinac N.A. William E. Davis, Niagara Mohawk's chairman and chief executive officer, will head the new holding company.

"After thorough, strategic analysis, I am confident we have selected the right model and the right leadership to assure our company's success into the 21st century," said Mr. Davis. The company that grew from approximately 150 forerunners, with its roots from the settlers who first tamed the water power of New York's great eastern watershed, looks forward with confidence and pride as it continues to provide power to the residents of Albany and New York State.

ORANGE MOTOR COMPANY

Orange Motors is one of the largest auto dealerships in the Northeast. It also has the distinction of being one of the oldest family owned businesses in the region. Orange Motor Company was founded on Friday, October 13th, 1916 by Charles Touhey. Before Charlie Touhey entered into the automobile business he operated a farm in Orange County, New York, South of Albany. As the story goes: Mr. Touhey was on a train enroute to Albany from Newburgh when the offer to purchase the Ford franchise in the Albany area was presented to him. He proceeded with the purchase, moved his family to Albany and started the Orange Motor Company at a small site on Delaware Avenue. Since that time the company has made three other moves in the area until its present location on Central Avenue.

Orange Motors primary business is the sale of new and used cars and the service of these sales. The company has been one of the premier dealers in the Capital Region and has always maintained a high profile in community affairs. The firm has also played an important role in the life of many employees over the years. The owners of the company have always instilled in their employees the importance of family values and these values have carried over to the customers a feeling of honesty and security. Orange Motors at this time has 130 employees on staff. This work force has been maintained for the last ten years. It is noteworthy that their tenure is outstanding. Employees are still working with over

forty years of continuous service and many have retired with twenty-five, thirty and forty years of service.

The present CEO of the company is Carl E. Touhey, son of Charles Touhey, the founder. Carl's brother Frank managed the company during the early 1960s. After Frank's death Carl took over the active running of the company and he has played a major role in the managing of the franchise. The business has grown from its early days as a facility with 10,000 square foot building to its present size of two buildings with over 80,000 square feet. The property has also expanded to over 8.5 acres of land on a major highway in the Capital city of the state.

Like most other automobile

Charles Touhey, the founder of Orange Motor Company, displays the end of an era—the last Model "T"

dealerships, they too have acquired other franchises. Orange Motors has a Mazda franchise and a Sterling Heavy Duty Truck franchise. Orange Motors has the reputation of being one of the most progressive automobile dealerships in the Northeast. The company is known to have one of the largest parts businesses in that area. They deliver parts as far as the Canadian border, 150 miles away and also have one of the largest service departments in the area. They service 150–175 cars per day. Their sale of cars, light and heavy trucks ranks them among the top twenty-five car and truck dealers in the New York district. Orange Motors' future plans are to continue to press forward in the pursuit of sales and development of well-trained employees. The future of Orange Motor Company is to continue its process of growth and to become a leader in the automobile franchise system in the State of New York.

The present Orange Motor Company.

PARSONS CHILD AND FAMILY CENTER

On December 2, 1829, the Society for the Relief of Orphan & Destitute Children in the City of Albany opened its doors and admitted its first orphan, a five year old boy. Little more was known of him other than his name, Lewis. He was the first of thousands of destitute and forlorn children who were housed, fed, educated and cared for by the institution that was to evolve more than a century later into Parsons Child and Family Center of Albany.

Although the culture in the City of Albany was ripe for its founding at that time, the orphanage would not have come into being had it not been for the dedication and determination of Mrs. Orissa Healy. In the weeks prior to its opening, letters written to her friend, Miss Eliza Wilcox, reveal a rising emotional involvement and a fierce, almost fanatical intensity that must have kept her working at a constant feverish pitch. Mrs. Healy expressed herself without reserve, "What shall I do? I hear the Macedonian cry from every little, wicked child in the streets."

News of Orissa Healy's plan quickly spread throughout Albany's churchgoers. Many contributions followed in those initial months—donations of cash, food, clothing and other goods needed to keep the orphanage operating. The list of benefactors includes Albany's most prominent citizens, as well as others whose names are unfamiliar today.

Martin Van Buren contributed $10; Erastus Corning, $20; Edward C. Delevan, $50; and Stephen Van Rensselaer, $100 to Mrs. Healy's cause. John G. Wasson donated 10 gallons of molasses, two fowls, 14 Christmas cakes, a bushel of apples, eight pounds of cheese, a pork ham and a piece of beef. His wife gave seven yards of bed ticking, 10 yards of factory sheeting and four pieces of tape.

In 1907, the Albany Orphan Asylum, as it was then named, moved to its present location on New Scotland Avenue, establishing one of

the earliest cottage type institutions in the country. In 1935, the Asylum officially became the Albany Home for Children and soon after hired the first trained social worker to its staff. Over time the Home developed new programs to aid more effectively those children suffering with dramatic emotional and social problems.

With this change of emphasis, the trustees decided to sell part of the former campus with the old cottage facilities and to construct modern, cottage-type buildings on the remaining 19 acres. The agency remains today in what has become the University Heights section of the City of Albany.

From humble beginnings, the Albany Home for Children evolved into what is today known as Parsons Child and Family Center. With an annual budget of $20 million, Parsons employs over 500 people and provides a wide network of services to more than 2,000 children and 5,200 family members in 30 counties.

What is it that makes Parsons so unique? In part, it is a real tradition of caring with an ability to

In 1829, the Society for the Relief of Orphan & Destitute Children in the City of Albany opened its doors to a handful of children. They were life's forgotten, orphaned and impoverished. In the next 169 years, that organization grew into one of the most progressive and effective treatment and counseling centers for children and families challenged by emotional difficulties—Parsons Child and Family Center.

respond to the ever-changing, complex needs of families and communities. The staff at Parsons firmly believe that children have a right to a stable, safe living environment that will allow them to establish permanent relationships with parents or parental figures. The staff believe that healthy children come from such living arrangements, and deserve to learn and grow in a nurturing setting.

From the beginning, Parsons has relied on ongoing support from the community. The special care, so vital for thousands of young lives, would not be possible without the generosity of individuals, businesses, corporations, foundations and volunteers who believe in and support Parsons Child and Family Center.

A.J. RINELLA AND COMPANY

In 1919 A.J. Rinella began operating a wholesale-produce distributorship serving small grocery stores, markets, restaurants and other clients in and around Amsterdam, New York. After a decade of learning the business, he moved to Albany to become the manager of a cousin's produce-supply company, Caruso Fruit. With ten additional years of experience in acquiring, storing and distributing produce, in 1948 he once again went into business on his own, starting a competing wholesale firm in Albany and concentrating during the years to come on building a growing clientele. Placing orders directly with brokers and growers in Florida, California and other fruit and vegetable-producing areas, A.J. Rinella received shipments at his Menands Market warehouse and distributed a wide array of fruits, vegetables and other food products to smaller wholesalers, mom-and-pop grocery stores and increasingly to larger markets primarily in the immediate Albany region.

By 1953 he was firmly established when he welcomed his son Joseph into the company, which they incorporated in 1957 as A.J. Rinella and Company, Inc. During the 1960s, the father-son team progressively expanded their delivery fleet to include some twenty refrigerated trucks, increased their catalogue of products to include the

Some of the A.J. Rinella trucks.

The third generation of Rinellas to own and operate the family produce business.

exotic as well as the customary, and expanded their operational territory to encompass a 90-mile radius of Albany, extending into large portions of western Massachusetts and southeastern Vermont.

Grandfather A.J. carried the title of president and father Joseph served as vice president, secretary, and treasurer when the third generation of Rinellas began to occupy the company in force, solidifying the firm's function as the stronghold of a family dynasty. Joseph's son A.J. went to work as a regular employee in the spring of 1978 immediately following his graduation from Paul Smith College with a degree in hotel-restaurant management. A second son, Peter, began learning the trade from the ground up in 1981. A third son, Paul, followed and completed the pattern in 1982.

The elder A.J. retired in 1985, leaving his namesake creation firmly established as one of the major produce suppliers in the Albany region. However, the first major catastrophe in the history of the business struck Rinella and Company in 1989 when a fire destroyed its warehouse and offices. Reacting to the calamity speedily, the Rinellas built a 10,000 square-foot new warehouse-office complex on the site of the old and diligently strove to ensure that business continued apace with as little adverse affect as possible. Joseph Rinella continued to run the company full time, consistently enlarging the company's line of products and its list of customers, until his death in January 1992.

Currently, Peter Rinella serves as president, Paul is vice president of transportation, and A.J. fills the multiple roles of vice president, secretary and treasurer. Collectively, they share the basic goals of maintaining the reputation for integrity and timely service that Rinella and Company has established over four decades and three generations and of continuing to add to the company's long list of satisfied customers.

ROYAL & SUNALLIANCE FINANCIAL SERVICES

The Royal Indemnity Company incorporated its subsidiary Royal Globe Life Insurance Company of New York on February 7, 1974, to sell insurance and annuities exclusively in New York, an endeavor prompted by the singularity of the state's insurance laws. Royal Globe received its license in August, 1974 and began business in September. In May, 1980, the company adopted its current name, Royal Life Insurance Company of New York.

The firm maintains its home office in Albany and sales offices in Syracuse and Manhattan. Executives and staff conduct their business through approximately 500 independent agents. From its beginning, Royal Life of New York has concentrated principally on serving middle-income families by assisting them in building retirement income through single and flexible premium fixed annuities, with a further concentration on serving small businesses and not-for-profit groups.

Through a complex corporate structure, Royal Life of New York traces its lineage through Royal Maccabees Life Insurance Company to Royal & SunAlliance Financial Services, a colossus created in a 1996 merger of Royal Insurance Company and the SunAlliance Group, a combination that shares a long and legendary history in the world of insurance.

The origin of the Royal & SunAlliance can be traced to London, England, in 1710 with the founding of the Sun Fire Office, which entered the United States market with the acquisition of the Watertown Insurance Company of New Jersey in 1882. They became the Sun Insurance Office in 1891, and earned the undiluted respect of its clients in 1906 by dispersing £333,000 following the San Francisco earthquake. In 1959, Sun merged with the Alliance Assurance Company, established in England in 1824, to form SunAlliance Insurance, which acquired London Insurance Company in 1965 to become SunAlliance and London Insurance, which evolved into the SunAlliance Group in 1989.

The Royal Insurance Company, formed in Liverpool, England, on May 31, 1845, expanded into the United States in 1851, opening agencies in New York, Baltimore, Philadelphia, Savannah, and Charleston. Royal also earned a distinguished reputation for integrity by paying in full every valid claim resulting from the San Francisco earthquake.

Beginning in 1891, Royal expanded its types of coverage vastly and grew to become a dominant force in the insurance industry through a series of acquisitions, culminating in 1919 with the absorption of the Liverpool and London and the Globe Insurance Company, then the largest merger in British history. By 1960 Royal had hundreds of branch offices peppered around the globe, with 175 in the United States alone.

Major acquisitions by Royal continued in England with the addition of Lloyd's Life Assurance in 1985 and in the United States with the Milbank Insurance Company, the

J. Tyler Lee, president.

Silvey Corporation, and American Overseas Holdings. In 1989, Royal Insurance Company acquired Maccabees Insurance Company, which was established in 1878 and has been headquartered in metropolitan Detroit for 90 years. The Royal name provided a great complement to Maccabees, as Royal had earned an outstanding reputation in the United States dating back to 1906.

Finally, in 1996 Royal and Sun Alliance merged to create the Royal & SunAlliance Financial Services companies, operating its U.S. life Company out of Southfield, Michigan, controlling $100 billion in assets and capital of $12 billion, and engaging more than 40,000 employees to provide personal financial services and commercial risk protection in more than 120 countries.

Royal & SunAlliance Financial Services headquarters in Southfield, Michigan.

ST. PETER'S HOSPITAL

The story of St. Peter's Hospital begins with a journey of faith. In the fall of 1863, four Sisters of Mercy left New York City on a Hudson River Day Line steamship with one-way tickets to Albany and just 80 cents between them. Their mission was a broad one: establish a new convent; tend to the sick; and lessen human suffering, especially among the poor. They had been sent "according to Gospel fashion, without purse," their Mother Superior wrote to them. It would take more than faith, these pioneering nuns soon learned, to practice that mission on a large scale, given their limited means.

Providence arrived in 1869 in the form of a $15,000 contribution to

A typical St. Peter's interior view of 1875; the rooms were spartan by today's standards. Water was provided in ceramic pitchers like the one behind the bed at center.

the Sisters of Mercy from the Cagger family, who presented the bequest in honor of the late Peter Cagger, an Albany lawyer, civic leader and philanthropist who had been killed in a carriage accident the year before. The Cagger donation made possible the founding of St. Peter's Hospital (named in recognition of Peter Cagger) on the Feast of All Saints, Nov. 1, 1869. Grateful citizens of Albany called it the hospital "with doors that never close." In the ensuing 129 years, the doors of St. Peter's have remained perpetually open to all in need, regardless of economic status.

The first site of St. Peter's Hospital was at the corner of Broadway and North Ferry, amid a busy commercial stretch along the Hudson River. The Sisters of Mercy had been instructed to go where the need was greatest and

the high toll of industrial injuries and manufacturing mishaps put the Hospital at a critical geographical juncture. The Hospital was located in a landmark building, a three-story brick structure converted for medical use from a glorious past that includes its use as home for three prominent Albany residents. Philip Livingston, a signer of the Declaration of Independence lived there, as did Stephen Van Rensselaer, son of the Dutch patroon, and Gov. John A. King—making it the New York State Executive Mansion during his tenure.

St. Peter's Hospital opened with 33 general-ward beds, two private rooms, an outpatient dispensary and just seven doctors—all of whom maintained private practices —on its staff. Where the Hospital built its reputation was from its exceptional nursing staff, noted for

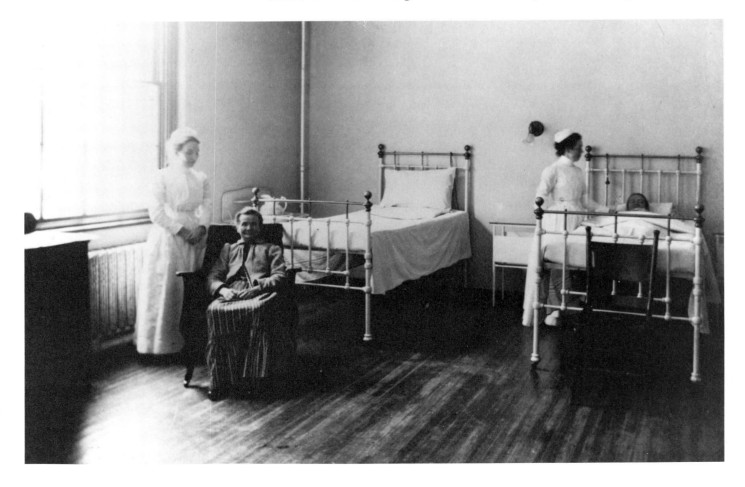

The original St. Peter's Hospital, at Broadway and North Ferry Street. Its origins dated to 1783.

the professionalism and compassion of its care. The Sisters of Mercy anchored the nursing operation and were the heart and soul of the institution from its beginning, under the direction of the superintendent, Mother Mary Paula Harris, a Southerner whose prayerful devotion and expert nursing care was legendary among wounded soldiers in Civil War field hospitals. Another aspect of its mission established early on was the $100 worth of medicine dispensed free-of-charge to the poor during the first two months of the Hospital's operation.

A healthy tension between ministry and business administration was born between Mother Harris and her superior, Mother Mary Vincent Sweetman, who wrote: "Be kind to the sisters and keep out of debts."

The sisters were joined on their journey of faith by a community eager to supply the funds and support necessary to move the Hospital forward and fuel its continuous growth and transformations. Physicians donated their services. The New York State Legislature gave St. Peter's Hospital a $10,000 grant in 1871 as a

result of the Hospital's incorporation after two years of operation in which capacity had tripled to 100 beds. The Hospital quickly outgrew the building, so a fourth story was added in 1873 at a cost of $36,000. The community pitched in once more by donating items to a fundraising bazaar held at the Martin Opera House and spearheaded by the Cagger family. The Hospital's new addition featured several innovations for the day, including

244

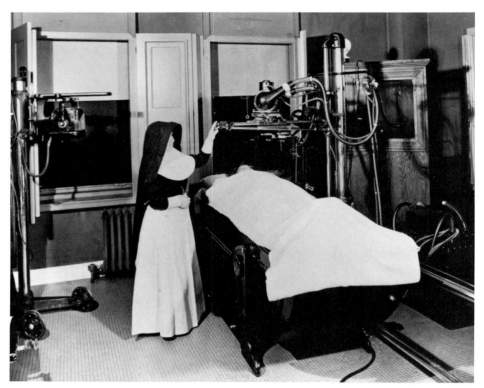

Sister Mary Eucharia, X-ray technician, with the Hospital's state-of-the-art X-ray equipment circa 1947. The Hospital claimed "one of the finest X-ray Departments in the Eastern United States."

large skylights and strategically situated windows to circulate as much fresh air as possible through the building. Special parlors on each floor were meant to promote convalescence, as were lounges where patients played checkers and chess, received visitors, and played the piano.

In that early era, St. Peter's Hospital assembled a team of outstanding physicians, led by medical director Dr. Thomas Hun, who was joined by Dr. John Swinburne, Dr. Samuel B. Ward, Dr. Henry Hun, Dr. S.O. Vanderpoel, Dr. J.V.P. Quackenbush and others. Multiple trauma from industrial accidents was the most common admission, followed by typhoid fever, rheumatism, tuberculosis, eye diseases and dyspepsia. The reputation of the physicians soon matched the highest esteem in which the nurses

were held. "This institution has grown year after year in public favor, until it holds a place second to none in the state," *The Evening Times* of Albany wrote in an editorial. Faith and community support merged once more when Mother Harris established the St. Peter's Hospital School of Nursing of 1899, one of the first such programs in New York State. The nursing school was chartered by the State Board of Regents in 1905.

The next chapter of the St. Peter's Hospital story, the middle phase, was marked by a dizzying array of expansions and an organized and sustained effort of fundraising by the St. Peter's Hospital Auxiliary. By the height of World War I, with an annual patient census of 2,000 and more wounded soldiers arriving daily, the staff was stretched to the breaking point. The Sisters of Mercy nurses offered their living quarters for patient care. Mrs. Margaret Brady Farrell, a major benefactor, gave a special $2,000 gift that eased the wartime medical

crisis. But the long-term facilities shortcomings only grew more dire. "A hospital cannot stand still," proclaimed the new Bishop of the Albany diocese, Most Rev. Edmund F. Gibbons, who launched a capital campaign to build a new hospital on Easter Day in 1923 that raised more than $200,000. Bishop Gibbons himself climbed aboard a steam shovel and broke ground on the site at the intersection of New Scotland Avenue and Allen Street on May 28, 1928.

The Hospital was not standing still. It was growing and moving uptown. Patients were transferred from the original downtown site to the new St. Peter's Hospital on August 25, 1930. Mother Mary Leo Doon was the hospital superintendent who provided the firm and steady leadership through the transition, the seventh superintendent in an unbroken chain of ten charismatic and skilled Sisters of Mercy managers who guided the institution in the first 125 years of its history.

More than its ever-expanding brick-and-mortar physical plant and its state-of-the-art equipment, the story of St. Peter's Hospital must focus on the people and their commitment to the Mercy mission of tending to the sick and lessening human suffering. At every critical juncture, an administrator rose to the challenge, such as Sister Mary Esther Redmond, who led the hospital through the hardships of the Great Depression and World War II and managed to double the bed capacity and complete the first $1 million additions despite the upheaval around her. Another giant of leadership was Sister Ellen Lawlor, president and chief executive officer for 24 years until her death in 1994, who transformed the community hospital into Mercycare Corp., a multi-faceted healthcare organization with more than 3,000 full-time employees, a constellation

The main entrance to the modern St. Peter's Hospital in 1997.

of healthcare delivery sites and $150 million in annual revenues. During her tenure, St. Peter's also participated in the creation of the Eastern Mercy Health System (EMHS) which united 13 institutions from Maine to Florida into a strong, financially viable healthcare system that strengthened the healing ministry and values of the Catholic Church. In the late 1990s, EMHS evolved into a larger more comprehensive network now known as Catholic Health East.

Sister Ellen's protégé, Steven P. Boyle, became the first person other than a Sister of Mercy to direct St. Peter's Hospital when he took over as president and CEO of St. Peter's and Mercycare in 1994. Boyle's tenure has been one of continued stewardship of the original Sisters of Mercy mission, despite a healthcare climate of uncertainty and an increasingly complex corporation with new challenges to go with an annual budget approaching $200 million.

St. Peter's Hospital and Mercycare have grown exponentially in the decades of the 1980s and 1990s, providing a full continuum of health care services throughout life—from prenatal to end-of-life care. These services are provided by Mercycare component corporations: the Hospital, St. Peter's Addiction Recovery Center, Mercy Cares for Kids (day care center), St. Peter's Auxiliary, Inc., Our Lady of Mercy Life Center (skilled nursing and residential care facility), the St. Peter's Hospital Foundation and The Community Hospice. Literally, tens of millions dollars worth of capital improvements and expansions have prepared the Mercycare System of Care to continue to provide quality healthcare in the 21st century as it did in the 19th and 20th centuries.

The story that began with a journey of faith in 1863 has come full circle at the end of 1998. St. Peter's Hospital, poised for the new millennium, is a living example of faith personified, of staying true to one's mission with the unshakable belief that by tending to the sick and lessening human suffering, the rest will work out. It is the story of an institution with a rich history of caring that has become a regional leader in Upstate New York providing the most modern treatment for today's illnesses and injuries. Most importantly, it is a story that will have a happy ending.

SAWCHUK, BROWN ASSOCIATES

In 1979, when Albany's largest and most respected commercial developer announced plans for a new suburban office park, it was surprised by the public perceptions resulting from misunderstandings and misinformation.

The Picotte Companies found its plans stymied and its impeccable image threatened. Active opposition and a reluctance by the company to talk with the media were shaping public opinion. Approvals were delayed. The project was in peril.

Meanwhile, Pamela Sawchuk was contemplating a career change. The veteran newspaper editor and award-winning feature writer observed the need for professional communications counsel in the Capital Region. In establishing an independent public relations practice, her first client was The Picotte Companies. She helped the company communicate effectively with all concerned. With greater understanding of the project, opposition declined. Improved communication provided greater community acceptance.

Today, the project—Corporate Woods—is the region's premier office park. And, as Sawchuk, Brown Associates prepares to celebrate its 20th anniversary, The Picotte Companies remains a major client along with more than 60 others who benefit from a relationship with what has become the largest independent public relations/public affairs firm in Upstate New York.

Throughout its first two decades Sawchuk, Brown Associates has developed in size and stature, enhanced by an impressive client list and the region's growing sophistication toward professional public relations. It serves regional, statewide and national clients with professional communications and public affairs counsel and services including public relations and public affairs strategy; media relations, community relations; crisis communications; publications, video and editorial services; marketing support; database communications and research;

David Brown, president, and Pamela Sawchuk, founder of the largest independent public relations firm in Upstate New York.

on-line communications and Web site counsel; and government communications. Over the years it has developed expertise in a wide range of areas, including economic development, education, employee relations, entertainment and the arts, environmental issues, financial services, health care, state associations, state and local government relations, telecommunications, travel and tourism and others.

The firm was selected in 1998 as an organizing member of the new, prestigious Association of Public Relations Firms (APRF) which was established to represent the leadership of the public relations agency industry in the United States.

Founded as Pamela Sawchuk Associates, it was incorporated as Sawchuk, Brown Associates in 1988, reflecting the principal role of David P. Brown, formerly executive news editor of the Albany *Times Union* and editor of the Sunday *Times Union*. Like his wife Pamela Sawchuk Brown, Mr. Brown had extensive journalism experience, more than 16 years as a reporter and editor for daily newspapers in New York and Virginia.

Over the years, the firm has built a strong staff of professionals from journalism, business, government and academia, including public relations specialists from national firms, who have served hundreds of clients.

The firm is organized into four core practice groups—health care/education, corporate/technology, travel/leisure and—because of its location in the capital of New York state—public affairs.

The communications-focused public affairs operation, which often works with lobbyists and law firms, was established in 1988. Its offers public affairs and government relations services including issues management, legislative and issues research, grassroots lobbying, media relations, speech writing, association communications, preparation of testimony, coalition building, political assessment/analysis, access to decision makers and seminars and legislative functions. The public affairs operation has received national honors from the Public Relations Society of America and *Inside PR* magazine.

Among the local, regional and national professional honors the firm has received are "Company of the Year" (under 100 employees) awarded by the *Capital District Business Review*; the Albany-Colonie Regional Chamber of Commerce "Small Business of the Year"; Presidential Citations from the Public Relations Society of America; "Silver Quill Award" honors from the International Association of Business Communicators, "Mark of Excellence" honor from the American Marketing Association; and a "Creativity in Public Relations Award" from *Inside PR* magazine.

Inside PR magazine, in its "Agency Report Card of Independent Firms," has selected Sawchuk, Brown Associates as one of the "12 best managed agencies" in the country. The 1998 O'Dwyer's report on American public relations firms ranks Sawchuk, Brown Associates as the largest in New York state outside of New York City. In addition, O'Dwyer's PR Services magazine has listed Sawchuk, Brown among the nation's leading regional public relations firms in the areas of health care,

environmental, travel/tourism and financial communications.

It is actively involved with the Internet, maintaining its own site on the World Wide Web—"The Albany Experience"—as well as assisting clients develop sites. *Inside PR* magazine has identified Sawchuk, Brown Associates as a leader among a "new generation of PR firms" on the Web.

The firm is the Upstate New York Associate of Hill and Knowlton, one

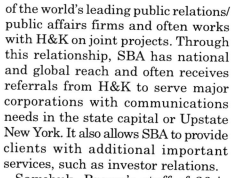

SBA professionals present a media training session in the firm's offices.

of the world's leading public relations/public affairs firms and often works with H&K on joint projects. Through this relationship, SBA has national and global reach and often receives referrals from H&K to serve major corporations with communications needs in the state capital or Upstate New York. It also allows SBA to provide clients with additional important services, such as investor relations.

Sawchuk, Brown's staff of 26 is actively involved and holds leadership positions in professional organizations (e.g., Public Relations Society of America, Women's Press Club, American Marketing Association), business groups (e.g., Albany-Colonie Regional Chamber of Commerce, Business Council of New York State, Center for Economic Growth) and a number of leading community institutions and organizations in the arts, education, health care and social services. In 1997, Pamela Sawchuk received the Albany–Colonie Regional Chamber of Commerce "Spirit of the Chamber" award, marking the first time this prestigious business honor was bestowed on a communications professional.

Among the firm's public affairs staff are, from left, Jonathan Pierce, Rose Raus and Jon Rucket, in front of the New York State Capitol building.

THE COLLEGE OF SAINT ROSE

The College of Saint Rose was founded in 1920 by the Sisters of Saint Joseph of Carondelet who dreamed of establishing the only catholic college for women between New York City and Buffalo. Under the leadership of Sr. Blanche Rooney and with the encouragement of the Roman Catholic Diocese of Albany, the Sisters built an institution of higher learning dedicated to intellectual progress and an awareness of the spiritual dimension.

On June 28, 1920, the New York State Board of Regents granted a provisional charter that allowed the College to award bachelor's degrees in the arts, sciences and music. The Class of '24 consisted of 19 young women and 8 professors.

In 1927, the Middle States Association of Colleges and Universities accredited the College without the customary period of probation. By the College's Silver Anniversary in 1945, the College had grown from 19 to 360 students and from one house and a garage to 14 houses and two major buildings. By the mid-40s, over 1,000 graduates had been awarded degrees and the College was fast becoming a leading educator of teachers for the Capital Region.

The curricula also grew and intensified and in 1949, the College became the first Catholic women's college in New York state to be given

The College of Saint Rose began with a vision, $1,000 and the house pictured below, Saint Rose Hall. The first 19 students attended class, ate their meals and made their home in this building. It is known today as Moran Hall.

the right to award masters' degrees in the arts, sciences and education.

The College's largest change since its founding came about in 1969, when it became fully co-educational. Thomas Hart, a four-year Marine Corps veteran, who served in Vietnam, became the College's first full-time, male day student.

As the College reached its 50-year milestone in 1970, new seeds of tradition were being sown. The College legally became an independent institution while maintaining its Catholic traditions. Dr. Alphonse R. Miele became the College's first lay president in 1970, followed by Dr. Thomas A. Manion, Dr. Louis C. Vaccaro, and the current president, Dr. R. Mark Sullivan.

In 1971, The College was again at the educational forefront establishing the Experienced Adult Program (EAP), enabling adult students to receive undergraduate credit for documented life learning experiences. The EAP was one of the first

Today, the 27,000 square foot Science Center is the entryway to the 25-acre Saint Rose campus. The College serves nearly 4,000 students with 36 undergraduate and 21 graduate programs.

programs of its kind in the country and still stands as a national model. The College's athletic programs also blossomed throughout the '80s and by 1991, the College's Golden Knights were invited into the National Collegiate Athletic (NCAA) Division II.

There is no doubt that the dreams of a few can impact the lives of thousands. The College has awarded degrees to more than 23,000 students and the early vision of the Sisters of Saint Joseph of Carondelet continues to form the underpinnings of the institution. The College's mission remains the same: to provide quality educational opportunities to students of all backgrounds and create an atmosphere in which students are empowered to improve themselves and the world around them.

SIENA COLLEGE

Siena College is an independent, coeducational liberal arts college with a Franciscan tradition. Since its founding by seven Franciscan friars, Siena has enjoyed a reputation as a community where care and concern for the intellectual, personal, social and spiritual growth of all students is paramount. Located in Loudonville on 155 lush, green acres, Siena is just three miles north of Albany, New York State's capital city.

It all began in 1937 when the Franciscan Friars of the Province of the Most Holy Name founded a Catholic college for men residing in the Capital Region in New York State called St. Bernardine of Siena College. As a site for the college, the 40-acre Garrett Estate in suburban Loudonville, New

Seven founding Friars.

York was purchased, and a single building was converted to temporary use as a college building. Groundwork for the first new structure, Siena Hall, was begun in early 1938. That same year the college received its provisional charter.

Early growth of Siena was fast-paced. By 1939 a coeducational evening division was added. One year later the total enrollment grew from an original enrollment of 91 to almost 1,000 students. By

1941 a second building, Gibbons Hall Gymnasium, was completed. Siena received its permanent charter in 1942. That same year the College altered its program to meet defense needs, training Navy personnel, as well as regular students. By the end of World War II, an era of new growth emerged, due in large part to the number of ex-servicemen who comprised of, at that time, 75% of the student body.

Today, Siena's 2,700 undergraduate women and men choose from among 23 majors in liberal arts, science and business. Siena offers more than a dozen special signature and certificate programs. Some additional 700 women and men are enrolled in graduate degree programs and continuing education courses.

Since the early years, Siena has experienced continued growth and expansion with the addition of a multitude of academic, sports, and residence building facilities. Groundbreaking for the new J. Spencer and Patricia Standish Library began during the spring of 1998 and is expected to be completed in the fall of 1999 to facilitate growth and technology as Siena moves into the 21st century.

More than 160 women and men comprise the full time faculty at Siena, with more than 81% holding doctorate degrees. In addition to their teaching, the faculty are actively engaged in scholarship, research, writing or artistic performance. Siena's student-focused professors are at the heart of a challenging, supportive learning community that prepares and challenges students for careers, active roles in their community, and for the real world.

Siena remains a community of shared living and learning shaped by its Franciscan heritage. Throughout its history, Siena has been committed to building a college, which nurtures the academic, social and spiritual growth

Siena Hall.

of its students in an environment modeled after the principles of St. Francis of Assisi. He was a man of God who recognized the goodness of all creation, who welcomed every human being as brother or sister, and who esteemed all labor no matter how humble. Siena affirms the unique worth of each person and the responsibility of individuals to cooperate in the creation of a just and peaceful society.

Siena College, since the beginning, has worked to develop all facets of the student in preparation for an ever-changing world and a diverse society by approaching education, "one student at a time."

St. Francis Hall, "The Friary," circa 1938.

TIMES UNION

As is the case with most major enterprises, the *Times Union*—the dominant newspaper in New York's Capital Region—began in much humbler circumstances.

On April 21, 1856, the *Morning Times* published its first edition, the beginning of the newspaper we know today. One of its three founders, Alfred Stone, was an experienced newspaperman, having been involved with the *Albany Morning Express*, which he founded in 1847 and sold in 1853.

The new *Times* was published in the old *Express* offices at State and Green streets in Albany, with Stone, David M. Barnes and Edward H. Boyd as co-owners. Stone couldn't get rights to the *Express* name for his new venture, even though the people who bought his former newspaper were using a different title, so the name "Times" was selected.

Through various mergers, the name underwent a series of short-lived changes, finally becoming *The Evening Times* on Sept. 25, 1865. *The Albany Weekly Times* was created as a companion publication to *The Evening Times* in 1872.

Today's view of the Times Union offices.

The newspaper claimed no ties to any political or other group, stressing its motto, "Independence Now, Independence Forever."

On May 29, 1882, another competitor entered the field when the *Evening Union* was established with John H. Farrell as editor and publisher. The marriage of the *Times* and the *Union* took place on Nov. 19, 1891.

When Farrell died just before the turn of the century, Martin H. Glynn, a Kinderhook native of Irish background, became editor and publisher. His journalism and political careers were intertwined.

He was elected to Congress in 1898, to the office of state comptroller in 1906, and became lieutenant governor under William Sulzer in 1912. Later that year, Glynn moved into the governor's mansion when Sulzer was impeached.

Glynn resumed the publisher's role at the *Times-Union* (the name by now had become hyphenated) in 1915, but during a long illness—which eventually claimed his life on Dec. 15, 1924—he sold controlling interest of the newspaper to William Randolph Hearst who was in the midst of expanding his legendary newspaper empire.

In 1937, Hearst made a move that decades later helped propel the *Times-Union* into the No. 1 position among newspapers in the region. He ended 72 years of afternoon publication by moving the newspaper into the morning field.

As changing American lifestyles and the emergence of television as an evening news source made morning newspapers increasingly dominant, particularly in white-col-

Current Times Union facility in Colonie, N.Y.

lar areas such as the Albany market, Hearst's decision paid off handsomely.

On Oct. 14, 1960, the Gannet Co. sold its popular Albany newspaper, *The Knickerbocker News*, to Hearst. By that time, Hearst's *Times-Union* had been moved to a modern plant on Sheridan Avenue in Albany, a building that became home to both the *Times-Union* and *The Knickerbocker News,* which were published under the corporate identity of Capital Newspapers.

Gene Robb, who was publisher of Hearst's *Times-Union,* became the first publisher of Capital Newspapers, and held the position until his death in 1969, shortly before completion of the *TU's* present headquarters at Wolf and Albany Shaker roads in the town of Colonie. This puts the *TU* in the heart of the region's largest suburb, at the crossroads of major interstate highways, and within minutes of the newly expanded Albany International Airport.

Robb was succeeded by Robert J. Danzig, who held the position of publisher before becoming general manager of Hearst's newspaper division in early 1977. Successor publishers were J. Roger Grier, Joseph T. Lyons—under whom the two newspapers were combined into today's *Times Union* on April 16, 1988—and Timothy O. White, the present publisher.

Under White, the *Times Union* company expanded its franchise to become the dominant multimedia news source in the Capital Region.

In recent years, the *TU* has broadened its reach with a news bureau network of five locations, and a circulation depot network of eight locations.

It also has under one umbrella the daily and Sunday newspapers, various specialty publications such as the four-times weekly *Saratoga TU* and *Rensselaer TU* and the weekly *Capital Region TU,* and numerous seasonal publications such

The old Times Union *plant in Albany, N.Y.*

as a glossy polo magazine geared to the Saratoga summer season.

But beyond the print product, the company made major strides during the 1990s to create ways for consumers to obtain news, information and advertising data on demand. The two major venues are the award-winning Electric Times Union site on the World WideWeb, and SourceLine, the interactive audio news and information service that truly is among the top such enterprises in the nation.

―――――――――――

One time home of The Knickerbocker News, *merged into the* Times Union *on April 16, 1988.*

TRANS WORLD ENTERTAINMENT CORP.

From Frank Sinatra to Garth Brooks...from Barbra Streisand to Madonna...from LPs and Beta tapes to CDs and DVD. Though the names, styles and media have changed dramatically in the last 25 years, one thing has remained the same: entertainment sells. Robert J. Higgins realized that back in 1972, when he established Trans World Music Corp. in Colonie, NY—a company that would later become one of the largest specialty music and movie retailers in the nation.

Today, Trans World owns and operates over 500 retail entertainment stores across 36 states, the District of Columbia and U.S. Virgin Islands. The company's chains include some of the best known names in the industry, including Record Town, Coconuts, Strawberries, F.Y.E. (For Your Entertainment) and Saturday Matinee. At its corporate headquarters in Colonie, NY, Trans World employs 900, and nationally, over 6,000—making it one of the leading employers in the Capital Region.

Founded in 1972 as a wholesale distributor of prerecorded music, Trans World first entered into the retail business in 1973 under the guidance of President/CEO Higgins, a lifelong Albany resident. The company's first store, Record Town, opened in Colonie, NY at Karner Road and Albany Street. The Record Town concept soon became the flagship chain for Trans World, and the company began to expand throughout the Northeast.

The mid-'70s saw the emergence of an amazing retail phenomenon: the suburban mall. As the new indoor shopping centers sprouted across the country, Trans World stores were at the forefront of the trend. The first mall-based Record Town was opened in Plattsburgh, NY in 1975, selling products such as vinyl records and 8-track tapes.

A few years later, a new music trend was on the horizon: audio cassettes, a superior alternative to

Trans World Entertainment Corporation Chairman, President & CEO Robert J. Higgins pictured outside an F.Y.E. (For Your Entertainment) superstore. Founded in 1972, Trans World now operates over 520 retail stores in 34 states, the District of Columbia and the U.S. Virgin Islands.

Paul Castle Photography

the 8-track. To capitalize on this exciting new music medium, Trans World launched its Tape World concept in 1979.

As the music business thrived, the early '80s brought even more changes. In 1982, Higgins decided to

focus the company where he envisioned the growth would be—which was retail—and exited the wholesale business. In 1986, the company went public—trading on NASDAQ under the symbol "TWMC." In 1987, Trans World capitalized on the strip mall trend and acquired the Coconuts name—adding a powerful new chain of free-standing stores to its ever-growing arsenal.

Big things were happening for Trans World, and Wall Street took notice. Business was booming. More and more stores were developed. Trans World's stock price soared.

With the boom of VCRs, sell-through video stepped into the limelight in the late '80s. Once again, through Higgins' vision, Trans World was leading the charge. In 1989, the company unveiled its Saturday Matinee concept, specializing in movies on video. An even more

Record Town, which was Trans World's original store concept in 1973, continues to be one of the company's leading chains. In 1990, Trans World introduced the Record Town/Saturday Matinee combo store, pictured below.

Laslo Regos Photography

Laslo Regos Photography

Trans World strengthened its market share in October of 1997, after acquiring 90 Strawberries locations (including the one pictured above), making it the dominant specialty music and movie retailer in the New England area.

exciting concept was introduced in 1990—a combination Saturday Matinee/Record Town format, a music and movie superstore.

In 1993, Trans World launched another revolutionary store concept: F.Y.E. (For Your Entertainment), the first-ever entertainment superstore designed for a mall setting. With over 25,000 square feet of selling space, the F.Y.E. concept includes not only music and movies—but also books, t-shirts, games and even an arcade. As this publication goes to press, the chain is being rolled out in locations across the country.

As its store formats and product mixes became more diverse, the company was ready for a new name. In 1994, it became known as Trans World Entertainment Corporation. Around the same time, the company began a plan for restructuring, as always following the leadership of Higgins. Seeing an industry trend long before its competitors, the company began to consolidate its stores and streamline its operations. Just two years later, Trans World was a far stronger company—positioned to take the lead in its industry.

Marking Trans World's 25th anniversary, 1997 was perhaps the most momentous year yet in the company's colorful history. It achieved record-setting sales and profits, and its stock price hit an all-time high. The company greatly expanded its free-standing business with the acquisition of 90 Strawberries stores. *Forbes* recognized it as the top-performing retail stock of 1997, and *Billboard* magazine named Robert Higgins "Video Person of the Year." Halfway through 1998, the company was breaking records again.

The history of Trans World is a story of innovation...a story of tenacity...a story of a president/CEO with foresight and vision...a story of a company at the top of its industry. As Trans World enters into the new Millennium, there is no telling who the next big stars will be or even how the world will watch or listen to them. However, one thing is certain—entertainment sells. And Trans World will be a part of it.

Trans World Entertainment's corporate headquarters (pictured below) are located off Route 155 in Albany, where the company employs over 900 in its newly remodeled home office and distribution center.

Tom Killips Photography

UNIVERSITY AT ALBANY

The University at Albany, State University of New York, had its beginnings as the New York State Normal School. Established by legislation passed on May 7, 1844, it became New York's first state-chartered public institution of higher education. Its mission was "the instruction and practice of teachers of common schools in the science of education and in the art of teaching." It began with 29 students and four faculty in an abandoned railroad depot on State Street, in the heart of the city of Albany.

Throughout the 19th century, the Normal School trained a student body from around the State to become schoolteachers and administrators. In time, the Normal School became the New York State Normal College, one of the first normal schools in the nation to make the transition to collegiate status. With a revised four-year curriculum in 1905, the College became the first public institution of higher education in New York State to be granted the power to confer the bachelor's degree. By 1914 there were 556 students and 44 faculty members. The master's degree was offered, and with this came another name change—the New York State College for Teachers.

In 1948 the State University of New York (SUNY) system was created, comprised of Albany and many other institutions throughout the state. In 1962, Albany received a new broader mission: to create a university center of undergraduate and graduate education, research and service. It also acquired a new name—the State University of New York at Albany.

By 1969, when the institution observed its 125th anniversary dramatic changes had taken place. Enrollment grew to 10,000, and the faculty grew to nearly 700. A new uptown campus, designed by the renowned architect Edward Durell Stone was completed to accommodate this growth and to give the institution a new image befitting its aspirations.

Through the 1980s, the education, research and service programs grew and matured. The Rockefeller College of Public Affairs and Policy was created in 1981 to bring together schools with an orientation toward public policy: criminal justice, public affairs, information science, and social welfare. In 1983, the New York State Writers Institute was established by Pulitzer Prize winning author

An aerial view of the University at Albany's uptown campus.

William Kennedy. Further growth took place in 1985 when the School of Public Health opened as a joint endeavor with the New York State Department of Health—the only school of its kind in the country with such affiliation.

During the 1990s Albany firmly established its national reputation as a research university. A third campus was acquired—the East Campus—when The University at Albany Foundation purchased the former Sterling Laboratories, and turned it into a facility which houses health related and technological disciplines and a business incubator. In an important study titled The Rise of American Research Universities: Elites and Challengers in the Postwar Era, released in 1997, Albany was ranked 17th in research and scholarship among the nation's top public universities. With business incubators at the East Campus and the Center for Environmental Sciences and Technology Management, and the Center for Advanced

Thin Film Technology (CAT), the University at Albany is a major force in the economic development of the Capital Region.

Today, Albany's eight degree-granting schools and colleges offer 221 degree programs to approximately 12,000 undergraduates and 5,000 graduate students. Its faculty is recognized nationally and internationally. And, the University at Albany is preparing

Built in 1997, the Center for Environmental Sciences and Technology Management (CESTM) is home to the University's Atmospheric Sciences Research Center, National Weather Service Forecast Office, and the Center for Advanced Thin Film Technology.

for the 21st Century by implementing a $130 million Capital Facilities Master Plan that will enhance the University's reputation as a premier center of scholarship and research.

Draper Hall, downtown campus, was built in 1909 and inspired by Jefferson's design for the University of Virginia.

THE SWYER COMPANIES

The Swyer Companies are comprised of construction, real estate development, and property management companies, dedicated to providing the highest level of quality and service in the greater Capital District.

The legacy of Lewis A. Swyer is reflected in the glass and steel structures his company developed and constructed. That legacy is a reflection of fifty years of accomplishment.

If the past is a prologue, then the major works of the Swyer Companies are reflections of even greater things to come. For fifty years, the Swyer Companies have articulated their vision through innovative planning, fresh architectural concepts, and functional structures. It is from this strong foundation, that The Swyer Companies will help shape the future.

The L. A. Swyer Company, builders and construction managers, was founded in 1948 by Lewis A. Swyer. It has kept pace with the enormous change that has characterized America since the Second World War. The advent of modern building materials, the rise of trade unions, the proliferation of suburbs and the decline of urban centers, are all factors that have reshaped the architectural profile, and have challenged the modern developer/builder. One of the biggest challenges today is the many difficult environmental considerations that need to be addressed.

The Swyer Companies are equipped to handle every phase of a project, from the environmental impact statement to property management. From raw land to finished product, Swyer provides and manages any resource necessary to complete the project.

From the internationally recognized Saratoga Performing Arts Center, to the highly efficient and dynamic design of 80 State Street in downtown Albany, the L. A. Swyer Company builds structures that define the architectural content of the surrounding area. The Albany

80 State Street, a highly efficient and dynamic designed first class office building located in the heart of Albany's downtown business district.

Law School Library, although contemporary in design, complements the nineteenth century cut granite exteriors of the existing law school buildings. It may be fairly said that in one way or another, sooner or later, every Albanian will be affected by a Swyer Company project-through working in some of the over seven million square feet of offices, shopping in stores, attending classes in schools, enjoying the performing arts, or transacting business in

banks built by Swyer.

Stuyvesant Plaza, owned and managed by The Swyer Companies, is a unique shopping center in Albany noted for its distinctive collection of sixty original stores and restaurants. The majority of the businesses are locally owned and operated. This quality tenant mix makes Stuyvesant Plaza one of the most successful shopping centers in the area.

Next door to Stuyvesant Plaza is Executive Park, a twenty-acre first class office complex anchored by the ten story Executive Park Tower. "We always believed a perfect day would be to work in the 'Park,' then shop in the 'Plaza'."

The Swyer Companies currently own substantial property in downtown Albany. In addition to the first class 80 State Street project located in the heart of Albany's business district, it owns future developable land at 747 Broadway. There, the Company hopes to build its next commercial project to again add to the magnificent and historic Albany skyline!

Stuyvesant Plaza is a unique shopping center in Albany noted for its distinctive collection of sixty original stores and restaurants."

URBACH KAHN & WERLIN PC

Urbach Kahn & Werlin PC, Certified Public Accountants (UK&W) was founded locally more than 30 years ago and has grown as a result of a commitment to both quality service and client satisfaction. Founding partners Eli Werlin, Howard Kahn and Sidney Urbach, together set a tone and standard for practice that was unwavering; a commitment to exceeding client expectations, an environment where only the highest professional and ethical standards were accepted. That tradition, and the service philosophy it fostered, continues today.

Headquartered at 66 State Street, the firm is acknowledged as one of the 45 largest CPA firms in the United States serving its diverse client base from six offices located throughout the Northeast, in Washington DC and in California. In addition, UK&W is a founding member of Urbach Hacker Young International, a worldwide organization of independent accounting and consulting firms, offers flexible benefit plan services through UKW Benefits, LLC and information technology support through WORD Information Services. The diversity and growth of Urbach Kahn & Werlin is evident the moment you step into the 66 State Street office; an ever-growing office directory welcomes you to Urbach Kahn & Werlin PC, WORD Information Services from Urbach Kahn & Werlin and the UKW Economic Consulting Group!

UK&W offers a wide range of services, each supported by experienced professionals; from the more traditional assurance services of accounting, auditing and tax to value added services like health care consulting, employee benefits plan design and administration, economic consulting, business valuations, litigation support, information technology and more. The firm maintains long-term experience and expertise in a number of industries

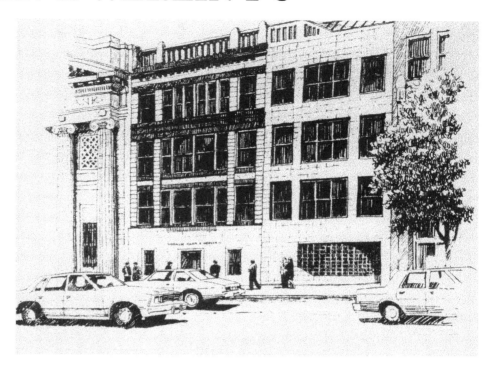

Offices of Urbach Kahn Werlin PC

including health care, the not-for-profit arena, government, high-tech, education, manufacturing, real estate/construction and financial institutions. The firm's specialists work together as a strategic planning team to understand their clients businesses.

UK&W is actively involved in the on-going development of the accounting profession itself, enjoying significant profession-wide recognition and stature through firm membership in the American Institute of Certified Public Accountants (AICPA) SEC Practice Section, Group B, and individual appointed and elected positions on senior level committees of various professional organizations including the AICPA Board of Directors, Ethics Committee, AICPA Auditing Standards Board and SEC Practice Section Executive Committee, the New York State Society of Certified Public Accountants and more.

Always furthering the goals and objectives of their firm are the many specialists who make up the UK&W team. These include accountants, tax advisors, attorneys, employee benefits specialists, valuation

specialists, personnel consultants, actuaries and computer consultants. Specialists work together as a strategic planning team to understand clients' businesses. In addition, the firm pledges the commitment and involvement of senior staff and Shareholders at all phases of an engagement to ensure the consistency and quality today's business challenges demand.

UK&W is also actively involved in each community in which it resides. Whether it's a leadership role in the Albany-Colonie Regional Chamber of Commerce or the Downtown Albany Business Improvement District, involvement in the Juvenile Diabetes Walk To Cure or a golf tournament benefitting the American Cancer Society, UK&W is committed to area and civic development through the Capital Region and beyond.

Urbach Kahn & Werlin PC is committed to meeting the needs and exceeding the expectations of its client base, not only on a local level, but through the world-wide resources of Urbach Hacker Young International.

WAMC/NORTHEAST PUBLIC RADIO

In October 1958, WAMC-FM gained Federal Communications Commission (FCC) approval to broadcast and officially signed on the air. Funded by the Albany Medical College Department of Postgraduate Medicine, the station was started three years prior by several physicians with an interest in radio. In a makeshift studio, they broadcasted daily conferences and programs on medical education over a two-way radio.

Today, WAMC/Northeast Public Radio is a ten-station network heard in portions of seven states by more than 300,000 listeners during a four-week period. It boasts an award-winning news department which has been recognized repeatedly by several broadcasting organizations for its excellence in radio journalism. WAMC's National Productions produces thirteen programs ranging in topic from health to politics and most of these shows are nationally and internationally syndicated. Its music programs include classical, folk, jazz and world music. In addition, WAMC airs a host of programs from National Public Radio (NPR) and Public Radio International (PRI).

"There's no stopping us," says chair and executive director, Alan Chartock. "Everyone has worked together to make this station an important part of our region."

Alan Chartock, chair and executive director, prepares to go on the air.

WAMC must raise $125,000 immediately, or leave the air.
So throw Beethoven a line. Keep "Jazz Alive" alive.
Keep "All Things Considered" afloat.

Home in on our signal and
Save Our Station

Send your tax-deductible contribution to:
WAMC, 684 Madison Avenue, Albany, New York 12208

WAMC 90.3 FM
National Public Radio
Serving Eastern New York and Western New England.

The famous S.O.S. poster that helped save WAMC.

WAMC's positioning was not always so bright though. In 1980, WAMC's survival was in jeopardy when the Medical College informed station management that it would no longer be able to support the station because of its own financial difficulties.

This marks a defining turning point in the history of WAMC. Between 1981 and 1982, WAMC left Albany Medical College and became the independent, non-profit educational corporation it is today. This was accomplished by a group of concerned WAMC staff, listeners and volunteers who took on the challenge of keeping the endangered station on the air.

The group worked to cover the accrued operating expenses of the station, in addition to cutting costs and sustaining the station for the coming years. Part of this effort included implementing an active grant committee, a call for underwriters and streamlining WAMC's staff.

The key to WAMC's survival, however, was its first fund drive, under the leadership of Alan Chartock and a dedicated board who put in countless hours to assure success.

According to Chartock, "By this time I was already doing the "Legislative Gazette" program...and after doing a show one afternoon I came upon the then general manager..." who was quite upset. "When I asked him what was wrong he explained about the funding. I told him we should go on the air and ask the listeners for the money—that I had seen this work on public radio in the city...I began to spread the word through my column and my contact with other people who wanted to help save the station."

There was a tremendous public response to this first, five-day fund drive, aptly titled "Save Our Station" or S.O.S., which raised over $125,000 and proved that listeners were deeply concerned about maintaining WAMC. Enough funds were raised in this initial drive to cover the deficit and carry the station through the next year.

On July 31, 1981, the station was incorporated as an Educational Corporation chartered by the New York State Board of Regents. On June 30 of the following year, the newly incorporated WAMC took over the station's FCC license.

During the transfer of the station, costs had been reduced by relocating WAMC from the building which had been rented by the Medical College to another local station's studios. By 1984, it became necessary for WAMC to find a new space. The "Home of Our Own" campaign raised enough money for WAMC to purchase the building it still calls "home" at 318 Central Avenue. The building had housed an auto dealership and an electronics store among other things and was redone to house the offices and studios of WAMC in 1986.

In October 1987, WAMC began to expand its broadcasting capabilities with the addition of satellite station WCAN in Canajoharie, New York. Today, WAMC's network is comprised of the following FM frequencies: WAMC, Albany; WAMK, Kingston; WOSR, Middletown; WCEL, Plattsburgh; WCAN, Canajoharie; WANC, Ticonderoga;

W205AJ, Oneonta; W226AC, Troy; W299AG, Newburgh; and, WAMQ, Great Barrington, MA. WAMC's internal expansion has been equally as rapid. Beginning with a staff of six in the small college studio in 1981, the station has a current staff of nearly 50.

WAMC's National Productions was formed in response to the financial needs of this rapid expansion. In 1986, the first educational program, "The Health Show," was produced and quickly followed by "51%." Today, "The Health Show"and "The Environment Show" are aired by over 200 stations each nationwide. As impressive is the fact that more than 500 stations in the United

WAMC's building located at 318 Central Avenue in Albany.

States carry one or more of WAMC's programs. In addition, many of WAMC's programs are heard internationally via Armed Forces Radio Network and Voice of America.

The News department has been equally successful. It has been recognized by the New York State Associated Press Broadcasters' Association, the Massachusetts and New York Broadcasters' Associations, the Radio-Television News Director Association and numerous other organizations.

Through the years and all the many changes one thing has remained constant: the love and support of the WAMC family. The listener support that began during S.O.S. remains the driving force behind all endeavors at WAMC. Without member support, WAMC would not exist today. Not only does member support comprise the single largest component of WAMC's budget, but the attitudes, opinions and tastes of WAMC's listening population shape much of WAMC's programming. In the end, WAMC is a cooperative project between staff, members and volunteers who share a commitment and love for the station and its many activities.

Alan Chartock (left), Chair and Executive Director, and David Galletly (right), Assistant Executive Director, work hard to obtain pledges from WAMC listeners during a recent fund drive.

WHITEMAN OSTERMAN & HANNA

For almost a quarter century, the law firm of Whiteman Osterman & Hanna has been building upon the vision of its four founding members from the Rockefeller administration and the talented group of prominent attorneys who have joined the firm over the years.

Today, Whiteman Osterman & Hanna, according to the Albany Times Union, "enjoys the muscle of a Wall Street firm and the low-profile demeanor of an Albany address" as it serves major corporations, institutions and organizations. Its work in the state capital of New York has not only served clients well but has also had a significant impact on public policy issues. The firm has been recognized by those in both the public and private sectors as among New York's premier law firms, one of the most astute about New York government and its impact on its fields of special expertise: environmental, healthcare, regulated industries, business, education, and labor and employment law.

Whiteman Osterman & Hanna, Albany's largest law firm with nearly 50 attorneys and a staff of 70, has played major roles in landmark New York cases, from the resolution of the New York City watershed issue to settlement of the Love Canal environmental situation. Its clients include MCI, American Express, GE, Occidental Chemical, the New York Stock Exchange, Albany Medical Center and the Metropolitan Museum of Art. The firm occupies two top floors of One Commerce Plaza, an Albany landmark building directly across the street from the State Capitol, from which it has vistas of the nearby state government complex, the Hudson River and beyond, reflecting its position of serving statewide and national clients from an Albany perspective.

But the view was not always so clear. The four "formerlies" (formerly counsel to the Governor, formerly chief counsel for the Department of Environmental Conservation, etc.)

Albany Times Union.

Whiteman Osterman & Hanna's four founding partners, John Hanna, Michael Whiteman, Melvin Osterman & Joel Hodes.

who founded the firm acknowledge anxious times at the outset. However, their entrepreneurial anxiety and concern that interesting work might be long in coming proved unfounded. The firm's early ability "to facilitate the interface between the regulators and the regulated," as Michael Whiteman puts it, helped attract major clients, interesting work and many of the best and brightest lawyers in the region.

The firm has developed a reputation for innovative solutions, cutting-edge counsel and professional leadership. Through integrated, firm-wide collaboration, it offers clients a broad scope of legal counsel, drawing from its experience and expertise in education, energy, telecomunications, environmental and land use, government relations, healthcare,

Whiteman Osterman & Hanna occupies two top floors of One Commerce Plaza, an Albany landmark building directly across from the State Capitol.

Jeff Goldberg/Esto.

international trade, business transactions, corporate and professional immigration, labor and employment, litigation, and trusts and estates matters. For example, it recently established a Healthcare Business Group, a fully-integrated interdisciplinary "task force" that provides health facilities, professionals and insurers with the specialized skills and knowledge about healthcare regulation business and finance that are indispensable in today's complex healthcare workplace.

Since its founding, the convergent arena of government, business and the community has been key to the firm's growth. Its depth of knowledge and experience in government service is unparalleled in the region. Members of the firm have served as Counsel or Assistant Counsel to four recent Governors of the State of New York. The Whiteman Osterman & Hanna Public Affairs Roundtable is a highly regarded forum bringing together leaders of government, business and the community to discuss significant issues of mutual concern. The firm is also active in the community, with attorneys holding key leadership positions in business organizations, educational institutions, arts organizations, and civic and community groups.

ADELS-LOEB INC.
(circa 1981)

It was a new item, a radical departure from American masculine tradition, when Louis Adels, founder of New York City's L. Adels Company, first introduced the wrist watch to the American market in 1917. Adels did well with the new product, once he overcame the qualms of American "he-men," and his firm, now the Winton-Nicolet Watch Company, remains in business today. Louis's brother Moe, of M. Adels and Company, was a diamond importer in New York City for more than 50 years; brother Harry settled in Troy around 1919, opening Adels Jewelers, a retail store still in operation. Louis's sister Etta and her husband, Max Segel, opened Segel's Jewelers in Schenectady. In 1923 Samuel Adels, Pearl Adels Loeb, and Pearl's husband, Martin Loeb, opened Adels-Loeb in one of the shops in the North Pearl Street facade of the once-prestigious Kenmore Hotel.

After six years at the Kenmore location, in late 1929, Adels-Loeb moved into larger and more modern quarters in the newly constructed National Savings Bank building on the southwest corner of South Pearl and State streets. The firm has remained there ever since. The refined details of the store's art deco interior largely remain—meticulously joined cabinets, and glass doors and interior windows acid-etched in floral patterns, cherished survivors of an age when even the utilitarian was made gracefully amenable. Enough remains of that original interior in Adels-Loeb to form a picture of the store as it was in 1929.

Pearl Adels Loeb alone survives of the company's three founders, and at the age of 80 works in the store each day, known to her clientele for her understanding, merchandising, and fine taste. David Loeb, son of Pearl and Martin Loeb, entered the family firm in 1949; a registered jeweler of the American Gem Society and a certified gemologist, David eventually became president of Adels-Loeb.

Adels-Loeb weathered nearly 60 years of operation by adapting to the changing times without losing sight of its tradition of friendly, scrupulous service, fine quality merchandise, and unassailable integrity. As the heyday of downtown Albany waned, as inflation, recession, and the advent of large suburban shopping centers came to pass, Adels-Loeb adjusted. Business hours were modified and Adels-Loeb, once Albany's largest retailer of sterling silver, no longer displayed even place settings. Lunch hour downtown today brings a cross section of professional people and workers of all sorts into the store, Albany's oldest credit jewelers. Appraisals, watch and jewelry repairs, and engraving mark this most versatile old-time jewelry store.

After 57 years in business at the center of downtown Albany, Adels-Loeb is intimately associated with the reawakening commercial life of the inner city. As in the interior of its store, Adels-Loeb itself preserves and employs the best elements of its past, "doing business in the old-fashioned way—with warmth, with knowledge, and with integrity."

Left:
Opening day at the new Adels-Loeb store in 1929 revealed a beautiful art deco interior and an extravagant quantity of cut flowers.
Right:
A very sophisticated display attracted window-shoppers on South Pearl Street in 1929. (Courtesy, Glen S. Cook, photographer)

THE DAVID M. CAREY INTERESTS
(circa 1981)

The Albany Hyatt Billiard Ball Company

Twelve thousand elephants were slaughtered every year to provide the ivory for the world's billiard balls at the height of the mid-19th century's billiard craze. As ivory grew more costly, one billiard ball firm offered a $10,000 prize for a successful ivory substitute. Albany printer John Wesley Hyatt sought that prize in 1868; his discovery was celluloid, the world's first plastic and a cornerstone of modern technology. Hyatt became, according to the Smithsonian Institution, "one of the most important men in the development of modern chemistry in the United States." Hyatt's discovery was accidental, but experimentation led to a number of uses, celluloid eventually being used for combs, photographic film, umbrella handles, and for the detachable celluloid shirt collars that made Troy the "Collar City."

Hyatt raised $2,000 from investors and borrowed work space in the Albany machine shop of Peter Kinnear. Kinnear made the molds for casting the celluloid, a flammable plastic, and although Hyatt's early billiard balls had an alarming tendency to explode on impact, Albany Billiard Ball Company was in business, the world's first plastics manufacturer. Kinnear purchased stock in Hyatt's venture, eventually gaining control as John Hyatt, unfortunate in his investments, encountered financial difficulties. Under Kinnear's management, the firm grew rapidly. Hyatt's celluloid composition billiard ball gained universal acceptance and was used by England's King Edward VII and by Kaiser Wilhelm II. Two generations of Kinnears followed Peter into the firm, the last selling the business in 1968.

Cheaper, foreign-made billiard balls flooded the U.S. market and Albany Hyatt Billiard Ball Company fell on hard times, nearly closing down under a succession of owners. In 1977 David M. Carey acquired the troubled firm

Above:
John Wesley Hyatt was a journeyman printer who tinkered with various inventions in his room at Hawk Street and Washington Avenue. He invented Ice Creepers (which attached to shoes) and manufactured Dominoes and Checkers there.
Below:
Architect Charles Ogden (1858-1931) designed the Albany Billiard Ball Company building for his father-in-law, Peter Kinnear, in 1890. The Delaware Avenue site remains the firm's headquarters. Both photos courtesy the Knickerbocker Press.

and, employing new marketing principles, adjusted prices and once again became highly competitive. By 1981, Albany Hyatt Billiard Ball Company, one of the firms composing the David M. Carey Interests, was once more in financial good health, 113 years after John Hyatt gave birth to the Age of Plastics.

Pedersen Golf Corporation

The pioneer custom golf club maker in the United States, Pedersen Golf Corporation is one of the six oldest club-making companies in the nation. The Pedersen brothers founded their company in Mount Vernon, New York, in 1926, moving it to Connecticut four years later. The golf clubs Pedersen made were, and are, used by many of history's great golfing professionals. The company always made classical, high-quality clubs and emphasized a custom fit for the average golfers, who, the Pedersens felt, needed it most to enhance their playing abilities. In 1970 Pedersen was acquired by F.O. Mossberg Corporation, and in 1979 by David M. Carey, who promptly returned it to New York State. Applying the same management techniques which revived a faltering Albany Hyatt Billiard Ball Company, Carey continued Pedersen's innovative tradition.

MAYORS OF ALBANY

1686-93	Pieter Schuyler	1778	John Barclay	1860-61	George H. Thacher
1694	Johannes Abeel	1779-82	Abraham Ten Broeck	1862-65	Eli Perry
1695	Evert Bancker	1783-85	Johannes Jacobse Beeckman	1866-67	George H. Thacher
1696-97	Dirck Wesselse ten Broeck	1786-89	John Lansing, Jr.	1868-69	Charles E. Bleecker
1698	Hendrick Hansen	1790-95	Abraham Yates, Jr.	1870-73	George H. Thacher
1699	Pieter Van Brugh	1796-98	Abraham Ten Broeck	1874	George H. Thacher (resg.
1700	Jan Jansen Bleecker	1799-1815	Philip S. Van Rensselaer		Jan. 28)
1701	Johannes Bleecker, Jr.	1816-18	Elisha Jenkins	1874	John G. Burch, ex-officio
1702	Albert Janse Ryckman	1819-20	Philip S. Van Rensselaer	1874-75	Edmund L. Judson
1703-05	Johannes Schuyler	1821-23	Charles E. Dudley	1876-77	A. Bleecker Banks
1706	David Davidse Schuyler	1824-25	Ambrose Spencer	1878-83	Michael N. Nolan
1707	Evert Bancker	1826-27	James Stevenson	1883	John Swinburne
1709	Johannes Abeel	1828	Charles E. Dudley	1884-85	A. Bleecker Banks
1710-18	Robert Livingston, Jr.	1829-30	John Townsend	1886-87	John Boyd Thacher
1719-20	Myndert Schuyler	1831	Francis Bloodgood	1888-89	Edward A. Maher
1721-22	Pieter Van Brugh	1832	John Townsend	1890-93	James H. Manning
1723-24	Myndert Schuyler	1833	Francis Bloodgood	1894-95	Oren E. Wilson
1725	Johannes Cuyler	1834-36	Erastus Corning	1896-97	John Boyd Thacher
1726-28	Rutger Bleecker	1837	Teunis Van Vechten	1898-99	Thomas J. Van Alstyne
1729-30	Johannes De Peyster	1838-40	Jared L. Rathbone	1900-01	James H. Blessing
1731	Johannes ("Hans") Hansen	1841	Teunis Van Vechten	1902-08	Charles H. Gaus
1732	Johannes De Peyster	1842	Barent P. Staats	1909	Henry F. Snyder
1733-40	Edward Holland	1843-44	Friend Humphrey	1910-13	James B. McEwan
1741	Johannes Schuyler	1845	John K. Paige	1914-16	Joseph W. Stevens
1742-45	Cornelis Cuyler	1846-47	William Parmelee	1917	Joseph W. Stevens
1746-47	Dirck Ten Broeck	1849	Friend Humphrey	1918-21	James R. Watt
1748-49	Jacob C. Ten Eyck	1850	Franklin Townsend	1922-25	William S. Hackett
1750-53	Robert Sanders	1851-53	Eli Perry	1926-40	John Boyd Thacher 2nd
1754-55	Johannes ("Hans") Hansen	1854-55	William Parmelee (died in	**1941**	**Herman Hoogkamp (acting)**
1756-60	Sybrant G. Van Schaick		office)	**1942-83**	**Erastus Corning 2nd and Frank S.**
1761-69	Volckert P. Douw	1855	Charles W. Godard		**Harris (acting while Mayor Corning**
1770-77	Abraham Cornelis Cuyler	1856-59	Eli Perry		**was in the U.S. Army 1944-45)**
				1983-93	**Thomas M. Whalen, III**
				1994-	**Gerald D. Jennings**

GOVERNORS OF NEW YORK

1777-95	George Clinton	1851-53	Washington Hunt	1901-05	Benjamin B. Odell, Jr.
1795-1801	John Jay	1853-55	Horatio Seymour	1905-07	Frank W. Higgins
1801-04	George Clinton	1855-57	Myron H. Clark	1907-11	Charles Evans Hughes
1804-07	Morgan Lewis	1857-59	John A. King	1911-13	John Alden Dix
1807-17	Daniel D. Thompkins	1859-63	Edwin D. Morgan	1913	William Sulzer
1817	John Taylor	1863-65	Horatio Seymour	1913-15	Martin H. Glynn
1817-23	DeWitt Clinton	1865-69	Reuben E. Fenton	1915-19	Charles S. Whitman
1823-25	Joseph C. Yates	1869-73	John T. Hoffman	1919-21	Alfred E. Smith
1825-28	DeWitt Clinton	1873-75	John A. Dix	1921-23	Nathan L. Miller
1828	Nathaniel Pitcher	1875-77	Samuel J. Tilden	1923-29	Alfred E. Smith
1828-29	Martin Van Buren	1877-79	Lucius Robinson	1929-33	Franklin Delano Roosevelt
1829-33	Enos J. Throop	1879-83	Alonzo B. Cornell	1933-43	Herbert H. Lehman
1833-39	William L. Marcy	1883-85	Grover Cleveland	1943-55	Thomas E. Dewey
1839-43	William H. Seward	1885-92	David P. Hill	1955-59	Averell Harriman
1843-45	William C. Bouck	1892-95	Roswell P. Flower	1959-73	Nelson A. Rockefeller
1845-47	Silas Wright	1895-97	Levi P. Morton	1973-75	Malcolm Wilson
1847-49	John Young	1897-99	Frank S. Black	**1975-80**	**Hugh L. Carey**
1849-51	Hamilton Fish	1899-1901	Theodore Roosevelt	**1981-94**	**Mario M. Cuomo**
				1995-	George E. Pataki

ACKNOWLEDGMENTS

For the completion of this book—the first overall view of the city's history since Codman Hislop's fine work of 1936—credit belongs to many people, most of whose names do not appear on the title page.

Before all others, I am indebted to that unique group of Albany scholars who over the generations have undertaken tedious efforts to preserve and pass on the city's heritage at a time when it was in its most vulnerable state: chiefly E.B. O'Callaghan, Cuyler Reynolds, and, above all, Joel Munsell.

Within the past decade, Albany has been blessed with a renewed interest in her rich past. I have drawn upon the contemporary scholarship and encouragement of Margaret Conners Harrigan, Stefan Bielinski, Charles Gehring, and Don Rittner, as well as Alice Kenney, Tammis Kane Groft, Dorothy Filley, Roderic Blackburn, and Alison Bennett, who with Charlotte Wilcoxen have shown us that the city's history has not all been written, and that our understanding of our roots is an ever-evolving process.

It takes a special gift to create an atmosphere in which an entire community will come to know and value its past. Much of our most fascinating history is contained in folklore and oral tradition, quoted from the keen minds of average people in the twilight of their years. My thanks goes to the late Edgar Van Olinda and Bill Schirving, as well as to their fellow columnists Charles Mooney, Cecil Roseberry, and my long-time friend Raymond Joyce, Sr., whose widely read newspaper columns have done much to bring the city's history and traditions into all our homes over the years.

William Kennedy, the late John Boos, and, of course, Morris Gerber deserve special mention for their welcome dissemination of Albany memories.

In addition to the many citations credited within the book, several people deserve special recognition for their dedicated assistance given to either myself or Dennis Holzman in our two year search for rare photographs and information. Kathleen Roe of the N.Y. State Archives and James Corsaro of the State Library, Manuscripts and Special Collections, were invaluable in their aid. Marguerite Mullenneaux of the Albany Public Library has been my standby for many years. The staff of McKinney Library of the Albany Institute of History and Art—James Hobin, Kenneth MacFarland, Suzanne Roberson, Christine Ward, Daryl Severson, and others mentioned above—showed a degree of cooperation far beyond the call of obligation.

For their contributions to the photographic aspects of the book we are further indebted to Joseph McCormick, Arthur O'Keefe, Lindsay Watson, and the wonderful expertise of Lou Carol Lecce.

I extend my gratitude to Martha Noble, who spent innumerable hours in proofreading; to Margaret C. Tropp for her editing and arrangement of a rambling manuscript into a readable book with chapters of a common theme; to Robert Arnold for his updating of the city's chronology, a task of great value that has long needed doing; and to Emerson Moran for his condensing and writing of several "sidebar" sections in the text.

Some have helped in this endeavor far more than they realize. To Brother Conrad and the late Brother Alfred of CBA, James Magee and Robert Flacke of Fort William Henry, as well as to the late Fr. Michael McCloskey and the excellent history department of Siena College, belongs the credit for giving me what ability and confidence I needed to commence this work.

Encouragement is a quality of inestimable value without which I could not have started, much less completed, this task. In addition to much helpful advice rendered, I am especially endebted to Mayor Erastus Corning and Albany Institute Director Norman Rice for unselfishly helping me at every juncture of the long and often trying journey.

I express gratitude to those who have remained close to me over the years: Dick Conners, Jane McNally, Mel Wolfgang, George Marguin, and the dedicated staff in City Hall and the department of Human Resources; also to my students in Old Albany for the constant input of information which they continue to provide, years after our formal relationship has ceased.

I am immeasurably grateful to my family: to my parents John and Margaret Gaffie McEneny, for the love and education imparted to me; to my brother Terry, who has never failed to support me in anything I have ever attempted to do; and to my Aunts Alice McCullen and Josephine Belser, who are my constant mentors.

Finally, this book could never have been written without the irreplaceable support of my best friend, Barbara Leonard McEneny, whom I had the good sense to marry 13 years ago.

—John J. McEneny
August, 1981

I again thank the many friends and colleagues listed above who helped me in the original writing of this book, and in contributing to my ever-growing appreciation of history. I also wish to thank my friend and fellow traveler in our search for the often illusive truth in Albany's history, Bill Kennedy, for his constant encouragement and for writing the introduction to this edition. I would be remiss, however, if I did not now add to that list the name of my younger daughter, Maeve Leonard McEneny, whose patience and dedication are responsible for her father finally entering the world of computers and word processing.

—John J. McEneny
August, 1998